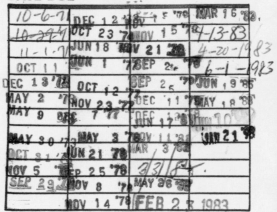
Kraus, Richard
History of the Dance

WITHDRAWN

DATE DUE

10-6-7	DEC 12	5 '78	MAR 16 '83
10-29-7	OCT 23 '7	NOV 15 '78	4-13-83
11-1-7	JUN 18	NOV 21 78	4-20-1983
OCT 11	JUN 1 '78	SEP 2 78	6-1-1983
DEC 13 '7	OCT 12 7	SEP 25 '79	JUN 9 85
MAY 2 '7	NOV 23 77	DEC 11 '7	MAY 18 85
MAY 9 8	DEC 7 77	DEC 13 78	JUN 10
MAY 30 79	MAY 3 '78	NOV 11 '81	JUN 21 98
OCT 31	JUN 21 78	MAR 3 82	
NOV 5 '7	SEP 25 78	3/31/8	
SEP 29 7	NOV 8 '7	MAY 26 82	
	NOV 14 78	FEB 2 8 1983	

HISTORY
OF THE
DANCE
in Art and Education

RICHARD KRAUS

Professor of Education
Adviser, Dance Education Curriculum
Teachers College, Columbia University

HISTORY
OF THE
DANCE

in Art and Education

Prentice-Hall, Inc., *Englewood Cliffs, New Jersey*

13-390054-1

Library of Congress Catalog Card Number: 69-13716

Prentice-Hall International, Inc., *London*
Prentice-Hall of Australia, Pty. Ltd., *Sydney*
Prentice-Hall of Canada, Ltd., *Toronto*
Prentice-Hall of India Private Ltd., *New Delhi*
Prentice-Hall of Japan, Inc., *Tokyo*

Printed in the United States of America

Current printing (last digit): 10   9   8   7   6   5   4   3   2   1

To Ethel and David

PREFACE

This book is intended to be read by both the general reader interested in dance and the student taking a course in the fine and performing arts, the humanities, or the history and philosophy of dance. It developed from my teaching of courses and seminars in dance history and dance education at Teachers College, Columbia University, over the past two decades. Because during this period I found no single book which dealt satisfactorily with the full history of dance as an art form and which also examined the place of dance in education, I have attempted to provide in this single, carefully documented volume:

1. An analysis of the history of dance through the ages, tracing its role as religious ritual, art form or popular entertainment, and viewing it in relation to the social context of each period and other major art forms

2. A contemporary examination of theater dance, particularly on the American scene, stressing the newer modern dance and ballet companies, the emergence of avant-garde dance and the growth of regional ballet activities, and the growing contributions of government and private foundations to the performing arts

3. A review of dance education as it has developed on three levels of education in the United States (elementary, secondary, and higher education), along with a presentation of its objectives, current practices, and problems

In preparing the chapters on dance history, I have drawn heavily on the research and writing of a number of dance historians: Curt Sachs, E. Louis Backman, Lillian B. Lawler, Lincoln Kirstein, Gaston Vuillier, Agnes de Mille, Joseph Marks, Marian H. Winter, E. D. Andrews, Olga Maynard, among others. In so doing, I have drawn quotations rather liberally from these sources. The reader who seeks fuller information about a particular period or topic of dance history is urged to go directly to the original source. Similarly, a number of references have been drawn from the recent or current writing of such critics as John Martin, Walter Terry, Doris Hering, and Clive Barnes, with respect to recent developments in theater dance. The section on dance education draws heavily on the professional literature in this field, on reports and studies, and on the author's own observation and systematic research.

History of the Dance in Art and Education necessarily has certain limitations. First, a number of topics are presented in a somewhat limited format. For example, the book deals rather briefly with dance forms other than those found in Western society; the remarkable and beautiful dance of the Orient is mentioned only in passing. Also, the place of dance in film and television, current ventures in dance research, and the use of dance as therapy or as popular recreation are treated with less attention than these topics deserve, but space simply does not permit an expanded treatment.

A second limitation concerns the constantly changing nature of the dance world. Even as this book goes to press, it is apparent that certain new developments in theater dance and dance education cannot be included. To illustrate, a major modern dance and ballet series of programs was sponsored by the Brooklyn Academy of Music in New York City in 1968–1969. Featuring thirteen leading companies and performing over 80 works over a five-month period, this series represented a landmark in the growth of popular interest in dance as a performing art. Because of the printing schedule, a description of it could not be included in the book. Similarly, in 1968 an issue of *Impulse* titled *Dance: A Projection for the Future* was published, describing a conference which had been held, with federal assistance, at the University of California at Los Angeles, and which discussed college dance programs at considerable length. Again, information regarding this conference could not be included in the present volume. The perceptive reader will therefore recognize that references to artists and companies, or to curricular practices, must be read with the understanding that they were accurate in the late 1960's. However, as with any of the performing arts, constant change and development is to be expected in the field of dance. One of the most striking new developments has been that in two states, California and Wisconsin, graduates of specially approved college dance curricula are now permitted to teach in public schools without physical education certification. Again, it has not been possible to include information about this recent development in the book.

The author would like to acknowledge the assistance and encouragement of a number of persons. Appreciation is expressed to Thais Barry, instructor in dance at Teachers College, for her stimulation and interest. Special thanks must be given to Genevieve Oswald, Curator of the Dance Collection of the Library and Museum of the Performing Arts at Lincoln Center, in New York, for permission to use a number of prints from that collection; thanks go also to Rosalie Stone of the Dance Collection for help in gathering the pictures that were used. Other photographs were obtained from such leading dance photographers as Jack Mitchell, Martha Swope, and Barbara Morgan, from the publicists of leading dance companies, and from the advisers of college dance groups. A number of college dance faculty members were helpful to me; specifically, I wish to thank Professor Elizabeth Hayes of the University of Utah.

This has been a fascinating book to write. Dance, as a vital and expressive art, both throughout history and in the present, is deeply revealing of man's personality and culture. As we stand today at the brink of a new age of leisure, faced with the possibility of an increasing involvement in all the arts by many more people, it seems clear that the history of dance is a history that is just beginning.

R. K.

New York, 1969

CONTENTS

I

MEANING AND
PURPOSE OF DANCE

One of the most striking aspects of the cultural scene in the United States today—and indeed throughout the Western world—is the rapid growth of dance activity, both as a performing art and as a form of educational experience. Existing ballet companies have been strengthened and have found new audiences. New ballet companies have been founded throughout the United States, several on a fully professional basis, and others as an outgrowth of regional enthusiasm, which supports workshops, festivals, and a network of dance schools and clinics. On the college and university level in particular, more and more institutions have introduced dance as a performing art into their programs. As one critic has written:

> . . . in retrospect, the Sixties may prove to have been the decade of organization, stabilization and popularization of dance in all its theater forms . . . . The way things have been going recently, the common man will soon be hard put to find a bush without a ballet company or dance troupe of some kind under it.[1]

Increasingly, dance, and particularly ballet, have received support for professional training, for subsidy of productions, and for reaching large new audiences. A single major grant given by the

[1] Allen Hughes, *The New York Times*, May 31, 1965, Sec. X, p. 12.

2

Ford Foundation, for example, provided a ten-year program which awarded over $7.7 million to the New York City Ballet Company and its affiliated School of American Ballet, and to several other companies: the San Francisco Ballet; the National Ballet of Washington, D.C.; the Pennsylvania Ballet of Philadelphia; the Utah Ballet in Salt Lake City; the Houston Ballet; and the Boston Ballet.

Attendance at major dance events has been steadily growing throughout the country, and an increased number of companies have held extended tours in cities large and small. State and regional councils on the arts have stimulated local dance workshops, classes, and performing groups. A number of cities and towns have Dance Councils; as of 1966, there were four major regional Ballet Associations, and over 80 small civic or regional ballet companies in the United States. While modern dance has not kept pace, in terms of the growth of large resident or touring companies, there is a considerable amount of choreographic experimentation and an increasing number of smaller companies performing in this field. Clive Barnes comments that this growth of interest suggests that Americans have discovered that there is nothing mysterious about dance:

> ... in the old days when dance was a cult, the especial province of dowagers swathed in diamonds and even gilded youths with gold-dust in their hair and star-dust in their eyes, in those long-distant, dizzy days of raging balletomania, the sensible man in the street regarded dancing, be it ballet or modern, as a crank fad. Well, the crank fad phase seems to be over, and theatrical dancing has won its place in the American world.[2]

Similarly, there has been a striking growth of dance activity in the field of education on two levels—within the formal curricula of schools and colleges, as part of general education, and in private dance schools and studios throughout the country. On the first level, dance is widely offered as a form of physical, creative, and social experience, usually within departments of physical education, in secondary schools. A recent survey revealed that over 270 colleges have impressive departments or major offerings in dance education; this number has expanded steadily since the early 1950s.[3]

In terms of community involvement in dance, the 1960 Census listed over 6,800 dance halls, studios, and schools (includ-

---

[2] Clive Barnes, *The New York Times*, May 19, 1966.
[3] *Dance Directory: Programs of Professional Preparation and General Educaion in American Colleges and Universities* (Washington, D.C.: American Association for Health, Physical Education, and Recreation, 1966).

ing professional dance schools for children) throughout the United
States. The social forms of dance continue to be popular, with a
single ballroom dance organization having over 450 franchised
studios throughout the country. Over 20,000 persons are employed
as dance teachers, in various kinds of settings. Television programs
and youth canteens or lounges feature teen-age "discotheque"
dancing, and thousands of adult folk and square dance clubs
provide informal social recreation to their devotees throughout
the country.

Thus we see a steady growth of involvement in dance for
students and spectators alike, and for both amateur and professional performers. The interest is nationwide, and it, too, is growing steadily.

Understanding Dance

To understand the reasons for the powerful appeal of dance,
and its growth as a cultural form in our society, it is necessary to
understand the nature of dance itself. So varied are the forms of
dance, and so different the motivations for carrying them on,
that it is difficult to offer a single definition or description that
encompasses all forms. There are at least six widely found forms
of dance, each with a unique character:

1. Ballet. The highly disciplined and codified stage art of
ballet, based on a centuries-old tradition of movement skills,
and with a repertoire today that is drawn from classical
performance and the most contemporary themes and choreographic approaches.

2. Modern Dance. Sometimes known as "contemporary"
dance, this highly individual form of artistic expression began
as a rejection of what its advocates saw as the formalism and
sterility of traditional ballet. Today, it still places emphasis
on the artistic expression of the individual performer, and
lacks a single approach to technique; however, its practitioners range from those who accept ballet as an indispensable
form of training to highly avant-garde practitioners who, in
performance at least, appear to be concerned with non-dance.

3. Social Dance. The most widely found form of participating dance, this ranges from the familiar ballroom dances
which were popular in past decades (the fox-trot, waltz,
tango, rumba, and other Latin-American steps), to the
pulsating and physically exciting rock-and-roll or "discotheque" dances of today's teen agers.

4. Musical Stage Dance. This hybrid form, as found on the Broadway stage or on television, usually combines elements of modern jazz, ballet, tap, and even ethnic dance. It tends to be a bright, spectacular, and highly polished form of dance, visually pleasing to a broad audience.

5. Recreational Dance. Many individuals perform the traditional folk dances of European countries, either because of their ethnic heritage or because they are part of an international folk dance movement. Similarly, American square dancing and round dancing are practiced by many thousands of enthusiasts in urban and suburban adult clubs. While these forms of dance—when done originally by the common people—were quite simple, today they are often extremely complicated, with new dances constantly being invented and introduced.

6. Ethnic Dance. This refers to the type of dance performed by ethnic groups—usually of a highly traditional nature, and often linked to religious practice and social customs. It differs from folk dance in that it is usually done as a form of spectacular entertainment, for an audience, while folk dance places emphasis on performance for the pleasure of the participant.

Thus we find a wide variety of distinctly different dance forms, ranging from social pastime to concert performance. Dance, in one form or another, appeals to all social classes and widely ranging levels of artistic taste. Some dances are centuries old; others were evolved quite recently. Dance has become an important part of our cultural, recreational, and educational experience. But, at the heart of all this, what *is* dance? Why does it continue to have such a strong appeal on all these levels, for both spectator and participant? What, essentially, is the meaning and purpose of dance in human life?

One might respond in several ways—in terms of the etymological source of the word, or through historical explanations of the term, or through the eyes of the philosopher, the psychologist, or the dancer himself. All of these viewpoints will be helpful in framing a definition.

To begin with—the word itself. According to Lincoln Kirstein, the English word *dance* is related to the French *danse*, which is believed to have been derived from the ancient high German *danson*, meaning to "stretch" or "drag." Each of these terms, along with other European variants (*dands, danca, danza, tanz*), is based on the root-combination of letters *tan*, found in the original Sanskrit, meaning tension, or stretching.[4] It is therefore apparent

---

[4] Lincoln Kirstein, *Dance: A Short History of Classic Theatrical Dancing* (New York: G. P. Putnam's Sons, 1935), p. 1.

that the idea of tension has, from the beginning of Western culture, been closely linked with dance. However, in a number of definitions dating from the time in which dance was becoming increasingly popular in the courts of Europe, one sees the stress on elegance, grace, and beauty. One authority, John Weaver, wrote in 1721:

> Dance is an elegant, and regular movement, harmoniously composed of beautiful attitudes, and contrasted graceful posture of the body, and parts thereof.[5]

Jean Georges Noverre, in 1760, described dance as follows:

> Dancing, according to the accepted definition of the word, is the art of composing steps with grace, precision and facility to the time and bars given in the music, just as music itself is simply the art of combining sounds and modulations so that they afford pleasure to the ear.[6]

Another early definition that places stress on order, precision, and graceful movement to the accompaniment of music is found in Diderot's *Encyclopedia* (ca. 1772):

> [Dancing is] ordered movements of the body, leaps and measured steps made to the accompaniment of musical instruments or the voice . . . .[7]

Clearly, these definitions were based on the kinds of ballroom or theatrical dance which were common in Europe during the 18th century. Dance was chiefly thought of as the graceful, formal, and highly stylized couple or set dances performed by members of the court, or as the equally stylized ballet of the period, performed as entertainment and narrative in its effect. One famed historian of the dance, Gaston Vuillier, made it very clear that only these forms were regarded as dance; indeed, among more primitive cultures, there was no dance:

> Like poetry and music, to which it is closely allied . . . the choreographic art . . . was probably unknown to the earlier ages of humanity. Savage man, wandering in forests, devouring the quivering flesh of his spoils, can have known nothing of those rhythmic postures which reflect sweet and caressing sensations entirely alien to his moods. The nearest approach to such must have been the leaps and bounds, the incoherent gestures, by which he expressed the joys and furies of his brutal life.[8]

[5] Anatole Chujoy, *The Dance Encyclopedia* (New York: A. S. Barnes & Co., Inc., 1949), p. 125.
[6] *Ibid.*
[7] *Ibid.*
[8] Gaston Vuillier, *A History of Dancing* (New York: D. Appleton and Co., 1897), p. ix.

But a true definition of dance must recognize that prehistoric man *did* dance; indeed, that this was a highly important part of his life, and was the ancestor of dance as we know it today. Sheldon Cheney, the distinguished historian of the drama, points out the significance of dance as an ancient form of primitive artistic expression:

> Man dances. After the activities that secure to primitive peoples the material necessities, food and shelter, the dance comes first. It is the earliest outlet for emotion and the beginning of the arts . . . .
>
> Not only did drama as such—the art of which *action* is a pivotal material—arise out of primitive dance . . . . Music, too, which can hardly be dissociated from the theatre's beginnings, traces its ancestry to the sounds made to accentuate the primitive dance rhythm, the stamping of feet and clapping of hands, the shaking of rattles, the beating of drums and sticks. Dance, then, is the great mother of the arts.[9]

Clearly, to describe dance in terms of a particular form (whether it be the ornate and graceful 18th-century French ballet, or the pounding rhythmic dance of a primitive ritual), gives only a partial picture. It is necessary to determine the essential nature of dance, rather than its outward form. What are the elements that distinguish this from other forms of human experience and expression? Two philosophers, James K. Feibleman and Thomas Munro, have attempted to analyze dance systematically, as a form of artistic experience.

Feibleman suggests that there are seven traditionally accepted fine arts: sculpture, dance, painting, architecture, poetry, drama, and music. Each of these has a basic concern, and a medium through which it finds expression. Thus, drama is the art which deals with the human social relations of life situations. Painting is the art which deals with the colors and qualities of two-dimensional space. Music is concerned with time, making use of sound vibrations in a temporal relationship. Feibleman defines dance as "that art which deals with the motions of the human body." Uniquely, it is ephemeral, in that it does not have a lasting product or record of performance.[10]

Accepting this as a concise statement which succeeds in distinguishing dance from other art forms, one must then explore the nature of "art." Thomas Munro points out that this is an extremely complex concept. There are many levels of art, ranging

[9] Sheldon Cheney, *Three Thousand Years of Drama, Acting and Stagecraft* (New York: Tudor Publishing Co., 1929), pp. 11–12.
[10] James K. Feibleman, *Aesthetics: A Study of the Fine Arts in Theory and Practice* (New York: Duell, Sloan and Pearce, 1949), p. 302.

from what might simply be a skill, or product of human manipulation, to the liberal arts, the fine arts, and the performing arts. Munro suggests that different types of art have different characteristics, in terms of how they are perceived, what their subject matter is, and whether or not they are directly functional. He suggests that there are:

Arts of simultaneous perception, such as architecture, sculpture, or painting, where we see all that is there to see, at once.

Arts of successive perception, which continue in time, changing form, such as music, dance, poetry, and drama.

Arts of space; some art forms are stationary, such as sculpture or painting. Others, like theater, or dance, are movable.

Arts that are imitative or non-imitative. Munro suggests that sculpture and painting are imitative, and that music and architecture are non-imitative. This distinction is not as useful today as in the past; however, if it is applied, dance may be both imitative and non-imitative.

Arts that are serviceable or non-serviceable; architecture and crafts are generally seen as serviceable in that they perform a "useful" function. Dancing, while less so, may perform a service, just as music or art may.

Munro discusses dance at length, pointing out that it is partly a theater art, partly a ballroom art, and partly a religious art. Finally, he states:

Dance is an art of rhythmic bodily movement, presenting to the observer an ordered sequence of moving visual patterns of line, solid shape, and color. The postures and gestures of which these are made suggest kinesthetic experiences of tension, relaxation, etc., and emotional moods and attitudes associated with them. They may also represent imaginary characters, actions, and stories. Dances are performed by one person or by two or more in mutual coordination; some animals can be trained to do simple dances. The movements are usually synchronized with, and partly aided by, musical or other rhythmic sounds . . . .[11]

Munro's analysis tends to be a description, rather than a definition. What is needed is a clarification of *why* dance is done. Suzanne Langer makes a strenuous attempt to do this, suggesting that ". . . the dancer expresses in gesture what he feels as the emotional content of music. . . ." The implication that the music must be the basis for dance performance, and the goal of the dancer merely to reflect what he feels to be the mood or emotional content

[11] Thomas Munro, *The Arts and Their Interrelationships* (New York: The Liberal Arts Press, 1951), p. 496.

of the music, is not satisfactory. Most choreographers would reject this view, pointing that that it is the dance which comes first, in most instances, and that music is then composed to accompany the dance. Again, Langer refers to dance as a "plastic art, a spectacle of shifting patterns of created design. . . ."[12] It is an illusion, a vivid representation, created, organized, formal—the play of power made visible.

While these passages give us a vivid sense of what concert dance is like, they are too restrictive in that they describe only a certain kind of dance. Langer's point, however, that emotional expression is at the heart of dance, is one which has been widely accepted by writers in this field, including the respected dance critic, John Martin. He comments that, no matter what the nature of the dance activity, in spite of many variations in outward appearances, all dance is essentially the same. His concept of "basic dance" is based on the view that emotional states tend to express themselves through physical movement. Often the movement is not representational, but it is a clue to the feelings of the person possessed by the emotional state. Dance, as Martin sees it, emerges when the dancer:

> . . . allows each of these impulses to express itself in movements which he deliberately remembers and develops in order to be able to convey to others something of his own intuitive reaction which is too deep for words. Thus, at the root of all these varied manifestations of dancing . . . lies the common impulse to resort to movement to externalize states which we cannot externalize by rational means. This is basic dance . . . .[13]

Here, then is a concept which, if it can be proved to apply in all situations, might well provide a unified explanation of dance. It is supported and amplified by the statements of two outstanding modern dance pioneers, Martha Graham and Doris Humphrey. Graham wrote:

> I am a dancer. My experience has been with dance as an art. Each art has an instrument and a medium. The instrument of dance is the human body; the medium is movement . . . . It has not been my aim to evolve or discover a new method of dance training, but rather to dance significantly. To dance significantly means "through the medium of discipline and by means of a sensitive, strong instrument, to bring into focus unhackneyed movement, a human being . . . ."[14]

[12] Suzanne Langer, *Feeling and Form* (New York: Charles Scribner's Sons, 1953), pp. 2–3.
[13] John Martin, *John Martin's Book of the Dance* (New York: Tudor Publishing Co., 1963), p. 8.
[14] Martha Graham, "A Modern Dancer's Primer for Action," in *Dance: A Basic Educational Technique*, by Frederick Rand Rogers (New York: The Macmillan Company, 1941), p. 178.

A somewhat different philosophy of dance purpose was expressed by Humphrey, who wrote:

> My dance is an art concerned with human values. It upholds only those values which make for harmony and opposes all forces inimical to those values. In part, its movement may be used for decoration, entertainment, emotional release, or technical display; but primarily it is composed as an expression of American life as I see it today .... I believe that the dancer belongs to his time and place and that he can only express that which passes through or close to his experience.[15]

This view that all dance has as its fundamental purpose the dancer's expression of his own emotions, or of his feelings about his life experience, would be meaningful if all dance were intended as communicative expression. Clearly, however, it is not. Much dance is simply ritual, practiced again and again because it is custom. Other dance involves social identification, or pastime, or simply a display of physical agility and grace. How then can one probe for the essential meaning of dance? Perhaps the anthropologist can help, if we seek to discover not so much the purpose of dance for the individual performer, but rather, its meaning for society. Sociologists have pointed out that dance is seen as a profoundly important social experience—a powerful rite shared by all members of the culture, and essential to its well-being. Margaret Mead commented about her anthropological studies in Samoa that "Dancing is the only activity in which almost all ages and both sexes participate, and it therefore offers a unique opportunity for an analysis of education."[16]

The cultural historian, Curt Sachs, has written that in the lives of primitive peoples and in ancient civilizations few experiences or communal functions approached the dance in importance. It is not viewed as an activity that is external to survival; indeed, he writes, it "provides bread and everything else that is needed to sustain life."

> It is not a sin proscribed by the priest or at best merely accepted by him, but rather a sacred act and priestly office; not a pastime to be tolerated only, but a very serious activity of the entire tribe. On no occasion in the life of primitive peoples could the dance be dispensed with. Birth, circumcision, and the consecration of maidens, marriage and death, planting and harvest, the celebration of chieftains, hunting, war, and feasts, the changes of the moon and sickness—for all of these the dance is needed.[17]

[15] Doris Humphrey, "My Approach to the Modern Dance," in *Dance: A Basic Educational Technique*, Rogers, p. 188.

[16] Margaret Mead, *From the South Seas* (New York: William Morrow & Co., Inc., 1939), p. 110.

[17] Curt Sachs, *World History of the Dance* (New York: W. W. Norton & Co., Inc., 1937), p. 4.

So important to the life of primitive man was dance, that it became a primary means of social identification. According to Havelock Ellis, when a man belonging to one branch of the African Bantu tribe met a Bantu of another branch, he would ask, "What do you dance?" The great power of dance for establishing a sense of tribal unity is vividly described in the following passage by the anthropologist Ruth Benedict. She writes of the Zuni tribe in the American Southwest:

> The dance, like their ritual poetry, is a monotonous compulsion of natural forces by reiteration. The tireless pounding of their feet draws together the mist in the sky and heaps it into the piled rain-clouds. It forces out the rain upon the earth. They are bent not at all upon an ecstatic experience, but upon so thorough-going an identification with nature that the forces of nature will swing to their purposes. This intent dictates the form and spirit of Pueblo dances. There is nothing wild about them. It is the cumulative force of the rhythm, the perfection of forty men moving as one, that makes them effective . . . .[18]

Among primitive peoples, then, one of the great purposes of dance was to establish social unity and provide a means of collective strength and purpose. Closely linked to this was the function of religious celebration or worship, in which dance was used as a means of communication. It represented a language for communication with the forces of nature—for becoming one with the gods. A number of examples of dance as religious worship among primitive tribes are illustrated in the chapter that follows.

What other fundamental urges are there that account for dance as a form of human expression? One, obviously, is the need to express oneself physically through rhythmic play, and through exploration of one's bodily powers and physical environment. Observe children playing—either toddlers in the crib or nursery school age children in a sandbox or play lot. They are constantly moving, crawling, lifting, clapping, kicking, running, manipulating their environment. Ted Shawn writes, in *Dance We Must:*

> We know that body movement is life itself—our movement begins in the womb before our birth and the new-born infant's need for movement is imperative and continuous. When we sleep there is constant movement, our hearts beat, our intestines work; in fact as long as there is life there is movement, and to move is hence to satisfy a basic and eternal need . . . .[19]

But movement alone is not enough. The quality of the movement experience is crucial. And dance has the capacity to promote a special kind of feeling—a sense of heightening of life, an exhilara-

[18] Ruth Benedict, *Patterns of Culture* (New York: Mentor Books, 1934, 1946), pp. 84–85.
[19] Ted Shawn, *Dance We Must* (London: Dennis Dobson Ltd., 1946), p. 9.

tion, a sense of joy. It has a unique capacity to blend, or combine, the physical and emotional aspects of our being in an integrated expression. The ability to release one's feelings in this way is a deeply therapeutic and healthful function. A distinguished psychoanalyst, Joost Meerloo, suggests that dance is such a widely found form of human expression and emotional release that those who cannot dance are "imprisoned in their own ego," and have lost the "tune of life." He describes them as "deeply repressed" and "forlorn." Through the ages, he writes,

> . . . sorrow, pleasure and ecstasy have been expressed by ritualized, festive dances. The rhythm of life brings the dance, and the dance brings the *saltatio*, jump, and the *ludus*, the playful activity. Every dance transforms man's innate passive rhythm—the mechanical beat in him—into the active rhythm of personal music. Dancing promotes man's vital pulsations, it changes mechanical repetitiveness into passionate and ebullient life. It lets man rediscover his body as a tool of expression.[20]

In Meerloo's view, dance is thus seen as a means of enriching life, of expressing man's deepest moods. In this sense, he supports Martin's view of the purpose of basic dance. However, as one examines certain forms of dance, such as the mechanical performance of tap dance, or folk or square dance, each of which is primarily social in nature and often involves designed movement with little emotional content or release, one must ask whether this purpose is found in all dance.

What other purposes does dance serve?

A commonly cited function is that of its role in courtship between the sexes. There is a theory that dance occurs psychologically among primitive peoples as a result of non-repressive sublimation of the libido. It is thus an expression of sexual drive, a means of displaying one's vigor or beauty, and part of the complicated ritual surrounding the entrance into adulthood and the act of courtship. Certainly, this is true in our own society, where young people dance on social occasions, or as part of the process of dating. Dancing provides socially accepted physical contact, and is a direct means of expressing sexual attractiveness; indeed, many of the teen-age dances performed today are frankly sexual and derived from primitive dance movements that were related to fertility symbolism.

But this too is true only of some dances, and there are many forms in which courtship or sexual attraction plays no part.

It is a mistake, then, to assume that *all* forms of dance have a common core or purpose or meaning. Instead, dance may have

[20] Joost Meerloo, *The Dance* (New York: Chilton Book Company, 1960), pp. 39–40.

many functions, but these vary, according to the society, the class, the age or sex, the religious structure, and similar factors about those who dance. Within varied kinds of societies, past and present, primitive and complex, Judeo-Christian or animist, one might find any or all of the following purposes for dance:

1. It is a form of social affirmation, a means of expressing national or tribal loyalty and strength.

2. It is a means of religious worship, as a form of ritual and direct means of communicating with the gods.

3. It is an art form, an outlet for self-expressiveness and personal creativity; within the mainstream of cultural inheritance, it may be the source of great works which are performed as part of a continuing tradition, or a basis for continuing artistic experimentation.

4. It may also be a form of popular entertainment, appealing to a broader audience than when it represents an art form with a high level of aesthetic worth.

5. Dance may serve as a means of expressing physical exuberance, strength, and agility.

6. It offers an important social and recreational outlet, both as a means of restoring oneself physically, and of finding social acceptance within group participation.

7. It provides a medium through which courtship can be carried on, and attraction expressed between the sexes.

8. Dance serves as a means of education, in the sense that it is taught to achieve the specific purposes of education within a given society, just as art, music, or theater are taught as cultural forms.

9. Dance serves as an occupation; in increasing numbers, it offers a means of livelihood to performers and teachers.

10. Finally, dance serves as therapy; for many it offers a form of physical and emotional release and rehabilitation; thus it is provided, along with other therapies, in many treatment centers.

Blending all of these elements together, one is able to isolate a number of factors that are useful in developing a definition of dance. These include the following:

1. Use of the human body. Here we are concerned only with those forms of dance which involve people in performance. While, as Langer points out, one might refer to the "dancing" of gnats in the air as a kind of dance motif or patterned movement, and while animals or birds frequently carry on dance-like and even ritualistic movements, in this context we will not consider these forms as dance.

2. Extends Through Time. Dance is not a frozen tableau, or a single gesture or picture of movement; instead, it is a continuing sequence of activity, extending through time, and may comprise a few moments, or may last for several hours or days.

3. Exists in Space. Dance is three-dimensional; it exists on a ballroom floor, on a stage, or in a village square.

4. Accompanied by Rhythm. Most dance is rhythmically patterned; it is performed either to the accompaniment of music, chanting, handclapping, or percussive beating. Even those dances which may be performed silently, or to the accompaniment of speech or arbitrarily devised or selected sound effects, usually have a rhythmic structure.

5. Serves to Communicate. Most dance has communicative intent, ranging from the literal characterization or storytelling of pantomimic dance or traditional ballet, to the expression of personal emotion or physical exuberance. Even dances which are intended as abstract, non-literal forms, convey a kind of meaning to the onlooker—depending on his ability to perceive or translate the movement in personal terms.

6. Has Movement Style and Form. Unlike a child's aimless and playlike exploration of movement, most dance has a characteristic movement style, and has a structure or form. This may range from the use of gestures or step patterns which are typically found in a particular type of ethnic or social dance, to the carefully choreographed sequence of individual and group movements that one finds in concert dance.

Using the word "art" in its broadest sense, that of involving human skill, one arrives at the following definition:

Dance is an art performed by individuals or groups of human beings, existing in time and space, in which the human body is the instrument and movement is the medium. The movement is stylized, and the entire dance work is characterized by form and structure. Dance is commonly performed to musical or other rhythmic accompaniment, and has as a primary purpose the expression of inner feelings and emotions, although it is often performed for social, ritual, entertainment, or other purposes.

One final distinction may be made. It has been suggested that there are two types of dance—the kind which is performed by people, usually as a mass activity, without an audience (or in which the idea of performance is secondary to the idea of doing the dance for oneself), and the kind of dance which is *meant* to be performed for an audience. John Martin phrased it in this way:

Dance falls naturally into two major categories: that which is done for the emotional release of the individual dancers, without regard to the possible interest of a spectator; and that, on the other hand, which is done for the enjoyment of a spectator either as an exhibition of skill, the telling of a story, the presentation of pleasurable designs, or the communication of emotional experience . . . .[21]

According to this view, most dances were originally of the first type and were meant to be performed as communal activity; the second type is considered to have descended from the first. Ballet and modern dance are essentially concert forms, meant to be performed on a stage and before an audience of spectators. On the other hand, such forms as social, folk, or square dance are primarily participant forms. However, this distinction breaks down in some of the present-day uses of dance. Thus, it is not at all uncommon for children or adults to study modern dance or ballet because of the enjoyment and personal benefits this brings to them, without ever doing a performance, other than possibly a recital at the end of the studio year. On the other hand, social, folk, square, and especially ethnic dance—which may all be regarded as primarily participant dance forms—are often done on a highly skilled level, and may provide the basis for performances or exhibitions. Often, national performing groups develop their dances to a high level of artistic quality. They may even combine (as in the case of the Moiseyev and other European "folk ballet" companies) traditional peasant and regional dance forms with balletic training and complex choreography which makes their performance very attractive to an audience. Too, in a number of concert works on the ballet or modern dance stage, folk and ethnic themes or movements are used as the basis for choreography. In the past, the court dances of the nobility, which were closely linked with the beginning of ballet, were carried on both as entertainment and for social participation; they, in turn, owed much of their origin to the folk forms of peasants.

Perhaps it would be better to say that, rather than dividing dance rigidly into "spectator" and "participant" forms, dance may range from the simple to the complex, and may under one circumstance or another, have as its primary purpose either performance or participation.

In order to better understand the current role of dance in our society, as a cultural form and as education, it is necessary to understand its historical development. The following chapters will therefore be devoted to an exploration of dance among primitive peoples—both past and present—and to its role in societies preceding our own.

[21] John Martin, *John Martin's Book of the Dance*, p. 20.

2

DANCE IN
PRIMITIVE CULTURES

As the preceding chapter has made clear, dance is found among all the peoples and civilizations of the world. Among primitive cultures, where we see its social and religious functions most clearly displayed, dance plays an important role throughout life. It is important, in thinking of primitive societies, to recognize that this term is based chiefly on assessment of the scientific, technical, and economic advancement of the culture. The patterns of education, religion, and social custom may be highly complex; the arts may also be extremely sophisticated. Here we are thinking of societies that are essentially tribal, living in rural surroundings, and depending on hunting or agriculture for their livelihood.

Within such cultures, past and present, dance has been a major form of social expression and religious ritual—a utilitarian and omnipresent art. Pearl Primus, the American Negro dancer who went to Africa to study the dance of her forebears, writes with the trained eye of an anthropologist:

The role of the professional dancer was of tremendous importance in Africa. He was necessary to all ceremonies, all feasts, all occasions which involved the health and well-being of the tribe. In return for his services the tribe fed and clothed him and provided for him in his every need. He was left free to dance . . . . Is it any wonder then that dance stands with music and art at the very top of the list of cultural contributions of the African to the world? Is it any wonder that the dancer developed to such an extent that he could spin his head on his neck so rapidly that the onlooker saw nothing but blur ... or that he could leap from the ground with feet outstretched in a wide sitting position and land on his buttocks only to spring into the air again unhurt? Is it any wonder that a group of fifty warriors could dance their spear dances and not one finger be out of place?[1]

Why was dance so important to primitive societies? What are its functions? Essentially, they are much the same as those listed in the previous chapter; dance is used as a means of worship, as a way of expressing and reinforcing tribal unity and strength, as a framework for courtship or mating, as a means of communication, and as a therapeutic or healing experience. It is likely that the use of dance as a means of aesthetic expression would rarely be found among primitive peoples; rather than form the audience for such a performance, they dance themselves. Nor was dance viewed as a means of recreation after labor; the life of primitive man does not make a clear distinction between work and rest, and rituals and playlike experience are thoroughly integrated with the productive work of the society.

How did dance begin among primitive peoples? Douglas Kennedy suggests that the religious aspect of dance generally had as its purpose communication with the unseen forces which provided food, promoted fertility, regulated the weather, gave good fortune in warfare—and thus controlled tribal welfare and human survival. Man danced originally to supplicate the gods, on all important occasions of life. Kennedy writes:

> As the faith behind such primitive religious impulses weakens, the dances which express it are not immediately abandoned, but they gradually change their character. The form of the ritual remains, but some of the magical content departs. The dancer becomes less and less of a medicine-maker and more and more a performing artist. In fact, the ritual changes imperceptibly into art. It was in some such manner that the folk dances in different parts of Europe grew out of old pagan rites as the pagans themselves were converted to Christianity and gradually lost their primitive beliefs ... in industrialized ... England, there are still a few ancient rituals directly descended from the pre-Christian era, and retaining, to a surprising degree, their aura of primitive magic.[2]

Probably one of the first uses of dance was as gesture, in order to communicate. Suzanne Langer writes at length of the develop-

---

[1] Pearl Primus, "Out of Africa," in *The Dance Has Many Faces*, by Walter Sorell (New York: The World Publishing Company, 1951), pp. 256–57.
[2] Douglas Kennedy, *England's Dances* (London: G. Bell & Sons, Ltd., 1950), pp. 31–32.

ment of language and symbolic gesture, showing how man developed certain stylized ways of expressing himself. Gradually, the use of expressive gesture, of facial expressions, of a combination of guttural sound and action to reinforce an idea led to the use of dance as a means of telling a story or giving information. Because of the lack of adequate speech, man was probably compelled to use easily recognizable gesture, sometimes supplementing the movement with the cries of animals or other natural sounds, or with whatever basic words he had developed. The elaborate East Indian *mudras*, or hand language used in dance, and the sign language of the American Indian are both examples of this kind of gesture-communication, elaborately systematized.

Ted Shawn suggests that the scope of what had to be conveyed gradually expanded, as culture became more complex. From the simple telling of a hunt or trip, much more elaborate or difficult ideas had to be conveyed through gesture. It became the practice to perform war dances in preparation for battle, or to celebrate victory; dances for weddings, births, christenings, and funerals. As society became differentiated, in terms of tribal or clan structures, and then in terms of levels of authority or special function, it became necessary to insure that the religious rituals of the group were carried out properly; a class of special performers came into being:

> Certain individuals were better dancers than others, were able to attain a greater degree of ecstasy, a nearer-perfect union with the God-given, than others. In these states, such magic-dancers were subject to visions and to prophetic utterances; these premier dancers were thus singled out for special respect and authority, and such a one was called the Shaman or medicine-man. Thus was born the priesthood.[3]

One of the important sources of inspiration of primitive dance was the movement of birds and animals. Prehistoric and early primitive man was undoubtedly acutely aware of the living things around him. He hunted them for food and clothing, he fought them for survival, and he knew well their courage, their beauty and their cunning. Most primitive people have an animist religion, in which they believe in animals possessing souls and being very much like people. Indeed, among many tribes the idea of reincarnation, and of transmigration of souls between humans and animals, is completely accepted. All this was woven in with a sense of mystery about the natural phenomena that surrounded man— the sun, the moon, the stars, night, day, the seasons of the year,

---

[3] Ted Shawn, *Dance We Must* (London: Dennis Dobson Ltd., 1946), p. 55.

life, and death. Most primitive tribes were, and many still are, deep believers in magic; they had no other way to explain the growing of a seed, or the entry of disease into a body, or lightning, thunder—or fate.

Thus, primitive man observed animals closely, felt one with them, attributed great powers to them; he drew, engraved, painted, carved, and told stories about them. He also danced them.

Without question, the dancelike movement of animals was one of the inspirations for the dance of primitive man. For it is true that many insects, birds, animals, and even fish carry out ritualized movement patterns that appear to be very much like our conception of dance.

George Wald, a professor of biology at Harvard, has noted that many human behavior patterns have evolved from those of animals. He suggests that fear and rage, for example, grew out of the need to prepare the body for sudden, strenuous action—either to fight or to flee. He has described, too, how certain movement patterns are used by bees, as part of their total social behavior, and as a means of communication and decision-making. His analysis is based on the work of an Austrian investigator, Karl von Frisch, who found that, by certain dancelike routines, a bee can tell others where it has found a rich store of nectar. Now, another researcher

> ... has discovered that dances are also used in searching for a site for a new hive. Worker bees fan out in this hunt. When they find a likely place, they return and dance before the swarm. The better the spot, the more prolonged and intense the dance. Other workers, told of the site through the dance pattern, go out to investigate and in turn give their opinion by a dance .... In this way the swarm achieves a consensus and flies out to build its new home ....[4]

Joost Meerloo describes dancing movements among fish, particularly the astonishing breeding behavior and courtship of the Cichlids, whose slow dancing movements, together with their extremely vivid color, provide what he calls a "slow motion waltz." Meerloo also refers to the unusual mass behavior of ants, in which they march in complicated and elaborate patterns and formations.[5]

Sachs has described the dance of an unusual storklike bird, the stilt bird of Cape York in northeastern Australia, only one of many birds which have been observed to fly or move around the ground in rhythmic and graceful patterns which resemble dance. These birds have been observed assembling by the hundreds in

[4] *The New York Times*, March 15, 1966, p. 40.
[5] Joost Meerloo, *The Dance* (New York: Chilton Book Company, 1960), pp. 45–46.

> In groups of a score or more they advanced and retreated, lifting
> high their long legs and standing on their toes, now and then bowing
> gracefully one to another, now and then one pair encircling with
> prancing daintiness a group whose heads moved downwards and
> sidewide to the stepping of the pair . . . .[6]

Perhaps most dancelike of all are the play forms, almost
approaching dance, which are carried on by chimpanzees. A
German investigator, Kohler, observed a number of these large
apes over a period of time, and describes them as having a variety
of behaviors to which newcomers joining their group were introduced. They used instruments and implements for reaching or
climbing; carried on a "sort of rhythmic play or dance," and made
a variety of murmurs, wails, and rejoicing sounds. Two of the
apes in particular, Tschego and Grande, developed a game of
spinning round and round like dervishes, in a spirit of friendly
play, which the other apes enjoyed greatly. The resemblance to
human dance became striking when one ape stretched out her
arm horizontally as she spun around, or revolved slowly on her
own axis. The group of chimpanzees sometimes trotted around
a post, marking a rough rhythm by accenting the movement of
one foot.[7]

Wild apes have even been observed to join hands and move
around rhythmically in a circle or weaving line, sometimes
bedecking themselves with leaves and boughs. Observing the
movements of animals carrying on such dancelike activities, it
is natural that primitive man would imitate them. He may have
believed that by impersonating them, he would gain their strength
or cunning—just as, to the primitive mind, obtaining the nail
clippings of a person may give him power over that person. His
purpose may have been to imitate the animal as part of storytelling, or for amusement, or to recount adventures. In any case,
just as animals are personified within folk myths, and appear
again and again in primitive carvings, so many primitive dances
are based on specific animal themes.

However, a superficial imitation of the movement of animals,
even when costumed by masks, skins, or horns, was not enough.
As Langer points out, man differs from animal in terms of ritual,
feeling, superstition, and scientific genius. His life is impregnated

---

[6] Curt Sachs, *World History of the Dance* (New York: W. W. Norton &
Company, 1937), p. 9.
[7] Suzanne Langer, *Philosophy in a New Key: A Study in the Symbolism of
Reason, Rite, and Art* (New York: The New American Library, 1942, 1951), p. 114.

with ritual—a complicated blend of reason and rite, fact and dream. Gradually, during the performance of ritual, primitive man's simpler imitative movements or gesture language became transformed into a more elaborate structure of symbolic acts, combining dance, acting, singing, and primitive speech, all wrapped around with complicated conventions and undergirded by an unquestioning belief in the efficacy of ceremony. All nature was embraced by such rites. Langer writes:

> The apparently misguided efforts of savages to induce rain by dancing and drumming are not practical mistakes at all; they are rites in which the rain has a part. White observers of Indian rain dances have often commented on the fact that in an extraordinary number of instances the downpour really "results." Others of a more cynical turn remark that the leaders of the dance know the weather so well that they time their dance to meet its approaching changes and simulate "rain-making." This may well be the case; yet it is not a pure imposture. A "magic" effect is one which completes a rite . . . he dances *with* the rain; he invites the elements to do their part . . . if heaven and earth do not answer him, the rite is simply unconsummated . . . .[8]

The power of religious belief among primitive peoples is tremendous. Often it is responsible for phenomena that otherwise could not possibly be explained on rational grounds. A dervish who dances for twelve or fifteen hours at a stretch, whirling steadily without faltering, demonstrates a degree of endurance and self-control that is almost beyond belief. A voodoo dancer in the West Indies who sits on a metal frame above a fire, her skin pressed against the glowing iron, is not burned. Trance dancers in Indonesia repeatedly thrust sharp daggers against their bare chests, so forcefully that the weapons are bent; yet they are not injured. Are these tricks? In some cases they may be, but too many illustrations of such primitive rites have been gathered to question the power of such magical belief. Perhaps the answer lies in hypnosis. Yet, for primitive man, the fact that such rites "worked" made him believe in them unquestioningly as a means of gaining divine protection. He sought the favor of the gods, or of nature, in every aspect of his life—for food, shelter, success in warfare, protection against the forces of nature, and in procreation.

A great concern of his, of course, was the magical act of perpetuating the species—of carrying on the tribe. Thus, many primitive dances are concerned with fertility, and are performed at ceremonies having to do with entrance into adolescence, courtship, marriage, and birth. Just as the primitive artist is usually

[8] *Ibid.*, pp. 138–39.

quite representational, except for those decorations which are intended as abstract design, so the primitive dance on such themes is usually quite frank. Hakansson writes on this point:

> ... primitive art ... is representational, conventional, and intended to be understood by the audience for which the artist creates. He decorates houses and equipment and he composes ceremonies concerned with birth, puberty rites, marriage, ancestors, hunting, harvestings, the seasons, and war. The primitive artist is really a craftsman. He is well integrated with the community in which he works. Whereas in our civilization the artist is a specialist and an outsider, a rebel against the conventions of his society, in the primitive community art is a necessity, not merely a form of entertainment ... art ... produces an esthetic effect that is both gratifying and vital, and is a useful social phenomenon, leading to participation of the artist-craftsman with the fellow members of his community in the use of his work—generally in dancing, rituals, and feasts.[9]

Hakansson points out that often art portrays dances and rituals which are part of initiation, clearly phallic in nature. Sex and sexual functions are expressed naturally, with a degree of distortion, or abstractly; often abstract decorations of art objects of primitive people are really stylized sex symbols and are recognized as such by the tribe that uses them.

According to Sachs, human fertility dances may be drawn from two different phases of sexual relations—the mating and wooing, and the act itself. In some cases, he says, moments of sexual intercourse may actually be made part of the dance. Quoting Koch-Grunberg, he describes a fertility dance of the Cobéna Indians of Brazil. The dancers have large artificial replicas of the male organ, which they hold close to their bodies with both hands.

> Stamping with the right foot and singing, they dance—with the upper part of their bodies bent forwards. Suddenly they jump wildly along with violent coitus motions and loud groans . . . . They carry the fertility into every corner of the houses . . . . They jump among the women—they knock the phalli one against another . . . .[10]

Sachs describes primitive dance as being essentially of two types: those which he considers to be out of harmony with the body, and those which are in harmony. In general, the dance which is "out of harmony" is one in which dancers work themselves into extreme nervous excitement. The song is panted out; movements are jerky and uncontrolled. The action is wild, eerie,

---

[9] Tore Hakansson, "Sex in Primitive Art and Dance," in *The Encyclopedia of Sexual Behavior*, eds. Albert Ellis and Albert Abarbanel (New York: Hawthorn Books, Inc., 1961), pp. 154–60.
[10] Sachs, *op. cit.*, p. 157.

ecstatic. Dancers may actually go into a trance corresponding to a medical description of clonic convulsion—a state of forceful flexion and relaxation of the muscles which may lead to a throwing about of the body in wild paroxyms. He gives as an example the dance of the secret society of the Wayee tribesmen in Unyamwezi, in Africa:

> . . . suddenly the dancers swing into violent motion. All the parts of their bodies begin to shake, all their muscles play, their shoulder blades roll as if they were no longer a part of their bodies. The drums resound louder and louder. Their bodies are bathed with sweat from head to foot. Now they stand as though changed to statues. Only the weird jerking of the muscles over their whole body continues. Then, when the excitement has risen to its highest point, they suddenly collapse as if struck by lightning and remain for a time on the ground as though unconscious. After a short time the play begins anew.[11]

He also classifies as "out of harmony" the type of dance that is based on a weakened convulsive state. Here, what had originally been a complete surrender to frenzy develops into a conscious art form; the movement is subordinated to the dancer's will, and the convulsion, or loss of control, is limited to a portion of the dancer's body. At no point does the dancer go into a full state of trance, nor does he usually inflict great suffering on himself.

In Sachs's terms, the primitive dance that is "in harmony" with the body is the one that does not "mortify or degrade" the body, but "exalts" it. Through repeated movement, the dancer achieves exhilaration. The dance is powerful, with strong motor reactions, every muscle stretched taut; it brings about a release from gravity with buoyant movements forward and upward. Actions involve leaping, lifting, slapping, stamping, striding, and lunging. Such dances are bold and positive.

Specific movements of primitive dance may include whirling, leaping, vibrating, and rolling of the pelvis, striding, and stamping. Certain dances, particularly in the Orient, tend to have a much narrower range of movement, and the movement itself may be much more subtle. Such dances frequently are performed on a limited base, with swinging, swaying, and suspension, with gesture language of the hands and arms. In certain dances on Pacific islands, particularly in the Marshall Archipelago, women sit on their heels; in others they sit cross-legged. Frequently, dances in such positions involve clapping in complicated rhythms, or the use of coconut shells or other instruments, to create percussive effects.

[11] *Ibid.*, p. 18.

The movement quality of much primitive dance has been well described by Agnes de Mille:

> All primitives . . . who go barefoot and hunt unprotected by armor, have certain characteristics in common. They stamp out rhythms. They run crouched low in imitation of animals or of the precautionary attitudes adopted when stalking prey or an enemy . . . .[12]

She suggests that, because of primitive man's nakedness and vulnerability, he bends to the ground to protect his vitals. Rhythm and complex foot movements are often stressed in primitive dance, rather than elaborate visual patterns or body movements. Dancing as part of primitive ritual is carried out over many hours; both endurance and intensity are stressed, as well as exact adherence to the rules for performance.

The themes of primitive dance are many. As indicated, many are animal dances, often with masks which give the dancer the godlike or magic power of the animal portrayed. Sometimes their skins or horns are worn. Such dances are performed as a prelude to hunting, or sometimes as part of fertility rituals. War dances are found in tribes throughout the world; often these are weapon dances, in which the motions of warfare are used, and in which dancers may sometimes work themselves up to a pitch of hysteria or trance. In many cultures ancient myths are acted out—often with the essential theme of the battle between good and evil, life and death, being reenacted. Other motifs for dance often include dances based on astral themes, portraying the sun, moon, or stars.

Among the American Plains Indians, the dancing ground frequently was laid out so that it had four sacred places, each named in honor of the deities who presided over the four cardinal points of the compass. Among the Cherokees, these points were known as the Sun Land (east), the Frigid Land (north), the Darkening Land (west), and Wahala (south). Each of these had a color assigned to it, and each color had symbolic meaning. White and red spirits were usually invoked for peace and health, red alone for success of an undertaking, blue for defeating a cunning enemy, and black for causing his death.

One of the most famous dances of the Plains Indians was the Sun Dance. Radin describes this, as performed by the Oglala Dakota. Basically, it is interpreted as a dance concerned with supplication to the deities for power and success in warfare, and it represents the cruelest kind of testing of the braves who took

[12] Agnes de Mille, *The Book of the Dance* (New York: Golden Press, 1963), pp. 32–33.

part in it. It was usually carried out by a warrior in fulfillment of a vow made at a crucial moment in his life when the help of the gods was needed. After a number of secret rites are carried out, to purify and prepare the initiate, there is a ceremonial search for a center-pole for the dance. When the proper tree is found, it is felled, brought to the camp, and erected. There is a period of fasting, prayer, chanting, and offerings to the gods, for a period of days and nights.

The Sun Dance itself involved a dramatic climax of self-inflicted torture. Medicine men would take up as much of the skin of the breast under the nipple of each dancer as could be held between the thumb and forefinger. A cut would be made and a skewer inserted through the flesh. The skewer would then be tethered to the center-pole, fastened by long ropes of woven hair or thongs. The warriors then danced, straining back against the thongs and staring up into the blinding white sun, until finally the flesh of their chest had torn loose and the thongs and skewers were pulled through.

> . . . as they dance, they hold eagle pipes in their mouths, this being a term for flutes made from one of the bones in an eaglet's wing. They had to be sounded throughout the time the young man was dancing. The dancing was done in the manner of a buck jump, the body and legs being stiff and all movements being upon the tips of the toes. The dancers kept looking at the sun, and either dropped the hands to the sides in the military position of "attention" with the palms to the front, or else held them upward and outward at an angle of 45 degrees, with the fingers spread apart and inclined toward the sun . . . .[13]

This ordeal frequently continued for many hours, until the warrior had proved his manhood by completing the ritual successfully. To understand such a dance, it is necessary to recognize that it is part of a total religious belief, a symbolic representation, a prayer which in many cases is hundreds of years old. In a sense, it is part of an elaborate drama which embraces all the arts and which is performed with the strictest adherence to authentic detail. Fergusson writes:

> Most of the Indian ceremonials are extremely elaborate, lasting for days and ending on the last day or night with the dance. Outsiders are usually permitted to see only the dance. The secret ceremonies take place in the kiva or medicine lodge and are open only to clan members or to the dancers. Sometimes they are historical or legendary in character, presenting the life of the whole people or of a

[13] Paul Radin, *The Story of the American Indian* (New York: Garden City Publishing Company, 1937), p. 313.

certain hero. Often elaborate altars are erected and painted with symbolic decorations, sand paintings are made and destroyed at specified hours and, with meticulous care for detail, costumes are prepared for the dance, masks are painted and decorated with feathers, prayer sticks are made. The dancers must be purified by means of fasting and medication, bathing the body, and washing the hair. Everything is done under the direction of the cacique or medicine-man, whose duty it is to see that nothing goes wrong, as the slightest slip may ruin the effect of the entire ceremony.[14]

American Indians of the Southwest performed dances that ranged from rituals of the utmost solemnity to others of a purely social and humorous character. As observed in the 1930s, certain dances were done for the cure of disease, notably the "medicine sings" of the Navajo tribe. These were elaborate nine-day ceremonials, which included prayers and the making of sand paintings in secret, sweat baths and medications for the patient, and finally the all-night dance . . . . They were conducted by medicine men, who knew every detail of the ritual, every song, every sand painting, word, and movement of the dance.

So varied are the dances of African tribes that it is difficult to characterize or classify them meaningfully. They embrace all the themes and motivations described earlier: war, the hunt, fertility, courtship, marriage, harvest, birth, initiation into adolescence or adulthood, and burial. Typically, many African dances are derived from motions performed during work. The rhythm that characterizes the dancers of this continent also pervades their labor; by singing and moving in unison, such tasks as rowing, carrying heavy burdens, or felling trees are made easier.

Although many of the functions of primitive dance have declined with the coming of civilization, often they continued to be performed as a matter of custom and national or tribal pride. Today, they may no longer be based on a conscious belief in magic; however, they are still seen as talismans of good fortune, and as expressions of patriotic unity. When over 1,000 Ethiopian troops were on their way to join the fighting in Korea in 1951, a newspaper account described them in this way:

> . . . a neat, well-disciplined contingent chosen for their fighting ability from among the finest units of the Ethiopian Army. Like all professional soldiers, they were deeply interested in the use of the Garand rifle [and had] frequent training periods; second only to this interest was their love for the symbolic dances of their country in which they engaged every noontime and evening . . . .[15]

[14] Erna Fergusson, *Indian Ceremonials of New Mexico and Arizona* (Albuquerque: University of New Mexico Press, 1931, 1951), p. xviii.

[15] *The New York Times,* July 1, 1951, p. 59.

Ten years later, in 1961, Sukarno, the then-President of Indonesia, made a point of forbidding his people to perform Western dances:

> . . . emotional, proud and determined to eradicate the scars of inferiority left by the Dutch on the Indonesians, Mr. Sukarno believes that everything Indonesian should be celebrated—from a made-in-Indonesia matchstick to Indonesian culture. He has assumed the role of impresario of the archipelago's music, dance and art. At informal palace receptions, he often puts Ambassadors through hours of knee-straining Indonesian dances.[16]

Typically, in a number of the emerging nations of Africa, a strong effort is made to retain traditional folk customs—particularly the dance. In 1966, King Sobhuza II, the Ngwenyama, or Lion of Swaziland, joined thousands of his people in a ceremonial six-day incwala, a central ritual in the life of Swaziland, symbolic of the renewal of the people, land, and king.

> The Ngwenyama, who wears three-piece suits when he addresses Parliament or dedicates factories, was dressed like his warriors. That is, he wore a headdress of fancy plumage, a leopard-skin girdle, and a mantle of ox tails. He danced barefoot on the earth of the royal cattle corral, where the ceremony took place. Many sophisticated young Swazis, European educated, took part. One university graduate said: "I used to shy away from these ceremonies. But there has been a remarkable change of late. We all realize now that this is our national land. It's something we've got to support and be proud of . . . ."[17]

In other countries, even those of Western world, where the pagan dances of earlier centuries have all but disappeared, there is a deliberate effort to retain and revive these forms, as evidences of the historical past. One example is England, where the efforts of Cecil Sharp led to the development of the England Folk Dance and Song Society, which has been instrumental in a widespread revival of English country, Morris, and sword dancing. Many of the original dances done by clubs and teams throughout the country date from pre-Christian days; some are directly suggestive of early pagan rituals. Thus, even in a heavily industrialized nation, elements of primitive dance survive in recognizable form. In other parts of the world, where village life, simple handicrafts, and agricultural pursuits have retained their traditional forms, primitive dances still exist and still hold much of their appeal for the peasantry—although the original magical belief that prompted them has largely slipped away.

[16] *The New York Times*, September 21, 1961.
[17] *The New York Times*, January 13, 1966, Sec. L, p. 9.

3

DANCE IN
PRE-CHRISTIAN
CIVILIZATIONS

It is reasonable to assume that prehistoric man danced; indeed, we have records of what appear to be war dances and shaman dances in cave paintings that date back tens of thousands of years, in what is now France. However, because of the limited number of examples, little is known of these dances. Based on other facts known about the culture of prehistoric peoples at various levels of development—in terms of their utensils, tools, weapons—it is possible to draw parallels with primitive tribes existing in the world today. Thus, conjectures may be made about their customs, their means of cultivation, their dwellings and communities, and similar aspects of their lives. However, these are largely speculation. Our first real knowledge of dance comes with the great Mediterranean civilizations that preceded the Christian era.

The ancient Chaldeans are said to have used the dance as education, and are accredited with the beginnings of the science of astronomy, which they taught by means of great symbolic ballets. Shawn writes that on a saucer-shaped plain outside one of their great cities, the population would assemble on a designated day. Each adult met at a temple built in honor of the planet under whose sign he was born. Then, arranging themselves in complicated patterns, accompanied by bronze horns and gongs, they proceeded to reproduce the movements of the stars, as children watched on the surrounding slopes.[1] Many of these elements were similar to the structure of ancient Indian dances, in North and Central America, although there is no evidence to suggest communication between these civilizations, widely separated in both time and space.

The early Sumerians had a vigorous musical culture; they developed in the third millenium B.C. lyres, pipes, harps, and drums, some of which they passed on to succeeding Babylonians and Assyrians. In Sumer, a sacred dance was practiced in various forms. In one, a procession of singers is recorded to have moved soberly, perhaps around an altar, to liturgies played on flutes. In another, dancers prostrated themselves before the altar or other sacred objects, as part of religious worship.

In ancient Assyria, many depictions of dancing men and women have been found, suggesting that dance was found both as part of religious practice and as part of the social life of the time. Processions led by men playing harps have been noted, and it is known that the great fire festival of Ashtoreth, the goddess of fertility, which was celebrated every spring, was noted for having wine-crazed dancers slash and mutilate themselves with knives to the orgiastic accompaniment of drums, cymbals, and droning oboes.[2] In Babylon, too, the occurrence of temple dancing has been confirmed; in the text of the Assurbanipal, it is stated that at a religious festival the performers danced a ring-dance, to musical accompaniment, around the idol of the god who was being worshipped.[3]

Dance in Ancient Egypt

However, it was in ancient Egypt, a civilization which lasted for 4,000 years, that dance for the first time reached a full flowering, and was richly recorded, in wall paintings and reliefs, and in the literary record of the hieroglyphs. The Egyptian culture was a complex one, and achieved an advanced understanding of astronomy and geometry, sculpture, architecture, and engineering, as well as initiating the use of paper and weaving processes. It also developed for the first time a varied class structure, with royal

[1] Ted Shawn, *Dance We Must* (London: Dennis Dobson Ltd., 1946), p. 16.
[2] Alfred Sendrey and Mildred Norton, *David's Harp: The Story of Music in Biblical Times* (New York: The New American Library, 1964), p. 14.
[3] E. Louis Backman, *Religious Dances* (London: George Allen and Unwin Ltd., 1952), pp. 2–3.

Egyptian dancing girls and a musician. From a tombstone fresco at Karnak, about 1420 B.C.

families, workers and peasants, slaves, a powerful priesthood, and, in later dynasties, troupes of professional entertainers.

Shawn writes that in Egypt, where the priesthood was all-powerful, dance was the chief medium of religious expression. The secret doctrines and mysteries of the Egyptian mythology, based primarily on the annual rise and fall of the River Nile (giving rise to a legend of resurrection and belief in human survival) were portrayed through symbolic dance dramas. In these, the central theme of the Egyptian religion—that of Osiris being slain and dismembered, with the parts of his body hidden throughout the earth, followed by the search of his sister-wife, Isis, to find and bury the body of the god—all this "was re-enacted constantly within the temples in dramatic dance form, and the young people were thus given their religious education. . . ."[4]

There was a complex and highly ritualized system of worship in ancient Egypt, concerned chiefly with death and rebirth, as indicated, and attached to certain holy cities associated with the cult. As part of this system, there began to appear trained dancers who performed regularly as part of religious service. Their main purpose was to propitiate the gods, and to reenact

[4] Shawn, *op. cit.*, p. 16.

through dance, music, song, and pageantry, the search for the dead body of Osiris, and its resurrection. Chiefly, these were connected to rituals of planting and harvest. Kirstein points out that annually such a mystery-play or tragedy was produced at Abydos; in the ritual, the priest, or first dancer, becomes the personification of the entire enacted legend. He is aided by a larger group of dancers, performing en masse.[5]

Other religious dances included a traditional festival performed in honor of the bull Apis, one of the most powerful of Egyptian gods. To carry on this ceremonial, a special bull was selected and raised; in his quarters, the Apeum, the priests or priestesses who attended him would perform secret dances, retelling the adventures of the god of whom the bull Apis was the living image. In dance parades inside and outside the temples, they would recount the life story of Osiris. Another traditional dance was the Astronomic, or Dance of Stars, which was performed by priests in their temples, without onlookers. This ritual, similar to that of the earlier Chaldeans, was based on the movements of the solar system, and was extremely significant to the Egyptians who plotted the seasons of the year, and thus regulated control of the dikes that gave fertility to the land.

Since they were so preoccupied with themes of life and death and indeed sought to conquer death by making the body of the buried nobleman immortal, funeral ceremonies were extremely important to the ancient Egyptians. On the occasion of the burial of important personages, a man skilled as a mimic was dressed in the dead man's garments and, having his face covered with a mask as nearly as possible resembling the face of the deceased, he immediately preceded the hearse. As the procession moved slowly along to the sound of solemn music, he performed a pantomimic dance to show the remarkable deeds achieved during the lifetime of the man being borne to his tomb.

But such themes were not the sole preoccupation of dance among the Egyptians. They enjoyed sports, acrobatics, and various forms of entertainment, and had complex orchestras, including copper cymbals, tambourines, bone clackers, drums, pipes, castanets, whistles, and other stringed and percussive instruments. Bands of female performers were attached to temples, and the royal houses also owned troupes of entertainers who performed on both sacred and social occasions. Slaves were taught both dancing and music, and in the later dynasties there developed a class of professional performers who were independent, in that they were

[5] Lincoln Kirstein, *Dance: A Short History of Classic Theatrical Dancing* (New York: G. P. Putnam's Sons, 1935), p. 7.

neither owned by the nobility nor attached to temples. Kirstein gives a number of examples of Egyptian dance at various periods:

As far back as the first Dynasty (ca. 3000 B.C.) a wooden relief shows King Semti dancing rhythmically to simple instrumental music.

An official of King Assa (ca. 2400 B.C.) brought from a distant land a Pygmy dancer, who was believed to have come from the spirit-world. Such dancers, who performed in a buffoonlike and grotesque style, were prized; there is an ivory statuette of a dancing Pygmy in the Metropolitan Museum of New York, dated about 1950 B.C.

Wall reliefs at Gizeh (ca. 1580–1150 B.C.) show "girls posturing with tambourines, clacking castanets curved and carved to form conventionalized fingers."[6]

Gradually the practice developed of having dancing as professional entertainment at private dinner parties. Although the upper classes had once danced, they gradually relinquished this practice to slaves or highly skilled paid performers. In the words of Curt Sachs, none of the "vast number of dance pictures and none of the literary sources reveals a real social dance" for the aristocracy. However, dance as entertainment continued to be popular for all classes; in later dynasties one would find in larger cities like Memphis or Alexandria small groups of roving mimes or acrobats who gave impromptu shows in public squares.

In a physical sense, what was the dance of ancient Egypt like? Because of the stylized treatment of figures in all reliefs and paintings, it is difficult to tell whether the poses and movements that are shown give a realistic picture of the actual dances that were done. However, the movement seems to have ranged from quiet, dignified walking steps, with arms outstretched, to difficult acrobatic positions, such as the famous "bridge" position, or handstands. In some cases, vigorous striding, leaping, or running movements are shown. There are hieroglyph names for dance figures and positions. Some of the movements suggest turns in the air, and one wall relief dated about 1,500 B.C. seems to show a figure doing what would in ballet be called an *entrechat*. Other acrobatic actions, such as tumbling, somersaults, and splits, were also common.

Dancers sometimes performed as soloists, or in groups of two or three; occasionally they formed larger corps of performers.

What was the influence of Egypt, then, in terms of the development of dance? Certainly, it consisted of the extent to which dance found a formal place in religious practice, as well as its use as a

[6] *Ibid.*, pp. 11–12.

form of popular or courtly entertainment. The scope and variety of dance movement, as well as the development of a professional class of dancers within the increasingly differentiated Egyptian social structure, were additional important developments. Without question, Egypt was influential in terms of spreading its cultural forms throughout the Mediterranean world. Even beyond the Mediterranean, at Cadiz, it seems that dancing essentially Egyptian in character was established. Havelock Ellis writes:

> The Nile and Cadiz were thus the two great centers of ancient dancing, and Martial mentions them both together, for each supplied its dancers to Rome.[7]

Dance Among the Ancient Hebrews

While there are no wall reliefs or paintings to tell of dance as performed by the ancient Hebrews, there are abundant references to this practice in the Old Testament. Numerous Biblical allusions show that dance was highly respected, and was particularly used on occasions of celebration and triumph:

"And David danced before the Lord with all his might" (2 Samuel 6:14).

"Then shall the virgin rejoice in the dance" (Jeremiah 31:13).

"Let them praise his name in the dance: let them sing praises unto him with the timbrel and harp" (Psalms 149 1:3).

Throughout the Bible, there are such references. When the prodigal son returned home he was welcomed with "music and dancing," to signify reconciliation and joy. When David slew Goliath, the passage read, "Is not this David the king of the land? Did they not sing to one another of him in dances, saying—Saul hath slain his thousands, but David his ten thousands?" Exodus tells of the dance of celebration by Miriam and the other women, with the timbrel in hand, after the crossing of the Red Sea. After the victory of Judith over Holofernes, we read that they put a garland of olive upon Judith and her maid, and that "she herself went before all the people in the dance, leading all the women." And when Israel was depressed by enemies, war, and captivity, the passage goes, "The joy of our heart has ceased, our dance is turned into mourning."

[7] Havelock Ellis, *The Dance of Life* (Boston: Houghton Mifflin Company, 1923), p. 54.

What were the types of dances performed by the ancient Jews? Several forms are described in the Old Testament. A circular, or ring-dance, is the dance around the Golden Calf portrayed in Exodus 32:6,19. In other passages, we are told how David took the Ark to David's City, in a processional march. Along the way, he stopped from time to time to prepare sacrifices, and to dance with all his strength before the Lord and his Ark.

Other dances are described as hopping dances or whirling dances, usually carried on in celebration. And still other passages refer to use of the dance in divine service, although no formal provision was made in the Mosaic law for music or dance in the service of the Lord.

Probably the early Hebrews were strongly influenced by the religious and secular customs of the Egyptians during their four centuries in Egypt; indeed the Jewish cult had come to life in countries in which the Jews were surrounded by peoples who had regarded the dance as an essential element in religious worship. Sendrey and Norton write:

> In both religions, processional dances were used in ritual ceremonies. National festivals alike include popular dancing. The harvest festival was celebrated by both people with fertility dancing, the husband-man of Israel rejoicing, like the Egyptian, with palm and willow branches . . . . Even the Egyptian belief that their gods themselves indulged in dancing had its parallel in a conception of the Hebrews . . . .[8]

As evidence that the ancient Hebrews must have danced on every possible occasion, both in daily life and for special occasions and ceremonies, Sendrey and Norton point out that Biblical Hebrew has no less than twelve verbs to express the act of dancing. The Hebrew word most frequently used is *hul*, or *hil*, meaning "to whirl." Sachs interprets this as "to turn, "a word used both for a sword swung in a circle, and for the whirlwind. From this is derived the word for dance, *mahol* (the source of the girl's name Mahelah, or, today, Mahalia). At least two psalms have in their headings the instruction, *al mahalath*, suggesting that they were meant to be performed with some kind of dance. Another interesting term is the word *pasah*, which has two meanings: "to pass over," or "to spare" (thus *Pesah*, the Feast of the Passover), and "to limp," or "to dance in a limping fashion." Some Biblical scholars have thus speculated that the Passover ceremony owes its origin to the peculiar limping dance that may have been performed at spring festivals of the early Hebrews.

[8] Sendrey and Norton, *op. cit.*, p. 207.

In addition to ritual processions or circle dances, or dances of celebration, dance was performed on certain other occasions; some of these have lingered as customs throughout the history of the Jews. Wedding dances were performed in ancient times; centuries later, during the Middle Ages, it was the custom for the bridal party to dance all the way to the house of the wedding. Dignified rabbis were not above dancing before the bridal couple with myrtle and olive branches. Although mixed dancing was common in the earlier pagan cultures, men and women were customarily separated in religious dances. The rabbis of the Middle Ages only permitted those who were closely related (husband and wife, brother and sister, or father and daughter) to dance together. In Eastern Europe during this later period, the extremely orthodox Hasidic Jews made a practice of having the men only dance certain ritual dances during religious worship.

Although no mention is made in the Old Testament of funeral dances, it is probable that these too were carried on by the ancient Jews. Certainly, they had observed them as performed by Egyptians and in other surrounding lands. Even among the modern Sephardim (Jews of Spanish and Portuguese descent) there are funeral customs of walking around the bier while chanting prayers, which suggest that they are derived from earlier funeral processional dances.

Thus we see that among the ancient Hebrews there was great interest in and respect for the dance. However, certain prohibitions began to appear. Dance is not mentioned formally in the Mosaic code. Men and women were not permitted to take part together in certain dances. And, finally, a distinction was made between those dances which are of a sacred or holy nature and those which resemble pagan ceremonies—such as dancing around the Golden Calf, a form of idolatry. This distinction made by the early Jews, whose faith was the first of the great monotheistic religions, was to be made even more sharply by the Christians, in the centuries that followed.

Dance in Ancient Greece

Just as among the early Egyptians and Hebrews, dance was held in great esteem by the ancient Greeks. They speculated on its antiquity and saw it as divinely inspired. It seemed to them that the stars and planets in the sky were doing some sort of cosmic dance; indeed, Urania, the patroness of astronomy, was also a

Muse and a patroness of the dance. Lawler points out that the gods were thought of as fathers of the dance, and almost all of their greater divinities were portrayed in literature or art as dancing. In the *Laws*, Plato suggested that dance arose from the natural desire of all young creatures to move their bodies in order to express emotions—especially joy. But, he went on, the sense of harmony and rhythm which actually makes dances out of natural and instinctive movements is the specific gift of the gods and the Muses.[9]

The Greeks did not really think of dance as a separate entity. Instead, it was closely linked with other kinds of experiences. Thus, the word *orcheisthai*, which is translated in English "to dance," actually suggests rhythmical movements of many sorts— the feet, hands, head, eyes, or entire body. It might even describe marching, the playing of games, juggling, or tumbling, just as in Egypt professional dancers were also acrobats. Another Greek word was *mousiké*, the "art of the Muses"; this embraced music, poetry, and the dance, which, to the ancient Greeks, were all part of the same thing.

The sources of information about Greek dance are many. Among the literary sources are the words of songs written for dance, lines of poetry (including the great Homeric epics), the writings of philosophers, and many other forms of literature, including the work of later Roman historians and essayists. Archaeological sources, such as statues, wall reliefs, carvings, and paintings on walls or pottery, all frequently provide actual pictures of dancing. Because of the conventions they employed, and their lack of realism, however, most of these do not give an accurate picture of what Greek dance movements were actually like. And, of course, our knowledge of the music that accompanied dance in this early period is extremely limited.

The earliest references to dance within the region of the Aegean Sea are to the dances performed on the island of Crete from about 3,000 to 1,400 B.C. Archaeological excavations at Knossos and elsewhere on the island show the Cretans performing a variety of games, sports, dancing, and musical activities during this period.

One of the oldest of the dances was that of the Curetes, a wild leaping men's dance, with much shouting and clashing of weapons. Other warlike dances were performed, as well as simple circle dances, patterned dances of women, dances with animal masks or heads, and fertility dances which involved "front and

[9] Lillian B. Lawler, *The Dance in Ancient Greece* (Middletown, Conn.: Wesleyan University Press, 1964), p. 14.

back somersaults, flying leaps and rapid kicks, standing on their heads, standing and walking on their hands or forearms, or bending far backward like wheels."[10] Lawler suggests that so complicated were these actions that it seems likely that the performers had long and rigorous training, and may have been professional entertainers, although members of royal families were also known to dance. Another famous dance of ancient Crete was the "maze" or "labyrinth" which, in its weaving, spiraling pattern, was thought to have been based on the palace of Minos, at Knossos.

In any event, the colorful and spectacular dance of Crete was said to have inspired the dance of the Mycenaean Greeks, who came into being during the Bronze Age, on the mainland of Greece. These vigorous and talented warriors fortified their steep hills into impregnable fortresses, and sallied forth to conquer the Cretan cities, as well as other neighboring powers—such as the Trojans, in Asia Minor. Theirs was the civilization which Homer celebrated in the epic poems of the *Iliad* and the *Odyssey.* Several passages in these works describe dance as it was carried on by the Mycenaeans. In the *Odyssey*, Odysseus orders Telemachus to assemble all the servants in the palace after the slaying of the suitors; a lively dance is held and the palace resounds with the noise.

A vivid picture of dance is given in the eighteenth book of the *Iliad*, where Homer describes the armor of Achilles. Three dances are described as depicted on the shield. One of these portrays a dancing place where young men and maidens danced, holding their hands on one another's wrists:

> The maidens had soft linen garments, and the youths wore well-woven chitons, faintly glistening with oil. The maidens had fair garlands, and the youths had golden daggers hanging from silver belts. And now they ran around with skillful feet, very lightly, as when a potter, sitting by his wheel, which fits in his hands, tries it to see if it runs. And then again, they would run in lines to meet one another. And a great throng stood around the colorful dancing-floor, enjoying the sight; and among them an inspired musican was singing and playing on his lyre, and through their midst, leading the measure, two tumblers whirled . . . .[11]

As Greece moved into its classical period, the Greeks no longer worshipped animals, as they had in their earlier years. Instead, they worshipped a number of deities cast in the shape of men and

[10] *Ibid.*, p. 38.
[11] *Ibid.*, p. 45.

women. Many myths surrounded these gods and goddesses, each of whom had special attributes, powers and cults. Thus, fertility rites were often offered to Dionysus, the god of fertility and wine; indeed, the term *tragedy* is believed to have originated with the bacchic rites that were offered in his honor. Some of the mythological companions of Dionysus were believed to be satyrs, or "goat-men"; when dancers performed these roles at festivals, they wore goat costumes and footwear. The Greek word for "goat" is *tragos*, and goat-dancing contests carried on during the 6th century B.C. came to be known as competitions in *tragoedia*, or "goat song." Thus the word *tragedy*. Again, the term *orchestra* originally meant the circular dancing place of the theater.[12]

Among the other deities who had dances and festivals performed in their honor were Apollo and his sister Artemis, at Delphi on the island of Delos in the Aegean; indeed, Apollo was said to have dictated the laws of choreography. Similarly, Athena, Hecate, Demeter, and Persephone all were worshipped by their own special cults, at different holidays during the year.

One of the most common uses of dance in ancient Greece was in education. The leading Greek philosophers strongly supported this art, as an ideal integration of the body and spirit. Aristotle defined education as a blend of music and gymnastics, and Socrates urged that it be taught more widely, saying that those who honor the gods most beautifully in dances are best in war. Plato wrote "to sing well and to dance well is to be well-educated," and devoted a great deal of attention to the importance of the dance in education in his treatise on the *Laws*. He emphasizes the fact that there are two kinds of dance and music—the *noble*, concerned with what is fine and honorable, and the *ignoble*, imitating what is mean or ugly:

> He would have all children, boys and girls alike, instructed from an early age in noble music and dancing, and would spur them on with contests . . . . He would give to officials absolute power to exclude from the schools and from public performances all unworthy rhythms and harmonies, steps and gestures. Music and dancing should be consecrated to the gods . . . inasmuch as the gods themselves dance and create dance . . . . Noble dances should confer on the student not only health and agility and beauty of the body, but also goodness of the soul and a well-balanced mind . . . .[13]

The Greeks learned to dance at an early age, with most of the instruction apparently at the hands of private teachers. They

[12] *Ibid.*, pp. 76–81.
[13] *Ibid.*, p. 124.

practiced a variety of physical disciplines; they were extremely athletic and their movements were full and vigorous. Vase paintings show free running, skipping, and jumping, always in natural, easy poses, with little artificiality or acrobatics for its own sake. Particularly among the boys, dancing was taught as an aid to military education in Athens and Sparta. In the *palaestra* (wrestling school) and *gymnasium*, they took part in Pyrrhic dances and others designed to prepare them to execute battle motions. The dances fell into several categories:

Podism: quick, shifting movements of the feet, to train the warrior for hand-to-hand combat.

Xiphism: mock battle, in which groups of youths would practice the arts of warfare in dancelike form.

Homos: high leaps and vaults, to prepare them for leaping over high logs and boulders, or for scaling walls and fortresses.

Tetracomos: stately group formations, in which soldiers would advance on the enemy en masse, or protect themselves through interlocked shields.

Not only were these dances learned, as in Sparta, at training schools for boys, but they also were performed regularly at the Panathenaic Festivals, and were carried on regularly as part of the continuing training of soldiers. Shawn writes:

> We have records today of some eighteen named Pyrrhic dances—solo, duet and ensemble—which were mimetic warfare dances, by which the soldier attained the mind-body coordinations, the muscular strength, the discipline, which made him supreme on the field of battle.[14]

So esteemed was dance that it was accepted practice for statesmen, generals, philosophers, and other outstanding Greeks of the Periclean Age to perform solo dances before audiences of many thousands, on important public occasions, or on return from a military campaign or victory. Sophocles, the Athenian poet, while still young, was chosen to play the lyre and lead the victory dance after the battle of Salamis. Epaminondas of Thebes, one of the most distinguished of Greek generals and statesmen, played musical instruments, sang, and danced, and did so before audiences in his adult years. Aeschylus and Aristophanes danced in various performances of their own plays, and the *Dithyramb*, one of the principal dances of the Dionysian festivals, was often led by celebrated poets and statesmen.

The Greek satirist, Lucian (who lived in a later era in Rome), remarked that the Greeks valued dancing to such an extent that:

[14] Shawn, *op. cit.*, p. 18.

... the most noble and greatest personnages in every city are the dancers, and so little are they ashamed of it, that they applaud themselves more upon their dexterity in that species of talent, than on their nobility, their posts of honor, and the dignities of their forefathers.[15]

X The Greek theater, of course, was closely linked to dance in its inception. Aristotle stated that Greek tragedy arose from the *Dithyramb*, in which the spring rites of fertility and rebirth took formal choral and dramatic form, and were ultimately made into plays. The original Greek communal dance, practiced in the *orchestra* or dancing floor, ultimately became the *choros* that was an essential element in Greek drama. Throughout the classical period, the dance held an important place in the performance of tragedy which was more like "an impressive semi-operatic spectacle than a drama, as we use the word today."[16]

There were specific types of dances in Greek drama:

Emmeleia: this was a grave, serious type of dance, typically used for tragic themes; it embodied a code of symbolic gestures through which the dancer could tell the entire story of a dramatic work without speaking.

Kordax: this was the characteristic dance of comedy, and has been described as obscene and ignoble; it involved suggestive rotations of the body, kicking one's buttocks, slapping one's chest and thighs, and similar movements.

Sikinnis: this was the dance typical of the Greek satyr plays during the sixth century B.C. It was lively, vigorous, and disrespectful, with much horseplay and acrobatic movement; often it involved satirical reenactment of mythological themes.

Not only was dance featured in the Greek theater; it also was an essential element in the entertainment of guests known as *Komos,* or *Komoi.* It was the practice to have afterdinner entertainment of singing, juggling, playing musical instruments, and dancing. At first this was done by the host or guests. Gradually, however, a class of professional dancers developed—and these performers displaced the amateurs. By the 5th and 4th centuries B.C., such performers were widely found, and had developed a high degree of specialized skill. In some cases, slaves were trained as dancers and then performed for pay. Apparently, there were star performers even in those days; one inscription on the island of Delos indicates that a single dancing girl was paid far more than an entire dancing troupe that accompanied her.

Following the conquests of Alexander and his return with

---

[15] Ethel L. Urlin, *Dancing, Ancient and Modern* (New York: D. Appleton and Co., 1914), pp. 29–30.
[16] Lawler, *op. cit.*, pp. 81–82.

Eastern captives, Greek dance began to show Asiatic influences, with gesture language used increasingly. During the Hellenistic and Greco-Roman periods, the *pantomimus*, or pantomimic dancer, became highly popular. A solo dancer, wearing different costumes and masks, would make use of flamboyant gesture and mimicry to tell a story in several scenes, each episode being separated by musical interludes. This form of entertainment was found most widely in Rome, during the peak of power of that Empire.

In Greece we see a civilization in which dance began as an essential element in religion, and an important and respected means of military training. Gradually, it became part of the developing Greek theater and then of popular entertainment. Always, it was widely respected by the Greeks; one of their seven Muses, on an equal plane with the Muses of epic poetry and music, was Terpsichore, the Muse of Dancing. But the respect held for dance was based on the total philosophy of the Greeks, during the age of Pericles—their belief in the integrity of mind, spirit, and body and their keen interest in all the arts as essential expressions of man's spirit. It was different in Rome.

Dance in Ancient Rome

Dancing was much less important to the Romans than to the Greeks from whom they borrowed much of their culture. The educated Romans looked upon Greece as the source of culture and civilization; Roman aristocrats spoke Greek, employed Greek tutors, and copied Greek arts and literature. Early Roman art was vigorous, simple, and well-proportioned. However, as the nation grew wealthy and powerful, it ceased to value such qualities in art; indeed, war and lust for conquest brought thousands of captives and great wealth to Rome. The Romans ceased to create and perform within the arts themselves. Instead, they were entertained by their slaves and captives, of many nationalities. When this happened, dance—along with other forms of popular entertainment, became brutal and sensational.

Shawn comments that while the Romans were great organizers, military conquerors, and lawmakers, within the arts they only borrowed. Ultimately, they debased all they touched. So it was, he says, with the dance:

> Here in Imperial Rome we find the dance first completely theatricalized—then commercialized; and as the religious life of Rome gradually decayed and became orgiastic, so the religious dances became occasions for unbridled licentiousness and sensuality . . . .[17]

[17] Shawn, *op. cit.*, p. 17.

How did it all begin?

During the earliest period of recorded history in what was to become Rome, the men of certain corporations, or societies, were grouped together under the name of *Salii*, which some have interpreted as derived from *saltio*, the Latin word for "dance," and *saltantes*, the word for "dancers." The *Salii*, who included sowing priests who purified the fields, warriors who performed weapon dances, and the priests of Mars (god of war), carried on spring processionals which had a somewhat dancelike character. During this period, other choral dances were done, with choruses of older and younger men who marched around in a circle to the rhythmic beating of their shields. Other feasts and holidays throughout the year were celebrated, with dancing that was apparently of a dignified and restrained nature:

> . . . at the Palilia, or festival of Pales, solemn and magnificent dances were performed in the fields by shepherds, who during the night formed circles around blazing fires of straw and stubble. The Floralia, or festival of Flora, gave rise to the May Day customs still surviving in parts of England . . . .[18]

These customs continued for centuries. A Roman writer, Suetonius, comments at a much later date on the processionals of the *Salii*, held as a three-week ritual in March and October. Clad in embroidered tunics and high conical caps, armed and bearing shields, they trooped through the public places of the city, dancing and singing sacred songs.[19]

Other customs included the religious festivals of the *Lupercalia*, the *Saturnalia*, and the *Ludiones*. The *Lupercalia* were held during the Kalends of March, in honor of the god Pan. The priests of this cult, the Luperci, danced naked through the streets of Rome, armed with whips, with which they were said to have struck at the crowds of spectators. The *Saturnalia* was a great feast, held in mid-December, in honor of Saturn. It was a time for revelry, feasting, drunkenness, dancing in the streets, and for class distinctions to be set aside. Kirstein comments that this pagan holiday was adopted by Roman Christians for Christ's Mass, or Christmas, and that it became, in ensuing centuries, the occasion for many dramatic dances.[20]

Dance also played a part in the early Roman theater, although much of this was the work of imported Greek performers, or players from Istria who were brought to Rome in the middle of the 4th century B.C., to placate the gods with entertainment, and to

[18] Urlin, *op. cit.*, p. 35.
[19] Kirstein, *op. cit.*, p. 46.
[20] *Ibid.*, p. 47.

distract a population that had been racked by plague. The dancers and pantomimists from Istria were known as *istriones;* their name was the source of the modern word "histrionic." They wore goat-skin shepherd's cloaks; the name for these, *saturae,* is said to be the source of the term "satire" or "satirical." Their performances were farcical enactments which parodied the lives of gods, heroes, or everyday men, often in rustic settings. They were carried on usually without speaking, relying on gesture to tell the story. Kirstein comments that dance, in the form of the *choros,* had little place in the Roman theater. Romans preferred the excitement and color of mass spectacles which were provided in their huge circuses and arenas, to the thoughtful and literary works that were found on the Greek stage.[21]

Since this was the case, the stage became unattractive as a profession; actors and dancers in performing companies tended to be Greek or south Italian slaves, formerly owned by rich noble-men and now rented out to theatrical managers to perform. Vuillier comments that for a long time, no women appeared on the stage; their parts were taken by young men, and this may have been one of the causes of the degeneracy of dance in Rome.[22] Later, women, who among the Greeks were not even permitted to take part in tragedy or comedy, appeared in Rome in pan-tomime.

For a period of time beginning at about 200 B.C., it became fashionable for Roman patricians to dance. Etruscan and Greek choreographers taught private dancing classes, attended by the sons and daughters of the nobility. Dance became an important social grace. Later, dance was inveighed against, as a softening of the fiber of Roman citizenry; indeed, one emperor, Scipio Afri-canus, closed the dancing schools by edict, in about 150 B.C. However, it was hardly necessary; the Romans had little real inclination or aptitude for dancing themselves. The only real popularity of dance over a period of time was extended to the pantomimic dance which developed as an independent stage form under Caesar Augustus, about 22 B.C. This became a tremendously popular form of entertainment, for two essential reasons.

First, Romans had little real appreciation for dance as an expression of artistic beauty or emotion. However, they enjoyed the lively spectacle of pantomime dance. Second, by the time of Caesar Augustus, Rome was filled with a huge, heterogeneous population of varied origins. They spoke not only Latin, but Greek, Syrian, Gallic, Teutonic, and many other languages. It

[21] *Ibid.,* pp. 40–43.
[22] Gaston Vuillier, *A History of Dancing* (New York: D. Appleton and Co., 1897), p. 39.

was impossible to present spoken dramas that could be understood by all these varied spectators, particularly in the huge theaters with poor acoustics. Therefore, the pantomime became developed to an extremely fine degree and achieved immense popularity.

This dance form was much like an early stage of Greek tragedy, in which one actor, with the aid of varying costumes and masks, portrays a number of characters in a single tale. Instead of speaking or chanting, the pantomimic dancer performed with dance and gestures alone. Lawler comments that the effect on the public was tremendous:

> . . . spectators sometimes sat in the theaters for whole days, watching the dancers almost as if hypnotized; they thought of the dancers as virtually divine, and Seneca calls the craze for their performance 'a disease'—*morbus*. Women swooned, high officials of the state hung on every move, and Roman emperors summoned the dancers for command performances . . . .[23]

Vuillier wrote:

> We can form but a faint idea of the perfection to which the art of pantomime attained among the Romans. It ranged over the whole domain of fable, poetry and history. Roman actors translated the most subtle sensations by gestures of extraordinary precision and mobility, and their audience understood every turn of this language, which conveyed far more to them than declamation . . . the strength, the infinite gradations of this mute expression, made the dancing of the ancients a great art . . . .[24]

Among the many performers were two outstanding artists, Pylades of Sicily, and Bathyllus of Alexandria, both former slaves who were freed by their owners. Both were lionized by the public, became extremely wealthy and arrogant, and had admiring cliques which, in different liveries, used to battle angrily in the streets to support the reputation of their favorites.

Public opinion was divided about them; some emperors favored them while others opposed or banned them. Marcus Aurelius put a limit on the wages they might be paid and on their production expenses. The developing Christian Church kept up an unremitting attack on them, and yet at one time, when Rome was suffering from famine and even orators and teachers were banished, three thousand dancers were allowed to remain in the city—so vital was this entertainment considered to be. Yet, more and more, moralists spoke out against the pantomime. Lucian,

---

[23] Lawler, *op. cit.*, p. 140.
[24] Vuillier, *op. cit.*, p. 37.

in the 2nd century A.D., had one of his characters, Crato, ask in a dialogue:

> [How can anyone] sit still and listen to the sounds of a flute, and watch the antics of an effeminate creature got up in soft raiment to sing lascivious songs and mimic the passions of prehistoric strumpets to the accompaniment of twanging string and shrilling pipe and clattering heel?[25]

The controversy continued, but gradually the popularity of the pantomimists declined and many of them were forced to withdraw from the cities, and to perform in smaller towns. Probably their last performances were in the late 4th and early 5th centuries A.D. Dance itself had become increasingly disreputable by this time, in the eyes of many of Rome's leading citizens and writers. It was seen as corrupt, immoral, and inappropriate for a person of good society. Sallust wrote of a noblewoman, "She played and danced more gracefully than a respectable woman should," and Cicero wrote the following condemnation of an art which had indeed declined from the lofty stature it had held in the Greek civilization:

> Cato calls Lucius Muena a dancer. If this be imputed to him truly, it is the reproach of a violent accuser; but if falsely, it is the abuse of a scurrilous railer.... For no man, one may almost say, ever dances when sober, unless perhaps he be a madman; nor in solitude, nor in a moderate and sober party; dancing is the last companion of prolonged feasting, of luxurious situation, and of many refinements.[26]

In essence, dance suffered from the sickness that had seized the entire Roman empire. The sturdy, simple patriotism of the Roman citizen had given way to a decadence that demanded "bread and circuses." Tremendous public spectacles were staged, featuring the torture and slaughter of thousands of captives and slaves taken during Roman conquests. The taxes of entire provinces were expended on these cruel entertainments, which the public increasingly demanded. A variety of performers offered their talents—singers, dancers, jugglers, musicians, animal trainers, acrobats—but most of all the Roman citizens demanded violent and sadistic spectacles. There were chariot races; gladitorial contests pitting captives of war, condemned prisoners, and professional fighters together; cleverly staged "sea-fights" with slave-manned galleys in flooded ditches; and a variety of other brutal spectacles. These were carried on in huge arenas. The Circus

[25] Kirstein, op. cit., p. 50.
[26] Ibid., p. 45.

Maximus was said to have held at one time three hundred and fifty thousand spectators.

Two emperors, in particular, were identified with these monstrous games: Caligula, who was extremely fond of singing and dancing, and who frequently performed in the circuses, and Nero, under whom the persecution of Christians was unrelenting. Tacitus wrote that many Christians:

> ... were dressed in the skins of wild beasts, and exposed to be torn to pieces by dogs in the public games, that they were crucified, or condemned to be burnt; and at nightfall serve in place of lamps to lighten the darkness, Nero's own gardens being used for the spectacle.[27]

Dance itself was often used for gruesome purposes. The historian Plutarch records the fact that often condemned criminals, clothed in rich garments and wearing wreaths, were compelled to dance in the crowded arena until their clothing, which had been treated with some secret chemical, suddenly burst into flames and they died agonizingly.[28]

Because of all it stood for, the Roman way of life was bitterly condemned by the early Christians, who suffered under it, yet survived it. And, because dance was so integral a part of the corruption of the Romans in their later days of empire, dance too was condemned by the Church Fathers. But this relationship, after the fall of Rome and through the Dark and Middle Ages, was a strangely contradictory one. Dance became linked to the Christian Church in many ways, and at the same time was violently condemned by it, as centuries passed.

[27] *Ibid.*, p. 57.
[28] Lawler, *op. cit.*, p. 142.

4

DANCE IN
THE MIDDLE AGES

The history of dance—as of all the arts—following the fall of
Rome, is closely linked with the development of the Catholic
Church in Europe. As the preceding chapter has suggested, the
early Church Fathers were filled with bitter antagonism toward
the Roman way of life, and all its excesses. By religious conviction, they rejected this hedonistic philosophy, and instead moved
toward a fanatical asceticism.

It must be understood that, after the fall of the Roman
Empire, Europe was overrun with warring tribes and shifting
forces. The organized power of Rome, which had built roads,
extended commerce, and given protection to the arts and the
centers of learning, was at an end. Within this vacuum, during the
Dark Ages. the Christian Church offered a unity and form of
universal citizenship in Europe. The church and the feudal lords
who emerged, each controlling his own fiefdom, were the sources
of authority in this era. They were closely interlocked, and it was
the church that was the sole custodian of learning and education,
and the source of morals. H'Doubler suggested that the characteristic feature of early Christian thought was its otherworldliness,
placing a sharp emphasis on the reward to be gained after death,
and condemning all carnality and hedonism:

The paramount consideration of all living was to save the soul. Consequently, the body was looked upon as a hindrance. To exalt the soul the body was ignored, punished, and bruised. Anything that expressed the livelier feelings of instinctive human nature or in any way suggested former pagan ways and ideals of living, was banished into the realm of wickedness . . . .[1]

Theatrical entertainment in particular was prohibited. As early as A.D. 300, with the coming of the first Christian emperors, a council at Elvira decided that the rite of baptism could not be extended to those connected with the circus or pantomime. In 398, at the Council of Carthage, an edict excommunicated those who attended the theater on holy days. Kirstein points out that, after the Lombard invasion of 568, shows and games were rarely mentioned in Rome itself. For two or three hundred years, they are reported to have been carried on in the Eastern Empire, and isolated professional entertainers probably wandered through the countryside, but the great spectacles and organized shows of Imperial Rome were at an end.

However, dance continued to be performed under the most unlikely of auspices—within the Church itself. There is much evidence to suggest that the early Christian Fathers approved of the use of dance in religious ceremonials, provided that its form and intent were holy and not profane. Dancing was a formal part of the Christian service and litany until about the 12th century, when the pressures against it mounted and it became widely banned—although even then it continued to be performed in some areas.

What form did dance take within the Christian Church? The earliest examples are described by the Catholic Father Héliot, in his history of religious orders of monks. A number of Christian sects, the Therapeutae, withdrew into the wilderness in order to avoid persecution, assembling on Sundays and other holy days in groves of oases to dance ring-dances and sing psalms and hymns. Since, after all, worship of this kind had been practiced by all those of earlier faiths, it is not surprising that the first Christians engaged in it. The Therapeutae had a highly developed cult dance, according to Backman. Following a night watch (*vigilium*), the participants

> grouped themselves into two facing choral groups, one of men and one of women. Each group had a leader. During the alternate singing of songs, the singers sometimes remained stationary, sometimes

[1] Margaret H'Doubler, *Dance: A Creative Art Experience* (New York: F. S. Crofts and Company, 1940), p. 13.

they moved forward, sometimes backward, sometimes to right and sometimes to left, as circumstances required. Then they united in a single chorus . . . .[2]

Dating from about the year 160, there exists a remarkable hymn, known as the *Acts of John*, quoted in the Catholic Dictionary as being known to Augustine. It offers a version of the Lord's Supper where Christ, taking leave of his disciples, instituted the custom of Holy Communion. However, instead of the traditional symbolic acts of breaking bread and sipping wine, Jesus is described as having his disciples surround him with hands joined, singing and circling around. The word "dance" is actually used in the *Acts of John*.

There are many references to dance as part of worship during the 4th and 5th centuries, along with frequent warnings about forms of dance which were considered dissolute.

Epiphanius, who was made Bishop of Salamis on Cyprus in 367, gave a sermon on Palm Sunday on the entry of Christ into Jerusalem. The festival of celebration is described in these words:

> Rejoice in the highest, Daughter of Zion! Rejoice, be glad and leap boisterously thou all-embracing Church. For behold, once again the King approaches . . . once again perform the choral dances . . . leap wildly, ye Heavens; sing Hymns, ye Angels; ye who dwell in Zion, dance ring dances . . . .[3]

Those who have interpreted this work conclude that it describes not only the spirit of the ceremony, but also literal dances done within the Church. This view is supported by the writings of Basilius, Bishop of Caesarea, who lived between 344 and 407. Basilius wrote frequently of the existence of the dance in the time of early Christianity, including one passage which suggested that pagan rites such as dawn ceremonies which greeted the sunrise were also found in the early Catholic Church:

> Could there be anything more blessed than to imitate on earth the ring-dance of the angels and at dawn to raise our voices in prayer and by hymns and songs glorify the rising Creator?[4]

In many other ways, the Catholic Church based its practices on the rituals of earlier religions. When the heathen tribes of Europe and Asia Minor were converted, the missionaries (most of whom were Roman) built their churches on existing shrines or temple sites. Often they established the Christian holy days

[2] E. Louis Backman, *Religious Dances* (London: George Allen and Unwin Ltd., 1952), p. 11.

[3] *Ibid.*, p. 24.

[4] *Ibid.*, p. 25.

at the same times as earlier pagan festivals. Such implements of Catholic ritual as the bell, candles, incense, singing, and dancing had all been found in heathen faiths. Thus, it was natural that dance would be included in the services. However, the leading Church Fathers made a point of opposing those forms of dance which they saw as sinful or dissolute, and which smacked of Roman degeneracy.

Ambrose, Bishop of Milan in the late 4th century, wrote profusely in support of church dance, taking his text from Luke 7:32, "We have piped unto you and ye have not danced." However, he also warned against being "snared" by the appeal of indecent dances and the stage:

> . . . No, the dance should be conducted as did David when he danced before the Ark of the Lord, for everything is right which springs from the fear of God. Let us not be ashamed of a show of reverence which will enrich the cult and deepen the adoration of God. For this reason the dance must in no wise be regarded as a mark of reverence for vanity and luxury, but as something which uplifts every living body instead of allowing the limbs to rest motionless upon the ground or the slow feet to become numb. St. Paul danced in this spirit when he exerted himself for us . . . .[5]

Thus, dance, when it expresses vice and luxury, is condemned. When it is virtuous and performed in honor of God, it is praised. St. Gregory of Nazianzus, an eminent theologian of the 4th century who became Bishop of Constantinople, delivered a stern exhortation to the Emperor Julian, which has frequently been quoted:

> . . . if you wish to dance in devotion . . . then dance, but not the shameless dance of the daughter of Herod, which accompanied the execution of the Baptist, but the Dance of David to the true refreshment of the Ark, which I consider to be the approach to God, the swift encircling steps in the manner of the mysteries . . . .[6]

History tells us that the Abbot Meletius, on the advice of Gregory's writings, permitted dancing in his churches in England, during the early 7th century. Records of the famous Echternach processional carried on in Luxembourg during Whitsun week, in which clergy, choir, and congregation danced to the church and around the altar, indicate that this is a survival of a medieval dancing custom. It is carried on in commemoration of St. Willibord, who lived around 690. Many other illustrations support the view of Curt Sachs that dance continued to be practiced widely by those Europeans who had been converted to Christianity, but who retained many of their earlier pagan customs:

[5] *Ibid.*, p. 26.
[6] *Ibid.*, p. 31.

Even with Christianity the theme and content scarcely change their outer garb. The charms for fertility still occupy the central position; with undiminished power they dominate at Shrovetide, the first of May, and at weddings, at midsummer, and at funeral ceremonies .... Maypole and fire dances, sword dances, mask dances ....[7]

As the Dark Ages began to draw to a close, there was continuing confirmation of the use of dance in Christian worship. A hymn which dates from the 10th century, for early morning Mass during the celebration of Easter at the Monastery of Moissac in France, has these lines:

His [Christ's] life, His speech and miracle,
His wondrous death prove it.
The congregation adorns the sanctity,
Come and behold the host of ring-dances!

A second form of religious dance was to be found in certain church festivals which were carried on in the latter part of the Dark Ages, and apparently through the Middle Ages. These were particularly popular with the lower clergy—the monks, choirboys, and younger priests and subdeacons—and often they were highly disrespectful of the upper clergy. Just as in primitive religions, these festivals included various forms of acting, singing, dancing, and the playing of games. John Beleth, who lived in the 12th century and was Rector of the University of Paris, described four kinds of dance in use at church festivals: the Deacons' Festival dance on St. Stephen's Day, the Priests' on St. John's Day, the choirboys' on Innocents' Day, and the subdeacons' on the Feast of the Circumcision. It was the last of these which came to be known as the Festival (or Feast) of Fools. This was a New Year's celebration by the lower clergy which became a dramatic burlesque of the regular church service, with a caustic and licentious lampooning of the higher church dignitaries. From the end of the 12th century on, the Feast of Fools (sometimes called the Feast of Asses) spread through France and most of the other European countries. According to the records of Sens Cathedral, the festival typically included dancing, singing, drinking, and the parodying of religious offices—even those of the Cardinal and Pope.

As described in a circular letter issued by the Theological Faculty of the University of Paris in 1444, the practices were "abominable"; priests and clergy who took part in it appeared in masks at divine service:

[7] Curt Sachs, *World History of the Dance* (New York: W. W. Norton & Co., Inc., 1937), pp. 248–49.

. . . or with distorted faces, or women's clothes, or dressed as bawds
or actors, perform ring-dances, sing indecent songs, eat coarse bread
. . . and play dice . . . leaping and jumping they course through the
church without shame . . . .[8]

The letter of the Faculty condemned these practices, and
specifically forbade dancing, feasting, and drinking at the altar,
and wearing masks or paint on one's face during the festival.

Other ceremonies which were of a dramatic or dancelike
nature were carried on outside of the formal service of the church,
but with a greater degree of approval by the authorities. A
Children's Festival, or Festival of the Choristers, at which a child
bishop was elected, was celebrated usually on Innocent's Day,
December 28; this custom is believed to have begun in the 12th
century. Elsewhere, ceremonies included various games, acting,
singing, and feasting—without, however, the ridicule of the higher
clergy or the regular service that made the Feast of Fools so objectionable. At the Cathedral of Auxerres, during the 13th century,
a religious mystery play was carried out which made use of a sort
of ball game played on a labyrinth design on the floor of the
cathedral's nave. This custom is believed to have been based on
pre-Christian ceremonies in early Greece.

Particularly in France and Germany, there were many great
processions which were carried out to ward off distress or bring
relief from pain or epidemics. These were recorded as having taken
place regularly in the 9th and 10th centuries, and from the 12th
to the 16th centuries. As they marched, the worshippers often
carried relics of saints and martyrs, crosses and banners, and
images of the Holy Virgin. The movement involved rhythmic
steps with the procession stopping at certain stations and performing sacral dances: ceremonial greetings, bows, turns, advancing,
and retiring. One description of this ceremony describes it as a

> . . . moving chorus advancing in harmony and with a sort of cadence
> through the various parts of the church. The processions passing
> through the choir and aisles, swinging the censer, do so to measured
> movements prescribed in the ritual . . . representing by their sym-
> bolical movements and figures holy and mystical dances.[9]

Another source, from the 9th century, uses the phrase,
". . . the holy relics were borne amidst happy dancing." Because
they marched with crosses, banners, and relics, and because of
their reverence, those taking part in these processions were not
condemned by the church.

[8] Backman, *op. cit.*, pp. 50–53.
[9] *Ibid.*, p. 85.

Kirstein suggests that, with the beginning of the Middle Ages and extending until about 1400, a variety of dramatic activities was carried on with religious themes, but not as a formal part of religious service. These included "mystery plays" which dealt with events found in both the Old and New Testaments; these striking displays were put on in church squares or public market places. So-called miracle plays tended to be portrayals of the lives of the saints and martyrs. Somewhat later appeared the "morality plays," which were concerned with depicting the truths of moral behavior; essentially, they were allegorical representations of he struggle between good and evil, virtue and vice.

All of these apparently stemmed from earlier pagan sources, although their themes were Christian. Kennedy suggests that conversion to the new faith did not eliminate many of the older forms of religious drama. Indeed many of the earlier pagan rituals were adopted by the early Church Fathers, in the yearly cycle of miracle and morality plays which helped to convert many ignorant and illiterate peasants to Christianity:

> . . . outside the control of the Church popular custom continued to practice one relic of the old religion in the form of a midwinter drama/dance performance, in which was portrayed by the actor/dancers a contest between life and death. The European folk dances performed during the winter season . . . all include some scraps of this old drama of life and death . . . acted on or near Christmas Day, it is a symbolic death and resurrection. This death and revival drama, performed at the turn of the year, is known in every European country. As one would expect, it is found most complete among the primitive peasantry in Eastern Europe.[10]

Certain phenomena, however, which were carried on outside the control of the Church, and which involved dance, aroused more serious condemnation by religious authorities. One of these was the Dance of Death, or *Toten Tanz*. This was a custom believed to have originated in France, which then filtered into Germany, Italy, Spain, and England. It was carried on throughout the Middle Ages, and apparently was at its peak during the 14th and 15th centuries, when many references to it appear in songs, poems, and dramas, or are depicted on murals in cemeteries, churches, cloisters, and vaults.

The Dance of Death reveals the great preoccupation of mankind during this period with death. Backman points out that among primitive peoples, the dead often were regarded as

---

[10] Douglas Kennedy, *England's Dances* (London: G. Bell & Sons, Ltd., 1950), p. 36.

dangerous and hostile to the living. Legends of vampires, were-wolves, and ghosts were found throughout Europe during the Dark Ages, and many customs had been devised to prevent the dead from "returning." These included binding together the feet of the dead, driving nails into their feet, carrying on a death watch—and, in many instances, singing and performing games and dances during wakes or after the grave had received the corpse.

Particularly in northern European countries, it was customary for such rites to include music and dancing. Backman suggests that the belief was that music exorcised the dead, forced them into compliance at being taken to the grave, and prevented them from walking the earth again; church bells were thought to drive demons away, and to comfort and protect the dead.[11] In addition, there was a widespread folk belief that the dead themselves liked to dance in churchyards and cemeteries in a sort of *danse macabre*. According to this superstition, they attempted to entice the living into the ranks of their ghostly dancing; however, those who danced with them would then die within the year. In the Dance of Death, then, one finds the suggestion that the living themselves dance toward their own death; death is a wedding dance and one dances in death toward the bridegroom.

Stegemeier points out that, in its earliest form:

> . . . the Dance of Death is actually a Dance of the Dead . . . in which the dead bodies lure the living from the various ranks of society in their midnight frolic. Later, the dead are conceived of no longer as corpses, but each as the personified figure of death himself.[12]

Death appears in the ritual, and in the many songs, poems, and pictures of the Dance of Death, as a dancer. He compels humans of every station and age, however reluctant, to dance with him. Each in turn is taken, according to a graduated social scale—saints and sinners, rich and poor, young and old. A document in the archives of the church at Caudbec, France, described a dramatic dance held in 1393, in which actors represented the various ranks and professions and in which, after each repetition of the dance, one of the dancers withdrew and disappeared. In essence, this was a parable, depicting Death as the universal leveler. It says, "Death avenges all wrong, and all, no matter how powerful in the living world, must at last yield to him."

The point was made more explicit when the characters in

---

[11] Backman, *op. cit.*, 135–36.
[12] Henri Stegemeier, *The Dance of Death in Folk Song* (Chicago: University of Chicago Libraries, 1939), p. 6.

the dance were assigned exact roles—from pope to emperor to cardinal to the lowliest monk or subdeacon; from kings, princes, and barons to minstrels, peasants, and laboring men. As recorded in France, each dancer steps forward in turn according to his rank; Death dances grotesquely, questions them, and finally leads them all into the tomb.

The Dance of Death has been interpreted as a form of social and religious satire, and the healthy reaction of the people against the strict asceticism of the Church. It is also seen as an evidence of the awakening spirit of democracy in the dying Middle Ages, in that it protested against the tremendous power and wealth of the ruling classes, as well as the miserable lives led by the common folk. In essence, it was "a desperate statement of the common man's disillusionment with the entire social, political, and religious scheme under which he lived; Death leveled all ranks and stations and proved them ultimately vain. . . ."[13]

The Church was well aware of this symbolic meaning. From the 4th century well into the 18th century, there were many prohibitions against dancing for the dead in graveyards, particularly against dances which were ribald and indecent, or which involved drinking and feasting. The Roman Synod under Leo IV ordered at the beginning of the 9th century that:

> In witness of the true and living God, the devilish songs which are heard at night on the graves of the dead are to cease, as well as the noise which accompanies them.

And a later resolution says:

> Whoever buries the dead should do so with fear, trembling and decency. No one shall be permitted to sing devil songs and perform games and dances which are inspired by the devil and have been invented by the heathen.[14]

However, these and later prohibitions failed to put an end to the Dance of Death. As late as the 1930s, Backman reports a *Bal de La Mort* carried on in certain regions of Catalonia, as part of the church processions during Holy Week. This took the form of a quadrille, performed by twelve men and three women, wearing black clothes on which white skeletons had been painted. Their faces were covered with masks representing skulls. One of the dancers carries

---

[13] John Martin, *John Martin's Book of the Dance* (New York: Tudor Publishing Co., 1963), p. 22.

[14] Paul Nettl, *The Story of Dance Music* (New York: Philosophical Library, 1947), p. 44.

a scythe, another a pendulum clock, and a third a banner. The musician, with only a drum, is clad in armour, enveloped in a black mantle. They follow the Corpus Christi procession and therefore are a part of the popular church dance. The one who carries the scythe must not take part in the dance, but just swings his scythe toward the bystanders. The others dance and hop . . . .[15]

A number of other, similar phenomena appeared during the Middle Ages, reflecting belief in witchcraft, religious fanaticism, and the lingering influence of heathen superstition. In a sense, they represented the common man's primitive fear of death, in the midst of famine, war, and plagues.

"Witch dances," carried on in the dead of night, paid homage to the devil with wild bacchanals, accompanied by grotesque costumes and masks, sacrifices, and sexual excesses (just as angels were thought to dance heavenly ring-dances in honor of God). The *Witches' Sabbath*, carried on during the night of April 30th, was a traditional time for such rites, which took place in dark and lonely places. Another craze which spread over Europe from the 11th to the 14th centuries was *St. Vitus' Dance*, or, as it was sometimes known, *St. John's Dance*, named after the patron saint who was supposed to protect the afflicted. Here, men, women, and children danced in wild delirium; they performed frenzied leaps and turns, writhing as if suffering from epileptic seizures, screaming out uncontrollably and foaming at the mouth. Similar to this was *tarantism*, a form of seizurelike dance which was thought at first to be the result of the bite of the tarantula spider, and which then became deliberately performed in order to avert the effects of the tarantula's poison. Eventually, as the superstitious belief in this 'remedy' diminished, it was continued as a traditional folk dance appearing in many Italian provinces—the *Tarantella*.

The infliction of self-punishment, performed as an act of atonement, was recorded as early as the year 1000, based on the use of the lash in masochistic self-torture as referred to in Paul's Epistles to the Corinthians, "Thus do I tame my body as I make it unconscious of pain. . . ." From the 13th to the 15th centuries, flagellation songs and dances were widely performed in Europe, beginning in Italy and spreading beyond the Alps—often with approval of the church authorities.

But the most striking and unusual dance expression of the Middle Ages and early Renaissance was the so-called *danseomania*, or dancing mania, which flourished throughout Europe from the 11th to the 14th centuries. Martin comments that the people of

[15] Backman, *op. cit.*, p. 153.

Europe had been so affected by a succession of natural calamities (wars, plagues, fires) that they sought an outlet for emotional strain in the dancing manias:

> Whole communities of people . . . were stricken with a kind of madness that sent them dancing and gyrating through the streets and from village to village for days at a time until they died in agonized exhaustion . . . .[16]

Kirstein refers to the dancing mania as a form of pathological aberration which was widely documented by writings of the 13th and 14th century, particularly in Germany and the Low Countries. Sometimes it affected children, sometimes large numbers of adults. In 1237, a party of German children danced from Erfurt to Arnstadt, many dying along the way. In 1278, a bridge at Marburg collapsed beneath a company of dancers and all were drowned. In 1347, several hundred men and women danced from Aix-la-Chapelle to Metz, despite the efforts of priests to break the spell that had seized them.[17]

Clearly, these outbursts represented some form of possession, equivalent perhaps to what Sachs had described as "convulsive dance," found among primitive tribesmen. There had been instances cited of men and women who began to sing and dance suddenly in the churchyard, disrupting divine service. In some cases, when they refused to stop, they were cursed by the priest to dance the whole year through, until the ban was withdrawn by a higher church official. A 12th-century writer, Giraldus Cambrensis, described such an outburst:

> You may see men or girls, now in the churchyard, now in the dance, which is led round the churchyard with a song, on a sudden falling on the ground as in a trance, then jumping up as in a frenzy, and representing with their hand and feet, before the people, whatever work they have unlawfully done on feast days . . . .[18]

The participants in this ceremony were said to move their limbs stiffly and jerkily, until they fell senseless to the ground. When they awoke, they were "seized with fury," and leaped about "with wild gesticulations." The height of the dancing manias came about when the Black Plague, or bubonic plague, raged over Europe, killing thousands and wiping out entire villages and cities. This occurred in the year 1349, and in the decades following,

[16] Martin, *op. cit.*, p. 22.
[17] Lincoln Kirstein, *Dance: A Short History of Classic Theatrical Dancing* (New York: G. P. Putnam's Sons, 1935), p. 88.
[18] Sachs, *op. cit.*, pp. 253–54.

it became customary for huge crowds to wander through the countryside, particularly in Germany and the Low Countries. They danced as if bewitched, and all the rites of exorcism that were tried failed to drive out the mysterious demons which had possessed them. Petrus de Herenthal, a 14th-century monk, described such dances carried on during the year 1374. There came to Aachen, he says, a curious sect of men and women from various regions of Germany:

> Persons of both sexes were so tormented by the devil that in markets and churches, as well as in their own homes, they danced, held each others' hands and leaped high in the air. While they danced their minds were no longer clear, and they paid no heed to modesty though bystanders looked on . . . they cried out names of demons . . . and that they were dying . . . .[19]

Those possessed, who were sometimes called "choreomaniacs," were frequently accused of being heretics, and of flaunting the devil willfully. However, it seems clear that they did not behave in a spirit of revolt toward the Church; indeed, they apparently accepted the efforts of priests to bless or exorcise them. Nor were they apparently punished, as other heretical sects were. Nonetheless, the fact that they were forced to *dance* uncontrollably as part of the spell that had been cast over them confirmed the essential paganism of dance, in the eyes of many Church Fathers.

The dance epidemics continued well into the 17th century, although they appear to have reached their peak of virulence during the 14th and 15th centuries. At a later stage, they appear almost to have been taken for granted as a fairly mild, recurrent illness from which certain people suffered, or as a practice carried on regularly as part of community tradition. The great dance procession at Echternach, the procession of the hopping saints, is considered to be a descendant of this phenomenon of the Middle Ages.

As suggested earlier, secular forms of dance had from the very beginning of Christianity been the subject of opposition by the Church Fathers. Gradually, even the dances that were done in the church came under increasing attack during the Dark and Middle Ages. The Council of Toledo, held in 539, urged that dancing and singing at saints's festivals and processions be rooted out of Spain. The Council of Auxerres, 573–702, forbade the public to dance in choir dances, or nuns to sing in them. Again, the Council of Toledo, in 633, attacked the Festival of Fools, with its singing, dancing, and feasting in churches. At the beginning of

[19] Backman, *op. cit.*, p. 191.

the 10th century, Patriarch John III threatened to excommunicate women who visited graves to play music and dance. The Council of Avignon decreed in 1209 that, in night watches for the saints, "there shall not be performed in churches play-acting, hopping dances, indecent gestures, ring-dance, neither shall there be sung love songs or ditties. . . ."

Nonetheless, the prohibitions continued—which must have meant that the dances themselves continued to be carried on.

Odo, Bishop of Paris in the 12th century, is reported to have prohibited dancing in churches and processions, and especially funeral dances in graveyards at night. Much later, in 1667, there was a decree of the Parliament of Paris forbidding religious dances in general and particularly the public dances of January 1 and May 1, the torch dances of the first Sunday in Lent, and those which were held around bonfires on the Vigil of St. John. One reason, apparently, why dancing managed to survive was that the clergy, who sold dancing indulgences, and who therefore derived much income from these fees, resented these prohibitions and refused to enforce them.

But, even within the Church itself, some dancing practices managed to continue well into the Renaissance period. Father Menestrier, a Jesuit scholar living in the 17th century, tells of seeing in Paris churches the senior canon leading choirboys in a ring-dance during the singing of the psalm; indeed, the Paris Liturgy reads, "The canon will dance to the first psalm." In his history of dance during the medieval era, Menestrier wrote:

> Divine service was composed of psalms, hymns, and canticles, because men sang and danced the praises of God, as they read His oracles in those extracts of the Old and New Testaments which we still know under the name of Lessons. The place in which these acts of worship were offered to God was called the choir, just as those portions of comedies and tragedies in which dancing and singing combined to make up the interludes were called choruses . . . .[20]

In Spain, there were concerted attempts to end religious dance, including a decree by the Bishop of Barcelona to prohibit the so-called *eagle dance*, in 1753, and another royal decree in Madrid in 1777, which attempted to end all dancing on holy days in churches or churchyards, or before images of the saints. Backman concludes that, while these attempts were ultimately successful in ending dancing by the clergy, they were never able to suppress popular church dances in which the communicants

---

[20] Troy and Margaret Kinney, *The Dance* (New York: Tudor Publishing Co., 1936), p. 30.

participated. To this day, such religious dances are still held in Spain, particularly on saints' days and other important holidays.[21] And, until comparatively recently, similar ritual forms have been presented in the Rhône region of France and in Brittany. Urlin writes:

> Dancing still forms an important part of the Breton Pardons. After the bells have been tolled, Mass said, and the statues of the Saints decorated and clad in national dress, and after offerings have been made to them of corn, flax, sheepskins and cakes, dancing is inaugurated to the sound of the national *binyou* around a moss-grown dolmen.[22]

Although the Church had condemned dance as entertainment at an early point, and apparently had succeeded in wiping out organized forms of theatrical presentations, there continued to be wandering entertainers during the Dark and early Middle Ages. These performers, who were apparently combinations of singers, dancers, poets, musicians, actors, and jugglers, wandered through the countryside performing in village squares. Sachs points out that such an entertainer was known in Germany as *spielmann*, which is derived from *spielen*, "to dance." Another name was *joculator*, which later became *jongleur*, or "juggler." Sometimes they were known as *minnesingers*, and sometimes as *troubadors*. Increasingly, during the later Middle Ages, as the restrictions of the Catholic Church were less strongly enforced, these entertainers were welcomed in the castles and chateaus of feudal lords.

In addition to the performances of professional entertainers, the common people amused themselves by doing dances that were essentially social in character. There were two basic types of medieval dancing performed by peasants—the round dance and the couple dance. The round dance, or *Reigen*, was the more popular form. Sometimes called the *Chorea*, or *Carole*, this was usually performed by a long chain of dancers holding each other by the hand, and moving about in an open or closed circle, or in an extended line. Early German dancing, for example, is reported to have been habitually performed in rows or circles. Couple dances were less common, and did not become widely popular until the 15th century—partly because they were considered somewhat scandalous when first seen.

Sachs makes a distinction between the two dance forms—the couple dance is pantomimic in character, whereas the round dance

---

[21] Backman, *op. cit.*, pp. 95–107.
[22] Ethel L. Urlin, *Dancing, Ancient and Modern* (New York: D. Appleton and Co., 1914), p. 41.

Peasant dances at the May feasts. From a 15th-century prayer book miniature in the Bibliothèque Nationale, Paris.

is not. As an example of the former, Nettl cites a poem written in southern Germany, about the year 1000. It describes a dance passage between a young man and a young lady to the music of a harp player; the action is quite suggestive of the Bavarian folk dance, the *Laendler*, as performed today:

> Now the young man gets up, and then the maiden, and then a chasing and hunting begins, sometimes with loud, then with soft music. They fly hither and thither, as when the falcon hunts the dove in the air. He has reached her, the hunt is finished,—but no,—she escapes again, and the game begins anew. Truly their art would fascinate the critics, so skillfully do the dancers master the dance, the leaping, the gesture of the hands.[23]

The dances performed by peasants were extremely boisterous and robust, often frank in their sexuality and earthiness. Their names and brief descriptions suggest this character:

Hoppaldei: peasants rushing around like wild boars, moving

[23] Nettl, *op. cit.*, p. 51.

in couples as though they wanted to fly; arms waving, shoulders heaving and rolling.

Ahselrotten: a shoulder-rolling dance, lively, flirtatious, erotic.

Springeltanz: a wild dance in which the performers hopped and leaped about.

Houbetschotten: a shrugging of shoulders, while sliding along the floor, shaking the head.

Gimpel-Gampel: described both as a boisterous leaping dance, and as a skipping dance.

Peasant dances were copied by the nobility, but in more refined and courtly form. Court dances were part of the chivalric way of life, and stressed coquetry, with much posturing and preening. Because of the heavy, long gowns and trains of the noblewomen, and their elaborate headdresses and jewelry, the ladies of the court were not able to move freely. Indeed, their dance steps at first tended to be little more than gliding, curtseying, and posing. Most of the dances done at first were known as *"basse"* dances, which meant that the action was low; close to the floor.

Nettl describes two courtly dances, as described by poets of the German "minnesinger" period, about the 13th century:

> The women carried their trains . . . in their hands and smiled . . . and with their eyes signalled with love-sick and secret glances . . . the knight walked between two ladies, holding each by the hand and the page walked between two maids. The fiddlers stood close at hand. [The dance] is performed slowly with solemn steps, in long peaked shoes. All the dancers advanced like this is a long row with dragging steps, and two fiddlers play the music.[24]

In addition to their robust spirit, the peasant dances tended to have large movements and wide-stepping figures. In part, this may have been because of their costume, as well as the fact that they danced on grass or on the beaten earth of the town square. In contrast, when the court danced in a ballroom (the first of these is reported to have been built at Frankfurt-am-Main in 1350), the smooth floor of wood or polished marble made it possible for dancers to do graceful gliding or turning steps, while keeping contact with the floor. As an additional contrast, while peasant dances tended to be performed either in couples or rather free formations of both sexes, the courtly dances were precisely defined in group formations.

For example, there was the *"Treialtrei,"* danced by twelve people with four ladies and two gentlemen facing a similar group.

[24] *Ibid.,* p. 56.

In another dance mentioned by Nettl, one gentleman faced two ladies.

In the middle of the 15th century, when the Ottoman Turks captured Constantinople, many of the scholars in this eastern capital of the Roman Empire fled to the West, bearing with them knowledge of the classical culture of Greece and Rome, which they had preserved. They came to the cities and castles of the nobility in France, Italy. Germany, and other lands in Europe, which were ready in spirit for an infusion of artistic elegance, classical learning, and, in effect, a rebirth of culture. Gradually, the severe asceticism and preoccupation with spiritual concerns which had characterized the early Middle Ages gave way to the more worldly-minded spirit of the Renaissance. The gradual rise of a capitalist class produced men who were ready to be patrons of learning and art—within a world which was increasingly secularized. No longer did art have to justify itself through religious content.

Within this context, and with a breaking down of the old restraints, the dance which had once been banned by the Church was now wholly accepted in the courts of the early Renaissance. The minnesingers, jugglers, and jesters now became valuable adjuncts to the courts of Italy and France in particular. A special profession developed—that of the dancing master.

> He accompanied the prince or the count to whose court he was attached on all journeys, and, in fact, he occupied a position of trust and confidence in his patron's household. He was at the same time an arbiter of etiquette, where the instruction given the young men and women of noble family was considered an essential part of their education.[25]

Thus, history had come full circle. After a period in which the arts, learning, music, and dance had been submerged beneath the fanatic asceticism of the Church, there was again an atmosphere in which they could flourish and in which music, drama, and dance, in particular, could reach new heights of artistic development and popularity. This was to be the Renaissance.

[25] *Ibid.*, p. 71.

5

THE EARLY HISTORY
OF BALLET

With the coming of the Renaissance, most notably in 15th-century Italy and France, all the arts—and particularly dance, drama, and music—had a rebirth of interest and artistic experimentation. The old restraints were loosened during the Renaissance, and learning, literature, the stage arts, and indeed all creative expressions of the human spirit were no longer dominated by clerical ideals and purposes. Instead, they were to serve the secular goals of the wealthy and powerful kings and queens who had emerged throughout Europe—along with the luxury-loving members of their courts. The revival of interest in classical scholarship and in the arts of ancient Greece and Rome led to a fresh concern with mythology, ancient history, and the great heroes of past centuries. With the invention of printing, it became possible to widely distribute printed dance music; at one stroke, there was a flood of music published for such instruments as lutes, guitars, organs, and other string and keyboard instruments. The character of music itself changed abruptly. As Horst points out, the pale, austere, rhythmically irregular music of the medieval period—as exemplified by the Gregorian chants—shifted to more brilliant and spirited music with pronounced rhythm and a single strong melodic line.[1]

[1]Louis Horst, *Pre-Classic Dance Forms* (New York: Kamin Dance Publishers, 1953), pp. 1–2.

In the 15th and 16th centuries, a great dance movement swept throughout the courts of Europe, accompanied by a surge of creation of new musical forms. Essentially, this movement had two aspects. One was the creation of a variety of new court dances, performed by the nobility themselves as a form of aristocratic amusement and, more than this, a means of educating courtiers in social deportment and grace. The second was the development of a number of major entertainments, or spectacles, which ultimately gave rise to the art of ballet in France.

The court entertainments did not suddenly spring into life, as a form of extravagant display. Throughout the Middle Ages, there had been customs and performances which held in them the seed of the Renaissance spectacles. Under religious auspices, there had been festivals, miracle and mystery plays, and a variety of other celebrations, many of which were theatrical in character. Banquets in the homes of great nobles had increasingly placed reliance on entertainments by the resident troubador or dancing master and members of the court themselves; often these were elaborately costumed and provided colorful displays. The knightly tournaments were also exciting and vivid displays of wealth, costume, and ritualized combat. Even the trade guilds of the later Middle Ages had developed the practice of performing allegorical plays which involved singing, dancing, and acting.

Thus, out of the life of the Middle Ages came both inspiration and a readiness for new forms of artistic performance. These took the form of great banquets in the Italian and French courts, usually at times of weddings or as homage to visting royalty, or in celebration of the coronation of kings. Each of these banquets featured elaborate spectacles, with singing, dancing, and acting, richly costumed and sometimes with specially designed and built stage sets. Sometimes they were held in the castle itself, in the banquet hall, and sometimes at the entrance to the city gates or at a bridge leading to the city. Their themes were diverse, ranging from the acting out of stories from Greek mythology and fables, stories of the Crusades, tales of Roman history, Christian ceremonials, and episodes from the Old Testament. A number of such examples follow:

Charles V of France presented a major spectacle to the German Emperor Charles IV in 1377. Like many other entertainments, it portrayed a major episode of the Crusades. Two heavily armed wagons drove up to the banquet table. One represented the city of Jerusalem, held by Saracen defenders, and the other a galley holding soldiers of Godfrey of Bouillon. After a long, stylized combat, the crusaders successfully stormed the city.

Similar pageants were held in England, when Henry V returned from victory at Agincourt in 1415, and when Henry VI and his French wife Catherine returned in 1432 from their coronation as King and Queen of France and England; this was held at the foot of London Bridge.

In 1462, King René of Provence put on an entertainment that was both religious and social, on the eve of Corpus Christi. Lacking any single theme or plot, it offered tributes to the royalty of the day, and also portrayed, in a series of separate dramatic episodes, the Roman gods, Mars and Minerva, Pan, Pluto, and Proserpine; fauns, dryads, and tritons; King Herod persecuted by devils; ancient Jews dancing around a Golden Calf; Christ and the Apostles; Death with a scythe, and the Magi following a star.

A fete was organized by Bergonzio de Botta in 1489 to celebrate the marriage of Galeazzo, Duke of Milan, with Isabel of Aragon, when he passed through the town of Tortona, in Italy. This display involved music, dance, poetry, and pantomime as part of a great banquet, which told the story of Jason and the Argonauts. While it involved a number of other myths or folk tales from Greek and Roman mythology, the work was somewhat

Equestrian ballet, "Guerra d'Amore," in honor of Cosimo de Medici, Grand Duke of Tuscany. Engraving by Jacques Callot, published 1615.

more unified and consistent in its conception (each act or entree, celebrating the guests of honor, was performed as a new course was brought to the festive board) than previous entertainments had been.

One of the most popular themes of such entertainments was the *Moresca*, or *Moresche*, which depicted the battles between the Moors, or Saracens, and the Crusaders. This was found both as a form of popular folk ritual and as a subject for court displays. Other aspects of the same theme included the re-occupation of Spain by the Christians, and the attack on Jerusalem by the Crusader Godfrey. To illustrate, at the celebration of the conquest of Granada in 1493, a pantomimic pageant with triumphal arches, a procession of Spanish royalty, Moorish dances, and bullfights was performed. Usually in these performances, the Moors were depicted as black men, and it is believed that there may have been a connection between the *Moresca* and the Morris Dance—a traditional English folk dance in which it was the custom for certain of the dancers to blacken their faces.

In England, Henry VIII staged an elaborate Masque in 1510, based on the folk tales about Robin Hood. In the Vatican, in 1518, Ariosto's "Suppositi," a sacred representation which included much dance, was presented, with decorations by the great Renaissance painter, Raphael. Similarly, other Italian artists like Andrea del Sarto and Leonardo da Vinci were said to have painted the decorations for other religious spectacles.

Throughout all of these, dance served as a means of pantomiming the action. In many of the entrees, or interludes, other dances which had become popular during the Renaissance were performed. These were the so-called court dances, or "preclassic" dances, which were performed in couples or small groups, and which now covered a wide range of music, mood, and movement styles.

Dancing had become an everyday adjunct to court life in all of the palaces of the Renaissance. Queen Elizabeth of England was said to have made Sir Christopher Hatton her Lord Chancellor, not because of his particular wisdom in the law, but because "he wore green bows on his shoes and danced the pavane to perfection. . . ." But there was more to it than this. During the Middle Ages dancing had become widely accepted in the courts throughout Europe, and training in it was now viewed as indispensable to the education of a nobleman. De Mille points out that the invention of firearms meant that whereas before brute strength and endurance had been prize qualities for a courtier who also was a soldier, now intelligence and alertness counted for more. Just as the giant Percherons which had formerly been warhorses (to bear the lords clad in weighty armor) were replaced by lighter and more graceful Arabian thoroughbreds, so during the Renaissance, "clothes became lighter, manners daintier, dueling more expert and dancing more skilled . . . ."

De Mille points out that all courtiers took dancing lessons every day. The steps were simple, but precise, with intricate floor patterns and great emphasis on deportment and manner. The sequences were practised endlessly and when they were performed at court functions, there was no improvisation.[2]

What were the court dances of the Renaissance?

At the outset, they had been divided into two broad categories—the *Basse Danse*, in which the feet did not leave the floor, and the *Haute Danse*, in which there were higher skips and jumps. However, both of these were broad types, with no precisely designed steps or floor patterns. The term *"branle,"* which later described a separate dance, was in the early period only a step sideways with balancing of the body, or swaying. A number of extremely simple dances were described as having been performed during the 15th century by aristocrats of the French, Italian, Spanish, and German courts. Often, they were known by one name in one country, and another name elsewhere. For example, one of the best known early dances was the *Saltarello*, called *Alta Danza* in Spain, and *Pas de Brebant* in France. The action was not, as the name implies, a high jumping or leaping step; instead it was a fast forward and backward step, along with hopping actions to the side.

Other dances of the period were the *Piva*, *Saltarello Tedesco*, and *Calata*; however, none of these apparently had prescribed forms. Neither their descriptions nor the music to which they were danced were recorded for history. It was not until the end of the 16th century that rules were formulated for the proper steps for each dance, and for the appropriate dance music to be played. This meant that, in terms of progress in dance, a whole system of movement and a vocabulary of steps and patterns were developed. In terms of music, the need for contrast in rhythm and musical form meant that each dance soon had its characteristic accompaniment; the composers of the period grouped the selections that were played into a certain order, giving birth to the musical suite—which ultimately became the sonata form.

The most famous dances of the period were the *Pavane*, the *Galliard*, the *Allemande*, the *Courante*, the *Sarabande*, the *Gigue*, and the *Minuet*.

---

[2] Agnes de Mille, *The Book of the Dance* (New York: Golden Books, 1963), p. 63.

Pavane. This was a dance of ceremonious splendor and great dignity, which is said to have originated in the court of Spain during the Inquisition. Its mood was solemn and religious (the name is derived from the Latin *pavo*, or peacock) and it suggests this stately and pompous fowl. The Pavane was apparently used on some religious occasions; Arbeau wrote in 1588, in his *Orchesographie*:

> Our musicians play it when a damsel of good family is taken to Holy Church to be married, or when musicians head a religious procession of the chaplains, masters and brethren of some notable guild . . . .
>
> . . . It is used by kings, princes and great lords, to display themselves on some day of solemn festival with their fine mantles and robes of ceremony; and then the queens and princesses and great ladies accompany them with the long trains of their dresses let down and trailing behind them. These Pavanes are also used in masquerades (or ballets) where there is a procession of triumphant chariots of gods and goddesses . . . . [3]

In terms of its footwork, the Pavane was a *Basse Danse*, involving a simple walking step performed by one or more couples, advancing and retreating. It was done in a slow tempo, and one source describes it as a "grave kind of dance borrowed from the Spaniards, wherein the performers make a kind of wheel or tail before each other, like that of a peacock." The Pavane continued to be popular from about 1530 to about 1670; it was used as the opening dance of great festive balls, usually being followed by the spirited Galliard.

Galliard. Arbeau described the Galliard as a blithe and lively dance, of which there were at least 20 different versions. Its source was said to be Italy, where it was also called the *Romanesca*. It included a number of leaping, kicking, and leg-thrusting steps, and was most popular from the last quarter of the 16th century to about the middle of the 17th. Among its variations were the *Tourdion*, a somewhat restrained form of the dance, and the *Volté*, a very gay dance, in which the women were turned and lifted by their partners. Sometimes the Galliard was considered to be immodest; one author referred to it as an "invention of the devil, full of shameful and obscene gestures."

When the Pavane, in 4/4 time, was followed by the lively Galliard in 3/4 time, as a customary sequence at court balls, the first musical suite was born. Many musical compositions were composed with this contrasting structure.

Allemande. This dance eventually replaced the Pavane as the first part of what was to become the four-part classic suite. The

---

[3] Thoinot Arbeau, *Orchesographie* (1588), quoted in Horst, *op. cit.*, p. 7.

Allemande is considered to have been a very ancient German dance, simple and grave in demeanor. One writer, in 1584, described it as "knights in armour, treading a warlike almain."

After it was introduced at the French court, the Allemande gained rather flowing and sentimental characteristics; it was usually danced in 4/4 time, played in a slow and dignified tempo. Its unique aspect was that it required partners to keep their hands joined throughout the entire dance, as they turned and performed various patterns; after it was no longer performed as a separate dance, this action was still perpetuated in folk and country dancing. In square dancing today, to turn one's partner or corner by the hand means to do an "allemande."

Courante. Destined to become the second dance of the four-part classic suite, the Courante was said to have originated both in Italy and France, and had three distinct versions. The first phase of the Courante came from Italy, and was brought to France by Catherine de Medici. Played with running passages of eighth notes in quick 3/4 time, it was colorfully described: "It is danced with short passages of coming and going, and has a very pliant movement of the knees, which recalls that of a fish when it plunges lightly through the water and returns suddenly to the surface."[4]

The second form originated in France, and was the more popular version of the Courante. It was apparently a pantomime dance; as described by Arbeau, it was danced by three couples in a row, showing gestures of courtship and flirtation. Movements including running and gliding and, as the dance continued to be performed through the years, it gradually became more solemn and noble in its attitudes. According to Horst, the Courante was a great favorite for about two centuries, from 1550 to 1750.

Sarabande. Destined to become the third dance of the four-part suite, the Sarabande, like the Pavane, was of Spanish ancestry, and was a solemn dance which was widely used in religious processions and Masses. It appears to have been performed as early as the 12th century, although it was not introduced at the French court until about 1588. The dance was like a grave and proud *Minuet,* involving much advancing and retreating, with couples passing between lines of other dancers almost as a processional. Some thought that it originated first with the Moors in Spain, and it was often performed with castanets. The Sarabande was played in two parts, in 3/4 time, in a slow tempo.

Gigue. The fourth dance of the four-part classic suite was the Gigue—a lively and exciting dance which apparently was found in varying forms in many countries of Europe. The earliest form

[4] Horst, *op. cit.*, p. 35.

recorded was in Italy, where the name was derived from the *giga*, a small stringed instrument. Horst points out that the German name for fiddle was *geige*, and traditionally the Gigue, or Jig, has always been performed to spirited fiddle music, played in 3/8, 6/8, 9/8, or 12/8 time. The Gigue was most popular in the 16th and 17th centuries, although it continued to be done for centuries after, as a sort of individual folk dance step, or a music hall turn.

Other dances described by Horst as being performed during the preclassic period of the 16th and 17th centuries were the *Minuet* (which continued to be widely performed as late as the 19th century); the *Gavotte*, originally a lively and flirtatious peasant dance; the *Bourrée*, an earthy and vigorous dance, also of peasant origin; and the *Rigaudon*, a light, gay dance with running, hopping, and turning steps.

As court music became more complex and the courtiers more skilled dancers, the original two-part suite of the Pavane and Galliard was replaced, about 1620, by the four-part suite of the Allemande, Courante, Sarabande, and Gigue. Many great composers of the 17th, 18th, and 19th centuries wrote in one or another of these forms, including Purcell, Bach, Handel, Couperin, and Lully; among later composers who derived inspiration from them were Satie, Ravel, Schoenberg, Debussy, and Prokofieff. Although the court dances of the Renaissance were not ballet as such, they may be said to have provided the vocabulary of movement of much of the early ballet in France and Italy.

Dance historians usually assign the date of the first ballet to 1581, when the so-called *Ballet Comique de la Reine* was produced at the court of Henry III of France, at Fontainebleau. It was a tremendously elaborate and expensive spectacle, put on by the queen mother, Catherine de Medici, who, when she came to France to wed Henry II, had brought with her a company of highly trained musicians and dancers from the city of Florence. The *Ballet Comique* was produced in honor of the queen's daughter-in-law; it was the work of Catherine's valet de chambre, Balthasar de Beaujoyeux, an Italian. It was a mixture of Old Testament tales and Greek and Roman mythology; basically, its theme was that of Circe, the Greek enchantress. Original music, poetry, and songs were composed by professionals of the court, and elaborate sets and scenic devices, including fountains and aquatic machines, accompanied the performance. Over 10,000 spectators saw the performance, which lasted from ten in the evening until four in the morning, and which had cost between three and five million francs to produce.

Although the quality of performance and the splendor of the entire work far exceeded any court entertainment that had been produced before, it was chiefly because the *Ballet Comique* attempted to confine itself to a single major dramatic theme that it is regarded as the first real ballet to have been presented in Europe. The performance was regarded as a major artistic success; copies of its poetry and music were printed and sent to all the courts of Europe.

From this point, France was viewed as the center of the development of ballet, while Italy served as the home of the developing opera of the Renaissance.

The term "ballet" itself was derived from the Italian *ballare*, meaning "to dance," and from the word *ballo*, referring to dances as performed in a ballroom. *Ballate* were songs used to accompany dancing in Tuscany in the 13th and 14th centuries, and Chujoy points out that during the later years of the Renaissance the Medici princes wrote *canzone a ballo*, or dance songs. The word *balleti* was the diminutive of *ballo*, and is the direct source of the word *ballet*. At first it meant performances of patterned dances and had no specific theatrical meaning. Balthasar de Beaujoyeux, choreographer of the *Ballet Comique*, defined ballet as "a geometric combination of several persons dancing together."

Gradually, however, the term came to mean a form of theatrical storytelling through dance. The *Encyclopedia* of Diderot, published in France about 1772, says, "Ballet is action explained by a dance ... specifically theatrical, spectacular, and done to be seen. . . ." Another 18th century conception was, "The stage is, as it were, the canvas, on which the composer (choreographer) renders his ideas; the choice of music, scenery and costumes are his colors; the choreographer is the painter." A somewhat more detailed statement by Perugini is:

> A ballet is a series of solo and concerted dances with mimetic actions, accompanied by music and scenic accessories, all expressive of a poetic idea or series of ideas, or a dramatic story provided by an author, or choreographer.[5]

In addition to considering ballet in terms of its outward form, one might also view it historically, as the traditional concert dance form of the Western world. Conceived in Italy, it came to life in France in the court of Louis XIV in the latter part of the

---

[5] Mark Perugini, *A Pageant of Dance and Ballet*, quoted in Anatole Chujoy, *The Dance Encyclopedia* (New York: A. S. Barnes, & Co., Inc., 1949), p. 36.

17th century. It developed through the contributions of individual dancers, choreographers, and teachers, in the centuries that followed, reaching a peak of creativity and popular appeal during a so-called Golden Age, in the 1830s and 1840s. In this period, a complex system of movement and floor patterns was developed, as well as a teaching system that allowed ballet to be taught with relative exactitude in the courts, opera houses, and academies of Europe, and fundamental concepts of form and style which distinguished it from other dance forms.

How did the ballet make these advances?

Following the *Ballet Comique* in 1581, a number of other outstanding court entertainments were presented, none of comparable scope or artistic excellence. One of these was performed in the Salle de Bourbon, in 1615, to celebrate a royal marriage in France. Vuillier described it thus:

> Thirty genii [being the chamber and chapel musicians of the King], suspended in the air, heralded the coming of Minerva, the Queen of Spain. This goddess, surrounded by fourteen nymphs, her companions, appeared in a mighty gilded car drawn by two Cupids. A band of Amazons accompanied the car and made a concord of lutes . . . . Forty persons were on the stage at once, thirty high in the sky, and six suspended in mid-air; all of these dancing and singing at the same time.[6]

Altogether, over eighty such ballets were performed at the French court of Henry IV (whose reign was from 1589 to 1610), in addition to numerous balls and masquerades. Such works were known in France as Masques, since all the dancers wore masks— a custom that was not abolished in ballet until as late as 1773.

Louis XIII, who followed Henry IV, was another great patron of the dance. Under his reign, many ballets were performed; the king himself played a leading role in *La Délivrance de Renault* in 1617, and composed dance music for other works. A fairly typical work of this period was the *Mountain Ballet*, an allegorical entertainment in which the scenery consisted of five great mountains—the Windy, the Resounding, the Luminous, the Shadowy, and the Alps. In the midst was a Field of Glory, which the inhabitants of the mountains wished to capture:

> Fame opened the ballet and explained its subject. Disguised as an old woman, she rode an ass and carried a wooden trumpet. Then the mountains opened their sides, and quadrilles of dancers came out, in flesh-colored attire, having bellows in their hands, and windmills

---

[6] Père Menestrier, quoted in Gaston Vuillier, *A History of Dance* (New York: D. Appleton and Co., 1897), p. 90.

on their heads. These represented the Winds. Others rushed out, headed by the nymph Echo, wearing bells for head-dresses, and on their bodies lesser bells, and carrying drums. Falsehood hobbled forward on a wooden leg, with masks hung over his coat, and a dark lantern in his hand . . . .[7]

Typically, such works usually consisted of a series of dances, ranging in number from about 10 to about 30, by different groups of dancers who dramatized related phases of a common theme. At the end, general dancing was held, in which all the members of the court participated along with those who had performed in the entertainment. With the exception of those few professionals who were attached to the court as dancing masters, musicians, and composers, all were amateurs. Martin points out that during the reign of Louis XIII, a single performance in an evening often was not enough; the king and his fellow dancers trooped from the royal palace to other mansions of the nobility, repeating the performance. Frequently the evening was brought to a close with a final performance on a platform erected in front of the City Hall, with townspeople as spectators. At the end, the king and courtiers stepped down to the street and danced with the wives and daughters of the townspeople. The king's company was all male, since at this time noblewomen did not customarily dance in the formal court ballet. The roles of girls and women were usually taken by boys and slender youths wearing elaborate wigs and masks.[8]

A giant step in the progress of ballet was taken during the reign of Louis XIV, the Sun King, who was probably as enthusiastic and helpful a patron as the dance has ever known. The king himself was an excellent dancer as a young man, and delighted in performing himself. He took daily lessons from his dancing master, Pierre Beauchamps, for over 20 years, and, only when he was too heavy to dance gracefully, in middle age, did he stop performing.

Because of his great interest in ballet, Louis employed a number of outstanding musicians and dancing masters, among them Jean-Baptiste Lully, an Italian-born muscian and dancer who ultimately became the director of the Royal Academy of Music and Dance. Another key figure was Pierre Beauchamps, a brilliant dancer who formulated many of the beginning principles of ballet and became *maître de ballet* at the Royal Academy.

[7] Vuillier, *op. cit.*, p. 87.
[8] John Martin, *John Martin's Book of the Dance* (New York: Tudor Publishing Co., 1963), p. 29.

Louis XIV in the Ballet Royal de la Nuit, 1653.

Beginning in 1651, when he was thirteen, Louis XIV danced in public in the *Masque of Cassandra*. He continued until 1670 as a leading performer, dancing in 26 grand ballets, not to mention the intermezzi of numerous lyrical tragedies and comedy ballets. Throughout his reign, many ballets were danced at the Tuilleries and others at the Louvre, at Versailles, and Fontainebleau. One performance, the *Ballet du Carrousel*, was held on a large open space in front of the Tuilleries in 1662; in this ballet Louis XIV danced at the head of the Roman armies, while his brother led the Perisians, the Prince de Condé commanded the Turks, and the Duc de Guise the Americans. In other works, such as the *Grand Ballet du Roi*, performed at the Louvre in 1664, figures of Roman mythology and history were portrayed in a conglomerate sequence of tales. In addition to these separate ballets, a number of ballets were danced in the operas of Lully and other musicians of the period.

Dancing until this time had been an amateur art, and was performed, usually, within the ballroom. Typically, the king and his household sat at the end of the hall on a dais. Along the other sides of the room, spectators sat in long galleries on the edge of the floor. There was no stage, and the dancers were close to the audience. The dance movement was fairly simple, being based in large degree on the pre-classic court dances of the period. The dancers were encumbered by extremely heavy wigs, masks, and costumes; some of these weighed as much as 150 pounds. For amateurs, the noblemen of the court were excellent dancers. Every courtier could dance; de Mille comments that their style was always noble and controlled—the demeanor of a king. Gestures were symmetrical and harmonious, all opening from a central axis, based on the turned-out leg and *port de bras* (fencing position).

The nobleman, in de Mille's words, "danced as he was used to moving in all court procedures":

> . . . [with] movement characterized by arrogant confidence, affected yet elegant, ornate, swift and commanding, highly disciplined; with erect posture, lightness, strength, brilliance, and cat-like use of the foot . . . .[9]

But, in the Sun King's view, this was not enough. Realizing that from a technical standpoint ballet could be developed much more fully, in 1661 Louis XIV asked his ballet master, Beauchamps, to establish rules for ballet, to describe the foot and arm positions and all the known patterns of movement. This Beauchamps did, thus establishing the basis for ballet technique that was to develop through the centuries. In addition, in 1661, the king granted a charter to the Royal Academy of Dance, which was to provide a home for professional instruction in the art of dancing. This art, according to the letters patent founding the Academy:

> . . . has ever been acknowledged to be one of the most suitable and necessary arts for physical development and for affording the primary and most natural preparation for all bodily exercises, and, among others, those concerning the use of weapons, and consequently it is one of the most valuable and useful arts for nobles and others who have the honor to enter our presence not only in time of war in our armies, but even in time of peace in our ballets.[10]

Apparently, the Academy did not function for a decade. Then, in 1671, Lully obtained the charter of the Royal Academy of Music and combined that with the Academy of Dance, to form a single strong organization. Within two years, the new academy

---

[9] De Mille, *op. cit.*, p. 81.
[10] *Ibid.*, p. 90.

which joined both arts was given the use of the Theater in the Palais Royal, built about thirty years before by Cardinal Richelieu, and occupied until the death of Molière by that famous playwright and his company. This magnificent theater was built in the recently developed manner of the new Italian theater; it had an elevated stage on which the action took place, at one end of the hall, beneath a proscenium arch. All the spectators sat in front, rather than on three sides of the dancer, as in the past.

The use of Richelieu's theater had two important effects on the development of ballet as a professional art at this time.

First, since the dancer had only to be concerned with how he would look from one direction, it became necessary to think of the audience, in front, as a focus. When moving from side to side across the stage, the best way to do this while facing the audience was to turn the hip and knee out, so the feet pointed to the side instead of straight forward. Gradually, the turnout became more and more pronounced, and became the basis of the five positions of the foot in classic ballet which Beauchamps recorded about 1700 and which are essential to all ballet technique even today.

A second important effect of the new theater and its stage was that for the first time the performers were markedly separated from their audience. No longer did dance represent a somewhat casual, social activity, in which members of the court might intermingle freely with professionals. Over a period of decades, performance became the domain of the professional dancers who were trained in the Royal Academy and who developed an increasingly high level of skill that separated them, more and more, from the amateur performers in the nobility.

In *The Triumph of Love*, women for the first time performed on the professional stage. Lully succeeded in persuading some of the greatest ladies of the court, including the Dauphiness and a number of princesses, to dance professionally—still wearing masks, of course.

The ballet, however, became increasingly professional. Much of the technique was derived, as indicated earlier, from the court dances performed during the pre-classic period. However, gradually it moved from *danse terre à terre* (close to the earth) to *danse haute*, with leaps, springing steps, and such actions as the *entrechat*. The design of movement became vertical, rather than horizontal. Based on the five fundamental positions of the feet and the twelve positions, of the arm which Beauchamps had formulated, a wide variety of steps was developed and named; these became the basis of ballet technique and the *danse d'école*— or education in ballet.

Lully, who directed the new company that performed in the Palais Royal, felt that the Paris audience which now was permitted to attend performances in the new theater would enjoy plays that combined both dancing and singing. Thus, in the early days of the Royal Academy, its company performed in so-called lyric dramas. In these, while the dance may have slowed up the dramatic action, it was related to it, and served to carry the plot along. Gradually, however, in the early and middle 18th century, the so-called Opera Ballet came into being. This included both dancing and orchestral music; it dealt with many kinds of subject matter within a single work, and often the content of one act was not related to that of the following act. In essence, the dramatic action almost disappeared, and the stage work became a vehicle for singers and dancers to display their talents. Gradually, as the plot became less important, dancers tended to perform movement that was increasingly decorative and abstract—rather than story telling in nature.

In a sense, this reflected a change in the times. Vuillier writes:

> The opening of the eighteenth century was marked by a reaction against the majestic solemnity, the monstrous etiquette and the official piety that had prevailed during the later years of the Grand Monarque. The art of the new era inclined to artificiality . . . painters sought inspiration in love and joy, in sylvan delights, in dainty idylls . . . great financiers began to patronise dawning talent, and to encourage the growth of a luxurious elegance. It was a reign of daintiness and of taste . . . perhaps a little mincing and affected. Pictorial art lacked energy and deep feeling—lacked greatness, in a word; but it was pretty, it was seductive.[11]

It was at this time that a pattern developed with respect to the role of the sexes in dance, that has often been repeated since. The leading *organizers* of dance—the teachers, innovators, choreographers, theoreticians—were men such as Lully and Beauchamps. Lully was a musician and a dancer, but far more than this, a clever politician, wise in the ways of the court, who was able to mobilize the efforts of the king in his behalf. Further, he produced many works and composed operas and ballets. Beauchamps, while a brilliant performer who had introduced much technique and was known for his elevations, turns, *pirouettes*, and *tours en l'air*, was also a leading codifier of the dance. His system of dance shorthand, or notation, was the first of its kind and it was his analysis of the fundamentals of ballet movement that laid the groundwork for the development of this art.

[11] Vuillier, *op. cit.*, pp. 138–39.

While men monopolized organizational roles, women began to assume the role of stars—glamorous and brilliant dancers who won the acclaim of growing audiences. They no longer came from the nobility itself. Instead, they tended to come from poorer families, and to have learned their craft in the Academy. Now they performed on the stage of the Palais Royal before an audience that was still aristocratic for the most part, although with a sprinkling of wealthy bourgeois. Among these talented performers were Camargo, Sallé, and Prévost.

Marie Anne de Camargo, who lived between 1710 and 1770, is reputed to have been the outstanding French dancer of the 18th century. Her style was gay and light, her movements lusty and vigorous, with strong contrasts. While the technique at this time was still extremely limited, Camargo was considered an extremely expressive dancer; she made ballet a vehicle of interpretation. She had a particular ability for elevation, and was able to rapidly cross and recross her feet in the air (an action known as *entrechat*), and this gave her the courage to modify the traditional ballet costume. At this point, women wore stiff-hooped skirts that were heavily panniered, and reached the floor, as well as elaborate, heavy headdresses, masks, coats, and heeled shoes. In order to give her legs greater freedom, and to permit her ingenious improvisations to be seen, Camargo adopted a much shorter skirt than was the custom, and an undergarment which was the predecessor of ballet tights. In addition, she wore soft slippers which were the forerunners of ballet slippers.

Another great female star of the 18th century was Marie Sallé. Unlike Camargo, her style was not that of a brilliant virtuoso. Instead, she brought to ballet a dramatic realism and a natural expressiveness in movement. She, too, sought to abandon the traditional ballet costume and introduced flowing draperies modeled after Greek sculpture, particularly in the ballet *Pygmalion*, which she performed in London when her ideas became too radical for the directors of the Royal Academy in Paris. In fact, it was her intent to abandon the set uniform of ballet entirely and dress each character in its appropriate national style, or in terms of its place in the plot—a reform that has been suggested again and again by ballet innovators. So popular was Sallé, who lived from 1707 to 1756, that Vuillier wrote of her:

> She was idolised. The huge crowds that pressed about the doors of the theater fought for a sight of her. Enthusiastic spectators, who had paid great sums for seats, had to make their way in with their fists. Upon her benefit appearance in London, at the close of the piece, purses filled with guineas and jewels were showered on the stage at

her feet. The Cupids and Satyrs of her troupe, keeping time to the music, picked up this spontaneous tribute. On this memorable night, Mademoiselle Sallé received more than two hundred thousand francs, an enormous sum for that time.[12]

Another leading performer during this period, was Françoise Prévost, who danced during the early 1700s, and who was known for her lightness and precision, as well as for her dramatic ability. In addition, there were a number of leading male dancers, such as Louis Pécours, who starred in many of Lully's and Beauchamps' ballets, choreographed a number of works for the Palais Royal, and taught in the Academy. However, without question, it was the brilliant female stars who attracted the most fervently enthusiastic audiences.

As an increasing number of outstanding dancers developed in Paris, they began to travel from court to court throughout Europe, performing and beginning their own ballet schools and companies. It was at this time that rulers in Italy, Austria, Russia, England, and Scandinavia established royal opera houses and theaters, to which ballet companies became promptly attached. This meant, according to de Mille, that "the companies were established in permanent residence and guaranteed continuity and protection. All are still functioning as the ornaments of the state and repositories of great national works and technical styles.[13] Among the famous theaters and opera houses which were established at this time were: The King's Theater, in Haymarket, London, 1705; the Royal Danish Ballet, in the National Theater, Copenhagen, 1726; the Royal Opera, in Covent Garden, London, 1732; and numerous others in Naples (1737), Vienna (1748), Stuttgart (1750), Munich (1752), Moscow (1776), Milan (1778), and St. Petersburg (1783).

In some cases, ballet was founded as a separate company, under royal subsidy and protection; in others, it was a valued component of a major opera company. In each instance, support was assured that meant that a high level of training and performance could be maintained; ballet had now gained status that was to assure its continuity through the centuries.

In a sense, this represented a threat to the continuing creative development of ballet. Just as in any art form which becomes attached to the establishment, its ways became fixed and stereotyped in the middle of the 18th century. The choreographers of the early and middle 1700s made no attempt to reform the exist-

---

[12] *Ibid.*, p. 142.
[13] De Mille, *op. cit.*, p. 91.

ing Opera Ballet practices for several decades. Every opera had *Passepieds* in its prologue, followed by *Musettes* in the first act, by *Tambourins* in the second, and by *Chaconnes* and *Passepieds* in the acts following (these refer to dances popular during the period). No one dared to violate this formula, according to Vuillier:

> . . . in every opera, each leading character had to dance his special dance, and the best dancer always concluded. It was by this law, and not by the action of the poem, that the dancing was governed. And what intensified the mischief was that poets, musicians, costumiers, decorators, never consulted one another. Each had his prescriptive routine; each pursued his own old path, indifferent as to whether he arrived at the same goal as his neighbor. To reform all this was a Herculean task. No single individual could diverge from the beaten track until all abandoned it . . . .[14]

Few tried. Such famous performers or choreographers of the middle and late 18th century as Gaetano Vestris, distinguished member of a great ballet family; Jean Dauberval, a French dancer and choreographer who composed the famed *La Fille Mal Gardée*; Madeleine Guimard, a leading female dancer toward the end of the century who was extremely popular with royalty and conducted a leading salon; Charles Didelot, a dancer and choreographer in Sweden and at the Paris Opéra; and Salvatore Vigano, a leading Italian dancer and choreographer—all of these were generally content with their lot. It remained for one person, Jean Georges Noverre, to propose a set of sweeping reforms in ballet that ultimately changed this theatrical art in a number of radical ways.

Noverre, who lived from 1727 to 1810, made his debut as a dancer at the age of 16 in the Opéra Comique and was appointed ballet master four years later. Ultimately, he became a leading choreographer, critic, writer, and reformer of ballet. He was the first to fully envision its artistic possibilities, and to eliminate the conventionalized movements, gestures, and stage traditions. Noverre's book, *Letters on Dancing and Ballet*, published in 1760, stressed that dancing should not only be physical virtuosity, but also a means for dramatic expression and communication. Ballet had become a collection of miscellaneous short dances which tended to be thrown together to casually written music. These were presented at random in operas, with no relation to the action or plot, chiefly because they permitted the stars to show off their special abilities before the large audiences which only a performance of opera could obtain. Vuillier writes:

[14] Vuillier, *op. cit.*, p. 153.

... there were many clever dancers on the French stage, the Vestris, Gardel, and Dubervals, but it was impossible for them to execute dances properly .... They came on in enormous helmets, crowned by a mass of plumes, their faces concealed by masks. They advanced from the back to the front of the stage with prodigious bounds, displaying the suppleness of their figures with great effect; each one of them was careful to bring out his particular strong point, the beauty of his arm, the perfection of his leg; but this was hardly dancing in the true sense of the term ....[15]

Noverre's philosophy (one which he presented so vigorously that ultimately he was compelled to leave Paris and to seek posts elsewhere, in England, Vienna, and Stuttgart) comprised the following ideas:

Balletic movement should not only be technically brilliant, but should move the audience emotionally, through its dramatic expressiveness.

The plots of ballets should be unified in design, with logical and understandable stories that contribute to a central theme, and with all solos or other dance sequences that did not relate to the plot being eliminated.

The scenery, the music, and the plot should all be unified; a reform of costumes was necessary so that they would be appropriate to the theme of the dance, and music should be specially written so as to be suitable for the dance as well.

Pantomime, which had become increasingly conventionalized and meaningless, needed to be made simpler and more understandable.

These and many other suggestions were summed up in his writings on the *ballet d'action*—that is, ballet in which the dance actually promotes the dramatic representation, instead of interrupting it for meaningless displays of virtuosity. In his own work, Noverre collaborated with musicians closely. He sought appropriate subject matter first, worked out a libretto or poem, developed dance movements to express the content of the poem, and then explained the plot to the composer and asked that music be composed to fit this work specifically—rather than just setting a dance to existing music.

Noverre wrote:

A well-composed ballet is a living picture of the passions, manners, habits, ceremonies and customs of all nations of the globe ... if it be devoid of expression, of striking pictures, or strong situations, it becomes a cold and dreary spectacle ....[16]

[15] *Ibid.*, p. 160.
[16] Jean Georges Noverre, *Letters on Dancing and Ballet*, translated by Cyril Beaumont (published originally in 1760, republished by Dance Horizons, Inc., New York, 1966), p. 16.

Gradually, Noverre's ideas gained influence. When he urged dancers to ". . . break hideous masks, to bury ridiculous perukes, to suppress clumsy panniers, to do away with still more inconvenient hip pads . . ." he lent courage to leading performers who had long wished that costumes might be reformed. Thus, in 1772, when *Castor and Pollux*, an opera by Rameau, was being performed, Gaetano Vestris was scheduled to perform as Apollo, wearing a traditional enormous black wig, a mask, and a big gilded copper sun on his chest. Unable to appear, Vestris's role was taken by Maximilien Gardel who was determined to let the audience know that *he* was playing the role of the Sun God, rather than Vestris. He refused to wear the wig, the mask, and the copper sun. The public approved the change and from this time on, the use of the mask was abandoned by leading dancers.

Other disciples of Noverre, including Dauberval and Didelot, applied many of his reforms with respect to the development of ballet plots and the use of meaningful gesture—rather than the stereotyped hand language then in vogue. Noverre never completely succeeded in his wish to make ballet a completely independent theater art, rather than a decorative adjunct to opera. Nonetheless, he represented a force for the revitalization of ballet that was not to be duplicated until Michel Fokine left Russia for Paris, over a century later.

The next major influence to touch and modify ballet was the French Revolution.

The immediate effect of this violent overthrow of the French monarchy was to challenge the place of ballet in public life, as a form of entertainment that was essentially an aristocratic art, and identified with the pastimes of the very royalty that had fled the country in terror, or had been executed on the guillotine. However, dancers, as always, were adaptable. Before long, the Paris Opéra figured in the forefront of a number of fetes of the Republic; there were patriotic spectacles in which the performers were supported by large choirs singing patriotic hymns and cantatas. In one such fete, the Marseillaise was danced as a great public spectacle. In another, during the second year of the Revolution, a festival titled "Festival of the Supreme Being" dealt with revolutionary themes; it was designed by David, conducted by Robespierre, and presented by decree of the National Convention.

While the Revolution caused a temporary cessation to some forms of dance, it did not quench the French passion for this activity as a social art. According to Vuillier, scarcely was the ruthless execution of great numbers of Parisians (known as the Terror) at an end, than twenty-three theaters and eighteen

Mercier, a writer of the period, describes the scene:

> ... dancing is universal; they dance at the Carmelites, between the massacres; they dance at the Jesuits' Seminary; at the Convent of Carmelites du Marais; at the seminary of Saint-Sulpice; at the Filles de Sainte-Marie; they dance in three ruined churches of my section, and upon the stones of all the tombs which have not been destroyed. They dance in every tavern on the Boulevards, in the Champs Elysées, and along the quays. They dance at Ruggieri's, Lucquet's, Mauduit's, Wenzel's, and Montausier's. There are balls for all classes. Dancing, perhaps, is a means for forgetfulness ....[17]

And Parisians had much to forget. Strangely, one festivity was instituted—a so-called *Victim Ball*—to which were admitted only relatives of those who had died on the scaffold as part of the persecution during the Revolution. Mercier asks:

> Will posterity believe that people, whose relatives had died on the scaffold, inaugurated, not days of solemn general grief when assembled in mourning garb, that they might bear witness to their sorrow at the cruel losses so recently incurred, but days of dancing, drinking, and feasting? For admission to one of these banquets and dances, it is necessary to show a certificate of the loss of a father, a mother, a husband, a wife, a brother or a sister under the knife of the guillotine.[18]

When the Revolution came to an end, ballet, which had been suspended except for the sort of patriotic spectacles mentioned earlier, resumed. Now, however, under the Republic, its themes were quite different. There were now ballets dealing with the *sans-culottes* of the Revolution. Other works commemorated the American Revolution, and some ballets were choreographed which criticized religion and the Catholic Church—reflecting the viewpoint of the new government. All this represented not only an accommodation to the existing powers, but also the first breaths of a new idea—political and social democracy. It was linked with a concern with contemporaneous thought, and with the first stirrings of another sort of revolution—the Romantic Revolution.

With poetry, music, painting, and literature, the ballet was to be a vital part of this new artistic movement. Under it, ballet was to reach a new height of popularity and creative development.

[17] Henry Fourment, *Paris During the Revolution*, quoted in Vuillier, *op. cit.*, p. 197.
[18] Vuillier, *op. cit.*, p. 196.

6

THE GOLDEN AGE
OF BALLET

In the decades immediately following the French Revolution, ballet continued to change radically, in terms of its aesthetic content and format, technical style, and vocabulary. Instrumental in this development were three leading figures: Salvatore Vigano, Carlo Blasis, and Théophile Gautier.

Vigano, who lived from 1769 to 1821, had been a disciple of Noverre, and of the famed ballet master, Dauberval. He attempted to carry out Noverre's theories of unity of form and dramatic expression, and contributed much to the development of pantomime to replace the conventionalized gestures that were widely used in ballet to develop the plot. He attempted to develop what he called the *choreodrame;* this made use of groups of dancers who were treated in a plastic, almost sculptural way. He composed many of the leading ballets of his era, as ballet master at La Scala, and at other leading opera houses in Vienna, Venice, and other European cities.

Blasis (1787–1878) was, without question, one of the towering figures of ballet history. Blasis was an Italian dancer, choreographer, and teacher, who had been strongly influenced by both Noverre and Vigano. He had danced and composed in both France and England, and returned to La Scala in Milan as the outstanding ballet master of his time. He developed a comprehensive system for practicing and teaching the art of ballet; indeed his method of education is still widely influential today. He developed major theories involving the laws of equilibrium and balance, and geometric schemes governing the body's movement in ballet exercises. In 1830, he published his famous *Code of Terpsichore*, which contained a fundamental system of ballet instruction, a model that every ballet school has since used. In the Imperial Academy of Dancing and Pantomime in Milan, of which Blasis became director in 1837, the following practices were instituted: pupils were not admitted before the age of eight, or after the age of twelve (fourteen in the case of boys). They had to be medically sound, and of "good stock." Their training was fully mapped out: three hours of practice a day and one hour of mime. They were attached to the school for eight years and after that their careers as performers were assured by an ascending scale of salaries.[1] Blasis was a gifted student of sculpture and anatomy and so clear a writer that in his book he was able to make thoroughly understandable the mechanical basis of ballet technique. In addition to the bar work and other exercises that he developed, Blasis required his students to study character dancing, pantomime, and *adagio*. His writings provide a comprehensive picture of dance in his day, including many folk and national dances, descriptions of different techniques, and an analysis of dance as related to music, painting, and sculpture.

Without question, Blasis was the key figure in the development of the *danse d'école* during the early 19th century. It remained for Théophile Gautier to provide the inspiration that helped to plunge ballet into the thick of the Romantic movement in Europe.

Gautier was a poet, journalist, and dramatic critic of the Romantic era in France, with a great passion for the ballet. He took an active part in the development of this art during its so-called Golden Age. He did much to sponsor the careers of Fanny Elssler, Marie Taglioni, and Carlotta Grisi, who performed in *Giselle* (for which he wrote the libretto). As an extremely influential critic, Gautier helped to shape public taste and enthusiasm and influenced the entire course of ballet in the Romantic age.

Exactly what was Romanticism? Essentially, it was a revolutionary movement in art, which overthrew the rigid forms that had been established by the academic schools which had dominated artistic activity in the 18th century. In its origins, Romanticism was a literary movement; every art form became affected by literary sources, particularly by the poems and plays of Victor

---

[1] Arnold Haskell, *Ballet* (Middlesex, England: Penguin Books, 1951), p. 26.

Hugo. The Romantic poets and artists and composers were concerned with the occult and the supernatural; they depicted man's pursuit of the unattainable, exemplified in the hopeless love of a mortal for an unworldly being. Ivor Guest writes:

> ... [the 18th century] had been the Age of Reason, when artists tended to look outward and to concentrate on achieving a classical perfection in their works, often at the expense of feeling and meaning. The clarion call of the Romantics was liberation ... from bonds of classical restraint ... in an outburst of revolt, a new generation of artists, most of whom had grown up through the instability of war and revolution ... turned inwards on themselves; they sought more personal means of expression and let their imagination and their inspiration soar freely into the headiest heights of lyricism .... [2]

During the twenty years that followed the end of the Napoleonic era in 1815, Romanticism conquered all the arts in France, and spread throughout Europe. Earlier conventions were disregarded and new works were produced with meaning and emotional content that appealed to a fresh new audience. In a sense, Romanticism represented an attempt to escape the realities of life as it was. People had suffered badly during the wars of the previous decade, and the developing Industrial Revolution, with its mines and factories, was now bringing new suffering and wretchedness to millions of underprivileged throughout Europe. Thus, the Romantic movement, which offered color, fantasy, fairy tales, and folk legends—romantic love and beautiful dreams— offered a protest against the sordid quality of real life.

In ballet, this contrast between the bitter reality of life and the yearning for fantastic possibilities meant that a new kind of subject matter was to be used. Supernatural creatures fell in love with mortal men; dead maidens rose from the grave to haunt unfaithful lovers; there were moral victories of aerial and spiritual creatures over earthy and sensual beings.[3] Perhaps most typical of all ballets of this era was *La Sylphide*, choreographed by Philippe Taglioni for his daughter, Marie, one of the great ballerinas of this era. *Sylphide* depicted a woodland creature of supernatural origin, who fell in love with a Scotsman; the ballet is the tale of their tragic romance. For this work, a new costume was devised for the ballerina—full but filmy white skirts that reached halfway down to the ankles. Ballets of this type, which filled the stage with white-clad dancers, were called *ballet blancs*, or white ballets, because of the shimmering effect they created.

---

[2] Ivor Guest, *The Romantic Ballet in Paris* (Middletown, Connecticut: Wesleyan University Press, 1966), p. 2.

[3] John Martin, *John Martin's Book of the Dance* (New York: Tudor Publishing Co., 1963), p. 34.

As part of the yearning for the unattainable, dance itself became increasingly elevated. More and more, the ballerina defied gravity by soaring through the air and dancing *sur les pointes* (on the tips of her toes). In some ballets, female dancers actually "flew" above the stage by being suspended from wires, so that they could glide along overhead. Such devices were useful not only because of the ethereal roles they played, but as a symbol of the spiritual and exalted role which the Romantic ballet gave to women. Indeed, the ballerina was raised to a new height of glamor and popular favor, while the male dancer's role was reduced to being little more than a support for her brilliant solos. Kirstein writes that during the 1840s, male dancers were in a poor position, as compared to the period when Vestris, Dauberval, and Gardel were dancing. Even as partners, their roles were diminished and, with few exceptions, all solos were given to the ballerina, and the male dancer became little more than a support or a background for her.[4]

The predominant tone of the ballet was female, and the critics themselves ridiculed men who performed as dancers. One writer, Jules Janin, summed up the view of his fellows:

> You know perhaps, that we are hardly a supporter of what are called the grand danseurs. The grand danseur appears to us so sad and so heavy!... He responds to nothing, he represents nothing, he is nothing. Speak to us of a pretty dancing girl who displays the grace of her features and the elegance of her figure.... Thank God, I understand that perfectly.... But a man, a frightful man, as ugly as you and I, a wretched fellow who leaps about without knowing why, a creature specially made to carry a musket and a sword and to wear a uniform. That this fellow should dance as a woman does— impossible![5]

Even more cruel in his attacks was Gautier, who despised the male dancer almost as much as he worshipped the ballerina. According to Gautier, a ballet without men is the height of good taste, "for nothing is more abominable than a man who displays his red neck, his great muscular arms, his legs with calves like church beadles', his whole heavily masculine frame, shaken with leaps and pirouettes...."[6] The criticism was often inconsistent. On the one hand, Gautier criticized men for their masculine clumsiness; however, when they were too graceful, he attacked them also: "The dancers at the Opéra are of a nature to encourage

---

[4] Lincoln Kirstein, *Dance: A Short History of Classic Theatrical Dancing* (New York: G. P. Putnam's Sons, 1935), p. 253.

[5] Jules Janin, quoted in Guest, *op. cit.*, p. 21.

[6] Théophile Gautier, quoted in Deidre Priddin, *The Art of the Dance in French Literature* (London: A. & C. Black, Ltd., 1952), p. 41.

Pas de Quatre, danced in 1845 in London by Marie Taglioni, Carlotta Grisi, Fanny Cerrito, and Lucile Grahn. Color lithograph by John Brandard, in Cia. Fornaroli Collection.

the opinion which will only allow women in ballet [for they affect] that false grace, those ambiguous and revolting mincing manners which have sickened the public of male dancing. . . ."[7]

And finally:

> For us a male dancer is something monstrous and indecent which we cannot conceive . . . . Strength is the only grace permissible to men.[8]

By the middle of the 1840s so strong was the feeling against male dancers that they were kept out of the corps de ballet whenever a justification could be found. The device of the *danseuse*

[7] *Ibid.,* p. 41.
[8] *Ibid.*

en travesti (female dancers in male costumes) was then discovered, and women began to play the roles of hussars, sailors, and other customarily male parts. Although many talented male dancers continued to appear in Paris, the standard of their performance gradually lowered, and fewer and fewer young boys entered the Paris Opéra's School of Dance; it was a career that had less appeal for them.

The great stars of the period were five ballerinas, who flourished during the Golden Age of ballet, the 1830s and 1840s, when ballet was at its creative heights in terms of artistic inspiration and an expanding body of technique and brilliant choreography. These stars were Marie Taglioni, Fanny Elssler, Carlotta Grisi, Fanny Cerrito, and Lucile Grahn.

Marie Taglioni (1804–1884) was considered by many the greatest dancer of the century. She danced in Vienna, Italy, Germany, and France, and later in her life became a star of the St. Petersburg Imperial Theater. Her outstanding work was *La Sylphide*, which was a sensation throughout Europe and was considered to be the first great Romantic ballet. Taglioni was the first ballerina to develop the art of toe dancing; she was extremely light, almost floating, and had great elevation. She represented the mystical side of Romanticism; her technique was superb, but it was fragile and exquisite. Like other great dancers in history, she modified the traditional costume to suit her own style, wearing a light gauze skirt that became adopted by other dancers.

Taglioni's greatest rival was Fanny Elssler, who lived between 1810 and 1884. She was a Viennese dancer who symbolized the earthy side of Romanticism and was viewed as a "pagan" dancer; the stage image she conveyed was far more passionate than spiritual. She was an excellent technician, who danced with her entire body, and had great acting ability. Her movement was closer to the earth than Taglioni's, but had great style and precision. She perfected "character" dances of other lands—such as Hungary, Poland, and Spain. When she toured America in 1840 she was a tremendous sensation.

Fanny Cerrito (1821–1899) was a famous Italian ballerina and choreographer of the Romantic period, who danced in Naples, Vienna, London, and Paris. She was a spirited and beautiful dancer, with great technical skill, whose popularity was close to that of Taglioni and Elssler. Lucile Grahn (1821–1907) was a famous Danish ballerina who studied first in Copenhagen and then performed in Paris at the Opéra in *La Sylphide*, competing with Taglioni. She was considered the greatest classic technician of her time, and was noted for a quality of dreamy grace and abandon. Her teacher and choreographer was the renowned August Bournonville; his versions of *Giselle* and *La Sylphide* were among her great roles. Carlotta Grisi (1821–1899) was an eminent Italian ballerina of the Romantic period, who created the role of *Giselle* and was a protégé of Théophile Gautier. Her husband was Jules Perrot, the French dancer and choreographer. In addition to many starring roles in Paris, Grisi was a favorite in St. Petersburg and London, where she performed in Perrot's *Pas de Quatre*, with Taglioni, Grahn, and Cerrito.

Gradually the creative inspiration that had enabled ballet to reach its height in the 1830s and 1840s declined. Innovations were perpetuated as custom, and the great variety of new technical achievements that had been developed served chiefly as a means of displaying acrobatic brilliance. There were no great male dancers, and so one possible source of inspiration or stimulus was lost. With the decline of the great ballerinas of the period, interest in ballet itself declined in Italy, France, and England. The form itself had become set, and was monotonously repeated.

The typical ballet of the middle and later 19th century was a romance of ancient days or a fairy tale. It usually lasted for the entire evening, with three or four acts and intermissions that often lasted as long as forty-five minutes each, to permit the audience to stroll in the foyer. The plot was told through sign language of the hands, which often was not intelligible to the

Ballroom dancing in mid-19th-century Paris. Lithograph of the Bal Mabille by A. Provost, about 1850.

audience; dance numbers interrupted the ballet from time to time, with little relation to the drama itself. The sequence of performance was usually the same, with the high point of the evening being a grand *pas de deux* by the ballerina and her partner. Uninspired music was turned out in a cut-and-dried fashion by staff composers and artists; the whole point of the performance was to demonstrate the technical skill and beauty of the ballerina.[9]

Small wonder that public tastes declined, and that audiences became apathetic. Haskell comments that "two hundred years after the founding of the Academy, ballet in the country of its birth was artistically bankrupt ... merely a prelude to flirtation. ..."[10] In England, where there was no royal ballet or other state institution to support the art, matters grew even worse. Ballet became a popular routine on music hall programs, with poor music, decor, and choreography. In Paris, it hung on as part of operatic performance, although, according to Shawn,

> ... the "Golden Age" of the ballet was a period when the dancers were the supreme stars of the stage, and a bored public walked out into the foyer while the singing of the opera was proceeding .... At the beginning of this present century, the ballet was at a very low ebb indeed. Sterile, artificial, distinguished neither by greatness of execution nor of idea, written down to by the opera composers, it was now during the ballet that the audience preferred to walk about in the foyer, rather than watch the mechanical, lifeless performances ....[11]

Only in one country did ballet retain its popularity and prestige; this was in Czarist Russia. Here it remained firmly entrenched as a cherished ornament of the aristocratic regime, with a widespread audience that remained unquestioningly loyal to it.

Ballet in Russia had a long and respected tradition. As early as the time of Louis XIV in France, traveling "Muscovites" had visited his court to observe the court ballets. At the time of Peter the Great (1672–1725) it became government policy to westernize Russia, which had been sealed off from the rest of Europe for centuries. Peter the Great resolved to break down social customs which had kept his nation behind the times. Thus, he decreed that the boyars (wealthy landowners) must shave their beards and give up their "dignified and cumbersome robes," and that women might join men in social dances and assemblies which

---

[9] Martin, *op. cit.*, pp. 38–39.
[10] Haskell, *op. cit.*, p. 30.
[11] Ted Shawn, *Dance We Must* (London: Dennis Dobson, Ltd., 1946), pp. 21–22.

had heretofore been unknown. As in France and Italy, an interest in ballet as a stage art soon followed this introduction of social dance in the court. Almost from the beginning, however, it became a professional art, with the importation of distinguished foreign teachers and choreographers, and the training of skilled, paid performers. Haskell writes:

> The Empress Anne (1693–1740) founded the Academy, which survives today under a different regime, importing a Frenchman, Lande, to direct it, and thinking it of sufficient importance to include dancing in the curriculum of the cadets . . . . The most intense development took place with Catherine the Great (1762–1796) who imported a Frenchman, Le Picq, and the great Italian, Angiolini, to her court . . . enthusiasm and knowledge [of ballet] spread . . . .[12]

Particularly in Russia, where there were vast estates, courtiers had to provide their own amusements and cultural activities. Thus, when Catherine the Great favored ballet, the nobility followed suit, forming ballet troupes of their own, and spreading a great interest in ballet throughout the land. Gradually, these separate companies became merged in the two great ballet organizations in St. Petersburg and Moscow, with the dancers who joined these companies being given their freedom long before the serfs at large. In each center, excellent academies of ballet were begun, with standards as strict as those stipulated by Blasis for Milan. Haskell comments that ballet became the most cherished possession of the Russian Czars, with huge sums being expended to support its performance, and to import foreign dancers, choreographers, and teachers.

Charles Louis Didelot (1767–1837), an outstanding French dancer, choreographer, and teacher, was one of the greatest of these. Though born in Stockholm, he had an extensive career at the Paris Opéra and in London, where he choreographed a number of major works. He was brought to St. Petersburg by Czar Paul as ballet master of the Imperial Theater, and continued at this post into the regime of Alexander I. From 1801 to 1811, and then again after 1816, he remained in St. Petersburg, where he choreographed over fifty ballets. Most of these were in the Romantic tradition, and were characterized by interesting plots and expressive pantomime. Didelot was an excellent teacher, and during his reign the ballet school in St. Petersburg developed many outstanding dancers.

Other foreign performers who influenced the Russian ballet during the 19th century included Marie Taglioni, Jules Perrot,

[12] Haskell, *op. cit.*, p. 32.

Christian Johannsen, Charles Saint-Léon, Enrico Cecchetti, and Marius Petipa.

Following the debut of Fanny Elssler at the Paris Opéra, Taglioni left France, to accept a profitable three-year contract at the St. Petersburg Imperial Theater, from 1837 to 1839. While there, she performed in many of the great ballets then being done in Western Europe, and so introduced them to Russian audiences.

Jules Perrot (1810–1892), a leading French dancer and choreographer who had had an outstanding career dancing with the great Romantic ballerinas at the Paris Opéra, went to St. Petersburg in 1848. He was a leading dancer and choreographer there until 1859, producing nearly twenty ballets in that time— many of these based on realistic themes, with strong dramatic plots.

Christian Johannsen (1817–1903), a Swedish dancer and teacher who had studied under Bournonville in Copenhagen, went to Russia to perform in the St. Petersburg ballet in 1841. He became the leading male dancer there, remaining a *premier danseur* until 1869, when he devoted himself exclusively to teaching at the ballet school. In the decades that followed, he taught all of the great Russian dancers who developed in this period.

Charles Saint-Léon, who lived from about 1815 to 1870, was another leading French choreographer, dancer, and musician, who became ballet master of the Imperial Ballet in St. Petersburg in 1859. While there, he produced a number of original works, including the first ballet on Russian themes. He left Russia in 1867, returning to a post as ballet master at the Paris Opéra.

Enrico Cecchetti, an Italian dancer and ballet master, who lived from 1850 to 1928, starred at La Scala in Milan, in London, and was with the first major Italian ballet company to tour the United States. He came to Russia in 1887, where he made his debut at the Maryinsky Theater in St. Petersburg and shortly became the second ballet master at the Imperial Theater and instructor at the Imperial school. With interruptions for other assignments in Italy and Poland, he remained in Russia until 1909. He taught many of the great stars of the Russian ballet and became the private instructor of Anna Pavlova. As official instructor for the Diaghilev company he taught such outstanding performers of the 20th century as Leonid Massine, Adolph Bolm, Ninette de Valois, Alicia Danilova, Anton Dolin, Serge Lifar, and others.

Through the contributions of all these foreigners, the lavishly supported and prestigious Russian ballet gradually gained world eminence, blending the distinctive styles of the French and Russian dancers into a system of balanced training and performance.

In each of the other countries, there were strengths and weaknesses; but the Russians incorporated their strengths into what was to become a vigorous and extended technique of solid substance. In a history of the Russian ballet, one of its leading dancers, Nicholas Legat, wrote:

> The secret of the development of Russian dancing lay in the fact that we learned from everybody and adapted what we learnt to ourselves. We copied, borrowed from, and emulated every source that gave us inspiration, and then, working on our acquired knowledge and lending it the stamp of the Russian national genius, we moulded it into the eclectic art of the Russian ballet . . . .[13]

Without question, the most influential of all the foreign artists who came to Russia was Marius Petipa.

Petipa (1822–1910) was best known as a choreographer of the Imperial Ballet in St. Petersburg, and has often been referred to as the "father of the classic ballet." He studied in France and made his debut at the Paris Opéra opposite Fanny Elssler in 1841. He was regarded as an excellent dancer, with particular strength in the art of partnering. However, it is chiefly for his choreography and direction of the St. Petersburg ballet that he is known. Joining the Imperial Ballet in 1847, he remained active for over 50 years, during which time he became the dominant force in Russian ballet. He choreographed over sixty full-length ballets (which usually had four or five acts and lasted for the entire evening) and many shorter ballets and divertissements. Among his best known works were *Don Quixote*, *La Bayadère*, *The Sleeping Beauty*, and *Bluebeard*. He also restaged many great ballets which had originally been performed elsewhere, including *Giselle*, *Coppelia*, parts of *Swan Lake*, and *La Sylphide*.

In addition to his gift for choreography, Petipa was noted for his detailed research and planning for each ballet he produced or composed. He worked intensively with the composers and set designers who were attached to the Imperial Theater, but placed choreography high above all the other arts which contributed to the ballet. Thus, even in working with a composer of Tchaikovsky's stature, Petipa rigidly dictated the kind of music he wanted—the style, mood, length, beat, tempo, and dynamics. He developed a format for his full-length ballets which he applied consistently through the years: these patterns always involved three repeats of the same technical action and a fourth variant of it

---

[13] Nicholas Legat, quoted in Anatole Chujoy, *The Dance Encyclopedia* (New York: A. S. Barnes & Co., Inc., 1949), p. 411.

to complete the sequence. He established a routine pattern for the *pas de deux:* a duo, then the woman's solo, the man's solo, and a brilliant and fast duo to complete the sequence. Through the second half of the 19th century, his dominance was unquestioned in Russia, and indeed throughout Europe, for many of the leading dancers throughout the Continent came to study and dance with him. It was during his reign that the classic style and structure of the ballet became firmly fixed, and many of his works are still performed today as part of the repertoire of Russian ballet companies.

During this period, too, a class of spectators emerged who came to be known as "balletomanes." These were the enthusiastic and knowledgeable audiences that packed the Bolshoi and Maryinsky Imperial Theaters in St. Petersburg and other ballet houses in Moscow and throughout Russia. Ballet was cherished by the powerful and wealthy, as well as by intellectuals, students, young officers, and all classes that could afford to attend. Chujoy points out that most ballet performances in the Russian Imperial Theaters were given on subscription. With the exception of those seats reserved for the royal family and high public officials, all other seats in the orchestra and boxes and loges, as well as some in the balcony, were sold by subscription. These were highly valued and would often remain in the same family for generations; occasionally one would be sold at a very high price. Thus, the dominant audience for the ballet constituted "an exclusive circle" that knew the mechanics and tradition of ballet thoroughly, and was essentially a highly conservative audience that refused to accept change. There was a second kind of audience—the balletomanes who sat in the upper tiers of balconies and galleries who were mostly students, young officers, civil service officials, and clerks. They were dedicated to the ballet (to obtain tickets they usually had to stand in line through most of the preceding night, often in the frigid cold of the Russian winter) and were less conservative in their views.

Through the 1880s and 1890s, ballet in Russia became increasingly stodgy and stereotyped—following the same format that had been in effect for the previous three decades. The technique of the classroom was usually transferred directly to the stage, and thus contributed little to the dramatic action. Pantomimic sign language, that often was incomprehensible to the dancers as well as to the audience, was still used. The *corps de ballet* was usually used for purely decorative interludes that had no relation to the theme of the ballet itself. Costumes, music, and decor were all composed in a cut-and-dried way that contributed to the sterility of the performance and had little vitality or originality.

Finally, reform was not welcomed or even possible under Petipa. Thus it was that when two great Russians of the early 20th century, Diaghileff and Fokine, broke through the hidebound traditions of the past, it was not in St. Petersburg or Moscow, but in Paris.

7

DANCE IN AMERICA

Meanwhile, what was the development of dance on the North American continent? Certainly what happened in the American colonies, prior to the American Revolution and afterwards when it became an independent nation, could not be considered out of the context of what one historian has called the "Atlantic Civilization." Those who settled in New England, in the Mid-Atlantic colonies, and in the coastal region of the South were all Europeans—and they brought with them many of the attitudes and customs of their homelands. There was a steady flow of traffic back and forth, of colonists, journalists, performers, and publications. Clearly, a stone cast at the French court, or in London, spread ripples abroad.

Yet, there were certain distinct features in the New World that made life here very different—and particularly so for those concerned with the dance as art or recreation. One factor was the distance and danger of the ocean journey; this tended to reduce communication, and prevented vogues in the arts from being seized upon as rapidly in the American colonies as they were throughout Europe. Another factor was the difficulty of living on the North American continent—the fact that the first need of all was to survive. One had to plant crops, to cut down forests and clear fields, to build shelters, to protect oneself against the winter, against hunger, disease, and the unpredictable Indians who surrounded the colonies. In such a situation, it was difficult to justify amusements and public entertainment. This was a democratic society; there was no royalty that would view dance, theater, or other arts as a means of amusing itself or enhancing its own prestige, and that would therefore subsidize and protect performing companies.

Then there was the matter of religious attitude.

During the 17th century, there was a widespread condemnation of idleness and casual amusement. Dulles points out that in Puritan New England, where the stern rule of Calvinism prohibited any sort of play, the tradition was that life should be wholly devoted to work. There was no place for an "idle drone" in such a society.[1]

The Puritans had come to the New World in order to set up a society based on a Calvinistic interpretation of the Bible. They believed that they were a chosen people; the early government of Massachusetts, for example, was a theocracy, run by Puritan ministers, who thought that the Bible was the disclosed word of God, and that its meaning and intention on every subject had been made plain and explicit to them. Not all colonists in New England were Puritans, of course, but they were the dominant group and those who resisted them were often punished or banished. Typically, Massachusetts and Connecticut banned dice, cards, quoits, bowls, ninepins, "or any other unlawful game in house, yard, garden or backside. . . ." The theater was completely prohibited in a number of colonies; Connecticut adjudged as common rogues and served fifteen lashes on the bare back of anyone foolish enough to "set up and practice common plays, interludes, or other crafty science."

Just as there were ordinances against gambling, drama, and certain forms of music, so there were laws against dancing. In particular, the early Puritans forbade mixed dancing (between men and women), dancing in taverns, Maypole dancing (which they saw as an expression of paganism), or dancing accompanied by feasting and drinking.

Typically, a group of Puritan ministers in Boston issued a tract against dancing in 1684, titled *An Arrow Against Profane and Promiscuous Dancing, drawn out of the quiver of the Scriptures*. Yet, even as they condemned "mixt or promiscuous dancing," they indicated that dance could be a means of teaching "due poyse and Composure of Body," and that if a parent wished to have his children

---

[1] Foster Rhea Dulles, *A History of Recreation* (New York: Appleton-Century-Crofts, 1965), p. 5.

learn it, he should send them "to a grave person who will teach them decency of behaviour, and each sex by themselves."[2]

The same distinctions that had been made by the Church Fathers during the Dark and Middle Ages in Europe were again made in 18th-century America. The Reverend John Cotton who was to come to New England in 1633 and become the leading minister of Boston and New England, said while still in England in 1625:

> Dancing (yea though mixt) I would not simply condem. For I see two sorts of mixt dancings in use with God's people in the Old Testament, the one religious, Exod. XV, 20, 21, the other civil, tending to the praise of conquerers, as the former of God, I Sam. XVII, 6, 7. Only lascivious dancing, and amorous gestures and wanton dalliances, especially after feasts, I would bear witness against, as a great *flabella libidinis*.[3]

Others were less liberal than Cotton, and the court records during the 17th century, particularly in New England, frequently mention severe punishment for mixed dancing, dancing in taverns, and similar offenses. Yet, in spite of condemnation and punishment, settlers in communities large and small throughout the colonies of the North continued to dance. Beginning in the 1670s, dancing masters began to appear in the New England towns, and people of "quality" began to give balls. Indeed, the ministers themselves had sanctioned dancing schools provided that they were conducted by "grave persons" and did not teach "mixt" dancing. The dances that were most frequently taught were drawn from the newly published English work, John Playford's *Dancing-Master*. While these country dances had both men and women dancing together, they were in sets, or formations, and did not involve "couple dancing" as such. Since they taught good manners, and were desired by the more influential people in the community, they were accepted by ministers.

In other colonies, the attitude was less restrictive than in New England. In New Amsterdam, the Dutch settlers traditionally danced on special holiday occasions; also, dancing was encouraged at public fairs which were instituted to improve agricultural practices.

Further to the South, members of the ruling class in Virginia had much closer ties with England, and were of a higher social class in general, than the Puritans who had settled New England. They had both wealth and leisure because of the nature of the

---

[2] Joseph E. Marks, *America Learns to Dance* (New York: Exposition Press, 1957), pp. 20–21.

[3] John Cotton, quoted in Marks, *op. cit.*, p. 15.

land they settled and the large plantations which were worked by indentured servants and slaves. Thus, they were more inclined toward aristocratic forms of amusement, and able to indulge their inclinations. While the laws of the colony, applied by Governor Argall in 1618, "strictly banned any Sabbath-day dancing, fiddling, card-playing, hunting or fishing," these laws gradually fell into abeyance. In any case, dancing was permitted on other occasions and even justified, as an important aspect of education.

> Dance served an even more important role than that of social amusement. It was believed to be one of the accomplishments proper for a gentleman, and not having a knowledge of dance showed a lack of the proper education. Writers on aristocratic education expected a gentleman to dance well, but not to become so proficient that he rival the dancing master.[4]

For gentlemen, both dancing and fencing were seen as "ornaments to grace and accomplishment," and for young ladies, it was thought that "to lead a dance gracefully" was a commendable quality. Thus, by the end of the 1600s, Virginia was well supplied with dancing masters, as part of the life of her plantation owners which was closely modeled after that of country squires in the mother country.

During the 18th century, an increasing number of teachers of dancing were found in colonies of both North and South. Marks cites many examples of such masters advertising to the public: In 1712, George Brownell offered the young ladies of Boston, "Writing, cyphering, dancing, treble violin, flute, spinet, etc." Samuel Perpoint advertised in the Pennsylvania Mercury in 1728 and later in 1729 that he gave instruction in dancing and small sword. In Williamsburg, Virginia, Mrs. Neil stated that she was opening a boarding school of young ladies on the English plan, and that "The best Masters will attend to teaching Dancing and writing."

> Dancing masters, like preachers, doctors, lawyers, peddlers and many other trades and professions during the eighteenth and early nineteenth centuries, traveled from town to town, often advertising ahead that they planned to open a dancing school "if there be sufficient inducement."[5]

Probably the most famous traveling dancing master was Brownell, who taught in such widely scattered places as Boston, New York, Philadelphia, and Charleston, South Carolina, over

[4] Marks, op. cit., pp. 25–26.
[5] Ibid., p. 40.

a period of years ranging from 1712 to 1744. There continued to be a certain amount of resistance to dancing; one opponent of a school for dancing, fencing, and the violin in Providence, Rhode Island, wrote in 1763 that he would as soon have set up "a public stew or Brothel." But in general, social dancing had become widely accepted both as a form of recreation and as a means of education. Particularly for children of Southern planters, it was regarded as essential.

Typically, Thomas Jefferson, in making up a schedule for his daughter, to guide her in the use of her time, urged that she dance from ten to one, every other day.

Dance was seen as contributing to the ends of education. A book on education in Philadelphia in 1792 makes clear that ornamental accomplishments were not an end in themselves:

> . . . though the well-bred woman should learn to dance, sing, recite, and draw; the end of a good education is not that they may become singers, dancers, players, or painters; its real object is, to make them good daughters, good wives, good mistresses, good members of society and good christians.[6]

Toward the end of the century, an increasing number of balls and assemblies were held, particularly in the larger cities. It is probable that the colonists performed both the country dances, jigs, and cotillions which became popular during this period, and also such dances as the Minuet, Courante, Galliard, Rigadoon, and Gavotte, all of which were found in Rameau's text, *The Dancing Master*, which was found in libraries throughout the colonies. Certainly when, in 1762, sixty-nine couples attended a lavish ball given by Sir Jeffrey Amherst, which was described as the "most elegant ever seen in America," the dances done were similar to those found in the English court. Especially in the Southern colonies, dance now became part of a varied and colorful social life.

Both George Washington and Thomas Jefferson were known as zealous and enthusiastic dancers, who frequently attended concerts and the theater. Washington Irving, in his *Life of George Washington*, told how the "young ladies of Maryland rode to the assembly at Annapolis in scarlet riding-habits thrown over their satin ball dresses, kerchiefs drawn about the great masses of their puffed and pomaded hair, and after dancing through the night rode home again in the shadowy dawn."[7] The young John Quincy Adams, in Newburyport, describes going to a dancing hall with

[6] *Ibid.*, p. 47.
[7] Dulles, *op. cit.*, p. 57.

his friends during the 1780s, and dancing continually from seven at night to three or four in the morning.

Clearly, dance as recreation had taken hold in the colonies, by the time of the American Revolution. But meanwhile, what of dance as theater? Here there was less to report.

From the beginning, stage performers—whether they were actors, singers, dancers, or acrobats—were viewed with suspicion in the early colonies, especially in the North. Gradually, however, as the early bans against theater were relaxed and a leisure class began to develop, who had money to spend on commercial forms of entertainment, professional performances began to be offered. At first, these were given by amateur or semiprofessional groups, or dancing masters themselves, who seized on the opportunity to earn additional income, as well as to enhance their reputation by dancing before an audience. In time, the first truly professional troupes appeared on American stages; they came from Europe.

The first of these was an English company, headed by Lewis Hallam, which toured the colonies during the mid-1700s, to perform Harlequinades, spectacles, and incidental dances. Shortly thereafter, in 1767, the John Street Theater opened in New York and became the center of week-long performances of drama, pantomime, opera, and "ballet-spectacles" by various visiting companies. These were imported intermittently from Europe and probably visited other cities, performing wherever they could find a hall and a sponsor. The first native American performer of any reputation was John Durang, who had been born in Pennsylvania in 1768, and who made his debut in Philadelphia in 1785, with the Hallam company, which returned to the Continent after the American Revolution. There had been a cessation of theatrical activity during the American Revolution, due first to a prohibition of theater by the first Continental Congress in 1774, and then to an antitheater law passed by Congress in 1787. However, this law was repealed, and now an increasing number of foreign troupes visited the new United States.

In 1792, Alexandre Placide, his wife, and a well-trained company presented operettas, and ballets. Patriotric spectacles had briefly come into vogue during the Revolution, and Placide's company presented a number of these during the 1790s. Performances were diverse, including such unusual elements as "specialty dancers, acrobats, tightrope walkers" and similar features.

Perhaps the best example of this was John Durang, who gained in reputation during the 1790s and in fact established himself as the head of a famous dancing and theatrical dynasty—the first in the new land. While Durang was known chiefly as a dancer, he was also an "actor, singer, tightrope performer, acrobat, designer and scene painter, puppeteer, circus clown, and author." When he performed individually, he often did specialty numbers like an *Alamande*, or the *Hornpipe* for which he was most noted. Also, he performed in a group number known as *The Touchstone*, or *Harlequin Traveler*, which was an Italian-English pantomime, with such stock characters as *Harlequin*, *Scaramouche*, *Columbine*, *Pierrot*, and others. Later, he came into contact with well-trained European dancers such as Placide, and M. Francisquy, both of whom performed throughout the country. Typically, the Placides performed not only ballet, but acrobatics, tumbling, and dancing on the tightrope.

The first ballet to be regarded as a serious work in the United States was a performance of *La Forêt Noire*, in the New Chestnut Theater in Philadelphia, in 1794. This featured a well-known French dancer, Madame Gardie; Durang danced in the leading male role as her partner, and also performed in a variety of specialty numbers and character dances, including his famous *Hornpipe*.

By the turn of the century, an increasing number of European companies had visited the United States, and American audiences had become more knowledgeable and demanding, in terms of the dance art. However, there was no real center of theatrical art in the country, such as existed in European opera houses, where ballet had become firmly established. Nor was there any academy for the teaching of dance. The few Americans who established a reputation in this field usually received their training in a fragmentary way, from the European stars who came here to perform.

Increasingly in the early decades of the 19th century, theaters were built throughout the East. The leading centers of drama and dance were New York and Philadelphia; by 1830 there were three theaters in the latter city. In Richmond, Virginia, in 1819, a new theater, the Richmond, was built. It was an impressive structure with a dome that was 120 feet in circumference, that was "said to exceed in beauty the elegant dome of the National Theater in New York." Similarly, in other major cities, theaters were constructed and filled, with both dramatic, musical, and dance performances.

The French performers began to dominate ballet in America. One of the first of the foreign visitors who captivated American audiences was the ballerina Francisque Hutin, who showed them the first *pointe* footwork, in multiple pirouettes, that had been seen here. Other French artists, including Charles and Ronzi Vestris, and the Ravels, a family of acrobats and ballet dancers, toured the country during the 1820s. Gradually, terminology like *pas de deux* and *corps de ballet* began to enter the language; Americans were becoming somewhat knowledgeable in this new art.

The greatest European visitor of the century was Fanny Elssler, who arrived in 1840 and toured the country for two years. Somehow adapting herself to inadequate theaters and stages, untutored audiences, and makeshift *corps de ballet* (her partner was James Sylvain, an Irish dancer, whom she had brought with her from Europe), Elssler was the inspiration of almost hysterical acclaim. She was a prodigious success wherever she went:

> Champagne was drunk out of her slippers and red carpets were laid at her feet. Congress adjourned because so many of its members were absent, paying homage to the adorable Fanny. President Van Buren received her at the White House and the government treated her like a visiting dignitary. When she went out driving in her carriage infatuated young gentlemen took the horses from the shafts and harnessed themselves in their places. In the theater, Elssler had only to appear to receive an ovation . . . .[8]

In the time she was here, Elssler had a marked effect upon American tastes. She performed a number of the works which had been popular on European stages; her personal style, earthy, close to the floor, highly expressive and dramatic, received great acclaim.

Others who visited included the Paul Taglionis (he was the brother of Marie Taglioni); Jean Antoine Petipa and his son, the eighteen-year-old Marius, who was to become the dominant figure in Russian ballet; and even Enrico Cecchetti, who, traveling with his family, made his debut in 1857 at the Philadelphia Academy of Music, at the age of seven. While the tours of these outstanding European visitors did not succeed in creating an American dance tradition, they helped the development of a number of leading American ballet performers of surprisingly high quality. These were Mary Ann Lee, Julia Turnbull, Augusta Maywood, and the outstanding American male dancer of the century—George Washington Smith.

Mary Ann Lee was known as the first American to achieve nationwide fame as a performer of the classic ballet. Born in Philadelphia about 1823, she made her debut as a dancer at the Chestnut Street Theater in 1837 as Fatima in *The Maid of Cashmere,*

[8] Olga Maynard, *The American Ballet* (Philadelphia: Macrae Smith Company, 1959), p. 18.

the English version of a French opera. Later, she appeared in everything from Shakespeare to burlesque, and danced in everything from *La Sylphide* and *Giselle* to the *Sailor's Hornpipe*. Both Mary Ann Lee and Augusta Maywood, one of her early rivals, had received training in Philadelphia from the French performer, P. H. Hazard. They danced together and competed for public favor until Maywood left for Europe in 1838, where she was to spend the rest of her career. After performing in such works as *La Bayadère* and *La Sylphide* (most of the ballets performed at this time were copies of European successes), Lee herself went to Europe in 1844. She studied for a year in the ballet school of the Paris Opéra, where she took daily lessons from Jean Coralli, an outstanding teacher and the choreographer of *Giselle*. When Mary Ann Lee returned to the United States, she was not only much improved as a performer, but she brought with her a number of other European works, to introduce for the first time in America. Lee toured the leading cities of the United States with George Washington Smith, finally retiring because of poor health in 1847. She was generally regarded as an excellent performer, although not the equal of such foreign visitors as Elssler or Taglioni.

Julia Turnbull was regarded as Mary Ann Lee's strongest rival during the major period of her career. The two dancers starred in an original ballet, *The Sisters*, in 1839. Turnbull was soloist with the Fanny Elssler company during her tour of the United States, and performed principal roles in such works as *Nathalie*, *La Bayadère*, *Esmerelda*, and *Giselle*, until her retirement from the stage in 1857.

Augusta Maywood, born in 1825, was regarded as America's first great prima ballerina. She was an expatriate who spent the major part of her career in Europe, where she was ranked as being close in ability to the greatest dancers of the Golden Age. After a brilliant early career in New York and Philadelphia, she went to Europe. In 1839 she made her debut at the Paris Opéra. Regarded as an infant prodigy, she received the acclaim of Théophile Gautier. She toured widely, performing in Paris, Vienna, Lisbon, and ultimately, La Scala, in Milan. Forming her own touring company (including star dancers and an entire ensemble, rather than depending on local additions to the performing group) she remained in Europe throughout her performing career, and particularly in Italy, where she was regarded as the leading ballerina of the era.[9]

[9] Marian Hannah Winter, "Augusta Maywood," in *Chronicles of the American Dance*, Paul Magriel, ed. (New York: Henry Holt and Company, 1948), p. 119.

After Durang, who retired from the stage in 1819, the next widely known American male dancer was George Washington Smith. Smith's career encompassed almost two-thirds of the 19th century, since he first danced in public in 1838 and was still a teacher of dancing at the time of his death in 1899. Smith danced in everything from classical ballet works and opera to the circus. He partnered almost every one of the great ballerinas who visited this country, including Elssler, and staged and performed in many of the great romantic ballets, including *Giselle*, *La Fille du Danube*, and *La Jolie Fille de Gand*. He learned much of his classical ballet technique from Sylvain, Elssler's ballet master, and from Jules Perrot, in New York and Boston. It is believed, although not certain, that he also studied in Paris under Coralli, in the mid-1840s. Throughout his career, Smith received equal billing with the American and foreign ballerinas—the greatest of the time— with whom he performed. In Lillian Moore's view, he was America's first native *premier danseur*.

In the latter part of the 19th century, no dancers emerged on the American scene to equal these four. Indeed, ballet itself underwent a decline in the late 1850s. While other foreign performers toured the United States, including the troupe of Dominico Ronzani, who was later to become the leading choreographer at La Scala, ballet never took root here or flourished. America lacked major theaters and houses of opera, state-supported schools, and government patronage. Public taste was willing to support occasional foreign stars and touring groups, but did not value native American performers. Indeed, the major dance phenomenon of the latter part of the 19th century was *The Black Crook*, an elaborate and immensely popular musical play of questionable artistic merit.[10]

The Black Crook was performed for the first time at Niblo's Garden in New York in September, 1866. It was based on a melodrama with a trivial plot, which nonetheless provided the basis for a spectacular and original production, using props and decor from another performance whose theater had burned down. The plot included a remarkable hodge-podge of sorcery, demonism, and wickedness, with such characters as an alchemist, the Devil, fairies, demons, and baronial servants. The great feature of the musical was a "Great Parisienne Ballet Troupe," featuring Marie Bonfanti, star of the Paris Opéra and Covent Garden Theatre in London; the cast included many other leading dancers, with a company of 80 dancers in all. Part of the attraction of *The Black*

[10] George Freedley, "The Black Crook and the White Fawn," in Magriel, *op. cit.*, pp. 65–79.

Crook was its impressive and spectacular stage sets and effects. Another appealing aspect was the ballet success of "the 'witching Pas de Demons,' in which the demons, who wear no clothes to speak of, so gracefully and prettily disported as to draw forth thunders of applause." The show ran continuously for sixteen months to overflow houses, making almost a million dollars. It continued to be performed with added embellishments for forty years in various forms throughout the country, and was followed by many imitations, including one called *The White Fawn*. Throughout its various runs, the ballet remained a highlight of this landmark of the American stage and, while classical ballet was at a low ebb, this continued to keep the dance at a high level of interest in American theaters.

Overall, while occasional ballet performances continued to be offered, the classical dance had little prestige as America approached the turn of the century. In *The Black Crook*, the abbreviated costumes of the dancers had shocked many audiences, and the element of sex in their performance had been widely advertised by the management. Although other popular extravaganzas continued to be performed, with lavish productions and dancing girls on display, the quality of the dancing was of low caliber. Maynard comments that dancers were poorly paid and socially ostracized:

> The American dancing girls of the period had the worst of reputations, expecially as the management believed in advertising them as Parisians, and had them masquerade under Gallic names, with the supposed Gallic reputation for amorousness. They were required not only to dance but often to sing, act, and support comedians, trained animal acts, or starred singers, in variety shows . . . . How the performers endured the fatigue of their profession is a wonder. Many of them worked in factories by day and danced in the *corps de ballet* at night. Most of them were waitresses on the side . . . .[11]

With all this, interest in dance continued to grow, however. One evidence of this was the growth in the number of dancing teachers. In mid-century, there were eight dancing masters in New York City. In 1896, the New York directory listed 63 such teachers, who often combined instruction in the social dances of the time, and in ballet.

During the 19th century, certain other dance forms, in addition to theatrical dance, had enriched the cultural scene. Three of these are worthy of mention here: the continuing popularity of social dancing, the gradual development of a Negro dance art that was to make major contributions to entertainment in

[11] Maynard, *op. cit.*, p. 24.

America, and that strange phenomenon of religious dance carried on by the Shakers in New England.

At the beginning of the 19th century, social dancing had become widely popular and accepted throughout the young United States. In both North and South, religious objections to it had largely diminished, although, as new provocations appeared, resistance from the pulpit continued to be voiced from time to time. Dancing teachers were flourishing in cities and towns, and balls and assemblies were commonplace. A contemporary historian wrote that dancing had become "the principal and favorite amusement in New England; and of this the young people of both sexes are extremely fond."[12]

In the cities, where dancing masters conducted regular classes, and where education in dance had become a mark of aristocratic upbringing, instruction was formal and disciplined.

But on the frontier and in rural areas, where life was rougher, there were few dancing masters and no formal cotillions or rules of etiquette. Girls and women were scarce and often the action was rough and ready. Dulles quotes a description of the time:

> "None of your straddling, mincing, sadying," wrote Davy Crockett, "but a regular sifter, cut-the-buckle, chicken flutter set-to. It is a good wholesome exercise; and when one of our boys puts his arm around his partner, it's a good hug, and no harm in it."[13]

Dancing was carried on at country fairs, logrollings, and quilting parties, and at special holiday celebrations. After dinner and sports or games, the climax of every gathering was a dance. The men and women of the frontier loved to dance, doing Virginia Reels, country jigs, and shakedowns. It was a favorite form of entertainment everywhere, commented on with surprise by traveler after traveler amazed to find such rollicking gaiety in frontier settlements. Sometimes the fun was wild and unruly. Dulles describes what were known as "plank dances":

> "You stand face to face with your partner on a plank and keep on dancing," a countryman explained to one visiting northerner. "Put the plank up on two barrel heads, so it'll kind of spring . . . . They dance as fast as they can and the folks all stand around and holler, 'Keep it up, John!' 'Go it, Nance!' 'Old Virginny never tire!' and such kind of observation, and clop and stamp. . . ."[14]

Gradually, new forms of dancing came into being, and new settings for dance which aroused the condemnation of moralists.

[12] Dulles, *op. cit.*, p. 37.
[13] *Ibid.*, pp. 76–77.
[14] *Ibid.*, p. 162.

In the 1830s the waltz and polka emerged on the European scene, and soon became enthusiastically adopted on the dance floors of the New World. These whirling, giddy dances were shocking because they involved dancing in a facing, closed couple position. Ministers preached vehemently against "the abomination of permitting a man who was neither your lover nor your husband to encircle you with his arms, and slightly press the contour of your waist." Nonetheless the exciting new importations won their way into society:

> The New York Herald raved about "the indecency of the polka as danced at Saratoga and Newport . . . . It even outstrips the most disgraceful exhibitions of the lowest haunts of Paris and London." But the floor would be crowded on a Saturday night . . . .[15]

The upper social class had formal assemblies and cotillions; to match these, public balls, with admissions ranging from twenty-five cents to a dollar, came into being. In New York City, there was Mr. Parker's Ball at Tammany Hall, the Third Ward American Republic Ball at the Minerva Assembly Rooms, and the Native American Ball at the Park Theater. And, Dulles points out, there were counterparts of these in every town and city throughout the country; social dancing was the rage.

For the lower classes, there were less-respectable dance halls, cheap variety shows, concert saloons, and beer gardens—"branches of Satan's den" as those of Puritan conviction named them. In cattle towns and mining camps in the West, there were "hurdy-gurdy houses," where drinking, gambling, prostitution, and dancing might all be found together. In San Francisco, New Orleans, and other cities where living was easy, social dancing on this level became lumped together in the public mind with vice and sin.

Overall, social dancing continued as a favorite recreation. In the latter part of the 19th century, there were huge society balls for those of wealth and prestige in New York, Chicago, San Francisco, and the major society resorts. Dancing was a universal social pastime for those of the middle and upper classes; trade, professional, and fraternal organizations all gave annual balls. It was accepted that businessmen and their wives would attend dancing classes through the year, which would usually terminate in a *German*, or *Assembly*. Dulles cites a typical program of one such event: *The Lancers, Waltz, Polka, Military March, Quadrille, York, Portland Fancy, Caledonia,* and the *Virginia Reel*. Most of these were set or line dances, with the exception of

[15] *Ibid.*, pp. 151–52.

the waltz or polka. On a grander scale, Ward McAllister wrote in 1890 of a great society ball; the ostentation had begun to approach that of the royal courts of the Baroque era in Europe:

> For one ball the host built a special addition to his home providing a magnificent Louis XIV ballroom which would accommodate twelve hundred . . . . At a reception given at the Metropolitan Opera House, twelve hundred guests danced the Sir Roger de Coverly on a floor built over stage and auditorium, and were then served supper at small tables by three hundred liveried servants. It was a world of jewels and satins, of terrapin and canvasbacks, of Chateau Lafite and imported champagne . . . .[16]

To teach the dances, and to act as arbiters of social taste, there were many successful dancing masters. The best known and most successful of these was Allen Dodworth who, since childhood, had been a member of his family's fashionable band and orchestra. Dodworth was an accepted member of society himself, as a founder and first treasurer of the New York Philharmonic Society, and one of its first violinists. He had entrée into the leading ballrooms and private parties of the best society, and operated a fashionable dance academy that catered to the most exclusive and socially ambitious families in New York.

"The dancing school," as Dodworth saw it, "is not a place of amusement. . . ." Instead, it was a place where dance was taught in a rigorous and precise way; Dodworth was the author of a widely respected text on social dancing published in 1885. It contained a detailed system of dancing, with steps, diagrams, and musical phrases all clearly outlined, according to his established method. The precise foot positions, the carriage of the body, and the whole ritual of social behavior were taught inflexibly by Dodworth, who

> . . . battled with the world on the issue of dancing as a medium of education and cultured behavior, including health, morals, and manners. He demanded good teaching and not merely coaching in the transitory fads of the ballroom, and he strongly advocated the setting up of a standard of practice.[17]

By 1900, there were many other influential and successful teachers, and the private dancing academy was well established as one of the channels through which social-climbing families might pry their way into accepted society.

Another and quite different aspect of dance during the 19th

[16] Ward McAllister, *Society as I Have Found It*, quoted in Dulles, *op. cit.*, p. 232.

[17] Rosetta O'Neill, "The Dodworth Family and Ballroom Dancing in New York," in Magriel, *op. cit.*, p. 81.

Christy's Minstrels in *Skedaddle*, the celebrated "walk-round." Lithograph by H. C. Maguire.

century was the emergence of Negro dance and music on the North American continent. When African slaves were brought to America, they brought with them their folklore and religious traditions. Although they were converted to Christianity, many of the dances continued to be performed, now for reasons of custom and social entertainment, and also as a tenaciously lingering memory of magical belief. One name for such belief and practice was *Voodoo*, or *Vodun*. Almost as Italian peasants in the early Middle Ages danced the Tarantella to avert the effects of the bite of the tarantula spider, so the slaves in early 19th-century New Orleans were permitted to dance, as a kind of palliative to their miserable condition.

> The Sunday dances of the slaves in Congo Square, legalized by the Municipal Council of New Orleans, were an attempt of the "city authorities to combat Voodooism." They were supposed to act as a kind of safety valve to keep the slaves contented. The dances also became a remunerative tourist attraction at which voodoo music happened to be played . . . .[18]

[18] Marshall W. Stearns, *The Story of Jazz* (New York: Oxford University Press, Inc., 1956), pp. 44–45.

Public performances of these Negro dances were held in a large empty lot known as Congo Square, off and on from 1817 to 1885. Asbury describes the early days of such performances:

> At a signal from a police official, the slaves were summoned to the center of the square by the prolonged rattling of two huge beef bones upon the head of a cask, out of which had been fashioned a sort of drum or tambourine called the bamboula . . . . The favorite dances of the slaves were the Calinda, a variation of which was also used in the Voodoo ceremonies, and the Dance of the Bamboula, both of which were primarily based on the primitive dances of the African jungle . . . . The entire square was an almost solid mass of black bodies stamping and swaying to the rhythmic beat of the bones on the cask, the frenzied chanting of the women, and the clanging of pieces of metal which dangled from the ankles of the men.[19]

This lingering custom was unusual; in other parts of the South, the Negro had long given up his traditional native dances, and had developed hybrid forms of dance, either for his own amusement or as entertainment for his master. There are many accounts of Negro slaves acting as musicians and dancers on southern plantations during the 18th and 19th centuries. In many areas, an adapted form of the white man's dance was the only kind of dance permitted to him. Winter points out that Negro music making and dancing survived at all is remarkable, when one considers the Slave Laws of 1740, which remained among the basic regulations for Negro slaves for a century and a quarter. These laws were instituted after a slave insurrection in South Carolina in 1739:

> A group of slaves attempted an escape to Florida . . . and were captured in a bloody charge. They had marched "with colors flying and drums beating." The laws of 1740 stringently prohibited any Negro from "beating drums, blowing horns or the like" which might on occasion be used to arouse slaves to insurrectionary activity . . . .[20]

When drums were forbidden, Negro slaves devised substitutes; they used bone clappers like castanets, and other artifacts to provide rhythm: jawbones, blacksmiths' iron rasps—and handclapping and foot beating. The latter, with increasingly intricate heel and toe beats, was based on traditional African step dances.

One of these, the *juba* dance, resembled an elaborately varied jig; it was found wherever Negroes settled in the New World. The names *Juba* and *Jube* were slave names traditionally associated with dancers and musicians. Ultimately, "Juba" was to

---

[19] Herbert Asbury, *The French Quarter* (New York: Alfred A. Knopf, Inc., 1936), p. 243.

[20] Marian Hannah Winter, "Juba and American Minstrelsy," in Magriel, *op. cit.*, pp. 39–40.

become the sobriquet of the most famous of all Negro stage dancers.

Negro dance routines had long been known (either as originals, or as white men in blackface) on the American stage. Winter comments that by 1810, the singing and dancing "Negro Boy" was established with the traditional clown as a dance-hall or circus character. This role was played by impersonators who performed English or Irish jig or clog steps, to the accompaniment of popular songs which had allusions to Negroes in their lyrics. Only rarely did a genuine Negro appear. Indeed, the original "Jim Crow," known as a famous Negro performer in the early 19th century, was a white entertainer, "Daddy" Rice, who made an effort to use fairly authentic source materials in his act.

The first actual Negro to achieve distinction as a performer on the stage was Juba, who was born, probably free, under the name of William Henry Lane, in about 1825. Juba began performing professionally at about the age of 15, having learned much from an older Negro jig and reel dancer, "Uncle" Jim Lowe, who had not himself appeared in the regular theaters of the day. By 1845, Winter writes, it was widely accepted by professional entertainers that Juba was "beyond question the very greatest of all dancers. He was possessed not only of wonderful and unique execution, but also of unsurpassed grace and endurance."[21]

Winter describes his routine as imitating all the well-known dancers of the day and their special steps, and then going through his original specialties, including a comic "walkaround," in which he impersonated a number of different styles and characters. By 1845, Juba's position was so secure that he was able to tour with four white minstrel players and receive top billing as "Master Juba! The Greatest Dancer in the World." In 1848, he went to London, where he drew immense audiences and such praise as ". . . the dancing of Juba exceeded anything ever witnessed in Europe. . . . The style as well as the execution is unlike anything ever witnessed in this country. . . ."[22] Londoners of every class flocked to Vauxhall Gardens to witness his performance, and the critics were lavish in their praise of his tremendously agile and ingenious dancing.

At least partly due to Juba's influence, the traditional role of the "Gay Negro Boy" was adopted in British, French, and German circuses, and blackface clowns appeared in circuses and fairs. Because his material was essentially faithful to Negro dance steps and rhythms, as seen on Southern plantations, many white minstrel-show performers imitated him and other Negro dancers—

[21] *Ibid.*, p. 39.
[22] *Ibid.*, p. 50.

thus keeping a measure of authenticity in minstrel-show dancing. By contrast, minstrel-show music had little relation to its original source.

Although the American Negro continued to be the source of inspiration of music hall performances, Negroes themselves found it increasingly difficult to find employment on the stage. Winter comments that increasingly, the Negro was forced into playing a caricature of a superstitious, vain, ignorant, and child-like creature (often wearing a "fright wig," which could be made to suddenly stand on end at moments of "shock"). When he was allowed to appear at all as a musical or dancing performer, he was usually forced to play the role of the happy lazy plantation Negro, indulging in childish pranks. Sometimes, he was cast as a foreign performer; Zouave dancers and drill teams, or "Koo-i-baba, the Hindoo baritone," were examples of such exotic types that permitted the talented Negro performer to find a place on the stage.

The final irony, as America moved toward the close of the 19th century, was that Negroes were no longer permitted to share the stage with white performers. Racial segregation became increasingly widespread, and it might happen that a Negro performing group would appear on a stage during the afternoon, and a white group, in blackface, at night. Sometimes light-complexioned Negroes found it necessary to use burnt cork to make themselves as dark as white performers who did their act in blackface. Despite Juba's contribution, and the unquestioned ability of many great Negro dancers, singers, and musicians, there was little opportunity for such performers until several decades had passed.

A final aspect of dance in 19th-century America relates to a unique phenomenon that joined dancing and religion.

This was the appearance in New England and as far west as Ohio and Kentucky, of an unusual Protestant sect called the Shaking Quakers, or Shakers. Descended from a group called the United Society of Believers in Christ's Second Appearance, which appeared in Manchester and Bolton, England, as early as 1747, the Shakers actually traced their spiritual lineage far back to "an ancient heretical tradition for dancing as part of the adoration of God," as seen in early Christian sects. Andrews comments that:

> The worship of many spiritual sects was similar: the early Quakers and Baptists, the French Prophets, the Merry Dancers of England, the Kentucky Revivalists, the Girlingites or Shakers of the New Forest, the Shaker Indians of Puget Sound . . . .[23]

[23] E. D. Andrews, "The Dance in Shaker Ritual," in Magriel, *op. cit.*, p. 4.

Shaker dancing near Lebanon, N.Y. Lithograph, about 1825.

The small band of English colonists who came to be known as Shaking Quakers first made their appearance in this country in the region of Albany, New York, at about the time of the Revolutionary War. They had an extremely strict code; founding a religious order that was separate from the world, they rejected a "corrupt society," and forswore marriage and all "carnal" practices. Typically, the behavior at their early prayer meetings resembled the danseomania of the Middle Ages; a meeting in 1780 was thus reported:

> Everyone acts for himself, and almost everyone different from the other; one will stand with his arms extended . . . another will be dancing, and sometimes hopping on one leg about the floor; another will fall to turning around . . .; another will be prostrate on the floor . . .; some trembling extremely, others acting as though all their nerves were convulsed . . . .[24]

The Shakers expanded their order rapidly, developing eleven communities by 1792, with meetinghouses that had spacious halls which would permit expanded ceremonies, and with seats along the walls for outsiders. Gradually, the dancing, which had been

[24] *Ibid.*, pp. 3–4.

based on individualized expression, changed to a more organized and structured form, including first the "square-order shuffle," which was patterned on the vision of angels dancing around the Throne of God. Recognizing that a lively worship ceremony was impressive to onlookers and would help in conversion, the eastern leaders of the Shakers began to encourage the composition and performance of lively songs and dances. These included various formations, in circles, lines, and weaving patterns. Pantomime became increasingly used; "gestures, such as bowing, stamping, whirling, acting out "signs" . . . were incorporated into the structure of worship, assuming, to a lesser or greater degree, symbolic meaning. . . ."[25]

Sometimes the ceremony involved acting out "chasing the Devil," in which "true believers" would surround a "backslider," pointing their fingers at him and shouting "Woe, Woe, damn his devil," and attempting in other ways to save him for the Lord.

During the 1840s, there was a great revival of religious belief, and the Shakers developed increasingly complex and elaborate dance forms as part of worship. Andrews points out that a variety of formation dances were used during the "Great Revival"—lines, crosses, squares, stars, and other patterns. But now the dances took on new symbolic meaning.

> The devotees felt that they were indeed marching heavenward, that the circle was the perfect emblem of their union. The "wheel-within-a-wheel," three or more concentric circles turning in alternate directions around a central chorus, became a figure of the all-inclusiveness of their gospel; the outer ring the ultimate circle of truth, the Shaker dispensation; the singers, the harmony and perfection of God that were at the heart of life. In another exercise, "The Narrow Path," a single file of dancers, with heads bowed, placed one feet before the other as they trod the narrow way to salvation . . . ."[26]

Gradually, the Shaker communities that had flourished throughout the Northeast and Midwest declined; the songs and dances that were performed as an attempt to reach an ideal communion with God were abandoned early in the present century. In retrospect, the Shakers represented one extreme of religious practice—the use of dance in worship that was typical of pre-Christian or early Christian worship. Much more typical of the 19th century in America, however, was religious opposition toward dance. This varied, according to the particular denomination and the region of the country. As suggested earlier, along the

[25] *Ibid.*, p. 8.
[26] *Ibid.*, p. 10.

eastern seaboard, dance became widely accepted by the end of the 18th century, and aroused little opposition on the part of the clergy. However, in other parts of the country, fundamentalist Baptist and Methodists viewed dance as one of the great evils that threatened morality and chastity. Typically, one of the tracts distributed during the great religious revivals of the mid-19th century was titled "The Social Evils of Dancing, Card Playing, and Theater-Going."

Marks describes Cartright, the great Methodist itinerant preacher of the West, as delighting in telling of the many dances he successfully interrupted. Cartright described the Methodists of the West at the beginning of the century as plain and simple people who attended church regularly, forbade their children to go to balls or plays, and did not permit dancing schools or social dancing in their communities.[27]

Such attitudes were not universal. Sometimes it was dance itself that was seen as evil. Sometimes what was objected to was the custom of taking part in dance in crowded dance halls or public balls, with extravagant dress, drinking, foul air, and overheated exercise before going out into the cool night air. Opinion was divided among ministers themselves. In 1894, *The New York Times* carried out a survey of the attitudes of churchmen:

> Among the clergymen the division is as marked and as profound as it is among the laity. There are clergymen of the liberal school who not merely attend balls given by their parishioners but who applaud the waltz and the polka, and deny the responsibility of harm being inherent in either of them.
> On the other hand, many clergymen, both of New York and Brooklyn, make no effort to conceal their opposition to all forms and varieties of public dancing, and expecially the dances [waltz and polka] so vehemently denounced at the Brooklyn revival.[28]

Among the more liberal clergymen, it was considered acceptable to sponsor dancing in the church gymnasium, and one minister in Jersey City considered opening a dancing school for young people. It was his view that if they were going to dance, it should be in desirable surroundings; he approved of dance as wholesome exercise and a means of promoting graceful movement and carriage of the body.[29]

To sum up the state of dance at the end of the 19th century

---

[27] Peter Cartright, *Autobiography of Peter Cartright*, W. P. Strickland, ed. (New York: Carlton and Potter, 1857), p. 75.
[28] *The New York Times*, February 18, 1894, p. 12.
[29] *The New York Times*, December 17, 1897, p. 5.

in America, it was a time when social dancing had become extremely popular on all class levels, and when the dance in education had begun to gain broad acceptance—as a later chapter will describe. In terms of theatrical dance, however, and particularly ballet, the situation was at a low ebb. Amberg writes that during the 19th century, there was no continuous development or sustained tradition for ballet in America, in contrast to Europe, where the ballet:

> ...was a venerated art and a formal institution, affiliated with permanent opera companies, amply supported by official or private means and assured of a supply of well-trained dancers from their schools. In America the ballet was entirely left to private initiative, to enterprising impresarios or theatre owners or to the choreographers and dancers themselves. There was little opportunity for aspiring artists to study classic dancing and even less to see good performances.[30]

In America, there was comparatively little ballet as such, and what there was was poor. De Mille writes that the performers were pitied and scorned, and it was at this time that dance gained an unsavory name in the United States. No longer could it command respect as an artistic or theatrical enterprise.[31] On the music-hall stage, varied forms of dance were shown, ranging from acrobatics to toe-dancing, to variations of the "Little Egypt belly-dancer" theme, or the skirt-dancing and scarf-twirling effects of performers like Loie Fuller. In Europe, while ballet remained an established state institution, the art had declined markedly both in inspiration and its appeal for audiences.

To this sad state at the turn of the century, two pioneers addressed themselves. One was a European—Michel Fokine, and the other an American—Isadora Duncan. Between them, they changed the face of dance for the century that followed.

[30] George Amberg, *Ballet in America* (New York: Duell, Sloan and Pearce, 1949), p. 9.
[31] Agnes de Mille, *Book of the Dance* (New York: Golden Press, 1963), p. 128.

8

EARLY DEVELOPMENT
OF DANCE EDUCATION

Some critics have viewed the provision of dance education in American schools and colleges as a comparatively recent phenomenon, stemming from the influence of the "progressive education" movement of the first decades of the 20th century. Clearly, this is not the case. Dance has had a long and honored place in the curriculum, both in primitive societies throughout the world and during the long evolvement of Western civilization.

Margaret Mead has written informatively about the teaching of dance in Samoan village life. It takes place there as a highly individual activity, set in a social framework. Children learn to dance at small informal parties or entertainments, often in honor of visitors or wedding celebrations. Both visitors and hosts take turns in providing music and dancing. The chief's wife or one of the young men calls out the names of children, who come out on the floor to perform in small groups. As a group of musicians perform, everyone present joins in by singing, clapping, or beating on the floor with their knuckles. There is a minimum of preliminary instruction in dancing, and the form of the dance itself is highly varied.

No figures are prescribed except the half dozen formal little claps which open the dance and the use of one of a few set endings. There are twenty-five or thirty figures, two or three set transitional positions, and at least three definite styles . . . .[1]

Each child apparently uses the dancing of older children as a model for his own performance, although there is no set pattern, and individuals develop their own styles of movement. As the dancing goes on, the audience calls out praise, comments, and suggestions. Younger children are good-naturedly advised to move in certain ways, or to adjust their costumes, while the more expert older children receive a steady murmur of appreciative remarks: "Thank you, thank you for your dancing!" "Beautiful! Charming! Bravo!"

Within most primitive cultures, dance is thus learned—as a natural part of growing up, and through participation by children and youth in everyday social occasions or in special festivities or rituals. In some situations, they must learn and practice a special dance in preparation for a ceremony in which they will take part. In some others, where dance has become highly developed as an art form, groups of talented children receive instruction from expert adult dancer-teachers, but this is a less common arrangement.

As indicated earlier, the purposes of dance education were well understood by the ancient Greeks. Socrates expressed high esteem for dance, recommending that it be taught more widely:

. . . for health, for complete and harmonious physical development, for beauty, for the ability to give pleasure to others, for "reducing," for the acquisition of a good appetite, for the enjoyment of sound sleep. He confesses that he himself dances alone "at dawn," . . . and he openly expresses the wish that he may acquire greater skill in the graceful art.[2]

Aristotle also gave attention to the place of dance in education. Although he did not favor requiring it as a formal educational activity before the age of fourteen, he saw it as affording intellectual and aesthetic gratification of the highest type. In his view, it was useful in purging the young student's soul of "unseemly emotions," and it helped to prepare the future citizen for a honorable enjoyment of leisure.

Although dance fell into a low state during the Roman era and the Dark Ages, it once again came to the fore as an important part of the education of the nobility during the Renaissance.

[1] Margaret Mead, *From the South Seas* (New York: William Morrow & Co., Inc., 1939), p. 112.
[2] Lillian B. Lawler, *The Dance in Ancient Greece* (Middletown, Connecticut: Wesleyan University Press, 1964), p. 125.

Michel de Montaigne, the great French 16th-century essayist, wrote in his treatise *The Education of Children*, that education should include training for character and for life; that it should strengthen the body and also cultivate the mind:

> Our very exercises and recreations, running, wrestling, dancing, hunting, riding and fencing will be a part of his study. I would have his manners, behavior, and bearing cultivated at the same time with his mind. It is not the mind, it is not the body we are training; it is the man and we must not divide him into two parts . . . .[3]

The arts of music and dance, along with the skills of warfare and hunting, were an integral part of the education of courtiers in all of the castles of Europe. A leading Italian schoolmaster was Vittorino da Feltre (1378–1446), who was responsible for the education of the sons of Marquis Gian Francesco Gonzaga at Mantua, in 1423. Da Feltre was a humanist, who made Latin, Greek, and classical archeology the main body of instruction; youths from most of the princely houses of Italy, as well as the sons of nobility from other lands, came to him for instruction. Typically, he included in his curriculum the characteristic features of knightly education. There were special teachers of dancing, riding, fencing, and swimming, as well as excursions for hunting and fishing, and other sports.

With the growth of the Renaissance court dance, it became even more important for members of the nobility to learn to dance well. Thus one finds the examples of kings and all their courtiers taking regular dancing lessons, not only as youths, but throughout their active lives.

Many historians suggest that the modern physical education movement began with the appearance of a text, *De Arte Gymnastica*, dated 1569, and written by Hieronymus Mercurialis, a famous physician who lived in Rome. In this book, which was read throughout Europe and was widely cited by other authors and school authorities, Mercurialis sought to revive the gymnastic education of the ancient Greeks; among the activities he recommended was dancing. Another influential writer on education, who lived in the following century, John Locke, published a text, *Some Thoughts on Education*, in 1693. In this, he deals extensively with training not only the intellect, but also the constitution and health of the child. In addition to other forms of activity, he writes specifically of dance:

[3] Michel de Montaigne, *The Education of Children*, quoted in Emmett A. Rice, John L. Hutchinson, and Mabel Lee, *A Brief History of Physical Education* (New York: The Ronald Press Company, 1958) p. 73.

... besides what is to be had from study and books, there are other accomplishments necessary for a gentleman, to be got by exercise, and to which time is to be allowed, and for which masters must be had. Dancing being that which gives graceful motions all the life, and above all things, manliness and a becoming confidence to young children, I think it cannot be learned too early . . . .[4]

In many other writings on education of the 17th and 18th centuries, which placed increasing stress on physical activity and healthful living practices, dancing was included, usually from the point of view of its hygienic benefits and as a form of exercise. Typically, in the school for young noblemen founded in Denmark in 1623 by Christian IV, professional masters of riding, fencing, gymnastics, and dancing were appointed, as well as teachers in literary subjects. The German educator, Johann Bernhard Basedow, who founded the famous Philanthropium (a private academy) at Dessau in 1774, introduced what was probably the most complete course in physical training the world had yet seen, including dancing, which was primarily intended to achieve gentility and social graces.

Johann Guts Muths, another leading pioneer in the development of German education, published, in 1793, the text *Gymnastics for Youth*, in which he advocated dancing as a means of physical exercise, by writing, "Dancing is an exercise strongly deserving recommendation, as it tends to unite gracefulness and regularity of motion with strength and agility."[5] He promoted dancing vigorously in his gymnasium at Schnopfenthal, and was perhaps the first author to use the term "gymnastic dance":

A good gymnastic dance for the open air, approaching the heroic ballet for young men or boys, calculated to exercise their strength and ability, excite innocent mirth and youthful heroism and cherish their love of country through the accompaniment of song, is an extremely desirable object . . . .[6]

Other educators who were active in the beginning Turnverein movement introduced the so-called "folk roundel," which consisted of simple marching, hopping, skipping, and running movements and patterns. These were always accompanied by singing and sometimes by music, and were apparently the forerunners of what later came to be considered gymnastic dance in American

[4] John Locke, *Some Thoughts on Education*, quoted in Fred Leonard, *A Guide to the History of Physical Education* (Philadelphia: Lea & Febiger, 1923), p. 60.
[5] Johann Guts Muths, *Gymnastics for Youth*, quoted in S. C. Staley and D. M. Lowery, *Gymnastic Dancing* (New York: Association Press, 1920), p. 6.
[6] *Ibid.*

physical education. Similarly, the director of the Royal Central Gymnastic Institute in Germany, during the mid-19th century, introduced what he called "transition exercises," which seemed to be a blend of gymnastics and dancing, carried on in dance formations and executed according to command.

At the same time, there were many private teachers of dancing throughout Europe, who taught it as an art in schools of ballet, or as a social grace, in the homes of wealthy or royal families of the time.

Meanwhile, what of America? It has already been pointed out that, as religious attitudes condemning dance grew less severe in the American colonies during the pre-Revolutionary period, a great wave of interest in dancing developed. There was a steady growth of dancing schools; many private schools included instruction in fencing and dancing, or music and dancing, for both boys and girls. The purpose of such education was seen as the very opposite of frivolity; indeed, an example of dancing not being learned entirely for pleasure is suggested by an incident at the Philadelphia Assembly in 1781:

> "Come, miss, have a care what you are doing," shouted the Master of Ceremonies to a damsel who was permitting a bit of gossip to interrupt her turn in a contradance. "Do you think you are here for your own pleasure?"[7]

The development of dance in education during the 19th century in the United States was of course closely linked to the expansion of elementary and secondary programs, and to the establishment of private academies, seminaries, and colleges for women. In the early part of the century, schools for children of elementary school age rapidly increased in number, replacing in popularity the Latin grammar schools of colonial days. Treatises on education by European authorities became increasingly available in the United States. In particular, the works of Froebel, the German founder of kindergartens and champion of education for girls and women, began to affect educational philosophy here. Increasingly, there developed the conviction that the schools were responsible for physical as well as academic growth of children, and that activities other than the purely academic should be included in the curriculum.

During the first years of the new century, an increasing number of state colleges or church-supported colleges were founded, as well as the first women's colleges (which were founded

[7] Joseph Marks, *America Learns to Dance* (New York: Exposition Press, 1957), p. 51.

originally as seminaries) at Mount Holyoke and elsewhere in New England. In all of these settings, dance began to be taught. Some women educators, including Emma Willard and Mary Lyon, attempted to provide some form of physical education for their students. Emma Willard taught during the winter of 1807–1808 at Middlebury College in Vermont. It was an extremely bitter and snowy winter and, according to Marks, she later wrote:

> When it was so cold that we could live no longer, I called all my girls on to the floor, and arranged them two and two in a long row for a country dance; and while those who could sing would strike up some stirring tune, I, with one of the girls for a partner would lead down the dance, and soon have them all in rapid motion. After which we went to our school exercises again.[8]

While dancing was, as a rule, found more frequently in programs for girls and women than for male students, one of the first recorded examples of dance as part of the required program for men was in the military academy at West Point. It was included in the course of instruction which was submitted to President Washington in 1783. Its rationale, of course, was that each officer had to be able to conduct himself as a gentleman, and that instruction in dancing would help him do this, and would provide poise and social competence. However, it was not actually taught until 1817 when Pierre Thomas, the Academy's first fencing master, was permitted to organize a voluntary dancing class for cadets who requested it. In 1823, dancing was made a required subject in the summer encampment, with daily lessons for the third and fourth class which were taught by Papanti, a famous Boston dancing master of the period. A number of other military academies followed the example of West Point in including dancing in their course of instruction.

During the first quarter of the 19th century, dancing began to be found in schools for young children. It was seen chiefly as a means of acquiring poise, manners, and social confidence. As elementary education spread more widely, it came to be felt that the curriculum should be practical and useful. Thus, by mid-century, the justification for dance came more and more based on its healthful benefits. An educational writer of the time, the Reverend John L. Blake, wrote in *The Farmer's Every-Day Book* that dance should be provided in every country school, under the direction of the schoolmaster:

---

[8] Alma Lutz, *Emma Willard, Daughter of Democracy* (Boston: Houghton Mifflin Company, 1929), p. 37.

In the middle of the day, or prior to the commencement of the afternoon studies, let half an hour be spent in this fascinating exercise, as a reward of good conduct as scholars, and the prediction is made with confidence, that neither girls or boys will ever be tardy. Besides, it will refine the manners and the temper of the minds beyond calculation. Instead of diminishing progress in study, it will increase it. The design is by no means to fit them for the ballroom. It is simply to give them a healthful exercise; for boys, instead of playing ball—and the girls, instead of romping.[9]

In a number of cases, opposition to dance was evidenced. This was chiefly due to religious objection, both as a lingering remnant of the early Puritan view of dance, and also because of intensified religious attitudes about "sinful" social behavior which were inflamed during the religious revivals of the time. In addition to this, the American ideals of material accomplishment and usefulness made suspect any activity such as dance, which was manifestly connected with pleasure and pastime.

As a consequence, dance tended to be found more widely in private academies than in public schools, where it might be challenged on the grounds of utility or morality. Typically, in Cleveland in 1840, a citizen petitioned the city council to introduce music into the public schools. The council denied the request, claiming that it was illegal to teach music in the schools. At the meeting, one of the members of the council said that if music were introduced, dancing might also be taught; however, of the two, he preferred dancing. In some cases, when there was religious objection to dancing in public schools, teachers pleaded that it was a healthful recreation and exercise, and that it prevented children from carrying on more harmful activities.

In other cases, when dance was taught, it was in fact disguised as a form of musical gymnastics or as calisthenics. Thus, when Mary Lyon published a book of exercises at Mount Holyoke College in about 1853, teachers were warned that the exercises, done to music, should not be performed in a dancelike fashion—or they would arouse opposition. However, in Lyon's teaching, and also in the calisthenics taught by Catherine Beecher during the 1840s and 1850s in a girls' school in Cincinnati and at Mount Holyoke, the activity resembled dance greatly. The term "calisthenics" was adapted from the Greek *kalos*, meaning beautiful, and *sthenos*, meaning strength. The exercises involved simple movements to be accompanied by music, to produce grace of motion and good carriage. Foot positions and other elements of

[9] John L. Blake, *The Farmer's Every-Day Book* (Auburn, New Hampshire: Derby, Miller Company, 1850) p. 165.

the ballet were incorporated into these exercises, and the actions included marching, skipping, hopping, and similar steps—all done to music.

Between the period of the Civil War and the close of the 19th century, dance became a more fully accepted part of physical education, and thus of general education. Dio Lewis, a popular temperance and health lecturer, developed a system of graceful exercises using light dumbells, accompanied by music or drum beats for rhythm. In his book, *The New Gymnastics*, published in 1862, he praised dance as a moderately strenuous exercise, which developed flexibility, dexterity, and grace. In a school he conducted at Lexington, Massachusetts, girls took part in gymnastics twice a day for half an hour, and also performed dance as such, about three times a week. He described his gymnastics method as follows:

> ... persons of both sexes unite in all the exercises with great social enjoyment, thus adding indefinitely to the attractions of the place .... In the New Gymnasium, everything is set to music. Marches, free movement, dumbells, wands, rings, mutual-help exercises. No apathy can resist the delightful stimulus. The one hundred persons on the floor join in the evolutions inspired by one common impulse. Under the old system each person works by himself, deprived of the sympathy and energy evoked by music and the associated movement.[10]

Lewis was extremely influential in the developing physical education movement. He did not regard his system of "new Gymnastics" as dancing, commenting that the exercises "are arranged to music and ... possess a charm superior to that of dancing and other social amusements." However, they clearly resembled a modified form of dance, involving marching, leaping and skipping actions, with partners traveling around the floor together.

There was, more and more, in the latter decades of the 19th century, a readiness to accept dancing as such. Certainly, this was in part due to the fact that it was a popularly accepted social pastime among all classes in society. Indeed, when it was introduced at such a leading women's college as Vassar, and opposition was expressed, the trustees and officers of the college supported it strongly. Matthew Vassar, the founder of the college, said to the trustees in 1869:

> Years ago I made up my judgment on these great questions in the religious point of view, and came to the decision favorable to amusements. I have never practiced public dancing in my life, and

---

[10] Dio Lewis, quoted in Leonard, *A Guide to the History of Physical Education,* p. 261.

yet in view of its being a healthful and graceful exercise, I heartily approve of it, and now recommend it being taught in the college to all pupils whose parents or guardians recommend it.[11]

Similarly, years later, the president of Harvard University, Charles W. Eliot, wrote in a letter to Charles Francis Adams, "I have often said that if I were compelled to have one required subject in Harvard College, I would make it dancing if I could. West Point has been very wise in this respect. . . ."[12]

A major influence in helping to bring dance as art into schools and colleges was the work of the French dramatic teacher, François Delsarte. His American followers developed a Delsartian system of exercise which attempted to relate outer movements to inner states of feeling. This method, widely used in the 1890s, was introduced at Chautauqua, the famous adult education camp in upstate New York which began a nationwide movement during the later years of the 19th century and the early 20th century. The Delsartian system stressed freedom and harmony of movement, and had a vague rationale about making the body "a temple for the indwelling soul." Some called it "aesthetic gymnastics." It was based on exercises that stressed relaxation, making use of statue-posing and tableaux that purported to show the various emotions. Often it accompanied singing or the recitation of poems. In addition, it included a great many dance movements and maneuvers.

The Delsartian system in turn led to the introduction of a method which was termed "aesthetic calisthenics." This approach was formulated by Melvin Ballou Gilbert, a Portland dance teacher, who developed it as a substitute for regular gymnastic work for women. The method was introduced to physical educators in 1894 by Dr. Dudley A. Sargent, a pioneer in this field, and professor of physical training at Harvard, who organized what later became the Sargent School of Physical Education. Gilbert's method was based on:

> . . . the long-established five positions of the feet and the five positions of the arms, together with the positions of the whole body known as attitudes, arabesques, poses, elevations, groupings, etc. From these precepts are established, whereby the steps, attitudes and motions are systematic and in strict harmony with time and music.[13]

The Gilbert method gradually became known as *aesthetic dance.* During the early years of the 20th century, its practitioners

[11] Matthew Vassar, quoted in Marks, *America Learns to Dance,* p. 97.

[12] Charles W. Eliot, quoted in Henry James, *Charles W. Eliot, President of Harvard University, 1869–1909* (Boston: Houghton Mifflin Company, 1930), Vol. II, p. 163.

[13] Melvin Ballou Gilbert, "Classic Dancing," *American Physical Education Review,* June, 1905, p. 153.

were influenced by the work of Isadora Duncan and sought to make it a highly expressive and artistic form. While aesthetic dance made considerable use of ballet movements as well as such ball-room dance steps as the polka, schottische, waltz, and mazurka—all fitted into series of exercises or routines that might then be performed—it was modified in its level of difficulty so that it might be taught to large classes without difficulty.

Sargent had hoped that the Gilbert Method might be used with both men and women. However, as it became increasingly artistic and expressive, it was apparent that men and boys resisted it. Thus, "it became necessary to modify the dancing so as to give opportunity for a heavier kind of work...."[14]

This "heavier" and more masculine kind of work became known as *gymnastic dancing*. It rejected the balletic orientation of aesthetic dance; Staley and Lowery wrote of it as "any balance exercise that is free, serial, rhythmical," with coordinated simple movements, strenuous enough to be good exercise, and of a genuinely masculine makeup. The fundamental foot and arm positions, and the terminology of steps found in the aesthetic dance were discarded, along with the turnout, the difficult "technical steps," and the expressive emphasis.

Gymnastic dance made use of the terminology of gymnastics. It could be taught by the "physical director and not by a dancing master." The subject matter of gymnastic dance was drawn from various fields of physical activity: "folk dancing, aesthetic dancing, gymnasium exercises, athletic exercises, play and work."[15] Men, in performing it, wore gym costumes: shorts, athletic shirts, high stockings, and basketball sneakers. The dances were done in solos, couples, sets, and mass groupings. Often, they resembled the old drills of Dio Lewis, in that they involved maze running, skipping steps, galloping, as well as such folk dances as the Virginia Reel, the Hornpipe, the Highland Fling, the Czardas, and dances of other nationalities—usually performed as solo or group routines. Thus, in the early years of the 20th century, two forms of dance became established in college and secondary school physical education—gymnastic dance for boys and men, and aesthetic dance for girls and women. This separation of activity was typical of American physical education, which was one of the few curricular subjects in which boys and girls were divided into separate classes as a matter of custom.

It is important to recognize that the prejudice expressed by

---

[14] Dudley A. Sargent, quoted in Marks, *America Learns to Dance*, p. 102.
[15] Staley and Lowery, *Gymnastic Dancing*, pp. 82–83.

male physical educators against the Gilbert Method was largely because it seemed to be too expressive, difficult, and graceful for boys and men to perform comfortably. Men were, in this period, willing to dance, provided that the activity was vigorous, simple, and drawn from folk sources or based on robust, masculine themes.

EARLY DEVELOPMENT OF DANCE EDUCATION

A third form of dance that rapidly became popular in the early part of the 20th century was folk or national dance (the term "national" usually referred to those folk dances that were characteristic of a nation, and which were found within its borders, such as the *Irish Jig*, the *Italian Tarantella*, or the *Scottish Highland Fling*). As indicated, these dances had been the source of many of the gymnastic dance routines. Actually, they had been practiced in physical education since 1887 when Dr. William G. Anderson, a pioneer physical educator who was director of the Brooklyn Normal School of Gymnastics, introduced Irish jigs, reels and clogs, the buck and wing, and soft-shoe steps. Anderson taught all of these in Brooklyn, at the Chautauqua Summer Camps, and later at Yale and other institutions. In addition to this, in 1892 the Swedish Society of New York City began to collect and teach native folk dances of Sweden, lending considerable impetus to interest in folk dance among educators.

At the same time that much of the folk dance material became incorporated into gymnastic dance, it also developed as a separate stream of activity in physical education, and in the early recreational or playground movement throughout the country. Two collectors of traditional folk dances, Elizabeth Burchenal and C. Ward Crampton, did much original research in European countries. They published extensive collections of traditional folk dances which were still being performed in such countries as Germany, Denmark, Sweden, Finland, and the British Isles—as well as traditional American country dances. Through the efforts of Burchenal, Crampton, and Louis Chalif, who had been trained in Russian ballet but was also an influential teacher of folk dance, these became widely adopted in physical education syllabi and in community recreation programs throughout the country. They were seen as having important recreational values, and also as yielding intercultural benefits in a society whose citizens had come from many nations.

By the beginning years of the 20th century, dance had become widely adopted in schools and colleges throughout the United States. With the exception of a few finishing schools or girls' academies or colleges where it might be taught essentially as a social grace, it was viewed primarily as a form of physical education. Before long, physical educators developed an impressive litany of its benefits. Dr. Luther Halsey Gulick, an early physical educator who, like many of his counterparts, was initially a medical doctor, wrote rather mystically of the background of folk and national dances:

> The movements of folk and national dances . . . are . . . an epitome of many of the neuro-muscular coordinations which have been necessary to the life of the race. They have grown up very slowly through centuries until they have come to fit and express the very soul of the people, embodying its memories, expressing its psycho-physical traits and aspirations. Upon the basic neuro-muscular coordinations have been embroidered, for esthetic purposes, certain finer movements. The movements themselves, however . . . follow long-inherited tendencies toward neuro-muscular coordinations which arose under the selective influence of survival.[16]

Whether or not this meant anything, it sounded convincing, and physical educators were delighted to accept it as a rationale for an activity that was as enjoyable for students as dance. The physiological outcomes of dance were further described in great detail:

> . . . dancing . . . exercise removes excess accumulations of fat, replacing the same with healthy muscle tissue, thereby transforming a body that was soft, inactive, and soggy into one that is tonic and elastic. As a means of organic stimulation, dancing can be made vigorous enough to satisfy the most hardy nature . . . . The mental attitude of the dancer makes this possible. The dancer prosecutes the most vigorous steps with no thought for the work he is doing. He is aware only of his pleasure.
> From a physiological viewpoint, dancing is the best all-round exercise that we have in our program of physical training. There are no excessively difficult exercises from the standpoint of muscular strength, a fact that eliminates the possibility of structural strain, torn ligaments, tendons, wrenched joints, etc . . . .[17]

In detail, early physical educators who were proponents of dance praised its benefits for the circulatory system, the respiratory system, and the digestive process ("the jarring, twisting and jolting of the vigorous dance again plays its part here"), as well as being "an excellent curative measure for particular diseases," including chronic diseases of the digestive tract, flat feet, and diseases of the neural system.[18]

In any case, dance was now widely established, and was part of the teacher training program for both men and women in many

[16] Luther Halsey Gulick, quoted in Staley and Lowery, *Gymnastic Dancing*, pp. 22–23.
[17] *Ibid.*, p. 24.
[18] *Ibid.*, pp. 25–27.

departments of physical education throughout the country. It took many and varied forms, as illustrated by this description of end-of-summer performances at Chautauqua in the 1890s:

> The exhibitions by students of the School of Physical Education were the highlight of each Chautauqua season for years. Oldtimers still marvel at the amazing review Anderson's protégés presented each summer at the Amphitheater and on the ball diamond. They drew from six to seven thousand people with standing-room-only the rule .... In 1892, "1,000 pupils participated in the exercises closing the course, at which a vast audience was amazed as well as delighted at the feats of strength and agility shown." Old pictures show gymnasts, small dance groups, and large mixed classes of several hundred—including foreign pupils—doing wand drills and dances. Tumblers, Bolin's Swedish class, high bar work, Indian club drills, and the flambeaus (hoops of fire) set the pace with band music to fill any gaps. Minuets by tiny girls, Delsarte Health exercises, and dances—Swedish folk, English Morris, and clog—done to piano accompaniment, excited audiences.[19]

Three educators were to provide the spark that led eventually to the adoption of modern dance in American schools and colleges. They were Gertrude Colby, Bird Larson, and Margaret H'Doubler.

In 1913, Colby joined the staff of the Speyer School, the demonstration school of Teachers College, Columbia University, in New York City. A graduate of the Sargent School of Gymnastics, she was asked to develop a physical education program that would be natural and free, and which would permit self-expression. Gradually, she began to experiment with creative dance based on natural movement and on children's interests, a form that could be integrated with other curricular experiences in the school. Her approach made use of music as an emotional stimulus; it was not based on any carefully designed system of movement, and yet it had great appeal, compared to the stilted aesthetic dance, or the limited gymnastic dance that was in vogue at the time. Colby later joined the staff of Teachers College, where she taught a number of students who became leading American dance educators, including Martha Hill, Mary O'Donnell, Martha Deane, and Ruth Murray.

Colby gave the name of *natural dance* to her new method. In a sense, it was the forerunner of what was to become modern dance in schools and colleges. Before this was to happen, her method was to be influenced by the leading professional dancers

[19] Harold L. Ray, "Chautauqua, Early Showcase for Physical Education," *Journal of Health, Physical Education and Recreation*, November 1962, p. 39.

of the 1920s and 1930s, and also by other educators who were to provide it with a scientific rationale.

Closely associated with Gertrude Colby was Bird Larson, who was in charge of dance at Barnard College, on the Columbia University campus. While Larson recognized the value in Colby's natural dance, she also felt that there was a need for dance technique that would be based on the laws of anatomy, kinesiology, and physics. Having had an extensive background in corrective physical education, Larson experimented with a system of movement which would have its origin in the torso of the body, and which would in effect represent not a preconceived system of technique and dance patterns but a science of movement.[20] Her purpose was to encourage students to develop themselves through the dance, and she strove to enable each of her students to develop a dance art that was suited to his needs, capabilities, and limitations.

In 1916, Margaret H'Doubler, who had taught physical education at the University of Wisconsin, came to Teachers College to study for her Master's degree. As a part-time teacher at Columbia University between 1916 and 1918, H'Doubler carefully observed the experimental work of Colby and Larson. When she returned to the University of Wisconsin in 1918, she developed a dance program which was based on a scientific understanding of the nature of physical movement as well as a sound philosophy of creative expression.

H'Doubler succeeded in establishing a major in dance at the University of Wisconsin in 1926, thus achieving recognition for the dance in university education and bringing into existence a major center in the Midwest for the creation of a large dance audience. In addition, many teachers were brought into meaningful contact with dance education. H'Doubler wrote extensively, and her texts became influential in the professional preparation of dance educators and physical educators.[21] She also founded *Orchesis*, the University of Wisconsin dance club which served as a model for many college and university performing groups in the years that followed.

During the 1930s, three streams of dance activity were evident: folk and social dance; tap, clog, and character dance; and, most important, the new modern dance.

[20] Mildred C. Spiesman, "Dance Education Pioneers: Colby, Larson, H'Doubler," *Journal of Health, Physical Education and Recreation*, January 1960, pp. 25–27.
[21] Margaret H'Doubler, *Dance: A Creative Art Experience* (New York: F. S. Crofts and Company, 1940), and *Dance and Its Place in Education* (New York: Harcourt, Brace and Company, 1927).

Proponents of folk and national dance such as Louis Chalif, Mary Wood Hinman, and Elizabeth Burchenal had succeeded in spreading this activity very widely in schools and colleges throughout the United States. Burchenal, who was organizer and chairman of the folk dance committee of the Playground and Recreation Association of America, brought a wealth of material to the movement from original sources, and through her authoritative lectures and publications, trained many teachers over a period of several decades. Louis Chalif, through his special courses for teachers and a variety of publications, also spurred this activity forward. Mary Wood Hinman was active in the development of all kinds of dancing: gymnastic, Morris, Maypole, folk, national, and clog dance. She was instrumental in the establishment of Folk Festival Councils in number of American cities, and fought to gain acceptance for social dancing as a valid activity to be taught in schools:

> Social dancing . . . . Are we afraid of it, or are we lazy? Colleges and schools provide good surroundings and expensive equipment for basketball and archery, etc.; but many of them still leave out this one corecreational game, which becomes almost a necessity at some time in the life of a normal young person. The average boy or girl has seldom been given a straight-forward honest education in social dancing by the physical education department, where good surroundings demand group responsibility and pride in skills is the order of the day . . . .[22]

By the 1930s, Hackensmith writes, "Folk and social dancing were gaining in popularity in sections of the country unhampered by a prejudice against mixed dancing, and both gave promise of becoming valuable additions to the physical education program."[23]

Clog and tap dancing attained considerable success in schools and colleges during the 1920s and early 1930s. These dance forms were descended from traditional steps found in the Jig of the Elizabethan period, the shuffling and foot-tapping steps of Latin countries and the British Isles, and Negro plantation dances. In its earlier development, the term "clog dance" was used, based on the original use of shoes with wooden soles, which created rather crude and heavy rhythmic patterns. Tap dancing, which made use of leather soles with aluminum heel and toe taps, and of modern, popular music, with faster and more syncopated tempo

---

[22] Mary Wood Hinman, "Educational Possibilities of the Dance," *Journal of Health, Physical Education and Recreation*, April 1934, pp. 14–15.

[23] C. W. Hackensmith, *History of Physical Education* (New York: Harper and Row, Publishers, 1966), p. 453.

and rhythms, gradually replaced clog on the musical stage and, ultimately, in dance education. Duggan comments that

> Clog is to tap dancing, therefore, what natural is to modern dance—an immediate predecessor to designate this type of rhythmic work in educational institutions. The term *clog* persisted in education long after it had been replaced by *tap* in professional circles. This was due in part to the school's hesitancy to sponsor an activity associated with the theater. The name persists now partly due to habit and partly due to the fact that much published material was brought out during the period when *clog*, not *tap* dance, was the correct term for school teachers . . . .[24]

A number of physical education specialists were closely associated with the teaching and promotion of clog and tap dance, including Helen Frost, Marjorie Hillas, and Mary Jane Hungerford. Through the years, a rationale supporting the teaching of tap dancing as a "creative" activity was developed:

> The chief neuro-muscular value of clog and tap dancing comes from developing balance and coordination. Gestures and hand-clapping, combined with a wide variety of foot patterns, are the most common types of coordination which clog and tap involve. In addition, this type of activity makes a tremendous contribution to the development of a fluent motor response to rhythm. If taught by a leader properly equipped musically, it can make children thoroughly familiar with the elements of music—note value, beat, accent, measure, time signature, phrase, syncopation, and so on . . . .[25]

However, by the 1940s, emphasis on clog and tap dancing had declined sharply in schools and colleges throughout the country. Although they continued to have a few enthusiastic adherents, the dances were increasingly regarded as a mechanical form of activity which did not achieve the primary creative, social, and physical goals that were considered appropriate for dance education and physical education.

At the beginning of the 1930s, much of the creative dance which was taught in the schools stemmed fairly directly from the natural dance which had been taught by Colby. It tended to place great stress on free and unstructured movement, on self-discovery, and on spontaneous response to music. On the elementary level, many teachers were presenting "creative rhythmic movement" with a minimum of direction or actual instruction; rather, the teacher created the inspiration for the child to move.

---

[24] Anne Schley Duggan, "The Evolution of Tap Dancing," *Educational Dance*, February 1940, p. 2.

[25] Mary Jane Hungerford, *Creative Tap Dancing* (New York: Prentice-Hall, Inc., 1939), p. 108.

Teachers were encouraged to undertake the activity with younger children—whether or not they had dance skill themselves. In fact, one influential author thought it could be a positive handicap:

> ... dancing, like children's art, is not dependent on background. In fact, as in their art, it can be a good thing if the teacher is unencumbered with old ideas on the subject. What the teacher needs is faith and understanding. Faith that there is the capacity within the child to do surprisingly beautiful things when encouraged and freed by the teacher—understanding that children's dancing is not a thing of steps, of artificial movements to be learned by rote.
>
> The moment we concern a child with steps, we tie him up, inhibit his free movement, make him fearful, put false emphasis. The walk is ruined if we ask the child which foot he puts forward first. He just naturally walks following a desire within him. So also will the child dance . . . .[26]

Even for students on the high school or college level, many teachers at the beginning of the 1930s stressed an extremely free approach, based on Colby's natural dance theories. Betty Lynd Thompson wrote of "creative" dancing at this time:

> This form is taught in most large colleges and universities and in many high schools. It is developed along the lines of education and aims at developing personalities rather than dancers . . . . All of the movements are based on natural movements of the body, movements which we normally can do, but which are studied and practiced until they can be done with ease, perfect balance and coordination . . . .[27]

When the dancer has developed a degree of skill in the control of her body, when she becomes able to "sense the rhythm and the emotion of music," then, according to Thompson, she is ready to create dances herself. Essentially, the emphasis throughout this period was placed on personal creativity, and aesthetic expressiveness—without the conviction that the body had to be trained as a tool, or instrument, before it could perform effectively. The influence, however, of the concert dancers of the 1930s was to create a much greater interest in technical mastery, in expanding the range of dance movement, and in developing a recognition of dance as an art form—rather than a useful means of catharsis, or naïve self-expression.

How did modern dance come into being? It had its roots in the dance of Isadora Duncan, the work of Ruth St. Denis and

[26] Natalie Robinson Cole, *The Arts in the Classroom* (New York: The John Day Co., Inc., 1940), p. 69.

[27] Betty Lynd Thompson, *Fundamentals of Rhythm and Dance* (New York: A. S. Barnes & Co., Inc., 1933), p. xviii.

Ted Shawn, and the contributions of Martha Graham, Doris Humphrey, and Charles Weidman in America, and Mary Wigman in Germany. During the middle and late 1920s, two movements existed side by side. On the one hand, educators—primarily physical educators—were teaching creative dance under a variety of names, in the schools and colleges of the nation. On the other hand, professional dancers were holding their first recitals and concert tours throughout the land.

Before long, it became apparent that they needed each other. The dance educators in schools and colleges needed the professionals to provide a body of technique, and to explore the artistic potentialities of the new medium; in addition, many of them began to study dance in the studios or special workshops provided by professional dancers. In turn, the professionals needed the school and college people both to *attend* their classes, and to provide an audience for them, particularly on national tours with concert groups, when, it was soon discovered, the college or university town provided a welcome climate for programs that were experimental or controversial.

A more detailed analysis of this process, as well as of the development of modern dance itself, may be found in the chapters that follow.

9

MODERN DANCE:
THE EARLY DECADES

As suggested in the preceding chapter, the uniquely American dance form that was to appear in this country during the 20th century, and that was to have a profound effect on dance education, was the modern dance.

Beginning with Isadora Duncan, who broke away from the classical ballet and urged a new use of dance as a powerful medium of personal expression, the foundation was laid. Ruth St. Denis and Ted Shawn followed by providing a generation of Americans with their first awareness of dance as an exciting theater art. But it was the small group of dancers and choreographers who burst upon the scene in the late 1920s and early 1930s who may truly be said to have been the first modern dancers. These were the great early figures—Martha Graham, Doris Humphrey and Charles Weidman, Helen Tamiris, and the German dance pioneer, Mary Wigman. They were the pioneers, and it was thanks to their efforts that modern dance emerged as a unique and powerful art form.

How is modern dance to be defined? At the outset, many viewed it chiefly as a form of dance which rebelled against the formalism, decadence, and stereotyped choreography and productions of classical ballet. They welcomed a form of dance which they saw as responding to modern concerns, expressing a contemporary viewpoint, and, in essence, being a truly American form—rather than imported or foreign.

In rejecting the set vocabulary of movements of the ballet, and the artificiality of its arbitrarily imposed traditional forms and themes, modern dance was seen as being a true conception of the contemporary period—alive as today, and constantly changing. It was based on natural, expressive, basic movement, through which the dancer was able to express a broad range of feeling—rather than only the decorative, romantic, or pseudotragic emotions of the classical ballet. John Martin wrote:

> This is the prime purpose of the modern dance; it is not interested in spectacle, but in the communication of emotional experiences—intuitive perceptions, elusive truths—which cannot be communicated in reason's terms or reduced to mere statement of fact.[1]

In every way, through its stark and simple costumes, its simple and sculptural decor, its music composed by leading contemporary composers in most cases, modern dance was an expression of the contemporary scene. Typically, during one period in the 1930s, the titles of works performed on the modern dance stage included: *Strike, Heretic, Traditions, Stock Exchange, Lynch Town, Work and Play*, and *American Provincials*. But, like modern art, such preoccupations were cyclic; at other points, and in the hands of other choreographers, the themes of modern dance works might encompass Greek mythology; ancient or modern poetry, or other literary works; American folklore and legendry; major social issues; interpersonal relationships approached psychoanalytically; historical events; or, simply, abstract and lyrical works that had no theme or story line at all.

With no single tradition of instruction or universal system of technique, there were many approaches to modern dance. In general, the specific skills of ballet, as well as the emphasis on performing extremely difficult feats with an air of perfect aplomb and gracious ease, were rejected. Instead, the movement of modern dance tended to reveal the performer, rather than to mask him. A wide variety of nondiscursive gestures was developed; movement that was harsh, forceful, percussive—often primitive in quality—was developed. Instead of involving highly controlled leaps, turns, and other springing movements in the air, or dancing on the *pointes*, or holding the arms and feet in rigidly preordained poses, the body and limbs became flexible; they were held in any pose, they were wracked, torn, twisted, to suit the purposes of the

---

[1] John Martin, *Book of the Dance* (New York: Tudor Publishing Co., 1963), p. 138.

dance. The dancer might be dragged around the stage, or might roll on the floor or perform the most convoluted of actions.

Similarly, in terms of the use of the dancing group, the traditional ballet hierarchy of leading dancers—the ballerina and the premier danseur—secondary dancers, and the corps, all performing in a ritualized sequence, in which they played separate and largely unrelated roles, was discarded. Instead, modern dancers almost lost identity in their roles; the group itself was fluid, and treated as a sculptural whole.

Since modern dance was and is so eclectic, drawn from so many sources and subject to so many influences, it is difficult to define it further, either in its formative years or today—other than to describe the dancers and their works, and their influence on the American concert-going public. One final element, however, might be stressed, which characterizes modern dance, and that is—*freedom*. Always, its primary value has been placed on permitting the individual choreographer to develop and express his own art, without regard to preexisting forms and traditions. This does not suggest, as some have concluded, that modern dance has no discipline. Merce Cunningham has written:

> Since he works with the body—the strongest and, at the same instant, the most fragile of instruments—the necessity to organize and understand its way of moving is of great urgency for the dancer. Technique is the disciplining of one's energies through physical action in order to free that energy at any desired instant in its highest possible physical and spiritual form. For the disciplined energy of a dancer is the life-energy magnified and focused for whatever brief fraction of time it lasts .... The most essential thing in dance discipline is devotion, the steadfast and willing devotion to the labor that makes the classwork not a gymnastic hour and a half, or at the lowest level, a daily drudgery, but a devotion that allows the classroom discipline to be moments of dancing too ....[2]

Thus, although at the outset, modern dance might have been confused with the natural dance, or "interpretive dance" that flourished in the 1920s, it soon became a disciplined and demanding dance form. Ultimately, too, the complete rejection of ballet that had characterized the first years of modern dance gave way to an acceptance of the view that ballet represents a superb means of training and developing the body for dance. But this was much later.

What happened at the beginning? Isadora Duncan is usually referred to as the liberating spirit that gave expression to modern

[2] Merce Cunningham, "The Function of a Technique for Dance," in *The Dance Has Many Faces*, Walter Sorell, ed. (New York: World Publishing Co., 1951), pp. 250–51.

dance. Actually, there were a number of other rebels and pioneers who preceded her, and who helped to shape the form of dance that was to come. Among these were Émile Jaques-Dalcroze, François Delsarte, and Loie Fuller.

François Delsarte, a French teacher of music and acting, who lived from 1811 to 1871, had a remarkable influence not only on the actors of his time whom he taught, but also on Ruth St. Denis, Ted Shawn, and a generation of 20th-century German and Central European dancers. Delsarte sought to develop a logical system of expressive movement and gesture; in so doing he spent his life in observing people in a variety of circumstances, and particularly under stress:

> He even visited morgues and mines, after an explosion, to watch . . . how the bereaved betrayed their grief. From behind bushes in parks he studied children at play and . . . analyzed the differences in movement behavior between the attendants who loved children and those who did not . . . with cold scientific detachment he peered at humanity unconsciously registering its emotions and made copious notes . . . .[3]

Some of the great actors of his day were disciples of Delsarte. He developed a complex system of gesture, based on three zones of the body and of human expression. These were: *mental,* or *intellectual* (head and neck); *emotional* and *spiritual* (torso and arms); and *physical* (lower trunk and legs). In turn, each of these zones had three subdivisions, which were further divided in terms of function. The Delsartian method had nine fundamental laws of gesture, on which were based exercises to develop freedom and relaxation of every part of the body, and to serve as a discipline for learning gesture and pantomime.

Delsarte also developed a system of dividing movement into three majors orders, or types. These were "oppositions," "parallelisms," and "successions," terms which were widely used in modern dance vocabulary many decades later, as they had been transmitted to German modern dancers by Rudolf von Laban, who studied with a pupil of Delsarte. In addition, Ruth St. Denis and Ted Shawn made use of the Delsarte system by having one of his disciples teach in their school. Delsarte's influence was widely felt in the latter half of the 19th century in American schools, where aesthetic dance, based on a sort of modified ballet that made extensive use of his theories and gesture language, was taught as part of physical education.

[3] Margaret Lloyd, *The Borzoi Book of Modern Dance* (New York: Alfred A. Knopf, Inc., 1949), p. 29.

It was Shawn's view that Delsarte's teaching was the first to reveal what modern dancers call "tension and relaxation" or "contraction and release"; thus, it was he who laid the foundation for the German modern dance which, in turn, strongly influenced the American modern dance.[4]

Émile Jaques-Dalcroze, a Swiss music teacher and composer who was born in 1865 and continued to have a major influence on the teaching of music and dance from the late 19th century well into the 20th century, was a professor of harmony at Geneva, who developed a concern over the lack of expressiveness on the part of many music students. He determined to make use of physical movements to accentuate rhythmic awareness and musical creativity. He created a system of bodily exercises and approaches to the teaching of music and movement which, while not intended for theatrical purposes, strongly influenced many dancers and choreographers.[5]

In 1910, a college for instruction in the Dalcroze method was built in Hellerau, Germany, where Serge Diaghileff observed his students in action. One of Dalcroze's pupils, Miriam Rambach, who later became known in England as Marie Rambert, was assigned to teach the members of Diaghileff's ballet company; in particular, Vaslav Nijinsky was much influenced by the Dalcroze approach, and revealed its effect in his own dancing and choreography. A number of other European and Eastern dancers were disciples of Dalcroze, who continued through the years to teach in Austria. Many of the 3000 pupils he graduated scattered throughout the world, and taught the Dalcroze method in America, England, France, Sweden, and other lands—usually under the name "eurhythmics." Stated simply, his technique provided a basis for strengthening the dancer's or musician's sense of rhythmic and harmonic structure, through a progressive system of "music visualization" and other exercises.

Among Dalcroze's other influential pupils were Hanya Holm, Kurt Jooss, Ruth St. Denis, and Mary Wigman—either through his personal teaching, or through his disciples and writings.

Of the many other dancers who performed in the years preceding Isadora Duncan, who were not within the mainstream of the ballet idiom, one of the most unusual was an American performer, Loie Fuller, who lived from 1862 to 1928. In a sense, she provided a model for Isadora Duncan, as an independent performer with

[4] Ted Shawn, *Dance We Must* (London: Dennis Dobson, Ltd., 1946), pp. 48–49.
[5] Lincoln Kirstein, *Dance: A Short History of Classic Theatrical Dancing* (New York: G. P. Putnam's Sons, 1935), p. 286.

great popularity who found her audiences chiefly in Europe. However, the nature of Fuller's dance was far different from that of Duncan.

There were a number of popular dancers (known as "skirt dancers") in this period, who performed in American and English music halls, where variety performances were presented. Skirt dancing consisted of graceful, somewhat balletic steps, without toe dancing or lifts; the performers rustled extremely full skirts. Loie Fuller's contribution at the outset was to swath herself in yards of luminous veils; gradually she extended this to the point where she was dancing with 100 yards or more of diaphanous fabric which she manipulated with sticks under the play of colored lights. By the time she was well embarked on her career, electric lights had been invented, and she experimented widely with the use of moving lanterns of colored glass.

Although Fuller was said to be a mediocre dancer, who had had less than half a dozen dancing lessons in her life, the effect she created was spectacular. One description from a writer of the time tells how one could see,

> . . . at the back of the darkened stage, the indistinct form of a woman clad in a confused mass of drapery. Suddenly, a stream of light issued apparently from the woman herself, while around her the folds of gauze rose and fell in phosphorescent waves, which seemed to have assumed, one knows not how, a subtle materiality, taking the form of a golden drinking cup, a magnificent lily, or a huge glistening moth . . . .[6]

Isadora Duncan herself met Fuller in Berlin, and was much impressed by the magic that had been wrought with the help of colored lights, fabrics, glass mirrors underfoot, luminescent cloth, and skilled electricians:

> Before our very eyes she turned to many colored, shining orchids, to a wavering, flowing sea flower, and at length to a spiral-like lily, all magic of Merlin, the sorcery of light, color, flowing form. What an extraordinary genius![7]

Perhaps the lesson that Loie Fuller taught was that a single person dancing on the stage could create an image capable of gripping and moving a huge audience—and this without reliance on the traditional classic dance technique that heretofore was the weapon of star ballerinas who captured the public's adoration.

---

[6] Clare de Morinni, "Loie Fuller, The Fairy of Light," in *Chronicles of the American Dance*, Paul Magriel, ed. (New York: Henry Holt and Company, 1948), p. 209.

[7] Isadora Duncan, quoted in Kirstein, *op. cit.*, p. 268.

Isadora Duncan in *La Marseillaise*. Photograph by Arnold Genthe, 1916.

Isadora Duncan was to demonstrate the same effect—but she accomplished it without the aid of the brilliant stage effects that Fuller used. Her only instruments were her body and the power of her expressive personality.

Isadora Duncan was born in San Francisco, California. Her family was an artistic one; her mother taught music, and the young girl studied ballet as a child, but soon broke away from the classic dance form, which did not suit her spirit. Years later, she was to write about what she felt was the artificial idiom of ballet:

> The whole tendency of this training seems to be to separate the gymnastic movements of the body completely from the mind. The mind, on the contrary, can only suffer in aloofness from this rigorous muscular discipline. This is just the opposite from all the theories on which I founded my school, by which the body becomes transparent and is a medium for the mind and spirit.[8]

[8] *Ibid.*, p. 271.

At an early age, Isadora began to give dancing lessons. At the age of eighteen, she left for Chicago; then she gave concerts in New York at the Carnegie Hall Studios. In 1899, she danced in London and Paris, and began to develop an interest in Greek vases and statuary. Her fame began to spread; she danced in Budapest, Berlin, Italy, Greece, and then Russia, where she met Diaghileff and Stanislavsky and visited the Imperial Ballet School. Her first appearance in Russia, in 1905, stimulated a controversy between the traditional balletomanes and critics and those who proposed reform of the ballet. She is believed to have influenced Fokine strongly; indeed, throughout her career, dramatists, directors, painters, composers, all were said to have been moved and strongly affected in their own experimentation by Isadora.

There was nothing theatrical about her performance, in the sense of characterization, telling a story, or exhibiting brilliant dance technique. Instead, it was an art of personal expression, in which Isadora threw away the conventional corsets, ballet slippers, and tutus of the period, and danced barefooted and bare-legged in a filmy, short Greek tunic. She performed moderate lifts and leaps; ran, skipped. Her arms were often extended in an upsoaring gesture, never held in a fixed or formalized way; her neck and face were mobile and expressive. Overall, her movement was simple, but heroic:

> She reclined rather than fell; she kneeled to rise again; her movements were mainly upspringing. Although she vitalized the dance, gave it new weight and force, it did not have the dynamic range or accent of today's. It was more a harmonious plasticity, swinging, swaying, flowing rhythms, with no marked dissonances, no little vibratory movements . . . .[9]

The quality of Isadora's dance is well described in her own writing. She had a personal vision of America dancing, in which she saw

> . . . great strides, leaps and bounds, lifted forehead and farflung arms, dancing the language of our pioneers, the fortitude of our heroes, the justice, kindness, purity of our women and through it all the inspired love and tenderness of our mothers, that will be America dancing . . . .[10]

She danced to the accompaniment of great musical works of the time, and of earlier periods—including many selections which had never been considered works that were suitable for

[9] Lloyd, *op. cit.*, p. 4.
[10] Isadora Duncan, quoted in Walter Terry, *The Dance in America* (New York: Harper and Row, Publishers, 1956), p. 40.

dance. For over 25 years, she danced to music by Chopin—Mazurkas, Preludes, and Nocturnes, Ballades, Valses, and Polonaises. She used the operas of Gluck: *Orpheus et Euridice* and *Iphigenia in Aulis.* In 1904, she danced the Bachannal in Wagner's *Tannhauser* at Bayreuth; later, she was to perform to such powerful pieces as Wagner's *Forest Murmurs, Funeral March,* and *Ride of the Valkyrie.* She danced to three movements of Beethoven's *Seventh Symphony,* and in a later period to major works by Berlioz, Bach, Mozart, Scriabin, Rachmaninoff, Schubert, and Tchaikovsky.

She never did exactly the same work twice, and often improvised on the stage, as in her famous performances of *March Slav,* and the *Marseillaise,* at the time of World War I. Indeed, she had no system of dance as such, and no steps that she taught her own classes. Basically, she disapproved of schools, and would not teach her pupils to imitate her own dancing. Instead, she wanted to help them develop movements that would be their own.

Isadora continued to dance throughout North and South America and in Europe through the 1920s, until she was killed in a tragic automobile accident in Nice in 1927. Her life was marked by a number of tragedies and unhappy romances; indeed, she rejected the common morality of the time and led a tragic, unorthodox life.

What was Isadora's contribution to dance?

Certainly it was not in terms of technique or of a conscious system of dance. For several decades after her death, those who had performed in her group or studied with her, called themselves Duncan dancers. However, Kirstein refers to these "pitiful, aspiring devotees" of her art as giving recitals "which were only shadows of her violent impulse." Certainly, the interpretive dancing that flooded the country in the United States was due partly to her influence; however, it was also linked to the so-called aesthetic dance which was widely found in the late 1800s, for which she was not responsible.

Probably Isadora's foremost achievement was to cast dance in a new light. It was now seen primarily as a means of personal expression, as a powerful and emotional stage art, and as something which might be freed from the rigid classical technique and stereotyped performance found in the ballet of the day. While she had no direct successors, she set the stage for the next great dance artists who were to come along—Ruth St. Denis and Ted Shawn.

Born in New Jersey in 1877, Ruth St. Denis had little early dance training. It is said that she took only three lessons from Madame Bonfanti, the Italian ballerina who had been a star of *The Black Crook,* decades before. However, she was greatly inter-

Ruth St. Denis (center) in *Egypta*. Photograph by Sarony, New York, 1910. Denishawn Collection.

ested in the theater and, after touring as an actress, skirt dancer, and toe dancer, began in 1904 to take an interest in Egyptian dance art. She created what was first an Egyptian, and then a Hindu dance production—the ballet *Radha*—in 1906. Like her other works in this vein, it was authentically costumed, set to music that was composed with an Oriental flavor, but played with Western instruments. *Radha* was instantly popular, and St. Denis toured with it on the vaudeville circuit in the United States, the British Isles, and Europe. Gradually she composed other numbers, all on exotic themes: *The Nautch Dance*, *The Yogi*, and *O-Mika*, based on the Japanese Noh drama form. Audiences appreciated the colorful theatricality of her work, which she attributed in part to Loie Fuller, saying:

> She brought appurtenances—lights and veils—to dance and where would I be, pray, without my lights? where would Isadora have been without her simple lighting effects? where would the theatre dancers of today find themselves without Loie's magnificent contributions?[11]

She was greatly influenced too by the great spiritual quality and emotional force of Isadora Duncan, whom she had seen dance

[11] Walter Terry, "The Legacy of Isadora Duncan and Ruth St. Denis," in *Dance Perspectives No. 5*, 1959, p. 30.

in London in about 1900. Later she was to refer to Duncan as having a divine inheritance from ancient Greece, and as being "the embodiment of cosmic rhythm."

In 1914, Ruth St. Denis married Ted Shawn, who became her partner, and thus Denishawn was founded. Shawn had been born in Kansas City, Missouri, in 1891, and grew up in Denver where he entered college to study for the ministry. He was struck by diphtheria, was slightly paralyzed, and took up the study of dance as remedial exercise. Entering the field professionally, he studied ballet, opened a dancing school in Los Angeles, and made an early motion picture of dance. While touring the country he met Ruth St. Denis, and their marriage followed shortly.

These two great individualists remained together as a team until 1932. In that time, they organized 13 major tours of the country, helping to bring about a recognition of the American dance as an independent art form and, in effect, creating a new audience for dance among middle-class theater-goers who heretofore had seen only the pioneering Diaghileff tours. In addition to their tours, St. Denis and Shawn founded schools, first in Los Angeles and then in New York; there were a number of other branches and teachers of the Denishawn method in smaller cities throughout the country.

After they separated, Shawn formed his famous men's group, which toured the United States for several years; in addition, he founded and has since been the director of the Jacob's Pillow School of Dance in Lee, Massachusetts. Ruth St. Denis, who had by this time become known as the First Lady of American Dance, continued to run Denishawn House in New York City for a number of years. Later, in semi-retirement, she continued to experiment with, and to perform works based on a linkage of dance and other related arts with religious service; typically, at lecture-demonstrations, she would perform Psalms using the Indian *mudras*, or gesture language.

What were the great contributions of Ruth St. Denis and Ted Shawn?

First, St. Denis's dance was filled with theatrical appeal; she made great use of color, lighting, scenery, and exotic (and often abbreviated) costuming. She had a great preoccupation with religious themes and mysticism and, although her dance movement in ethnic-based works was not traditional in a true sense, nonetheless it gave a more accurate picture of authentic dance styles of exotic lands than ballet had ever done. St. Denis's movement skills were not highly developed; her technique tended to be largely a matter of "plastiques and poses, of manipulation of scarves

Ted Shawn and his male dancers in *Kinetic Molpai*. Photograph by Shapiro, Pittsfield, Mass., 1936.

and draperies, in decorative costumes, all very pictorial, and all done with an air."[12]

St. Denis had a very personal gift for movement and a facility for improvisation. She also, although she denied being directly influenced by Dalcroze, developed a choreographic technique of "music visualization," under which each dancer followed a specific instrument in an orchestral score—much as Dalcroze had done years before. Her talents then, were based chiefly on an instinctive theatrical sense, a quality of religious mysticism, and a great sense of mission, in terms of bringing dance to the American people that would be worthy of them.

Ted Shawn, in contrast, was less mystic and more analytical. He had a considerable respect for technical training in dance, and made use, in the system that was taught in the Denishawn schools, of varied elements—a barefoot adaptation of classical ballet instruction, ethnic and folk dance steps and styles, Dalcroze training, and even the beginning German modern dance. In 1930, the first course in Wigman dance technique was sponsored in America by Denishawn. All of this was brought together, particularly in Shawn's men's company and then at Jacob's Pillow, in an eclectic, but vigorous and impressive style.

In addition to his concept of dance training, Shawn made the following important contributions:

[12] Lloyd, *op. cit.*, p. 25.

He focused on the need to develop male dancers and fought to obtain recognition for dancing as a worthy art for men, throughout the United States on the concert stage and in colleges and universities.

He began the practice of commissioning music especially for his original dance works; composers such as Charles Wakefield Cadman, Deems Taylor, and Vaughan Williams were among the contemporary musicians with whom he worked. In addition, Shawn was among the first to make use of such composers as Debussy, Scriabin, and Satie.

He made widespread use of themes related to Americana—the early pioneers, the Indians, the American Negro, and the Spanish Conquistador. *Xochitl*, Shawn's production on an Aztec theme, showed movement that was stylized in the manner of figures seen on ancient Mexican reliefs; both he and St. Denis did intensive research in preparation for their dances. Other compositions of Shawn's were less literal; two of his works, *Labor Symphony* and *Kinetic Molpai*, were vigorous, abstract representations of primitive forces and masculine vigor.

Shawn was a great crusader for dance. He wrote a number of widely read books, including *Fundamentals of a Dance Education* and *Dance We Must*, and taught at a number of colleges, including Springfield College and Peabody—thus helping to gain recognition for creative dance as an educative medium.

Before Denishawn, America had largely been a wilderness of dance art and dance appreciation, consisting of hoofers, skirt

Ruth St. Denis and Ted Shawn in *Siamese Ballet*. Photograph by Lou Goodale Bigelow, 1918–19. Denishawn Collection.

dancers, acrobatic dancers, and vaudevillians. The only seriously regarded dance was European, and the greatest of the American dancers, like Augusta Maywood or Isadora Duncan, spent the major part of their careers in Europe. Denishawn exerted a tremendous influence on the youth of America; it has been commented that it converted as many to this form of dance as Pavlova did for ballet.

A final major contribution of Denishawn was that it provided a training ground for the great modern dancers who were to follow. In Martin's view, modern dance was not so much an outgrowth of Denishawn as a rebellion against it. Martha Graham, Doris Humphrey, and Charles Weidman were all leading Denishawn dancers and were deeply influenced by the training and theatrical experience they received in the company. However, when their original ideas for choreography, and their drive to create independently, were stifled within the Denishawn framework, they declared their independence.

This, in the late 1920s, modern dance as such came into being.

Generally accepted as the greatest single figure in American modern dance, and the symbol of it in the popular mind, Martha Graham has been described by the ballet choreographer Agnes de Mille, her close personal friend, as probably the greatest American choreographer, and an international cultural influence in fields extending beyond her own. Particularly, she has been one of the few persons to create new forms of movement.

> Her invention is prodigious. Like Picasso's, her art has changed deeply in style and technique many times during her career. For every new work, there was not only a new design in steps, but a new concept in technique and dynamics, a restudying of the basis of movement . . . .[13]

A tenth-generation American of New England stock, Martha Graham was brought up in California, after having been born in Pennsylvania in about 1898. As a teen-ager, she saw Ruth St. Denis dance and was impressed by her; in 1916, she entered the Denishawn School as a student. Three years later, she joined the company, with the leading female role in *Xochitl*. For several years, she performed with St. Denis and Shawn, both in the United States and abroad, and studied intensively with Shawn. Then, in 1923, she struck out on her own, dancing in the Greenwich Village Follies, and then teaching dance at the Eastman School of Music, in Rochester.

[13] Agnes de Mille, *The Book of the Dance* (New York: Golden Press, 1963), p. 157.

Martha Graham in *Letter to the World*. Photograph by Barbara Morgan.

In 1926, when she offered her first dance concert in New York City, she embarked on a career of choreography and performance that has been unmatched. During the period between 1926 and 1949, she composed over 100 dances, many of them full-scale theater pieces. She has covered a tremendously wide range of themes in her dances, frequently going through a period when a particular kind of subject matter served to preoccupy her for several works, until she had explored it thoroughly. Thus, the themes dealt with in her earlier years included the following: American Indian and primitive ritual, American pioneers, tragicomedy, Greek mythology, and both narrative and abstract works dealing with psychological insights and conflicts.

None of her dances can truthfully be assigned to just one thematic category; they are all extremely complex in terms of symbolic meaning, psychological implications, and literary illusion. As a creator of dance, Graham has been unfailingly experimental, uncompromising, often disturbing, and, to the uninitiated audience, frequently the source of bewilderment and angry resistance. One can imagine the reaction of students, faculty, and parents in a college auditorium in the 1940s, watching the following passage from *Cave of the Heart*, based on the Medea legend. Lloyd writes:

> The tension is terrific. There are spastic jerks and tremblings throughout the body. Tight, nervous, jiggling motions continue relentlessly in telegraphic dots and dashes . . . she walks about on her knees, folding in the lower half of her leg as she progresses . . . to the basin where stands the coppery-golden tree, to pick up the death-wreath for her rival; and to place in her bosom the symbol of the serpent heart, the red strip she is later to unroll for a fetish dance in an ecstasy of vengeance. A quieter passage is her stately entrance, dragging the dead body of the Victim in the folds of a black funeral cloth . . . the Adventurer falls upon the body of his beloved, and they lie together, limbs entwined in the death embrace . . . .[14]

Yet, with it all, critics and fellow choreographers deny that she is deliberately seeking to puzzle or to horrify the audience. Terry suggests that she is concerned with the universality of human emotions and behavior, and with the revelation of human character. He writes:

> Her dance purpose is to give physical substance to things felt, to lamentation, to celebration, to hate, to passion, to the experience of "frontier," to bigotry, to . . . underlying passions, dreams, fears and tragedies . . . . Far from being a cultist or an obscurist, she endeavors to remove the cloak of obscurity from the purposes and aspects of human behavior and to reveal in solid dance architecture the architecture of the inner man.[15]

In terms of technique, Graham has always avoided having a single set vocabulary or system of dance movement. She has certain movement principles and sequential techniques for the development of the body to the full range of its potential. These principles and techniques were in complete opposition to the serene and smooth control characteristic of classic ballet, in which all the strain, effort or uncertainty of the body is hidden. Instead, in Graham's technique, the "engineering, the effort" are revealed. "She threw aside all the traditional steps and techniques of ballet, the straight long leg, the pointed toe, the quiet even hips, the flexed foot, the relaxed hand; she stressed continuous unfolding movement from a central core . . . but added spasm and resistance . . . she made the floor a part of gesture; invented many beautiful falls and recoveries from the ground; she discovered a whole technique of balancing on bent knees, with her thighs as a hinge

[14] Lloyd, *op. cit.*, pp. 40–41.
[15] Walter Terry, "Martha Graham," in Anatole Chujoy, *The Dance Encyclopedia* (New York: A. S. Barnes & Co., 1949), p. 216.

and the spine cantilevered and suspended . . . she invented turns with a changing and swinging axis . . . ."[16]

In terms of music, Graham has commissioned many of the leading modern composers to write music for her, including, in an early period, many pieces by Louis Horst, Lehman Engel, and Wallingford Riegger, and, in a somewhat later period, Samuel Barber, Gian Carlo Menotti, Norman Dello Joio, William Schuman, Robert Starer, and Carlos Surinach. She has also danced to classical works by Cesar Franck, Gluck, Mendelssohn, Debussy, Bach, and Handel, among many others. In addition to using orchestral music, she has danced just to the spoken word, and to a variety of forms of accompaniment in between. Many of the musical works composed for Graham's dances have been recognized as outstanding contemporary compositions in their own right, such as Copland's "Appalachian Spring."

Similarly, she has set a whole fashion with respect to stage design and costuming through her own brilliantly imaginative costume designs and those of Edythe Gilfond, as well as by having leading modern artists and sculptors, such as Rouben Ter-Arutunian, Isamu Noguchi, Jean Rosenthal, Oliver Smith, and Arch Lauterer, design her sets for her. Graham has introduced a number of staging techniques that are now widely used: symbolic props and sets; the use of mobile scenery; the use of sculpturally designed props as a fully integrated part of the movement design of the dance work.

Most of the leading modern dancers of the 1930s and 1940s were Graham dancers—Erick Hawkins, Merce Cunningham, Jane Dudley, Sophie Maslow, May O'Donnell, Jean Erdman, Dorothy Bird, Mark Ryder, and many others. In more recent years, the leading roles have been taken by Bertram Ross, Helen McGehee, Ethel Winter, Matt Turney, Linda Hodes, Yuriko, Mary Hinkson, Robert Cohan, David Wood—all of them superb dancers of outstanding physical presence—many of them outstanding teachers or choreographers as well. One of Martha Graham's great contributions to the American modern dance was that she was the first to regularly use Negroes and Orientals in her company, in contrast to earlier companies which had established a rigid color line.

Through the 1950s and 1960s, Graham has continued to compose and present a number of major works of the American dance theatre—*Judith* (1950), *The Triumph of Saint Joan* (1951), both great solo performances; *Seraphic Dialogue* (a 1955 larger version of *The*

[16] De Mille, *op. cit.*, pp. 157–58.

Triumph of Saint Joan); *Embattled Garden* (1958); *Phaedra* (1962), and too many other critical triumphs to enumerate. Through this period too, she continued to operate her school in New York City, to offer special short-term courses for teachers, to present master courses at Connecticut College, and to tour both the United States and Europe to overwhelming acclaim.

Having been in her earlier years a controversial figure, because of her searching experimentation in modern dance choreography, Martha Graham today is so widely known and accepted that, if anything, she is regarded by many as traditional—as part of the "establishment." Nonetheless, it would be difficult to conceive of any force more vital to the creative arts on the American scene than she continues to be. Emily Coleman sums up her impact:

> How is one to say how many dancers, choreographers, actors and directors, have reflected in their own work the impact of Miss Graham's incandescent intensity on the stage? The precise degree of coloration may be impossible to gauge, but it is assuredly present. "Martha Graham is not only a great dancer," says Katharine Cornell. "She is also a great actress. She is one of the two or three great American creative artists in all fields.[17]

During the 1930s and 1940s, the other American modern dancer whose work was regarded as comparable to that of Martha Graham was Doris Humphrey. Born about 1895 and, like Graham, of New England ancestry, Doris Humphrey attended the Parker School in Chicago. There she received early training from Mary Wood Hinman, a well-known dance educator of that period, in ballroom, clog, folk, and aesthetic dance. Later, she studied ballet, and began to perform semiprofessionally, as well as to teach dance at summer workshops and in classes that she organized herself in Oak Park. In 1917, at Mary Wood Hinman's suggestion, she went out to Los Angeles to study with Ruth St. Denis and Denishawn. Shortly after, she joined the Denishawn company, and danced in many of its leading roles in tours throughout the United States and a number of Oriental countries. In 1928, she and Charles Weidman, with whom she had been working closely, left Denishawn and founded a school and small performing company in New York.

From that time until 1945, when she retired as a dancer because of arthritis of the hip, Humphrey was active as a dancer, choreographer, and teacher who was extremely influential in the development of dance in education in the United States. She was

[17] Emily Coleman, "Martha Graham Still Leaps Forward," *New York Times Magazine*, April 9, 1961, p. 44.

Humphrey-Weidman group in *The Shakers*. Photograph by Barbara Morgan, about 1941.

considered to be one of the great native choreographers of the United States. Commenting that her dance style was based on the "pseudo-Greek" approach of Denishawn, using light, fleet foot movements, and accompanied by a wide variety of music and expressive sounds, de Mille describes her impact as being more from composition and teaching than from technical development. She is considered to have been one of the greatest teachers of choreography as a fine art; she had the gift of releasing, rather than cramping, creativity.[18]

Her major works, some of which have been revived in recent years, included: *Air for the G String* (1928); *Drama of Motion* (1930); *Dance of the Chosen* (later named *The Shakers*) (1931); *New Dance Trilogy—New Dance, Theatre Piece, With My Red Fires* (1935–36); *Passacaglia in C Minor* (1938); *Song of the West* (1940); *El Salon Mexico* (1943); and *Inquest* (1944). Retiring as a dancer in 1945, she continued to choreograph a number of major works for José Limón and his company, including *The Story of Mankind* and *Lament for Ignacio Sánchez Mejías* (1946); *Night Spell* (1951); and

[18] De Mille, *op. cit.*, p. 162.

Ritmo Jondo (1953). During this period, while serving as artistic director of the José Limón Company, she also served on the faculty of the Connecticut College School of Dance and the Dance Department of the Juilliard School of Music in New York. A number of other major compositions were commissioned especially for the American Dance Festival in New London and the Juilliard Dance Theater. In 1958 she died, leaving a final unfinished dance work, *Brandenburg Concerto No. 4*, to be completed by Ruth Currier, and a book on choreography, *The Art of Making Dances*, to be published posthumously.

While Doris Humphrey's work was often highly moving, she tended to be less concerned with dramatic representation than with an abstract evocation of mood. She studied movement intensely for years, and developed a personal theory of dance movement as representing an arc between the pull of gravity and equilibrium—between fall and recovery.

She was gifted as a choreographer both in small groupings and in working with large-scale companies; her work ranged from a satirical comment on humanity and its foibles in *Theater Piece* or *Race of Life*, to a serene and abstract design in *Passacaglia*. Both through her own work and as choreographer and artistic director for José Limón, Doris Humphrey made a major contribution to the American dance theater.

Closely allied to Doris Humphrey during much of her career, particularly during its early period, was Charles Weidman. Born in Lincoln, Nebraska, in 1901, he joined the Denishawn school and company in 1920. His gift for pantomime soon became apparent, and he was recognized as the leading male dance comic and satirist of his day. Doris Humphrey was his first teacher, but they soon became co-performers on the stage. After touring with Denishawn for eight years, Weidman left the company and established a school and performing group with Doris Humphrey in New York in 1928. They danced in a number of works together through the years, and choreographed for each other. Weidman's most famous pieces were: *The Happy Hypocrite, Candide, Atavisms, Flickers, And Daddy Was a Fireman*, and *House Divided*, in which he depicted Abraham Lincoln during the Civil War.

Weidman staged the dances for a number of major Broadway musical shows, as well as separate dance revues. He taught at Bennington and a number of other colleges, was influential in training many dance educators, and numbered among his pupils such well-known performers as José Limón, Sybil Shearer, Jack Cole, and Peter Hamilton. His greatest gift was for narrative pantomime. Extremely inventive, he created movement that was fragmentary, mercurial, comic—making use of abrupt changes of tempo, rhythm, and dynamics. Lloyd writes:

> He jested in stroke and curlicue, lampooning right and left with his pencil-slim body, making jokes with his fingers and witty observations with his bare toes . . . . He could always be counted on to do the unexpected thing. The movement was choppy on the surface, but underneath flowed the current of human feeling; sometimes the surface, too, was smooth with serious intent.[19]

In such a work as *Lynchtown*, his group choreography had dramatic strength and a charged atmosphere that created a powerful effect; however, most of his work tended to be light, humorous, and entertaining, rather than deeply moving. Following his 20 years spent as a collaborator with Doris Humphrey, Weidman continued to perform with his own small company and to teach at a number of universities. In the mid-1960s, he established, with Mikhail Santaro, in New York City, the Expression of Two Arts Theater, which gives periodic performances demonstrating the linkage of the graphic and dance arts.

Another major influence on the developing modern dance came about through the work of two Europeans, Rudolf von Laban and Mary Wigman.

Laban was a Hungarian-born scholar who had studied painting in Munich and dancing in Paris, but whose major contribution was as a theoretician of dance and human movement. Beginning in the first years of the present century, he worked on experiments exploring the nature of human movement, and on a systematic analysis of so-called plastic rhythm. As early as 1910, in Munich, his first movement-choirs performed dancing for recreation. He was successful in developing huge civic festivals; throughout his life, he was concerned with the nature of work movements and the effective utilization of effort in labor. After directing his own dance company, which performed a number of experimental works, Laban became Ballet Master of the State Theater in Berlin during the 1920s. However, his most notable work was not in choreography, but in terms of his analysis of the physical laws governing dance movement, and the system of training for dance that he developed with his pupil and collaborator, Kurt Jooss.

According to his theory of *eukinetics*, all movement may be divided into two major categories: "outgoing" and "incoming." Laban developed a number of theories relating to *centrifugal* movement (movement originating in the center of the body and radiating or spreading out to the periphery) and *peripheral* movement

[19] Lloyd, *op. cit.*, p. 89.

(beginning with the extremities and moving to the center of the body). He carefully analyzed movement as to intensity, speed, and direction, making use of the object known as the *icosahedron*, the twenty-faced geometrical form which is a midpoint between a cube and a sphere. The essential concept of the icosahedron was that man's movements are both spherical and related to the three dimensions of space which are represented by the cube. Thus, movement takes place in three dimensions, and also on diagonals and inclines, limited only by the anatomical possibilities of the body; Laban used the imaginary points in space dictated by the icosahedron to develop a complicated movement scale that provided a systematic basis for dance training.

Laban also was known for his development of the movement-choir, a form of mass gymnastics somewhat similar to Dalcroze's music visualization, but with a greater degree of aesthetic purpose and emotional content than was found in Dalcroze's system. Following the Nazi takeover of Germany, Laban went to England, where he began an Art of Movement Guild. There, he had a major impact on the theory and practice of elementary education and physical education. Bruce writes:

> . . . his philosophy has impregnated the teaching of physical educa-
> tion, particularly as far as women are concerned. Laban's work has
> been taken most directly into the teaching of modern educational
> dance or free dance and dance drama as we see it in many schools
> and training colleges. Indirectly, his theories have become the basis
> of schemes of physical education, and have replaced to a great extent,
> in women's work especially, the anatomical and physiological
> approach which existed previously.[20]

Laban's major contribution has been his system of dance notation, called originally *kinetographie*, and now known as *Labanotation*. Of the many types of notation that have been proposed, this is today the best known and most widely used throughout the world.

Kurt Jooss, a German choreographer and dancer, who studied in Paris and Vienna and under Laban at the National Theater in Mannheim in 1921, later became his assistant and principal dancer. Jooss was supervisor of the dance group in the Essen Opera House and other German companies, and later, founded his own Jooss Ballet. However, having worked closely with Laban, Jooss had a concept of ballet that was far from the traditional classic style; in such experimental works as his famous *The Green Table*, the quality of the movement and choreography was very much like that of the beginning modern dance of the period.

[20] V. Bruce, *Dance and Dance Drama in Education* (London: Pergamon Press, 1965), p. 4.

The most influential of Laban's pupils and co-workers, however, was the German dancer, choreographer, and teacher, Mary
Wigman.

Mary Wigman is widely regarded as having been one of the
great germinal forces underlying the development of modern dance
in the 1920s. Although all her teaching was done in Europe, she
exerted tremendous influence in America through her three tours
of the United States in the early 1930s and through the many
American dancers who came to study with her in Dresden—as
well as through the work of her disciples. In terms of a basic philosophy of dance, use of movement and space, teaching ideology,
and the content of her dances, she was unique.

Wigman, who was born in 1886, and who continued to teach
in Germany when she was well into her seventies, studied with
Dalcroze at Hellerau and absorbed much of his teaching, although
she rejected his primary emphasis on musical elements. She next
studied under Laban, and was his teaching assistant in Zurich,
Switzerland, during World War I. While she absorbed much of
his intellectual viewpoint toward movement, her own approach
was a less systematic and more emotional one. Like Laban, she
rejected the vocabulary of movement as well as the total artistic
viewpoint of classic ballet; her approach to dance, in her first
performances in 1919, was almost acrobatic. In part, this was an
outcome of the environment in which she worked. Germany had
never had as strong a ballet movement as other European coun-

Mary Wigman in *Dance of
Silence* from the dance cycle *Autumnal Dances*. Photograph by S.
Enkelman, Berlin-Charlottenburg,
1937.

tries, and was receptive to new forms of art that were revolutionary in their approach, in the tortured years of inflation and political and spiritual turmoil following World War I. In such a setting, Wigman's radical new approach to dance found a welcome audience.

By 1926, she had formed a major school in Dresden, as well as lesser schools elsewhere, and had developed a performing group which became widely known. Her choreography tended toward full-length works, or "dance cycles," that were concerned with fundamental human emotions, superstitions, or relationships. When she performed in the United States in 1931 and 1932, she showed fragments of these larger works, performed by herself alone, without scenery and often without music. They had such titles as *Summer Dance, Witch Dance, Storm Song, Dream Image, Dance of Sorrow, Dance for the Earth, Lament, Death Call,* and *Dance into Death.* These were drawn from larger cycles, including *Visions, Sacrifice,* and *The Way.* In 1933 she appeared in the United States with her twelve-member company (all women) and American audiences had a fuller look at her art.

Her other works included a major antiwar statement in *Totenmal,* performed in Munich in 1930, and such later suites or cycles as *Woman Dances, Autumnal Dances,* and *Bright Queen* and *Dark Queen.* During World War II, Wigman's career was suspended; however after 1945 she resumed her teaching and choreography on a reduced scale in Leipzig. There, she produced Gluck's *Orpheus* as a dance-drama in 1947. In the years that followed, she taught in Leipzig and at a school in West Berlin, and choreographed for the Municipal Opera in Berlin and the National Theater in Mannheim.

What was the essence of Wigman's dance?

First, in terms of the content of her works, she was deeply concerned with primitive and symbolic themes, treated in a mystical and often grotesque manner; she is said to have had a typically Teutonic preoccupation with death and to have used it constantly as a symbol in her dances. Her general orientation was to deal not with intensely individual problems, but rather with the universal elements of life. The whole approach was highly mystical and evocative of feeling. Lloyd writes:

> . . . it was something primordial, something that dug deep into forgotten roots, an almost atavistic approach to man in relation to his universe, a return to the primitive through layers of civilization. It was something that stirred distant reverberations of things long past, something inexplicable, truly unutterable in words . . . .[21]

[21] Lloyd, *op. cit.,* p. 15.

In movement, the use of music, and staging, Wigman's approach was unique for her time. She had a tremendous range of movement, rejecting no possible physical expression, provided that it served her choreographic purpose. Her actions were described as "predominantly low-keyed." She tended to kneel, crouch, crawl, and creep; her head was often downcast, and the arms were rarely lifted high. She avoided all balletic movements and never danced on her toes, although she did use the turned-out knee and foot for the sake of balance.

Wigman's approach to music differed radically from that of Isadora Duncan's, in that Duncan had used music as a primary source of inspiration, whereas Wigman often danced without music, or with a simple melodic line of a woodwind instrument, or with primitive percussion accompaniment. She made much use of such Oriental instruments as Hindu drums and Balinese gongs, sometimes held in the dancer's hand. Dance and accompaniment were not composed separately, but developed together in an organic fashion.

In terms of staging, the total visual effect of Wigman's dance was stark, harsh, and gloomy. Many saw it as ugly and disturbing. Critics referred to her costuming as distressing, but original, and certainly successful in conveying the mood she sought. Costumes were simple, somewhat Asian or primitive in appearance, and usually made from dark, rough fabrics. She used platforms as part of her staging; her lighting was simple and stage effects in general, other than what could be created by the dancers, had little impor-

Mary Wigman Dance Group in *Der Weg*, about 1932. Hanya Holm Collection.

tance for her. Far more crucial was her sense of space as a vital element in staging and performance. Space, to Wigman, was not simply a vacuum to be filled, or an area in which the dancer moved. Instead, it was a force that was tangible—almost like water, through which the dancer must swim. She constantly saw it as a element which offered resistance to the dancer; in a sense, it represented the universe in which the dancer struggled.

Many critics and audiences did not readily accept Wigman's viewpoint.

Kirstein comments that although her influence on contemporary dancers was powerful, she had little to offer those who were primarily interested in theatrical dancing, or who wished to demonstrate dramatic ideas "larger than their own frustration." Describing her instructional system as basic and semiacrobatic, he sharply criticizes her custom of releasing students in the studio to freely improvise movements such as joy, terror, or grief, to percussive accompaniment. Unlike the traditional method of ballet instruction, he sees it as neither "brilliant, precise nor capable of repetition." Finally, Kirstein suggests that Wigman's dance was based on the era's "loose thinking" on progressive education and adolescent self-expression.[22]

Nonetheless, Wigman's impact was a major one. She broadened the scope of dance concern and represented a major influence on beginning modern dancers in America, who were operating in an educational and intellectual climate which *did* stress a growing concern with self-expression and a psychologically oriented creativity. In her work with such European dancers as Kurt Jooss and Harald Kreutzberg, a brilliant mime, she strongly influenced a number of performers who were essentially balletic. And finally, in her major disciple, Hanya Holm, she exercised a strong effect on the American dance scene that was to continue to the present day in those who were influenced by Holm.

Hanya Holm came to this country in 1931 to open a branch of the Wigman School here. Originally, she had studied at the Dalcroze Institute, and had been a leading dancer with Wigman's original dance company during the 1920s. Later, she headed the faculty of the Wigman School in Dresden, and acted as assistant director and a leading dancer in Wigman's major work, *Totenmal.*

Holm remained in the United States, fusing Wigman's original theories with her own creative impulses, to develop a new dance art that was uniquely American in outlook. Her major compositions included *Trend, Dance Sonata, What Dreams May*

[22] Kirstein, *op. cit.,* pp. 306–7.

Hanya Holm Dance Group in *Dance of Work and Play*, performed at Bennington College. Photograph by Barbara Morgan, 1938.

Come, Tragic Exodus, and *The Golden Fleece*, which was filmed in 1941. As a choreographer she was extremely gifted; her works had a remarkable plastic quality and were marked by originality of staging and much technical excitement. Music is extremely important in her work, unlike Wigman's, and she has had such modern composers as Norman Lloyd, John Cage, and Roy Harris write for her.

While never an outstanding dancer herself, Holm is an unusually gifted teacher, who exposes her students to a logical and detailed development of technique, and to working in various planes, directions, dimensions, and extensions that reflect Laban's original thinking. She stresses the centrality of the body that makes possible unified and integrated movement. At Bennington, Juilliard, at her own school in New York City (in 1936, the original name of Wigman School was changed to the Hanya Holm School of Dance), and especially at Colorado College, where she has been in charge of a summer dance workshop for many years,

José Limón as the Moor in *The Moor's Pavane*. Photograph by Walter Strate.

Hanya Holm has had a strong influence on American dance educators. She is also one of the comparatively few modern dancers who have been successful on the Broadway stage; two of her best known shows were *Kiss Me, Kate*, and *My Fair Lady*.

There were a number of other major choreographers and dancers during this period, on the American concert stage. Of these, two stand out as being close to Graham, Humphrey, and Wigman in their creative stature: José Limón and Helen Tamiris.

José Limón, born in Mexico and brought up in California, is without question a towering figure in American modern dance. John Martin has called him "the greatest American male dancer in his field," and Walter Terry has referred to him as "without peer in his generation of men dancers."

From an early interest in painting and music, Limón turned to dance in 1928. He performed and choreographed during the 1930s, mostly for small groups. He joined the Humphrey-Weidman

Company, becoming the leading male dancer, save Weidman himself. After World War II, he formed his own company, with Doris Humphrey, who had just retired from active dancing, as his artistic director. The company was well received, presenting a number of major works to critical acclaim, and traveling on several tours of Europe and South America sponsored by the State Department. Limón's work includes the retelling of an ancient legend of the conquest of Mexico by Spain, *Malinche*, with music by Norman Lloyd; *The Moor's Pavane*, the story of Othello, set to music by Purcell; and *Missa Brevis*, to music by Kodály. His own dancing has been sombre, powerful, and majestic; even when past the age of highest capability, he has always commanded respect. A number of his best works have dealt with Spanish or Mexican themes; one of these was *Lament for Ignacio Sánchez Mejías*, choreographed by Doris Humphrey to a poem by Garcia Lorca, with music by Norman Lloyd. Other Limón Company works choreographed by Humphrey included *Day on Earth*, to music by Aaron Copland, *Ruins and Visits*, to music by Benjamin Britten, and *Night Spell*, to Priaulx Rainier's music.

Limón's company originally included Dorothy Bird and Beatrice Seckler; later dancers were Lucas Hoving, Betty Jones, Ruth Currier, and Pauline Koner, all of them outstanding choreographers and heading their own companies as well. In addition to performing, José Limón has been a gifted teacher at the Connecticut Summer School of the Dance, at his own studio in New York, and at the Juilliard School of the Dance.

Helen Tamiris was another leading modern dance figure during the 1930s and 1940s. Born of Russian parents on New York's East Side, she studied at the Henry Street Settlement House under Irene Lewisohn; in addition to interpretive dance, she had ballet training at the Metropolitan Opera Ballet school. She learned Italian ballet from Rosina Galli and Russian ballet from Michel Fokine. She danced for a period of time in Broadway revues and night clubs, and with the Metropolitan Opera as well, including performances abroad in Berlin and Paris. Then, in 1927, she began a career as a concert dancer. Her aim was to be a dancer of her age and country and she felt that ballet, ethnic dance, or even Duncan dance could not help her do this. Modern dance could, and this indeed, to her, was one of its purposes—to deal meaningfully with modern problems, to help move audiences to a stage of concern and readiness for action.

Thus, most of her choreography dealt with important social themes; the works had titles such as *Revolutionary March, Dance of the City, How Long Brethren, Songs of Protest*, and *Adelante*, based on the Spanish Civil War. They were dances of camaraderie, protest, and affirmation, closely linked to the strong left-wing movement of the time. Negro spirituals and Caribbean ceremonials were also an important part of her customary concert program. Tamiris was an effective organizer; she brought together a Dance Repertory Company in 1930 which included Martha Graham, Doris Humphrey, Charles Weidman and, in the following year, Agnes de Mille. While its program was successful and well received, the Repertory Company did not continue. Instead, Tamiris danced independently and later, in the early 1960s, formed the Tamiris-Nagrin Dance Company with her husband, Daniel Nagrin, who had been a featured dancer with her in concerts and nightclubs and a leading performer on the Broadway musical stage and on television. Tamiris, too, was active on the Broadway stage during her career; among the shows that she choreographed were *Annie Get Your Gun*, *Show Boat*, *Up in Central Park*, and *Inside U.S.A.*

In addition to her gifts as a dancer and choreographer, Tamiris was a strong force for the promotion of modern dance as a movement. She was one of the main organizers of the First National Dance Congress, first president of the American Dance Association, and influential in having dance made part of the Federal Theater Program of the Works Progress Administration during the late 1930s. Tamiris also was associated with the Group Theater in New York, where she taught movement to actors, and was influential in the Broadway theater of her period.

A number of other dancers, who had been leading performers with these choreographers in the early period of modern dance, became choreographers and well-known teachers themselves during the 1940s and 1950s. These include Jane Dudley, Sophie Maslow, and Bill Bales.

Jane Dudley had been a pupil of Hanya Holm and was a featured dancer in the Graham Company; one of her best-known roles was *Letter to the World*. Like Tamiris, much of her choreography was done to social themes; she also had a strong concern with folklore and jazz rhythms. Her best-known works included *Harmonica Breakdown*, *Adolescence*, *Short Story*, *American Morning*, *Swing Your Lady*, and *New World A-Coming*. There was much comedy and sheer animal spirit in her work. Like most of the dancers of her generation, she has continued to teach, at Teachers College, Columbia University, at Bennington College, and at the New Dance Group in New York.

Sophie Maslow studied at the Neighborhood Playhouse and with Irene Lewisohn at the Manhattan Opera Ballet School.

One of her best-known works was *Folksay*, done to verses from Carl Sandburg's "The People, Yes," interspersed with folk ballads and stories. She also composed *Inheritance, Partisan Journey, Champion*, and *Festival*, the last of which was later developed into a full-length work, *The Village I Knew*. All her dances are lyrical and expressive of human drives and conflicts, but are not sharply partisan as many of the earlier "social protest" dances were. She has continued to choreograph major works for public festival programs in New York City, and to teach extensively.

Bill Bales, the third member of what came to be known as the Dudley-Maslow-Bales Trio, which was closely associated with the New Dance Group in New York, attended the Carnegie Tech Drama School, and studied ballet and Dalcroze eurhythmics. After developing an interest in modern dance, he was encouraged by Martha Hill, a leading dance educator at Bennington and later at New York University and Juilliard, to study with Charles Weidman. He danced in the Humphrey-Weidman Company, and taught on the faculty at Bennington until 1967. He has been a guest artist with Hanya Holm, and has choreographed many solo works, as well as his featured roles in the major New Dance Group presentations. Most of his choreography is based on Spanish, Mexican, and Negro themes.

There have been many other dancers in the period prior to mid-century, including such figures as Jean Erdman, Eve Gentry, Nona Schurman, May O'Donnell, Pearl Lang, Pauline Koner, Lester Horton, Ruth Currier, Katherine Litz, Eleanor King, Talley Beatty, Katherine Dunham, Pearl Primus, Sybil Shearer, and many others. It is not possible to describe all of their careers even in brief, other than to say that they have in most cases continued to teach, choreograph, and perform in one form or another into the 1960s. In a later chapter, the careers of several dancer-choreographers whose work achieved a high peak of public acclaim in the years following the mid-century point, are presented. This section includes a number who were professionally active during the earlier period, such as Erick Hawkins, Merce Cunningham, and Alwin Nikolais, as well as a number of somewhat younger dancers like Paul Taylor and Alvin Ailey, whose works are prominent on the contemporary scene.

After half a century of development, what then was the state of modern dance in the early 1950s? First, it was clear that it was an American art. The impulses that had given birth to Mary Wigman and other European experimenters were spent, and now the United States was the scene of contemporary dance activity.

Those Europeans who wished to study modern dance came here, to the studios of the major modern dancers, or to the colleges that offered specialized dance programs.

It was clear that what had begun as the creative expression of a comparatively few gifted individuals, who operated independently but were able to reach fairly large audiences through their tours and theater presentations, had changed considerably. Now there were many choreographers and many small companies throughout the country—located chiefly in the large cities where the cultural arts tended to find a sympathetic audience, and also in many university communities. For, particularly during the 1930s and 1940s, modern dance had swept through colleges and universities, exciting the interest not only of physical education departments—which usually placed dance in the hands of educators who had a special interest but often a limited background in dance—and also of others in the arts. There was a climate of comradeship among fine and graphic artists, stage people, poets, musicians, and dancers. All the arts were seen as having certain common elements, and efforts were made to link them in common courses combining the arts and humanities, and arts festivals.

However, the great surge of creativity and popular enthusiasm about modern dance was over. It was apparent that, although probably hundreds of thousands of college students—mostly women—had been exposed to modern dance over a period of three decades, this had not succeeded in building a large, literate, and supportive audience for modern dance. To the contrary: during the 1940s and 1950s, many performers found that it had become increasingly difficult to schedule and finance company tours throughout the country, or to have successful performances, extending beyond a day or two, in theaters in the large cities. Partly, this was the inevitable outcome of the growing costs of production. It was also due to the fact that the audience for modern dance proved to be limited—in terms of taste.

One of the problems was that, like all modern arts—modern poetry, painting, and theater—it was hard to understand, and people did not know how to receive it. Too few artists, and too few educators, had been successful in achieving a sense of how to view, or be open to, these pioneering, avant-garde forms. And, in dance, one of the great problems was its diversity. There was no single method or technique, and, in the dozens and perhaps hundreds of tiny groups that performed around the country (for anyone was entitled to call himself a performer, or a choreographer), the quality of both composition and performance ranged from the most abysmally weak to an extremely high level of competence. But, viewing this range, too many audiences, already insecure in terms of understanding and appreciating dance, had quick reactions that rejected compositions that were to them, pretentious, confusing, or silly, or that shocked or disturbed them. No longer did the notion that one needed only to express one's feelings to make a stage work worthwhile, have any meaning—if it ever did.

Similarly, the very rationale that led to the development of modern dance was under challenge. Originally, it had been developed to provide an alternative to ballet. One of its major premises was that ballet technique was outdated, arbitrary, and uncreative, and that the artistic works of ballet companies also were archaic and meaningless in a modern world. Thus, the early modern dancers tended to avoid balletic training in their studios (although many of them had had at least a modicum of such training); they dealt with thematic materials, and used choreographic approaches that were completely unlike those of the classic ballet. In a sense, it was this freshness of modern dance, its contemporary significance, its ability to say things that were personal and immediately meaningful to an audience, that captured its first fresh audiences— and that the audiences found lacking in ballet.

But, over the fifty-year period, ballet too had changed.

It was no longer the same art form that had been tired and stereotyped at the end of the 19th century. Instead, it was now a fresh and vital art that had gained tremendous new audiences and that, indeed, owed much of its spirit and contemporary outlook to the influence of modern dance.

What were the steps that led to the revival and enrichment of ballet, and to its recapture of public interest? The first of them took place in Russia and in France, in the early part of this century.

10

AGE OF INNOVATION
IN BALLET

As described in earlier chapters, ballet in Europe had reached a low ebb at the end of the 19th century. Only in Russia had it retained a measure of its former grandeur, and even there, under the artistic despotism of Petipa, it had become stereotyped and lacking in inspiration. It remained for two Russians, Michel Fokine and Serge Diaghileff, to make radical reforms and to embark the ballet on an age of innovation.

Michel Fokine was born in St. Petersburg in 1880; he entered the Imperial School of Ballet in 1889. Graduating nine years later, he entered the Maryinsky Theater ballet company as a soloist, instead of a member of the corps. He was a brilliant dancer, but ultimately became known as a choreographer and teacher, rather than a *premier danseur*. Fokine was much disturbed by the rigidity and sterility of Russian ballet, which he criticized in his writings. He described the nature of a typical *pas de deux* of his early years as a performer, commenting that each dance was little more than an exhibition of agility and physical virtuosity. There was little conscious choreography involved:

> We did whatever we felt we could do best. I did high jumps and Pavlova pirouettes. There was no connection whatsoever between our "number" and the ballet into which it was inserted. Neither

was there any connection with the music. We began our adagio when the music began and finished when the music came to an end.[1]

Gradually, Fokine began to teach and to assume responsibility for choreographing student performances. In 1904, he submitted a plan for the ballet *Daphnis and Chloe,* which revealed his philosophy for the first time. It was much like that of Noverre, stressing the need for unifying ballet as a meaningful dramatic enterprise, and for fusing its major elements of dance, music, and painting. This proposal was rejected, but three years later, Fokine's first major ballet, *Le Pavillon d'Armide,* was produced featuring two brilliant young performers, Vaslav Nijinsky and Anna Pavlova. However, he had little opportunity to put his ideas for reform into practice; typically, when he attempted to have dancers playing the role of Greeks dance with bare feet, the force of tradition was so strong that he was compelled to have them wear pink tights, with toes painted on them. Shortly after, Fokine was impressed by Isadora Duncan on her visit to Russia, and when the opportunity came to travel to Paris to stage several ballets for the Russian company that was going to perform there in the summer of 1909 with Serge Diaghileff as impresario, he seized it.

It was in Paris, during the years between 1909 and 1914, that Fokine rapidly achieved success as a choreographer. In that period, he staged a number of major works, some of which are still being performed today, including: *Prince Igor* (1909); *Les Sylphides* (1909); *Carnaval* (1910); *Firebird* (1910); *Le Spectre de la Rose* (1911); *Petrouchka* (1911); and *Le Coq D'Or* (1914). It was there too that his philosophy of ballet matured. His views were fully expressed in a famous letter to *The London Times* in 1914, in which he outlined five major principles which should govern the choreography and production of ballet:

1. It was necessary to create for each dance new forms of movement, suitable to the subject matter, period, or country of the ballet, and appropriate to the music, rather than to use ready-made movements straight from the classic tradition.

2. The dramatic action of the ballet should be continuously developed by means of movement, rather than having sections of pantomime to relate the story alternating with dance numbers that had no dramatic or narrative significance.

3. The traditional gesture-language, or pantomime, which often was unintelligible to the audience and even sometimes to the dancers, should be abandoned; instead, in its place, the

[1] Michel Fokine, quoted in Agnes de Mille, *The Book of the Dance* (New York: Golden Press, 1963), p. 138.

entire body of the dancer should be used to communicate ideas and feelings.

4. Similarly, the entire group of dancers should be used to develop the theme of the ballet and should be part of the plot, rather than having the corps de ballet provide decorative interludes that had no significance.

5. Ballet should reflect an active and equal cooperation of all the arts involved in it; music, scenery, dancing, costuming, all were crucial to a unified creative effort. Specifically, music should no longer be a series of separate and unrelated numbers, but should be a unified composition dramatically integrated with the plot.

Fokine's concern was to make the ballet a fully expressive art that mirrored life. For the period, his ideas were revolutionary. Fortunately, they were successful; the Paris audiences were immensely enthusiastic. In part, this was because the French ballet had become so lackluster, particularly in terms of male dancing. When the brilliant Russian dancers appeared on stage, in Fokine's colorful and dynamic ballets, using a range of movement that had never before been seen on the stage, disregarding the rigid conventions of past choreography, and dancing in a manner that involved real characterization, the audiences went wild. Fokine wrote of their excitement:

> After the Polovetznian Dances, the audience rushed forward and actually tore off the orchestra rail in the Chatelet Theater. The success was absolutely unbelievable.[2]

De Mille comments that in these early years in Paris, and in four years in England during World War I, ballet was transformed from a pretty entertainment to a major form of theater. Fokine based the choreography of his ballets on the locale and period in which they were laid. The music too was closely integrated with these elements. The style of the dances and their manner of execution were a sharp break from previous models; the classic technique was expanded to include freer and fuller arm and leg movements and a more supple back. The former rigid positions for the head and arm were now loosened, and the movement generally was more free-flowing and emotional. Costumes suited the period and plot; the old classic costumes were abandoned for these new works.

In 1912, Diaghileff replaced Fokine with Nijinsky as choreographer. Although he continued to create a few ballets for the company, Fokine left it in 1914 and from that time on worked inter-

---

[2] Michel Fokine, quoted in de Mille, *op. cit.,* p. 143.

mittently with opera-ballet companies in Copenhagen, Paris, Buenos Aires, and with his own company in New York. Fokine died in America in 1942; it was unfortunate that for over two decades, while he was at the height of his creative powers, he had not been associated with a major company of stability, for which he could have continued to choreograph his brilliant ballets. To understand the reason for this, it is necessary to know something of Diaghileff.

Serge Diaghileff, who lived from 1872 to 1929, was born a member of the Russian nobility. He studied both law and music, became interested in ballet and opera, and was given a supervisory post at the Maryinsky Theater. Because of his independence, he found it difficult to work there, and resigned shortly. He staged art exhibitions in St. Petersburg and Paris and, in 1908, became a theatrical impresario. It was in this role that he made his great contribution to dance. In 1909, he assembled a group of the leading Russian dancers of the Imperial Ballet, and arranged to present a season in Paris, during the summer vacation. His dancers for this first season included Michel Fokine, Anna Pavlova, Tamara Karsavina, Vaslav Nijinsky, and Mikhail Mordkin; the ballets were mostly the work of Fokine.

The next summer, Diaghileff's company appeared at the Paris Opéra, and such new works or revivals as *Scheherazade*, *Firebird*, and *Giselle* were added to the repertoire. In 1911, Nijinsky resigned from the St. Petersburg Company and Diaghileff decided to establish his company on a permanent basis, rather than have it continue as an informal offshoot of the Imperial Russian Ballet, with dancers appearing on leave.

In 1911, the company played a season in Rome, Monte Carlo, Paris, and London; in the following year it also appeared in Berlin, Vienna, and Budapest; after that, in South America and, in 1916, in the United States. There it created a sensation and spurred American interest in the ballet. Diaghileff's company toured steadily from 1916 to 1929, during what had become an international period for ballet—but one in which increasingly the art came to be considered almost exclusively Russian. In 1923, Diaghileff signed a contract with the principality of Monaco to become the official ballet of the Monte Carlo Ballet; its name was changed to Les Ballets Russes de Monte Carlo.

During all this time, although he used different choreographers, including Fokine, Nijinsky, Massine, Nijinska, and Balanchine, as well as a host of leading dancers, the Diaghileff company was preeminent in world ballet. What was the gift that accounted for Diaghileff's leadership?

He had remarkable ability as a manager and organizer and, while not a dancer himself, he had great artistic taste and judgment. Like Fokine, he recognized that ballet was a combination of choreography, painting, and music; he was able to get great artists in each of these areas to collaborate fully with each other.

In addition to the choreographers listed above, most of whom also were among his leading dancers, Diaghileff's stars included Tamara Karsavina and Anna Pavlova, Adolph Bolm, Alicia Markova, Anton Dolin, Alexandra Danilova, and many others. He was part of the total revolutionary movement in modern art and knew well the many painters and composers who were working, particularly in France, during this period. Among the composers whom he used for his ballets were Stravinsky, Ravel, Glazounov, Prokofieff, Debussy, Satie, and Milhaud—a roll-call of the leading musicians of his day. Similarly, among painters, such leading artists as Bakst, Benois, Derain, Picasso, Tchelitcheff, Roualt, Chirico, and Cocteau designed for his productions. But to all these, Diaghileff brought his own special ingredient. Kirstein points out that since he was not a creative artist himself, the exact role he played tended to be obscure and even mythical. However, without question, his contribution was tremendous;

Vaslav Nijinsky in *Afternoon of a Faun*. Photograph by de Meyer, Paris, 1911.

Anna Pavlova in *The Dying Swan.*

he influenced every aspect of art in his era, and brought together the great creative artists of his time in a "hotbed of collaboration."[3]

Gradually, through the 1920s, the great generation that had received its training and had reached stardom initially in St. Petersburg slipped away. Although the company continued to be known as Russian, it became somewhat more international in flavor and makeup. Kirstein comments that Diaghileff became known as a "purveyor of novelty," who presented the extraordinary. In the later years of the 1920s, he describes a gradual artistic decay of the company; the music became increasingly trivial, the dancing more and more capricious and fragmentary. A number of Diaghileff's leading dancers and choreographers had left the company long before he died in 1929. At his death, it dissolved completely, although attempts were made to carry on its tradition under a number of competing sponsors.

The Diaghileff period brought prominence to a number of great stars and choreographers who achieved worldwide reputation and, in some cases, artistic independence. Several of them had an impact on the development of ballet in America and at least one, George Balanchine, became without question the leading figure in American ballet over a period of several decades after the 1920s.

[3] Lincoln Kirstein, *Dance: A Short History of Classic Theatrical Dancing* (New York: G. P. Putnam's Sons, 1935), p. 279.

Diaghileff's two greatest stars were Vaslav Nijinsky and Anna Pavlova; their reputations were legendary.

Nijinsky is reputed to have been the greatest male ballet dancer of all time, although his dancing career lasted for only nine years, during two of which (1914–1916) he danced little. Of Polish extraction, but born in the Ukraine in 1890, Nijinsky attended the St. Petersburg Imperial School of Ballet, where he was considered to be a brilliant performer, although weak in his general studies. Shortly after his graduation in 1908, and his debut in Fokine's *Don Juan*, he accepted Diaghileff's proposal to go to Paris for his first season there. Nijinsky was an overwhelming success in several of Fokine's ballets and, two years later, in 1911, resigned formally from the St. Petersburg Company, to become a permanent member of Diaghileff's troupe. There, he continued as a *premier danseur* until 1913, dancing such great roles as *Le Spectre de la Rose* and *Petrouchka*. He temporarily left the Diaghileff company because of the impresario's anger at his marriage; although he later returned to it in 1916 for a tour of the United States and performed briefly after that in South America, Nijinsky's career came to a tragic end. He was mentally ill, and was confined to sanitariums for the remainder of his life.

What was the basis of the Nijinsky legend?

First, it stemmed from his great ability as a classic dancer; he was famed for his tremendous technique, his elevation, leaps, and pirouettes. He was believed to be the greatest jumper of all time, and could accomplish an *entrechat douze* (six full crossings of the feet in mid-air). Thus, in terms of sheer dancing brilliance, he deserved the reputation.

But Nijinsky was not just a classic dancer. He explored the possibilities of movement in a way that was akin to the beginning modern dancers of the 1920s. He was a remarkable choreographer who created four works: *Afternoon of a Faun, Le Sacre du Printemps, Jeux*, and *Till Eulenspiegel*. The first two of these aroused great controversy because of their radical break with traditional movement, and what some saw as a too frank depiction of sexual behavior on the stage. Both in his own works and in his dancing of certain of Fokine's roles, Nijinsky created movement that had never been seen before on the stage:

> . . . instead of tension, extension, elevation, feet turned-out, Nijinsky used relaxation, hugged-in shivers, jerky shakes, sub-human vibrations and feet turned-in . . . the grotesque, ugly, brutal and the strong he wielded like a weapon . . .[4]

[4] *Ibid.*, p. 289.

Anna Pavlova and Vaslav Nijinsky in *Le Pavillon d'Armide*, about 1909.

Even at his most experimental, however, Nijinsky did not reject the classic ballet technique; indeed, his highly unusual choreography was based on skills that could only be performed by a highly trained artist, trained in the *danse d'école*. It is difficult to predict what his contribution to the world of dance might have been, if his career had not been so tragically cut short.

In contrast was the role played by Anna Pavlova. Like Nijinsky, her name is legendary as the greatest dancer of her sex in ballet history, although it is hard to measure the basis for fame, or to compare her abilities accurately with those of present-day ballerinas. She was born in 1881, studied as a girl at the Maryinsky Theater's Imperial School, and was a featured performer in St. Petersburg for ten years. With Adolph Bolm, she toured Scandinavia in 1905, thus becoming the first great Russian ballerina to perform outside her country. She joined Diaghileff in Paris in 1909, but then left him and, forming her own company with Mikhail Mordkin, toured independently throughout the world for twenty years, until her death.

To millions, Pavlova was the embodiment of ballet. Chujoy comments that she took what had been an aristocratic, imperial art, found in the theaters and opera houses of Russia and Western Europe, and gave it to the common people in towns and villages throughout America:

> She played her great art in theatres and music halls, high school auditoriums and movie houses. She made available to the people an art form that before her had belonged to a chosen few, and thus elevated the people to an understanding, appreciation and enjoyment of it.[5]

Particularly in America, Pavlova's influence was tremendous. As Elssler had done during the Golden Age of ballet, she toured the country to tumultuous acclaim, making almost annual coast-to-coast tours between 1912 and 1925. Thanks to her, a generation of Americans became exposed to ballet as great art. What they saw was nothing like the revolutionary choreography or dancing of Nijinsky. Instead, Pavlova was a conservative and traditional dancer. Her performances on tour were not full-scale ballet, but involved a small company with herself featured with a leading male partner. Her dancing itself was "distinguished by its grace, airiness, and absence of visible effort. It was sincere, refined, marked by a vivid sense of style-atmosphere, and a genuine and deeply felt reverence for the poetry of movement . . . ."[6]

Other leading figures during the Diaghileff period included Leonide Massine, Bronislava Nijinska, and George Balanchine.

Massine, known both as an outstanding character dancer and as one of the leading choreographers of the 20th century, was born in Moscow in 1894. He graduated from the Moscow Imperial Ballet School, and was selected by Diaghileff in 1912 to join his company as a dancer. Shortly, he was assigned the task of ballet master, then that of choreographer to replace Nijinsky. From that time on (1915 to the late 1940s) Massine produced some 50 ballets for the Diaghileff Company, the Roxy Theater in New York during

---

[5] Anatole Chujoy, *The Dance Encyclopedia* (New York: A. S. Barnes, & Co., Inc., 1949), p. 358.
[6] Cyril Beaumont, quoted in Chujoy, *op. cit.*, p. 356.

the late 1920s, Colonel de Basil's Ballet Russe de Monte Carlo, La Scala in Milan, and Ballet Theater in America, during the 1940s.

Massine was known for two types of ballets. The first was the so-called symphonic ballet, in which he composed major works to the symphonies of Tchaikovsky, Berlioz, Beethoven, and Shostakovitch. Essentially, these were abstract dance works. His other metier involved story ballets, often with a high degree of comedy, satire, and character dancing; typical of these were *The Good-Humored Ladies*, *La Boutique Fantastique*, *The Three-Cornered Hat*, and *Capriccio Espagnol*. Throughout his work, Massine achieved a reputation for a high degree of musicianship and for great color, inventiveness, and choreographic soundness.

Bronislava Nijinska was also a leading dancer and choreographer for the Diaghileff Company. Born in Warsaw in 1891, the sister of Vaslav Nijinsky, she studied at the St. Petersburg School, joined the Maryinsky Theater, and, in 1909, went to Paris with Diaghileff. With some interruptions, she continued to choreograph for Diaghileff through the 1920s. She revived a number of works for him, and, for several years was his chief choreographer, creating such major works as *Le Renard*, *Les Noces*, *Le Train Bleu*, and *Les Biches*. Of these, *Les Noces* was the most striking. Set to Stravinsky's revolutionary music scored for pianos, percussion, and voices,

> ... it was a primitive Russian wedding ceremonial, with starkly simple scenery ... and an unornamented, architectural use of movement, mostly by solid groups of dancers. There was a marked kinship here to her brother's use of purely invented movement for expressive purposes, though in a more ordered and less violent form ... [the work displayed] a kind of inarticulate, archaic passion ... [it remains] one of the outstanding modern masterpieces.[7]

During the decades after the death of Diaghileff, Nijinska continued to choreograph for the Ballet Russe de Monte Carlo, the Markova-Dolin Company, Ballet Theater, and other opera and ballet companies throughout the world.

Without question, the member of Diaghileff's choreographic team who had the greatest influence on ballet in America was George Balanchine. Born in St. Petersburg in 1904, he entered the Imperial School of Ballet at the age of ten. After graduating in 1921, having appeared in many student performances drawn from the established 19th-century Imperial repertory, he began to cho-

---

[7] John Martin, *John Martin's Book of the Dance* (New York: Tudor Publishing Co., 1963), p. 57.

reograph a number of experimental works with a small group of young dancers in what was now Leningrad. However, there was much opposition to his work, and in 1924, Balanchine was permitted to leave Russia for a tour of Germany with a small group of young artists known as the Soviet State Dancers. Traveling on to Paris, they were auditioned by Diaghileff and absorbed into his company. At the age of twenty, Balanchine became ballet master, replacing Nijinska. He served in this role for Diaghileff for four and a half years, creating ten new works, restaging many others, and producing ballets during the opera seasons at Monte Carlo.

When Diaghileff died in 1929, the members of his company scattered. During his years with Diaghileff, Balanchine's maturity had been established. At the time he joined the company, he had been a young man of remarkable gifts, but immature in his judgment. Now, he had become a fully developed choreographer. Due to a severe knee injury in 1927, he was no longer able to dance in demanding roles. What was he to do? Two of his works, *Apollo* and *The Prodigal Son*, had aroused much interest, but thus far he had not achieved a major reputation.

He was invited to the Paris Opéra, to stage a new version of *Prometheus*, a two-act work to music by Beethoven. However, illness intervened; he had contracted tuberculosis and could not go on. After several months, he recovered, but the Paris assignment was gone. The period that followed was a rootless one for Balanchine. He concocted minor ballets and entertainments in revues in Paris and London. He served as guest ballet master in 1930 and 1931 for the Royal Danish Ballet in Copenhagen. He acted as ballet master for a new company under the direction of René Blum in Monte Carlo. However, he found himself in conflict with Colonel de Basil and left shortly, to be replaced by Leonide Massine. He organized another new company (Les Ballets 1933) at the Champs-Élysées in Paris. And then he was invited by a wealthy young American, Lincoln Kirstein, to come to the United States. With the cooperation of Edward Warburg, Kirstein had plans for the ballet in America. Taper writes:

> He was not content to have some Russian . . . company come here on tour, but, rather, it was his idea to have ballet take root and prosper as a vital, indigenous art in the United States—to establish a ballet company, a ballet repertoire and a ballet audience. Such a transplanting had succeeded only three or four times in the three hundred years since the first ballet company was chartered by Louis XIV, and each time it had taken a monarch with ample coffers to achieve it. Each time, too, it had been effected by the importation into the new country of a great ballet master from the old, who brought the art with him . . . .[8]

[8] Bernard Taper, *Balanchine* (New York: Harper & Row, Publishers, 1963), p. 161.

It was not an auspicious time to begin a ballet venture in the United States. The history of ballet in this country during recent years had been a fragmentary and discouraging one. While there had been a number of tours by foreign companies, such as the one-year tour by the Diaghileff Company in 1916, or Nijinsky's performances in 1916 and 1917, these had not served to arouse a permanent interest. Pavlova had appeared here first with Mikhail Mordkin at the Metropolitan Opera House, in 1910, and later had toured regularly until 1925. However, the Metropolitan itself, which might well have been the sponsor of a leading ballet company, never took sufficient interest to develop native talent, and relied heavily on European stars. For a period of years, it sponsored revivals of Fokine's ballets, staged by Adolph Bolm. However, these were not major works, and were apathetically received.

Bolm himself, who had been one of the leading stars of the Diaghileff Company, had remained in the United States and had formed a school and company. Later he was to work with the Chicago Civic Opera, to found Chicago Allied Arts, and to choreograph in Hollywood and with the San Francisco Opera. Michel Fokine himself came to the United States at the invitation of the impresario, Morris Gest; he staged musicals and also founded a school and company here. A third major European dancer was Mikhail Mordkin, who had been Pavlova's partner at the Paris Opéra and in her early American tours. After serving as ballet master of the Bolshoi Theater, following the Russian Revolution, Mordkin returned to the United States in 1924. He toured the country, taught ballet in New York and Philadelphia, and was to form the Mordkin Ballet (later to be assimilated into Ballet Theater) in 1937.

But, in 1933, the picture was not promising. It was a time of depression in the United States—hardly a good moment to introduce an art which was usually viewed as exotic, aristocratic, and certainly costly. Instead, at a time of crisis and unrest, modern dance, which dealt with significant social themes, seemed better attuned to the times. There appeared to be little reason for hope about a fresh attempt to interest the American public in ballet. Maynard writes:

> American dancers were desperate for a theatre to dance in, and they and the American audience believed that there was no American dance as a national art. They were wrong. The theatre was gradually being made, not in grand opera houses as it had been developed in Europe and Russia, but wherever Americans would dance. The audience, enormous, scattered and somnolent, did not know of its own existence, but stood, in reality, waiting for the momentous year of 1933.[9]

[9] Olga Maynard, *The American Ballet* (Philadelphia: Macrae Smith Co., 1959), p. 33.

The first company to break the ice was the Ballet Russe de Monte Carlo, for which Balanchine had served briefly as choreographer in 1932. Now Leonide Massine was the chief choreographer. Alexandra Danilova was the leading ballerina and there were several fine young Russian ballerinas in the company. The repertoire was drawn largely from the Diaghileff period, with emphasis on works by Fokine. The 1933 season, consisting of a brief series of performances in New York and then a tour of the country, was a critical success but a financial loss. Sol Hurok, who had arranged the visit, was convinced, however, that America was ready for ballet. He brought the company back year after year, and before long, it became a widely accepted and profitable enterprise.

This was still essentially Russian ballet; it remained for Balanchine and Kirstein to provide the foundation for what was to become an American art.

Their plans were to begin a new academy, to be called the School of American Ballet, and a performing company, to be called the American Ballet. The school began on a small scale in New York City, in 1934, and the first season for the company was in March, 1935. It presented a small repertory of Balanchine works: *Serenade, Dreams, Transcendence, Alma Mater, Errante,* and *Reminiscence*. Critical reaction was mildly negative, and the comment was voiced frequently that Balanchine was not an appropriate choice, if the intent was to develop a truly American school and style of ballet. The company set out on a short-lived tour in the fall of 1935; shortly after, it disbanded as an independent performing group, and joined the Metropolitan Opera as a resident ballet company, with Balanchine as ballet master. The contract was made, but much conflict rapidly developed between Balanchine and the opera management. Critic Virgil Thomson pointed out that the clash lay in part between the Russian style that Balanchine had brought to America, ". . . dynamic, explosive, sharply precise . . . full of enormous tension and vigor," and the Franco-Italian stage movement employed by singers on the opera stage, which was slow, broad, and much softer.

A second and even more serious difficulty arose when it became clear that the Metropolitan had no intention of scheduling regular separate ballet performances, which was the custom in great opera houses in Europe. Most of Balanchine's work for the Metropolitan was mutually dissatisfying, with the exception of his choreography of a new production of Gluck's *Orpheus and Eurydice*. With decor by Tchelitcheff, this performance, mounted in 1936, was greatly criticized and was discontinued after two performances. Yet, in the eyes of some, it was a major creative work.

In 1938, Balanchine and the Metropolitan dissolved their relationship. For several years, Balanchine turned to the Broadway stage, and choreographed the most popular musicals to appear during this era, including *On Your Toes*, *I Married an Angel*, *Babes in Arms*, *The Boys from Syracuse*, and a number of other hits, as well as several movies.

In this same period, in 1939, Kirstein made a second attempt at developing a performing company. This was named Ballet Caravan, and it included a number of the original dancers from the American Ballet Company, as well as others who had been trained by the School of American Ballet. Indeed, its avowed purpose was to promote dance as an indigenous art; it presented no ballets by Balanchine, but concentrated on the works of such choreographers as William Dollar, Lew Christensen, and Eugene Loring. Christensen's *Filling Station*, and Eugene Loring's *Billy the Kid*, to music by Aaron Copland, were among the first major ballets to deal successfully with American themes. In 1940, Ballet Caravan folded, but was revived in the following year as the American Ballet Caravan for a six-month good-will tour of South America.

In 1946, after a hiatus caused by World War II, Kirstein returned to the United States and, with Balanchine, formed the Ballet Society. Leon Barzin was musical director and Lew Christensen, ballet master. This membership organization gave performances of a number of Balanchine's works, including *The Spellbound Child* and *The Four Temperaments*, and later, *Symphonie Concertante* and *Symphony in C*, as well as works by Todd Bolender, Merce Cunningham, William Dollar, and Lew Christensen. It also offered its members special books and publications and admission to other theatrical events.

Then, in 1948, it joined forces with the newly established New York City Center of Music and Drama, under the title of the New York City Ballet. During the first years, the company performed in the New York City Center. Although it lacked a subsidy as such, the city's sponsorship and the deliberately low admission scale helped to build a large new audience for ballet. During the following decade, the company, under the artistic domination of Balanchine, achieved its reputation as one of the outstanding ballet companies in the world. A key factor in this growth was that the School of American Ballet had continued, during the twelve years since the demise of the original company, to train a number of outstanding young dancers, who were now ready to join the company. Among these were Tanaquil LeClercq, Jacques d'Amboise, and Edward Villella. Other principal dancers included Maria

Tallchief, Nicholas Magallanes, Francisco Moncion, and Todd Bolender.

The first season was brief, consisting of only fourteen performances. Artistically, it was considered successful. However, financially it was poor, because of the competition of the Ballet Russe de Monte Carlo, which had just concluded a smash four-week season at the Metropolitan Opera House, with such stars as Alicia Markova, Mia Slavenska, Agnes de Mille, Anton Dolin, Alexandra Danilova, and Frederic Franklin. In a second season, beginning in January 1949, the company was joined by Jerome Robbins and Antony Tudor as guest choreographers. This season was much closer to breaking even financially; the public had begun to take to the new company.

At the outset, however, it appeared as if the New York City Ballet would perform in the City Center only twice a year, for a total of about four or five weeks. This would mean that, even with rehearsal time, the dancers would be occupied for only thirteen weeks per year. Could many of the ranking dancers in the company be held under these conditions? Many of them had to go into musical shows, Ballet Theater, and other companies. However, under determined management and with the support of the City Center directors, the company continued; in the fall of 1949, attendance was larger and the deficit decreased. Then, remarkable recognition came for such a young company, when Ninette de Valois, director of the famed British Sadler's Wells Ballet, which was on its first American tour at the time, indicated that she was extremely impressed with the New York City Ballet Company. Balanchine was invited to come to London in the following spring to stage his *Ballet Imperial*, and shortly thereafter, the entire New York company was invited to perform for a season at Covent Garden.

This season, in July 1950, was under the auspices of the Arts Council of Great Britain, and was considered a quasi-official exchange visit for the Sadler's Wells Ballet season in New York in 1949. Sixty of America's leading dancers were in the company; it was the first international recognition of the United States in the field of ballet. The literary, art, and music worlds were well represented; all the London and Paris periodicals sent their first-string dance critics. And the reviews were highly favorable. One leading critic wrote:

> . . . they danced with such vigour and athletic enthusiasm that they had the audience in this hallowed theatre whistling its enthusiasm long before the end came . . . .

These fresh young Americans bring no mystery or sentiment to their dancing. They are rugged, tough and gay. The men attack feats of grace as a sport and the girls make almost a miracle of their execution of the classical routine. That is the strangest thing about their visit. They are not so much interested in the folksy style. They are pure classicists absorbed by the perfection of the old Imperial Russian Ballet.[10]

Although there was some criticism of Balanchine's revival of the Stravinsky-Fokine *Firebird*, and of Balanchine's "cold and undramatic" abstract ballet, in general the reception was highly enthusiastic. Chujoy comments that, despite some critical "coolness," the London audience was greatly impressed; indeed, much of the criticism served as excellent publicity:

> Controversial ballets like *Illuminations*, *Age of Anxiety*, *Orpheus*, and *Firebird* attracted wide attention. Technically difficult ballets, the so-called abstracts, never failed to bring out cheers. *The Prodigal Son* (with the real Rouault backdrop, which the company had had freshly painted for the London season) was probably the favorite of all . . . .[11]

In all, the visit to Great Britain, which included a tour of other cities, was a triumph and focused international attention on the New York City Ballet. The artistic prestige of the United States was enhanced. Increasingly, leading dancers who had not formerly been with the company joined it, including Jerome Robbins, Janet Reed, Melissa Hayden, Hugh Laing, and Diana Adams. The next seasons proved to be brilliant, and now the company was augmented by André Eglevsky and Nora Kaye. Through the 1950s, and then as it moved into its sumptuous new home, the New York State Theater in the Lincoln Center arts complex, it has gradually assumed the status of being one of the world's few great ballet companies, comparable, in the judgment of critic Clive Barnes, to the British Royal Ballet, the Royal Danish Ballet, and the two leading Russian companies, the Bolshoi in Moscow and the Kirov in Leningrad.

Under Balanchine, the New York City Ballet has developed an enormous and brilliant repertoire; its dancers perform superbly and its productions are handsomely mounted. If it has a major problem, it is that the company is so strongly dominated by Balanchine. Although, through the years, it has presented works by other leading choreographers, such as Todd Bolender, Antony

---

[10] Paul Holt, quoted in Anatole Chujoy, *The New York City Ballet* (New York: Alfred A. Knopf, Inc., 1953), p. 254.

[11] Chujoy, *op. cit.*, p. 261.

Tudor, Frederick Ashton, and Jerome Robbins, and a few works by younger members of the company, such as Jacques d'Amboise, it is still a showcase for Balanchine's choreography. And to some, his highly disciplined and unemotional "neo-classic" approach is too restrictive, lacking the color and variety that a great ballet company should have. De Mille gives a balanced view of Balanchine's work, commenting that, although he is highly musical himself, he demands of his dancers only that they "hear a downbeat" and stay in time with the music. He attempts to suppress all show of emotion; the dancer must be anonymous and is viewed essentially as a tool for the choreographer. Nonetheless, she finds his works deeply moving and exciting, because of the sheer inventiveness of his composition.[12]

The real question is not so much whether Balanchine will change the formula that has been so successful, but rather what the New York City Ballet will do, in terms of its artistic direction and inspiration, when he is no longer on the scene.

A second major thread that is traced through the development of ballet in the United States is that of Ballet Theater. This company has without question developed more native American performers than any other; its repertoire has been broad and diverse; it has mounted the works of all the great modern ballet choreographers; and it has presented superb ballet for over a quarter of a century to audiences throughout the United States and abroad.

Ballet Theater came into being as an outgrowth of the Mordkin Ballet, which had been founded in 1937 to provide a performing outlet for the students of Mordkin's New York school. In this little company, Lucia Chase and Leon Danielian were among the leading dancers, and the program consisted chiefly of older Romantic works which Mordkin had restaged. In the following year, the Mordkin Ballet was expanded by a number of leading dancers and by additions to the repertoire; Richard Pleasant became general manager of the company.

As the company began to gain an audience and a sense of artistic direction, it decided in 1939 to expand. Lucia Chase, who was not only a dancer but also an extremely wealthy patron of the ballet, and Richard Pleasant determined to form a full-fledged ballet company, to be known as Ballet Theater. It was to be under Pleasant's direction, and Mordkin's role was subordinated. In the first season of the new company, four weeks in the winter of 1940, works were presented by Michel Fokine, Adolph

---

[12] Agnes de Mille, *op. cit.*, p. 154.

Bolm, Anton Dolin, Antony Tudor, Agnes de Mille, Eugene Loring, and Bronislava Nijinska. The company included a considerable number of leading dancers, many of whom had been active in the Diaghileff Company in the 1920s, or in its successor organizations. Following the first season in New York, which was well received by the critics, Ballet Theater toured a number of other American cities, appearing in Chicago as the official company of the Chicago Opera.

In its second year, 1941, the company displayed a new and unusual structure. It had three separate wings, or branches, each under the direction of a choreographer-in-residence, who acted as regisseur, or stage-manager. Anton Dolin was in charge of the Classic Wing, Eugene Loring of the American Wing, and Antony Tudor of the New English Wing. This was part of Pleasant's much broader plan, which was to develop not a single ballet company, but rather a producing organization which would perform already existing works of all periods and national sources, as well as assist in the creation of new ballets from many contemporary viewpoints. Thus, Pleasant intended to develop a classical wing, a Fokine-Diaghileff Russian Wing, and contemporary American, British, Negro, and Spanish wings; there even was the intention of including modern dance in the company's repertoire.

Unfortunately, the plan was too ambitious and the financial hazards too great. Despite excellent reviews and enthusiastic audiences, Pleasant's plans could not be carried further and he himself was forced to resign at the end of 1941. At the end of that year, Sol Hurok undertook to book Ballet Theater. In the years that followed, the company traveled widely, performing in all of Europe, the Near East, and South America. Particularly until the 1950s, it offered a roll-call of the leading dancers to have appeared on the American scene: Diana Adams, Alicia Alonso, Agnes de Mille, André Eglevsky, Melissa Hayden, Robert Joffrey, Nora Kaye, Michael Kidd, John Kriza, Harold Lang, Alicia Markova, Janet Reed, Jerome Robbins, and many others. Similarly, it provided a vehicle for the most talented choreographers of the time to present their works, either for the first time, or in revival.

Among the masterpieces which became part of Ballet Theater's repertoire were the following:

Antony Tudor: *Dark Elegies, Lilac Garden, Pillar of Fire, Romeo and Juliet, Dim Lustre, Undertow.*

Michael Kidd: *On Stage.*

Agnes de Mille: *Tally-Ho, Fall River Legend, Three Virgins and a Devil, Rodeo, Black Ritual* (composed for a company of Negro dancers under Ballet Theater sponsorship).

David Lichine: *Helen of Troy.*

Jerome Robbins: *Fancy Free, Interplay, Facsimile.*

Frederick Ashton: *Les Patineurs.*

In addition, during the first two years of Ballet Theater's existence, Michel Fokine choreographed for it, and throughout its life, it has performed a number of works by George Balanchine. In Maynard's judgment, Ballet Theater in 1959 "has remained the only typical American ballet company for international audiences. Authoritative views in the foreign theatre consider its classicism strict and fine, yet vitally influenced by 'American' characteristics of speed, mobility of form and an urge for self-expression. Its American thematic ballets are considered the most representative of American ballet repertoire."[13] Certainly, it has been preeminent in two areas of performance, a strictly classic approach to the great works of the past, and what Martin refers to as a "modern dramatic-literary style."

Financial difficulties have plagued Ballet Theater throughout its existence. The original plan to have a company in which there would be no star system, no subdivision of dancers in a complex classification of levels, but rather simply "principals" and "company"—this had to go by the board, in order to develop glamour and encourage ticket sales. Similarly, during the years in which Hurok was in charge of Ballet Theater's touring schedule, its desire to be an *American* company was subordinated to the need for audience appeal. Instead it was widely advertised as Russian ballet, in an effort to capitalize on the reputation that had been established by Ballet Russe in years past. The company has always suffered from the lack of clear-cut artistic direction, and, particularly during the early and middle 1950s, has lost many of its leading dancers to other companies.

Nonetheless, it has continued to perform throughout America and in many other countries, and has continued to make a major contribution to the world of ballet, since 1957 under the name "American Ballet Theater."

The third major development in American ballet represented the continuation, particularly during the 1930s and 1940s, of the Russian ballet tradition that Diaghileff had first brought to the United States. As described earlier, René Blum and Colonel de Basil had founded the Ballet Russe de Monte Carlo in 1932, assembling many of the leading dancers from the original Diaghileff company. At first, the company was under the direction of Balanchine, then under Leonide Massine.

[13] Maynard, *op. cit.*, p. 119.

The first season in New York and London, in 1933, involved chiefly works by the two Russian choreographers; it was regarded as an artistic success but a financial failure. However, Sol Hurok promoted the Ballet Russe de Monte Carlo (the title had been changed to the singular) strongly, and with each succeeding year, the tours and seasons grew longer, and the audiences fuller and more appreciative. By 1935, the Ballet Russe de Monte Carlo was booked into the Metropolitan Opera House in New York; it had become an accepted part of the city's cultural life. Among the works presented at this time were several new symphony ballets by Massine, including *Les Présages, Choreartium,* and *Symphonie Fantastique.*

René Blum retired as co-director of Ballet Russe in 1936, with Colonel de Basil assuming full control. However, friction split the company and in 1938 Leonide Massine left it, returning to Europe, where he founded a new company with Blum. The history from this point is one of tangled relationships, rapidly shifting titles, and lawsuits over the use of ballets. The major company to retain the name and tradition, however, was the company which came here under Massine's direction in 1938. Among its dancers were such great stars as Alexandra Danilova, Alicia Markova, Mia Slavenska, Igor Youskevitch, André Eglevsky, Frederic Franklin, and Serge Lifar. It toured with great success during the years that followed, at first under Massine's direction and then, during the war years, under Balanchine. Beginning in 1942, its director was a former Russian banker, Sergei Denham, who proved to be a most successful entrepreneur.

At the outset, the company was clearly Russian in its origin and style; those Americans who joined it often changed their names in order to sound foreign. During the late 1930s, Ballet Russe ventured into Americana with such works as Massine's *Saratoga* and *Union Pacific.* However, these were not truly in the American genre, and not until Agnes de Mille's *Rodeo* was produced did the company produce a work that was really native in spirit and style. Cut off from Europe by World War II, Ballet Russe gradually become American in character, and more and more American in its membership. It has lost many of its leading dancers, some to age and some to the other leading companies—Ballet Theater and the New York City Ballet. Nonetheless, it has continued to be an exciting company, constantly on the move and bringing many American audiences colorful and well-performed ballets. Ballet Russe has never been noted as a source of great original choreography or artistic experimentation; instead, its distinguishing element is its dancing. Maynard writes, ". . . [its] dancing is *con amore*, forte is characterization, technique is virtuoso, excelling in speed and elevation . . . ."[14] Its repertory is heavily drawn from the past, including such works as *Giselle, Swan Lake, Coppelia*, and *The Nutcracker*. In addition, such works as Fokine's *Scheherazade*, Lichine's *Graduation Ball*, Nijinska's *Snow Maiden*, Massine's *Le Beau Danube* and *Gaite Parisienne*, and Balanchine's *Ballet Imperial, Danses Concertantes* and *Pas de Trois Classique* have been among its most popular works.

A final important development of the period prior to 1950 in the United States was that a number of native dancers and choreographers had emerged who, in turn, began to develop regional ballet companies and schools in cities other than New York. Unlike such gifted dancers as Augusta Maywood or Mary Ann Lee of the previous century, they were able to find a high quality of professional training and many opportunities for employment here in the United States. Three of the leading examples of such home-grown talent were Catherine Littlefield, Ruth Page, and Lew Christensen.

Catherine Littlefield, a leading American choreographer and ballerina, studied first in her mother's school in Philadelphia, and then under Albertieri at the Metropolitan in New York, and under Egorova, in Paris. On her return to the United States, she danced in Broadway musicals and was for several years a *première danseuse* for the Philadelphia Grand Opera Company. In 1935, she founded the Littlefield Ballet, which later became known as the Philadelphia Ballet—the first of its kind to be organized and staffed entirely by Americans. The company toured the United States and also performed in Europe in 1937, where it was well received; it continued to be active under Littlefield's direction until 1942. She also served for several seasons as the director of the Chicago Opera Ballet.

During her years as a teacher and ballet director, Littlefield helped to turn out a considerable number of fine young dancers, who later performed on Broadway or in the major ballet companies in New York. Among these were Joan McCracken and Zachary Solov, who danced for both the American Ballet and Ballet Theater, and who served for seven years as choreographer at the Metropolitan Opera. Littlefield herself restaged a number of classical ballets, including *The Fairy Doll* and *Daphnis and Chloe*. Her own beat known work was *Barn Dance*, which became part of the repertory of Ballet Theater.

Another leading American-born dancer and choreographer was Ruth Page, whose career centered in Chicago, although she

[14] *Ibid.*, p. 85.

danced throughout the United States and on a number of international tours.

Page studied with Adolph Bolm and Cecchetti; at an early age she accompanied Anna Pavlova on a South American tour, and appeared in the Broadway show, *Music Box Revue*. She was a leading dancer for Bolm in the Chicago Opera, for Diaghileff's Ballets Russes, and was the first American prima ballerina of the Metropolitan during the late 1920s. She toured widely through the United States and the Orient with Harald Kreutzberg, and was a guest performer with the Federal Theater Project. In 1938, she formed the Page-Stone Ballet Company with Bentley Stone. Among her best known works were *Frankie and Johnny*, *The Bells*, and *Billy Sunday*, all choreographed during the period of 1945 to 1948, and produced by Ballet Russe.

Ruth Page has been a leading choreographer of opera-ballet, and has converted into ballet form such works as *Carmen*, *Salomé*, *The Barber of Seville*, and *The Merry Widow*. Since the middle 1950s, her company, titled Ruth Page's Chicago Opera Ballet, has made major annual tours, with outstanding guest artists such as George Skibine and Marjorie Tallchief.

Lew Christensen, who was born in Brigham City, Utah, in 1908, has been one of the leading American male dancers and choreographers. Like Littlefield and Page, he did much to develop regional interest in ballet—in his case, in San Francisco. Christensen came of a musical and dancing family; his brothers, Harold and William, were also distinguished dancers and teachers. He received his training with an uncle and at the School of American Ballet in New York. He danced in vaudeville and was a member of the American Ballet Company in 1934, taking the title roles of *Orpheus* and *Apollo*, in performances at the Metropolitan Opera House. He also was a soloist, choreographer, and ballet master for Ballet Caravan during the period of 1936 to 1940. It was at this time that he choreographed *Filling Station*, *Pocahontas*, and *Encounter*—all part of Kirstein's effort to develop a number of young native choreographers. His choreography was marked by clean lines and a fine sense of clarity and design. Both in his choreography and in his performance, Lew Christensen had a strong gift for characterization. His most famous dancing role was that of Pat Garret, in Loring's *Billy the Kid*.

After a stint as ballet master of Ballet Society in 1946–1948, and as a faculty member of the School of American Ballet, he joined the San Francisco Ballet, which had been founded by Adolph Bolm in 1933 and was therefore the oldest extant company in America. Though originally formed as an auxiliary to the Opera, the San Francisco Ballet is now an independent organization, but it continues to dance the ballets that are part of the San Francisco Opera. In 1951, Lew Christensen succeeded his brother William as director of the San Francisco Ballet, and he has held this post since. There is a close tie between this company and the New York City Ballet Company. Kirstein has served as the artistic director of the West Coast company, and Christensen remains a director of the New York City Ballet. An example of this relationship is found in two of Christensen's later choreographic works. *Con Amore*, which he created for the San Francisco company, was first danced in the New York City Ballet by the leading dancers of the San Francisco Ballet. In 1959, Christensen choreographed *Octet* as a special ballet to be performed during the Tenth Anniversary Season of the New York City Ballet; thus, the bond remains strong.

In addition to these dancers and choreographers who played a strong part in developing regional ballet enterprises throughout the United States, several other choreographers of major stature were attached to the major New York companies; they will be described in the following chapter.

In summation, what was the effect of the first 50 years of the 20th century, in terms of the development of ballet as a theater art? It broke through the traditional ties that had imposed artistic sterility on it in Europe and that had weakened it as an expressive theatrical form, through the radical reforms of Fokine, and the brilliant productions of Diaghileff. During the 1920s, ballet became truly an international art of high esteem.

In America, the scene was marked, beginning in 1933, by an increasing amount of performing activity which was to culminate in the establishment of several major companies, one of which, the New York City Ballet Company, was to achieve major stature and public support. By 1950, there was little doubt that ballet had become a truly American art form, with native dancers, choreographers, and schools of high standards. There was now a large, vitally interested American audience, both for American companies and for visiting foreign troupes. This did not mean that the art was now on a thoroughly solid footing. Although great progress had been made in terms of the artistic quality of American ballet performance, and although a measure of stability had been achieved in terms of audience support, there was still much work to be done in terms of expanding the audience and achieving a real measure of financial security for ballet schools and performing companies.

11

BALLET TODAY

The bright promise that shone for ballet in the United States in 1950 was not an illusion. At that time, George Amberg commented that while there had been some form of ballet in America for over a century and a half, ballet as a native form of art was barely fifteen years old. It appeared as a consequence of the stimulus provided by the Ballet Russe, and was aided by expert training in the classical idiom provided by leading Russian teachers:

> Native talent emerged and an appreciative audience has developed and been consolidated. Recent attendances throughout the country have exceeded an estimated million and a half, not counting the enormous audience of the musical comedy.[1]

And, three years later, choreographer Agnes de Mille was to say, at a luncheon celebrating her best-selling *Dance to the Piper*, that dance in America had finally come of age. It was, at last, "stimulating, indigenous and important" to the country; it offered a career that was respectable. More men would be going into the profession, able to expect a "normal, happy life. There will be copyright laws for choreography. There will be literature for dancing,

[1] George Amberg, *Ballet in America* (New York: Duell, Sloan and Pearce, 1949), p. viii.

and a real school of choreography. I as a dancer rejoice in all this."[2]

If anything, the growth of ballet has exceeded the expectations that were held for it at mid-century. When the New York City Ballet offered its first season at the City Center, it was barely able to justify a two-week season. By 1955, its season had expanded to eight weeks; in the same season, Ballet Theater performed at the Metropolitan Opera House for three weeks. The Sadler's Wells Company filled the Metropolitan for five weeks, and a host of other companies from abroad had seasons in New York—Antonio and his *Spanish Ballet*, the *Comedie Française*, the *Azuma Kabuki Dancers*, the *Dance Theater-Berlin*, the *Yugoslav Folk Ballet*, and *Ballet Espagnol* —all just during the fall and early winter months.

All this was nothing, compared with what was to come.

By 1967, the number of indigenous and visiting ballet companies had strikingly expanded. During the months of April and May alone, in New York City, ballet-goers were able to see performances by five major companies. The British Royal Ballet, starring Rudolf Nureyev and Margot Fonteyn, was to give its longest season yet in New York City, and the first by any visiting dance company at the new Metropolitan Opera House in Lincoln Center. Simultaneously, in the New York State Theater, also in the Lincoln Center complex, the New York City Ballet Company was completing a highly successful New York season, before going on an extended six-month tour. In May, the American Ballet Theater, with guest star Erik Bruhn, moved into the New York State Theater for four weeks. During the same season, two comparatively new but highly regarded companies, the Joffrey Ballet of New York, and the National Theater of Washington, featuring Frederic Franklin, appeared at the City Center.

All this was an indication that the audience for ballet had grown tremendously. In a sense, it reflected the national interest which had given rise to a number of other major companies—in Boston, Philadelphia, San Francisco, Houston, and other cities—as well as dozens of surprisingly competent regional ballet companies throughout the country. In the words of dance critic Clive Barnes of *The New York Times*:

> ... within that brief period the United States has become, together with Russia and Britain, one of the major dance powers. The richness and variety of American dance are unmatched anywhere. Its possibilities—given proper financial support—are limitless.[3]

[2] Agnes de Mille, quoted in *The New York Herald-Tribune*, January 16, 1952, p. 13.

[3] Clive Barnes, "Dance Critic's Credo," *The New York Times*, *Theater Section*, September 12, 1965.

What was the full scope of ballet's development in the United States by the late 1960s? And what, precisely, was the meaning of the phrase—"given proper financial support?" The curious paradox, as the following pages will make clear, is that, while ballet companies have proliferated and ballet audiences have swelled, as part of the nation's cultural explosion, the whole financial base for the performing arts remains fragile and insecure. Within this picture, the role of government and of foundations is growing increasingly significant, as a means of supporting and encouraging the performing arts in our national life.

But first—the companies themselves.

Without question, the highest ranking company in the United States, and one which rates as a coequal with the best in the world, is the New York City Ballet, directed by George Balanchine. Its early promise, described in the preceding chapter, has been amply fulfilled. It is a handsomely mounted, vigorous, and exciting company, with superb dancing skills, and impeccably directed by Balanchine. Both in its extensive home seasons at the New York City Center (and since 1964, in the New York State Theater at Lincoln Center), and in its many tours abroad, it has been acclaimed by critics and public alike. In its season at the Bolshoi Theater in Moscow in the fall of 1962, it stunned the houses

New York City Ballet in the party scene from "The Nutcracker." Choreography by George Balanchine. Photograph by Martha Swope.

packed with Russian balletomanes with its versatility and fresh-ness.

In a sense, however, the New York City Ballet's great strength —the brilliant direction it is given by Balanchine—is also its weak-ness. For a number of years, both critics and members of the public have protested that the repertoire of the company has been so dominated by Balanchine's extraordinary body of work that the works of other major choreographers have not been included on his program. The charge is really one of artistic dictatorship. But in recent years the New York City Ballet has performed Robbins' *The Cage*, Tudor's *Dim Lustre*, and a number of other works by major choreographers of the Royal Ballet or Ballet Theater, such as Ashton's *Illuminations*. Also, Balanchine has presented a number of premieres by younger choreographers, such as Edward Vil-lella's *Narkissos*, or *La Guilande de Campra* of John Taras, or the *Irish Fantasy* and *Prologue* of Jacques d'Amboise. The New York City Ballet has even performed a specially commissioned work, *Summerspace*, by Merce Cunningham, who is primarily known as a modern dancer.

Yet, with it all, so prolific has Balanchine been, and so highly regarded are his works within the repertory, that they have tended to dominate seasons in New York and on tour. Typically, in the opening performance of the spring 1967 season at Lincoln Center, all of the works shown (*Raymonda Variations*, *Episodes*, *Ragtime*, and *Ballet Imperial*) were by Balanchine. A month or two before, six out of seven works shown on consecutive evenings at the State Theater were Balanchine's. The feeling has been frequently expressed that Balanchine and the management of the company arrogantly disregard the wishes of the ballet's patrons. This is coupled with a long-standing annoyance at the refusal of the com-pany to announce the names of those who will be dancing in advance. In a sense, this represents Balanchine's unwillingness to kowtow to the "star system," and his belief that the dancing is more important than any single performer; his critics translate this to mean that *his* dances are more important than anything. These views were strongly expressed by Allen Hughes, then dance critic of *The New York Times*, at the time of the company's move to Lincoln Center. Hughes commented that while the New York City Ballet had certainly matured as an artistic ensemble, it had failed to grow up as a theatrical institution:

> Up to now the public has allowed the company to ignore worthy works by choreographers outside the New York City Ballet in favor of second-rate items by Mr. Balanchine and choreographers of his choice. But how long will the regular public pay to see *Western Sym-phony*, *Con Amore* and *Fanfare*? How long will it be willing to buy

New York City Ballet in "Raymonda Variations." Choreography by George Balanchine.

repetitions of pieces like these when the best works of Sir Frederick Ashton, Antony Tudor and Agnes de Mille, to mention a few of Mr. Balanchine's contemporaries . . . are being ignored?[4]

Giving credit to Balanchine's genius as a creator, but questioning his competence as the "program chairman of our only resident ballet company," Hughes commented later (shortly before he was replaced as dance critic for the *Times*) on the unwillingness of the company to publicize the names of performers in advance. Pointing out that the principle of preeminence of works over personalities had now been firmly established, he asked when the public would be informed "who is going to dance what and when?"

> Or would this reveal too obviously the fact that very young dancers are being pushed at an inordinately fast rate while experienced dancers at the peak of their artistic accomplishments are dancing less frequently than they might be expected to?[5]

The implication of all this is that the New York City Ballet Company has flourished under a benevolent dictatorship. Asso-

[4] Allen Hughes, *The New York Times, Theater Section,* January 26, 1964, p. 18-X.
[5] Allen Hughes, *The New York Times, Theater Section,* November 8, 1964, p. 19-X.

American Ballet Theatre in "Les Noces," with choreography by Jerome Robbins to Igor Stravinsky's dance-cantata.

ciated with it is the charge that other leading ballet companies in the United States that have received important financial assistance from foundations in recent years are closely connected to Balanchine and the New York City Ballet. Thus, the dictatorship is said to extend beyond the limits of this one company and its audiences.

In contrast, this criticism of the New York City Ballet is the reverse of what is usually identified as the major weakness of American Ballet Theater—that throughout its history it has lacked the consistently strong guiding hand of an artistic director that is essential for any major performing company.

After its period of greatest success in the 1940s and early 1950s, the American Ballet Theater underwent a time of extreme financial difficulty, with a gradual decline in the quality of its performances. Nonetheless, under the leadership of Lucia Chase, its co-director, it continued to tour widely and to perform some of the major ballet works of the modern era. Fortunately, it received assistance in 1966 from the Federally sponsored National Council on the Arts, amounting to $350,000, on a matching-funds basis. This has been instrumental in helping the company maintain its extemely varied and expensive repertoire. In contrast to the New York City Ballet, the American Ballet Theater has offered in recent years such works as: MacMillan's *Romeo and Juliet*, de Mille's *Fall River Legend*

American Ballet Theatre in "Helen of Troy," choreographed by David Lichine to music by Offenbach. Photograph by Fred Fehl.

and *Rodeo*, Antony Tudor's *Pillar of Fire* and *Undertow*, and Robbins's *Fancy Free*. In addition, it has regularly performed such classics as *Giselle*, *Swan Lake*, *Sleeping Beauty*, and *La Fille Mal Gardée*, and has from time to time presented new, specially commissioned works.

Lacking a home of its own, American Ballet Theater has in recent years held a four-week season at the Lincoln Center's New York State Theater. In addition, in 1966–1967, it carried out a cross-country tour which took it to more than 90 American and Canadian cities; it has also frequently had seasons abroad.

No longer does American Ballet Theater boast a star-studded group of dancers such as those in its company during the 1940s, or even in the early 1950s, when Alicia Alonso, John Kriza, Igor Youskevitch, and Mary Ellen Moylan—all at the peak of their powers—comprised its leading dancers. Today, the company is forced to bring in guest performers, such as Erik Bruhn, of the Royal Danish Ballet, to provide this ingredient. However, the ensemble and solo dancers of the next rank are excellent, and provide this company with much hope for the future.

In general, it is recognized that a second major ballet company is needed in the United States, to provide contrast and to act as an artistic competitor to the powerful New York City Ballet.

American Ballet Theater, although it has not been able in recent years to mount important new works and thus could not add to the body of ballet literature, has provided this stimulus. Particularly in the late 1960s, the quality of its performances has been hailed by critics as markedly improved. The expectation is that, if its financial difficulties can be solved, it will continue as an important force in American and world ballet.

Two companies that have recently been formed and make their home in New York, and that have received much critical acclaim, are the Robert Joffrey Ballet—now known as the City Center Joffrey Ballet—and the Harkness Ballet, sponsored by the Rebekah Harkness Foundation.

Both of these are small companies, numbering roughly 28 to 38 dancers. Walter Terry comments that there is a real need for such small-scale companies, both for domestic consumption and for cultural export; the size of the company makes it much more adaptable and flexible, in terms of both the stages and financial arrangements that exist away from the large cities.

City Center Joffrey Ballet in the "multi-media" production of "Astarte," with choreography by Robert Joffrey, score by the rock group, the Crome Syrcus, kinetic scenery by Thomas Skelton, and projected photography by Gardner Compton. Tinette Singleton and Maximiliano Zomosa are featured. Photograph by Herbert Migdoll.

For years and years in America, there has always been a need for small ballet units, for inexpensive ensembles which could bring classical ballet at budget prices to towns, high school auditoriums, women's clubs. So there is nothing really new about the small-size ballet groups—what is new is what they used to dance and what they dance now . . . .[6]

In the past, Terry comments, such companies used to build their programs around abridged versions of the Russian classics, extracts from famous works, all sorts of *grands pas de deux*, and sometimes a novelty version of a dramatic or operatic work. Today, however, the small-scale companies are embarking on fresh, creative choreographic works that are particularly appropriate for their personnel and skills. Obviously, the huge ballet companies of the world—such as the New York City Ballet, the Royal Danish Ballet, the Royal Ballet of Britain, or the Bolshoi Ballet, do the "great old classics or the new spectacle ballets" better than the smaller troupes. However, these are extremely expensive, and the larger companies are less likely to risk commissioning new works than the "small-scale" companies. Terry points out that both the Robert Joffrey and the Harkness Ballets have racked up "impressive records" performing the new works of both young and veteran choreographers.

Curiously, these two companies have had a closely intertwined past.

Robert Joffrey, a gifted young dancer who had studied at the School of American Ballet and performed with Roland Petit's Ballets de Paris during its New York engagement, began his own school, the American Ballet Center, in New York in 1952. In 1956, he set out with six dancers in a rented station wagon, as the Robert Joffrey Ballet. They performed in 23 different locations in eleven states; after ten consecutive tours, they appeared in more than 400 cities in 48 states. The company also toured the Near and Far East for the State Department, appeared at the Kirov Theater in Leningrad as part of a ten-week tour of Soviet Russia, and gave a command performance at the White House.

In 1964, the Harkness Foundation, which had given financial support to the company for two years, wished to give its name to the company. When Joffrey refused this arrangement, the Foundation set up a separate Harkness Ballet, which drew away not only many of his better dancers, but also the rights to many of the ballets that had been produced by the company. Fortunately,

[6] Walter Terry, "The Not-So-Little Little Ballet," *The New York Herald-Tribune, Magazine*, April 24, 1966, p. 40.

City Center Joffrey Ballet in "The Clowns," choreographed by Gerald Arpino. Photograph by James Howell.

Joffrey was able to rebuild his company quickly, using many of the talented dancers in his Ballet School, and he was given assistance by the Ford Foundation in getting under way again. Since then, Joffrey has toured widely and successfully and been acclaimed by the critics for the Joffrey Ballet's seasons at the New York City Center.

Joffrey's chief choreographer is Gerald Arpino, a fresh and exciting talent whose works, *Nightwings, Viva Vivaldi, Ropes, Sea Shadow,* and *Arcs and Angels,* have been well received by audiences and critics alike. Other works performed by the Joffrey Ballet have included Anna Sokolow's *Opus '65,* Balanchine's *Donizetti Variations* and *Scotch Symphony,* Ruthanna Boris's *Cakewalk,* and a revival of the Kurt Jooss antiwar classic, *The Green Table,* first performed in 1932.

In 1966, the New York City Center formally affiliated itself with the Joffrey Ballet; this young, experimental company now has a permanent home and the promise of a rich future.

Meanwhile, the newly named Harkness Ballet, which consisted largely of Joffrey's original dancers and repertoire, got under way in 1964 with the assistance of a grant of $1 million from the Harkness Foundation to be spread over a 10-year period. Its first director was George Skibine; for the first three years of its existence the Harkness Ballet toured widely throughout the United States and in Europe. Its repertoire consisted of Skibine's *Sarabande* and *Venta Quemada*, as well as a number of works by choreographers who have been closely associated with modern dance. These have included Alvin Ailey's *Feast of Ashes*, Stuart Hodes's *The Abyss*, and John Butler's *Sebastian* and *Out of Eden*. Other well-received works have included Brian Macdonald's *Canto Indio* and *Time Out of Mind*.

The company has been noted for its brilliant productions, with colorful and handsomely designed costumes, decor, and lighting. Skibine has been replaced as artistic director by a committee consisting of Louis Castelli, Brian Macdonald, and Donald Saddler. It is too early to judge the extent to which it will find a place in the ballet firmament; its first New York season was held in the autumn of 1967, and generally, critical reviews of the young company were favorable. The Harkness Foundation has also founded a School of Ballet at Harkness House in New York City, under the direction of Patricia Wilde and with a staff of teachers that includes Jack Cole, Leon Fokine, Stuart Hodes, Matt Mattox, and Ramon Segarra. The elaborately remodeled and decorated mansion which houses the school also holds an exhibition gallery

Harkness Ballet in Stuart Hodes' "The Abyss," featuring Helgi Tomasson and Lone Isaksen.

for dance documents, art, scenery, and costume designs. It is the home of the Harkness Dance Training and Research Center, which is concerned with scientific analysis of movement motivation as applied to classical ballet training, under the direction of Jo Anna Kneeland.

In addition to these New York-based companies, there are several other ballet organizations in cities throughout the United States, that have earned a high level of recognition. Among these are the San Francisco Ballet, the Boston Ballet, the National Ballet of Washington, D.C., the Houston Ballet Foundation, and the Pennsylvania Ballet in Philadelphia.

The development of the San Francisco Ballet was discussed in Chapter Nine. It remains under the artistic direction of Lew Christensen, whose choreographic works comprise a major portion of its repertory; it also performs a number of works that are danced by the New York City Ballet. The San Francisco Ballet has gone on a number of Federally sponsored tours in the United States which, together with a repertory season of several weeks in San Francisco and a regular commitment to the Opera, means that the company has had regular employment for as much as forty weeks during the year. Even without foreign tours—which many companies count on to provide more performing time and income—this has given the San Francisco dancers and ballet staff substantial incomes and security during the year. The San Francisco Ballet has also sponsored a special workshop in choreography, which has resulted in a number of series of chamber ballet performances in recent summers.

One of the newest companies on the national scene is the National Ballet of Washington, D.C., founded recently under the artistic direction of Frederic Franklin. This handsomely mounted company, calling itself "America's classical ballet," features such traditional works as *Coppelia*, *Swan Lake* (*Act II*), *Les Sylphides*, and a number of other romantic ballets. It also, however, draws widely from the modern repertory, presenting such works as Balanchine's *La Sonnambula* and *Serenade*, Anton Dolin's *Pas de Quatre*, Juan Corelli's *Othello*, Job Sanders's *Bachianas*, and three by Franklin himself, *Homage*, *Danse Brillante*, and *Tribute*. It has presented a number of new, specially commissioned works: Michael Lopuszanski's *Through the Edge*, Anna Sokolow's *Night*, Jean-Paul Comelin's *Idylle*, and George Skibine's *La Péri*, which was a sensational success in its premiere in 1966 at the Paris Opéra. The company, which has toured widely, has brought forth highly favorable critical comments, including the statement by Barnes that in all of Europe, excluding the Soviet Union, there were probably fewer than a dozen ballet companies with the National Ballet's level of technique and artistry.[7]

Lacking, thus far, a permanent home base for its performances, the National Ballet will probably find this in the Kennedy Center being built in Washington. Probably, too, it will be strengthened with the addition of a major choreographer around whom its repertory can be built. The dancers of the National Ballet are young, but extremely gifted, and are expected to develop rapidly under Franklin's direction.

A third company has been recently formed which, like the National Ballet and the Pennsylvania Ballet, has developed close ties with the New York City Ballet and with Balanchine. This is the Boston Ballet, directed by E. Virginia Williams. Based in the Back Bay Theater, this company has received two major Ford Foundation grants, and has developed a strong list of subscribers and a number of bookings that have enabled it to employ its dancers regularly from October through April.

One of the major problems of new ballet companies is the task of building up a repertory for performance. Unlike the problem of a new opera company, symphony orchestra, or drama group, there is no convenient supply of ballet works as part of a standard repertory, which may readily be performed by such fledgling ballet organizations. The problem is twofold: acquiring rights to the ballet, and also being able to mount it properly. In the case of the Boston, Philadelphia, and Washington companies, Balanchine has made a large number of his own ballets available and has, in some cases, arranged to have leading dancers of the New York City Ballet visit them as guest performers.

Thus, the Boston Ballet has recently performed Balanchine's *Symphony in C,* and *Apollo,* with Edward Villella and Patricia Mc-Bride of the New York company as guest artists. Other works presented by the Boston Ballet have included Talley Beatty's *Phoebe Snow,* David Lichine's *Graduation Ball,* August Bournonville's classic *Flower Festival at Genzano (Pas de Deux),* and new works that were specially choreographed by John Butler, Anna Sokolow, and Joyce Trisler.

The Pennsylvania Ballet was started in Philadelphia in October 1962, under the direction of Barbara Linshes Weisberger. George Balanchine was artistic consultant. After only three years, it was providing more continuous employment for its dancers than all but one United States company—the San Francisco Ballet. Its Philadelphia performances are staged at the Academy

---

[7] Clive Barnes, *The New York Times,* March 7, 1966.

of Music. The Pennsylvania Ballet maintains its own school, and performs widely before school audiences and throughout its region, assisted significantly by two Ford Foundation grants.

Other companies throughout the nation which have been successfully presenting seasons in their home cities, as well as touring widely, have been the Chicago Opera Ballet, directed by Ruth Page, and the Houston Ballet Foundation, one of the recipients of the 1963 Ford Foundation grants to ballet companies, under the artistic direction of Nina Popova.

In New York City, one of the continuing disappointments of the ballet world has been the failure of the Metropolitan Opera to provide adequately for ballet in its productions—as other leading opera companies have done through the years. The Metropolitan management, through the years, has made an effort, through the employment of leading dancers as choreographers and directors, to have ballet become an increasingly important part of its staged performances. In the early 1950s, Janet Collins, a leading Negro choreographer, was given this assignment. Then, for several years, Zachary Solov was in charge of ballet at the Metropolitan and succeeded in mounting exciting ballets as part of such operas as *Eugen Onegin, Samson and Delilah, Carmen, Rigoletto, La Périchole, La Traviata,* and *Faust.* Leading ballerinas of the New York City Ballet, or Ballet Theater, such as Mary Ellen Moylan, Carmen de Lavallade, Alicia Markova, and Melissa Hayden, have appeared in these productions. Since 1963, Markova has been in charge of the Metropolitan Opera Ballet.

However, through the years, dancing at the Metropolitan has suffered through lack of a consistent management policy that would support the building of a strong permanent company, and that would sponsor separate ballet evenings. On the other had, this failure of the nation's leading opera company to develop a strong ballet component (a factor which has contributed greatly to the support of ballet in many European countries) is compensated for on the present scene by what appears to be a uniquely American phenomenon—the development of a far-flung network of highly successful regional ballet companies.

The term "regional ballet" is usually applied to those companies scattered throughout the United States which consist largely of nonsalaried dancers and directors, although their directors may occasionally perform professionally and may indeed have had extensive performing experience. They often are supported by organizations made up of members of the local community who are interested in the arts, and who contribute their services. They provide performance opportunities to local dancers and help to spread ballet interest in their regions of the country. They do not tour nationally, although there is often interchange among regions.

In general, two types of regional ballet companies exist: those whose members come from a single school, and those whose members may come from several schools. Invariably, they are incorporated as nonprofit organizations, and whatever income may be received through performance does not go back to the school, but goes rather to production expenses—costuming, scenery, rent for rehearsal space, and similar costs. Usually such companies require their members to pay annual dues, to sign a contract guaranteeing their commitment to the group, and to observe a rigorous schedule of classes and performances. The majority of members of regional ballet companies are between the ages of thirteen and eighteen, although the range may be somewhat older.

The regional ballet movement began with the formation of the Atlanta Civic Ballet in 1929 by a dedicated teacher and choreographer, Dorothy Alexander. Since then, the movement has swept the country. In 1955 there were thirty such companies, and by 1965, there were over two hundred regional ballet groups.[8] The growth continues steadily; in 1966, for example, the Southeastern Regional Ballet Association numbered 22 member companies. In the following year the number climbed to 25; the new groups were the City Center Ballet of Tampa, Florida; the Huntsville, Alabama, Civic Ballet; and the Savannah, Georgia, Civic Ballet.

Typically, the members of regional ballet companies are directed and taught by individuals who have received excellent training themselves and, in many cases, have performed for Ballet Theater, Ballet Russe, and the New York City Ballet. Teaching and directing is a natural outlet for such individuals, once they are past performing age, and may serve as an excellent livelihood. In addition to their efforts, many who join regional companies have been inspired by the highly polished performances of professional touring companies.

Most regional ballet companies offer a series of public performances during the year; sometimes their directors give lectures or demonstrations throughout their region, to spread interest in ballet.

Other activities of regional ballet companies include publishing newsletters or newspapers, making scenery, and being involved with all the business aspects of scheduling performances. Often

---

[8] Doris Hering, "Dance and Decentralization," *Dance Magazine*, December 1965, p. 124.

non-dancers in the community, such as lawyers, businessmen, and other professionals, are extremely helpful in filling posts or committee chairmanships having to do with publicity, fund raising, transportation, printing of programs and tickets, stage crew tasks, set design and construction, and the like. Typically, the organization chart of the Schenectady Civic Ballet in New York has a board of directors consisting of president, treasurer, secretary, producer, business manager, workshop manager, and artistic director, as well as several vice-presidents assigned specific tasks of administration.

The major problems of regional ballet companies involve raising funds (today, in addition to gate receipts, the Atlanta Civic Ballet gains support from performance fees, membership dues, and contributions from patrons or businesses); recruiting male dancers; and developing an organizational structure so that the professional choreographer-director is free from management and business responsibilities. Increasingly, the larger and more successful regional ballets throughout the country have been able to solve these difficulties.

One of the highlights each year for regional ballet companies is participation in festivals sponsored by regional ballet associations. The Southeast Regional Ballet Association was the first of these to be formed, and it has held an annual festival since 1956. Since then, three other associations have been formed: the Southwestern Regional Ballet Association with twelve member groups; the Pacific-West Regional Ballet Association with fourteen members; and the Northeastern Ballet Association, with twenty-three members. Customarily, a yearly sum of $100 is paid by member companies to support annual festivals, which represent a climax for the total year's activity. In addition to socializing, master classes, rehearsals, symposiums, and workshops are held, with, of course, the main event being performances by member companies. Works are selected through adjudication by experts, and customarily the general public is admitted to gala performances, while only association members view workshop or showcase performances.

Large audiences, often numbering several thousand, usually view regional ballet festivals, particularly the gala events. In addition, such events frequently offer workshops and special classes for the teachers and students who have come together. Often these are in areas other than ballet technique in a narrow sense; they may include modern dance, jazz, Oriental, and character dancing. The interchange that takes place among directors and teachers provides an important stimulus to the work they carry on in their own regions.

The goals of regional ballet companies are varied. However, a fairly representative statement of purpose is that of the Richmond, Virginia, Ballet Impromptu:

1. To establish a regional ballet company which shall be adjudicated in festival competition.

2. To present ballet programs of the highest quality for adults and children.

3. To elevate the art of the regional performing dancer to the highest degree possible.

4. To provide a medium of expression for regional choreographers, designers, musicians, and dancers.

5. To stimulate interest and support of ballet and ballet schools.

6. To solicit, and raise funds to further these purposes.[9]

Probably the fifth purpose, that of stimulating interest and support of ballet, is of greatest importance to those concerned with the health of dance as a performing art today. The growth of larger, professional companies around the United States must in large measure be supported by the existence of knowledgeable and enthusiastic audiences, young and old, throughout the country. Without question, a major contribution of the regional ballet companies is their development of such audiences. Recently, a Board of Directors of a National Association for Regional Ballet was formed, with the intent of promoting this broad movement.

A final influence which must be commented upon is the continuing presence of a wide variety of performing groups from other lands, on American concert stages. Ever since the colonial period in this country, foreign companies have toured in American theaters. Often, with indigenous theater dance so weak, it was the glamorous importation of dancers such as Fanny Elssler or Anna Pavlova which continued to inspire American audiences and to keep ballet interest alive. Today, with a flourishing group of native companies, they are no longer needed for this purpose. However, without question, the national ballet companies that tour the United States each year serve other valuable purposes. They offer performers, works, and artistic styles that are quite different from our own companies, and so provide a basis for contrast—or even a measuring stick for quality. In general, they fall into two categories: those companies which have been founded in a classic ballet tradition (although their works may have a strong modern flavor), and those which are essentially rooted in folk or ethnic materials, and which may be performed either by balletically

[9] Doris Hering, "Framework for a Regional Ballet," *Dance Magazine*, October 1958, p. 49.

trained dancers, in carefully choreographed works, or in their original forms.

Typically, in the first group, one would include such major companies as the Leningrad Kirov Ballet and the Bolshoi Ballet of Moscow, the Royal Ballet of England, and the Royal Danish Ballet. In the second are such companies as the Hungarian National Ballet; Kolo, the Yugoslav company; the Ballet Folklorico of Mexico; the Moiseyev Dance Company of Russia; Antonio and his Ballets de Madrid; the Philippine Folk Dance company, Bayanihan; and many smaller companies or solo performers, particularly of Oriental and Eastern dance forms.

The Bolshoi Ballet of Moscow, for most of its history, was regarded as secondary to the more celebrated Maryinsky Ballet in St. Petersburg. Even today, there is a strong feeling of competition between the Bolshoi, and Leningrad's Kirov Ballet, as the Maryinsky is now called. Yet, most regard the Bolshoi as pre-eminent today. It is a huge company; when it came to America several years ago, it brought over one hundred and thirty-five dancers and sent its famous ballet master, Asaf Messerer, six weeks ahead of the rest of the troupe to train an additional sixty-five American dancers for lesser roles in such giant spectacles as the full-length *Spartacus*.

It is brilliantly trained in the classical ballet technique; one critic has commented that, with their better-subsidized schools, the Russians have a tremendous advantage in the development of sheer dancing ability.[10] The general level of Russian performance is superb; the men in particular are capable of dancing with great zest and vigor—in an almost flamboyant style, and with unbelievable athleticism. The ballerinas of the Bolshoi, Galina Ulanova (as legendary for her time as Pavlova) and in more recent years, Raissa Struchkova and the superb Maya Plisetskaya, are among the very top rank of world dancers. The productions are splendid, and the entire effect highly theatrical.

Yet, for years, those visitors who saw the Bolshoi perform in Moscow, or who saw it when it visited Western Europe in 1956, or embarked on its first tour to the United States in 1959, were highly critical of its choreography. Of all the nations of the world, Russia, which underwent a national revolution in 1917, has been the most determinedly conservative in its approach to the arts. This has had two effects on its ballet choreography. First, it has continued until recently to base its repertoire very heavily upon the great works of the Romantic era—such ballets as *Giselle*, *The*

---

[10] Clive Barnes, *The New York Times, Theater Section*, May 8, 1966, p. 6-X.

Sleeping Beauty, Raymonda, Swan Lake, and *Don Quixote.* Even when works have been choreographed in fairly recent times, such as *Shurale* (1955), *Fadetta* (1952), and *Cinderella* (1945), they have dealt heavily with bird-maidens, gnomes, goblins, fairy princesses and godmothers, and pastoral romances.

A second preoccupation in more recent choreography has been dramatic subject matter that served the point of view of the Soviet state. Just as in Russian painting, literature, and sculpture, the ballets are expected to contribute in some way to Socialist ideology; Russians are serious about their art, and usually expect that it present a recognizable image or narrative. The chief choreographer of the Bolshoi, Yuri Grigorovich, commented recently that while he regarded pure classical ballet as the "highest form of dance," for him this did not mean plotless ballet:

> While I feel there can exist, must exist, dance form without subject matter, for myself I am interested in the total theatrical aspect, in a ballet theater that has a literary as well as a dance component.[11]

And, whenever possible, this literary component must be made to support Soviet doctrine. Thus, *Romeo and Juliet,* choreographed in 1946 by Lavrovsky, has been interpreted as an aspect of the class struggle; the Soviet ballet version of *Othello,* produced by Chabukiani, has similarly been seen as an example of racial conflict.

The initial impression many had of the Bolshoi's choreography was that it was ponderous, tedious, and, while technically excellent, so stodgy and traditional that it represented a throwback to the 19th century. Hering commented in 1959:

> Sometimes we felt as though we were returning to a neglected and worthy esthetic—the esthetic of realism. Sometimes that very realism seemed to be nothing more than a repository for outmoded sets, costumes and gestures . . . their reliance upon narrative mime seemed uncomfortably melodramatic . . . sometimes their approach to pure dance passages was merely athletic, with no sense of character revelation or dramatic furtherance . . . .[12]

Gradually, however, as the *Bolshoi* dancers and choreographers have been exposed to the performances of British and American Companies—including the Jerome Robbins State Department tour of Russia in the early 1960s—they appear to have broadened their view of choreographic possibilities. While they still mount huge

[11] Yuri Grigorovich, quoted in "The Fresh New Look of the Bolshoi," by Clive Barnes, *The New York Times,* May 15, 1966, p. D-5.
[12] Doris Hering, "First Impressions of the Bolshoi Ballet," *Dance Magazine,* June 1959, p. 38.

spectacles and present revivals of classical works as a major feature of their repertory, they are demonstrating a greater level of inventiveness, adventurousness, and even humor. Among the Bolshoi's leading dancers today are Vladimir Vasiliev, Ekaterina Maximova, Stanislav Vlasov, Rimma Karelskaya, Nicolai Fadeyechev, and German Sitnikov, performers who would be in the first rank of any company in the world.

In many ways, the Kirov Ballet in Leningrad is like the Bolshoi; the dancers are equally superb and the productions equally lavish. In a recent season at New York's Metropolitan Opera House, it performed classic works, *The Sleeping Beauty*, *Raymonda*, *Swan Lake*, Fokine's *Prince Igor*, a number of restaged works, and only one new ballet, *A Distant Planet*, dealing with the theme of space flight and reflecting contemporary social concerns.

The major difference is that the Kirov is somehow less flamboyant and more reserved than the Bolshoi, characterized by an air of elegant style. Directed by Konstantin Sergeyev, the Kirov numbers among its leading dancers Irina Kolpakova, Alla Sizova, Natalia Makarova, Kaleria Fedicheva, Vladilen Semenov, and Yuri Soloviev.

To understand fully the training that has gone into the making of these artists, one would have to examine the Russian system of ballet instruction. This is carried on through a network of state-supported and state-controlled schools throughout the member republics of the Soviet Union. Often, those pupils who are most talented find their way to the major centers of dance, such as Moscow or Leningrad, to complete their training and, hopefully, to join the Soviet's top companies. Rudolf Nureyev, in his autobiography, tells of his training in the Kirov School, before he joined the company, achieved stardom, and ultimately fled to the West. It was a highly conservative establishment, in which students worked between eight and eleven hours a day, starting early in the morning. There were usually two hours of instruction in art history and aesthetics each day, and then two hours of literature. This was followed by two hours of classical dance instruction which, in his words, was "so concentrated, so well prepared, and so absorbing that one session there was worth four hours' instruction anywhere else in Europe."[13] In the afternoon, students were given two hours on the history of the ballet and the history of music, and then another two hours of dancing, this time "character" work. In addition, academic courses were also scheduled during the week

[13] Rudolf Nureyev, "Nureyev: An Autobiography," *Dance Magazine*, May 1966, p. 40.

in physics, chemistry, geography, and similar subjects, as well as regular lessons in fencing. In the evenings, students would often observe rehearsals of the Kirov company, or see actual performances in the theater next door.

The competition was severe and the discipline rigid. The sense of uncertainty or lack of societal approval that affects many dance students in the West (in the sense that they recognize that the career they have chosen lacks widely accepted status) never affected Nureyev. He writes:

> The fact that ballet teaching in Russia is such a scrupulously regulated profession is, I believe, the main reason for our ballet's consistent high standard. Many European dancers (I don't know yet about the American ones) go endlessly from one studio to another in a misguided search for innovations and amplifications of their technique—and not always to teachers fully qualified for their work. The end result of amateur teachers in charge of shaping amateur dancers is that ballet gradually loses its purity and splendid traditions.
> How different in Russia! How severely controlled, how strongly rooted in tradition is the profession of the ballet teacher![14]

In a sense, the same conservatism that accounted for the unwillingness to venture into new choreographic directions is responsible for the rigid but productive system that creates a Nureyev—as well as a great number of other brilliant Soviet dancers. And it becomes understandable that an artist as individual as Nureyev, with extremes of temperament and deeply felt artistic conviction, would find it impossible to live under the Soviet system and would find his way to the West—to the Royal Ballet of England.

Of all the great foreign ballet companies, the most familiar to American audiences is the Royal Ballet, both under its present name, and as the Sadler's Wells Theater Ballet, the name under which it first came to the United States. Although it was not actually founded until just after World War II, this company had its roots in 1926 when Ninette de Valois established a ballet school in London, shortly after leaving the Diaghileff Company. For a period of years, she staged the ballets which were produced at the Old Vic Theater, and, when the new Sadler's Wells Theater was built, de Valois was asked to found a school there. She did so in 1931. The students of the Sadler's Wells Ballet School, known as the Vic-Wells Ballet, continued to dance at the Old Vic and in operas given at the Sadler's Wells. This went on into the 1940s;

14 *Ibid.*, p. 42.

during the war, the company performed at the New Theater, under the worst bombing raids, and so helped to maintain the morale of Londoners.

After the war, in 1946, the company began to perform at the Covent Garden Royal Opera House, rapidly gaining in public and critical esteem. One reason underlying its success was that many of the dancers during the 1930s had been performing in Marie Rambert's Ballet Club in London, which later became the Ballet Rambert. In this setting, many of the most distinguished figures in British ballet, such as Frederick Ashton and Antony Tudor, made their choreographic debuts. In it too, dozens of younger British dancers received their early professional experience.

It was the wartime service of the Sadler's Wells Theater Ballet that gave the company the affection of the British public and a later government subsidy (under the Arts Council of Great Britain) and, finally, the Royal Charter, in 1956. During the late 1940s and early 1950s, the company performed over thirty ballets by Ninette de Valois, Frederick Ashton's *Facade, Les Rendez-vous, Apparitions, Nocturne, Les Patineurs;* Robert Helpmann's *Comus, Hamlet, Miracle in the Gorbals;* a number of works by other choreographers, and classic ballets such as *Swan Lake, Giselle, Coppelia, The Nutcracker, Les Sylphides, Carnaval, Le Spectre de la Rose,* and similar works. Its leading dancers in this early period included Robert Helpmann as *premier danseur* and Margot Fonteyn, as *prima ballerina;* also Moira Shearer, Beryl Grey, Michael Somes, Elaine Fifield, David Blair, and Stanley Holden.

When, in 1951, the Sadler's Wells Theater Ballet toured the United States for the third time, it consisted of an extremely young company—the average age of the dancers was eighteen. A new choreographer, John Cranko, had created works that were now highlights of the repertoire: *Sea Change, Harlequin in April, The Fairy Queen,* and *Pineapple Poll.* Ashton's own works, including musical abstractions such as *Symphonic Variations* and *Scènes de Ballet,* the superb coronation ballet, *Homage to the Queen,* and *Birthday Offering,* created in celebration of the 25th anniversary of the ballet company (plus a wide variety of other works, some composed for other companies, such as the full-length *Romeo and Juliet* for the Royal Danish Ballet) had become masterpieces of the British company's repertoire. It was the point of view of both the critics and the public at large that Tudor, in particular, had gained the stature of one of the world's leading choreographers—comparable, perhaps, only to Balanchine.

The Royal Ballet has continued through the 1960s with an outstanding cast of superbly skilled dancers and an extremely diverse repertoire. Thus, in 1967, it revived Nijinska's powerful

Les Noces (first performed four decades before by the Diaghileff ballet); it continues to have new works by Antony Tudor (*Shadowplay*) and Ashton (*The Dream*, a one-act version of Shakespeare's *A Midsummer Night's Dream*); Kenneth MacMillan's *Song of the Earth*; a new production by Ashton of *Cinderella*; *Paradise Lost* by Roland Petit; and many other works both classic and modern. Indeed, a major criticism of the Royal Ballet is that, while it has wide variety in its repertoire (since 1946, when the company moved to the Royal Opera House at Covent warden, it has produced 106 different works) many of its ballets have been performed only briefly, and were then discarded.

There is a degree of concern in Britain about the future of the Royal Ballet, in terms of its ability to maintain consistently a strong repertoire for the company. In the view of many, Sir Frederick Ashton, who succeeded Ninette de Valois as director in 1963, while a brilliant choreographer, has failed to do justice to his own work, or to draw a clear-cut artistic policy for others.

The dancing of the Royal Ballet has continued to be outstanding. The leading dancers are Rudolf Nureyev and Margot Fonteyn, who are classified as guest artists and who have much the same glamor as Nijinsky and Pavlova in their day; indeed there is a constant controversy among balletomanes comparing Nureyev, a spectacular and highly dramatic dancer, to Nijinsky. Svetlana Beriosova, Merle Park, and Antoinette Sibley form a trio of excellent ballerinas, and such male dancers as Anthony Dowell, David Wall, Michael Coleman, Kenneth Mason, and Keith Martin, of the younger group, offer great prospects for the future. Its dancing, as described by Barnes, is a mixture largely of Russian and Italian styles, tempered by British attitudes and physical characteristics. He describes the Royal Ballet as favoring neatness, lyricism, and speed of execution, with typical British reserve rather than exaggeration.[15]

The Royal Ballet continues to place great emphasis on the Diaghileff concept that music, design, and choreography are equal partners in the ballet enterprise. Thus, in recent additions to the repertoire, outstanding sets and musical works are displayed. Kenneth MacMillan's *Song of the Earth* was choreographed to a remarkable score by Gustav Mahler; the stage design for Roland Petit's *Paradise Lost* is a vast white egg shape, a ramp and giant female lips on the backcloth, designed by the French "new realist" painter, Marius Constant. Other ballets have similarly unusual scores and sets.

By 1967, the Royal Ballet had made ten extensive tours to the

[15] Clive Barnes, "The Only Five Great Ballet Companies," *Harper's Magazine*, May 1966, p. 65.

United States. Perhaps its major effect was in the introduction of full-evening spectacle ballets. At first, the American audience, accustomed to the pattern of having three short, separate works in a program, found this difficult to accept. However, after exposure to the Royal Ballet, with its full-evening *Sleeping Beauty*, *Swan Lake*, and *Cinderella*, as well as similar long works by the two Russian companies, the New York City Ballet and American Ballet Theater have also begun to produce full-evening works.

A final comment on the relationship between the British and American ballets is that it has been heavily one-sided. Thus, although the Royal Ballet has frequently been to America, British audiences had seen only one two-week season by an American company during the decade preceding 1967. This may in part be due to the narrow loyalty of the British public; undoubtedly too, it is related to the fact that the British company is subsidized. Also, Sol Hurok has been extremely active in bringing foreign importations to America, whereas in Britain and Europe there has been no private impresario with comparable enthusiasm and ability.

There are, of course, other British companies of distinguished reputation. Actually, the Royal Ballet has a second company which is approximately the same size as the Covent Garden Company led by Fonteyn and Nureyev. This "other" Royal Ballet spends most of its time touring through the British provinces and on the Continent; it also has an occasional London season at Covent Garden.

In England, there is also the Festival Ballet which performs in the Royal Festival Hall on London's south bank. Founded by Anton Dolin and Alicia Markova in 1949, this is essentially a touring company which, like the American Ballet Theater, has had difficulty in maintaining a company of high quality and a diverse, well produced repertory of ballets. Like the American company, it has shown much improvement recently, and thus offers promise for the British ballet scene.

A fifth internationally famed company which comes very close in stature to the British, American, and two Russian companies just described is the Royal Danish Ballet. The history of this company is an ancient one. It was founded in 1748 and has been under royal patronage since that time. The school in which its young dancers are trained was founded in 1829 by August Bournonville, who was responsible for the initial development of the company, whose repertoire of classic ballets is still performed by the company, and whose system of dance training still gives the graduates of the Royal Danish Ballet School a unique character.

Since the middle of the 19th century, the Royal Danish Ballet has continued to perform such Bournonville works as *Napoli*, *Konservatoriet*, *Far from Denmark*, and *Valdemar*. While it had produced a number of outstanding dancers and excellent new works under the direction of its ballet master during the 1940s, Harald Lander, the company was not widely known. Then, after the first annual ballet festival in Copenhagen in 1950, it began to tour more widely. When it visited the United States for the first time in 1956, it received high praise from American critics. Typically, Hering wrote:

> Their pure dance passages are meticulously hewn. And their acting is a human experience. Americans are known for their realistic acting in modern works. But the Danes have found a way of extending this style into the traditional ballets, so that even the oldest ones like *La Sylphide* and *Napoli* (both more than a century old) emerge curiously alive and convincing. And from an acting point of view the Danes are equally at home in contemporary works like Frederick Ashton's *Romeo and Juliet* and Balanchine's *La Sonnambula* . . . .[16]

In summing up the merits of the Royal Danish Ballet at present, the question of its repertoire must be raised. Chiefly, this consists of the Bournonville works, a number of other classic ballets, and several modern ballets drawn from choreographers of other nations. For example, in its repertoire in the middle 1960s, the Danish company has included: Roland Petit's *Carmen*, Jerome Robbins's *Fanfare*, Frederick Ashton's *Romeo and Juliet*, David Lichine's *Graduation Ball*, and other works by Kenneth MacMillan, Balanchine, and other modern choreographers. Recently, several new works, including two ballets by the new, young ballet master, Flemming Flindt (*The Private Lesson* and *Three Musketeers*) have been introduced into the repertoire. Also, the Danes have veered into avant-garde experimentation with such works as *Tropisms*, choreographed by Eske Holm to "serial" music, and Ivo Cramer's *Catharsis*, also to music with electronic sequences. While the Royal Danish Ballet has a curious gift for taking the works of other companies, periods, and national origins, and endowing them with a uniquely different style and manner, its problem clearly will be to establish a modern Danish repertory to accompany the Bournonville repertory that is its unique possession.

In terms of dancing, the men tend to be somewhat stronger than the women, with Erik Bruhn, gifted both as a superb classical technician and as a fine dramatic dancer, standing out as the inter-

---

[16] Doris Hering, "The Danes: An American Debut," *Dance Magazine*, November 1956, p. 14.

nationally known *danseur noble*. Other leading male dancers include Flemming Flindt, Henning Kronstam, and Niels Larsen. It is agreed that none of the Danish female dancers are of true *prima ballerina* stature, although Kirsten Simone is generally thought of as a leading performer; other ballerinas include Anna Laerkesen, Viveka Segerskog, and Ruth Andersen.

In describing these companies in detail, it would be a mistake to suggest that there are no other national ballet companies of high quality.

In Canada, for example, there has been a strong upsurge of interest in and performance of ballet in recent years. There are three strong companies at present, including the National Ballet of Canada (the largest company), the Royal Winnipeg Ballet (the oldest company in Canada, about the size of the City Center Joffrey Ballet), and Les Grands Ballets Canadiennes, from the Province of Quebec. All three companies are subsidized by the Canada Council, a program for support of the arts that is modeled after the Arts Council of Britain; they also are granted funds by provincial governments, and are able to raise substantial contributions from private industry. The productions of these three Canadian companies are extremely impressive. In terms of dancers, the National Ballet of Canada maintains its own school and is developing capable performers. None of the three companies has yet, however, been able to produce new choreographic works of any consequence. Before it will be possible to consider the Canadians of major stature, they will have to develop the kind of individual creative talent that will add significantly to the repertory.

In France, long considered the birthplace of ballet, there has not been a major ballet company for several decades. The last one, under Diaghileff, was, of course, composed chiefly of Russian dancers. Two French choreographers of considerable promise have emerged in recent years. Roland Petit achieved fame in the late 1940s and early 1950s, choreographing a number of extremely appealing works for *Les Ballets des Champs-Élysées*. However, the critical consensus is that he has never matured fully as a choreographer and, while he has continued to create a number of important works for other ballet companies, Petit has certainly not succeeded in developing a strong French ballet. Maurice Bejart, a second dramatically forceful French choreographer, has produced a number of entertaining modern works, and is presently attached to a Brussels company, *Le Ballet du* xxe *Siècle*.

The historic Paris Opéra Ballet has continued to produce ballet through the years, both as part of the operas themselves and as independent productions. For almost thirty years, Serge

Lifar, who had been a leading dancer with Diaghileff, was director of the Opéra Ballet, and choreographed many of its works. One interpretation of the failure of French ballet to achieve stature in the modern era is that the close connection between ballet and opera has tended to encourage choreographic novelty and sensationalism for its own sake—almost a frivolous and dilettantish attitude toward the production of new works.

In such a situation, ballet does not flourish as an independent art, and the works of choreographers of the stature of Balanchine or Ashton have not been performed. Recently, George Skibine joined the Opéra Ballet as a leading dancer and choreographer, and it may be that this change in personnel heralds an upswing in the fortunes of the French ballet.

Other ballet companies are to be found in most of the larger European cities, as well as in many smaller ones. Typically, they are attached to the local opera house, performing during the opera season (which may last as long as ten or eleven months) and also putting on as many as twenty or more special ballet evenings themselves and sometimes having special ballet seasons of their own. Two such companies are to be found at the Bavarian Staatsoper in Munich and La Scala in Milan. Both companies maintain schools from which dancers enter the corps de ballet. They are fairly sizable; the Munich Staatsoper has 70 dancers, and La Scala a company of 46.

Both companies perform an international repertory, including a number of classic works as well as many dances by leading foreign choreographers. When possible, they invite the choreographer himself to stage his own work. Both at such occasions and at annual Festival Weeks, major choreographers from Britain, America, and the Soviet Union have come to Munich to stage their ballets—along with outstanding guest performers.

Independent ballet companies also exist in Holland (the Netherlands National Ballet), Sweden (the Royal Swedish Ballet, now to be directed by Erik Bruhn), throughout the member republics of the Soviet Union, and in other European and South American countries. Even Australia has a fairly new company of surprising quality. There thus appears to be a steady growth of ballet interest and support throughout the world.

However, it has become increasingly clear that this art, once the aristocratic ornament of kings and nobles, is one which—while it may arouse widespread interest and attendance—has great difficulty in supporting itself properly in a financial sense. It is unlike the legitimate theater, which may have as few as a handful of actors and a single set or two. Instead, a ballet company with an extensive repertoire must have a large number of dancers (Britain's Royal Ballet has about 140 dancers, and the Bolshoi in Moscow actually has over 240), plus different sets and costumes for each work that is to be performed, and an orchestra that in some cases is a full-scale symphony orchestra. Under these circumstances, even granted a full house, or a close-to-capacity audience throughout its home and touring season, ballet must operate at a considerable deficit. The alternatives of charging admission prices that are so high that much of the potential audience is excluded or of having subscription series that insure a regular, capacity attendance, are at least partially self-defeating.

The other alternative, of having foundation grants or governmental support for specific dance works, or of receiving grants to support special aspects of touring, training, or production, is becoming increasingly recognized as a desirable solution for the support of the performing arts.

Later chapters will describe this pattern of foundation and government support for dance—both modern dance and ballet—as it has evolved in recent years.

12

MODERN DANCE TODAY

As the preceding chapter has demonstrated, ballet has acquired an extremely broad audience since mid-century; to illustrate, some 14,000 people attended ballet performances at Lincoln Center in New York City on a single April day in 1967.[1] Ballet has also succeeded in forming a number of stable companies and organizations throughout the United States—several with major public subsidies or foundation grants—and in developing a broad network of regional performing companies.

The progress of modern dance has contrasted rather sharply with that of ballet during the 1950s and 1960s.

There are apparently more modern dance companies today than there were two decades ago, and certainly more performances are being given—particularly in large cities on the East and West Coasts. Although reliable statistics are not available to support this impression, an increasing number of colleges and universities appear today to be sponsoring performances by touring professional modern dance groups. Indeed, dance education in American colleges has expanded dramatically. In terms of worldwide influence, American modern dance companies have performed before

[1] Clive Barnes, "Pioneering with the Royal Ballet," *The New York Times*, April 30, 1967, p. 8-D.

audiences in Great Britain, Europe, and the Far East in recent years, to enthusiastic acclaim.

But it is also apparent that few modern dance choreographers have succeeded in breaking away from their narrow circle of devotees to reach a broader audience in the United States. The public remains comparatively uninformed about, and unexposed to, this branch of concert dance. It is also clear that the status of the modern dance choregorapher-performer has not improved significantly since mid-century. With few exceptions, it is not possible to earn a livelihood in the field of modern dance unless one's income is supplemented through teaching.

Certain changes have taken place in the field itself.

First, in terms of approaches to choreography, there appear to be three distinct groups active today. The first consists of those artists who were active and successful before mid-century, and who have continued to maintain their companies and develop as creative artists. The second includes those dancer-choreographers who have emerged since 1950, and who are moving ahead in exciting new directions. The third group consists of those avant-garde experimenters who, like their counterparts in "pop" and "op" art, are creating work that seems almost to be *anti*-dance, or *non*-dance.

The general tenor of modern dance purpose seems also to have changed through the years. The philosophy of the early modern dancers seems to have included a romantic but vague dream of building a new, vital, American form of dance. This concept is no longer heard. Nor is the psychoanalytically oriented view of dance as a means of emotional catharsis and self-release often expressed today. Most modern dancers regard what they are doing as a disciplined art form, and not simply as a convenient means of emotional release. Nor has modern dance continued to be used as a form of social commentary or propaganda, as it tended to be in the 1930s and 1940s. This trend has died out almost completely.

What other shifts have occurred? The most marked change is that modern dancers are rarely as opposed to ballet training as they were at the beginning of the modern dance period. Instead, many today recognize the fundamental value of classic dance training. In a number of other ways, the gulf that existed between modern dance and ballet has now been bridged; this is discussed in detail at the close of this chapter.

Another trend in modern dance relates to performance by Negro dancers. During the 1940s, the Negro dancer tended to be in companies like those of Katherine Dunham or Pearl Primus, performing works that were frankly in an ethnic idiom, based on African or Afro-Caribbean rituals and dance customs, or possibly on themes of Negro life in America. Today, more modern dance works as such are performed by companies of Negroes, or racially mixed companies. Not infrequently, their themes deal with race or race history—but they are part of the modern dance movement, and not a separate little stream of activity. A related influence is the growth of modern jazz, so-called, which reflects the primitive dance rhythms and movements that stem from African and Caribbean sources. A similar trend may be seen in commercial dance on television or the stage, or in night-clubs.

Another aspect of growth of modern dance has been the development of organizations for its promotion, such as the Dance Teachers Guild (now the National Dance Guild), or the successful continuation of centers and special summer camps devoted to it—such as the Connecticut School of Dance, at New London, Connecticut. In all, the picture includes much strength, as well as much weakness. To understand the total modern dance picture,

Martha Graham and Company in "Clytemnestra." Photograph by Martha Swope.

it is necessary to examine the work of leading modern dancers and choreographers during this period.

Preeminent among these figures is Martha Graham. She continues to be a major influence among modern dancers—almost as Balanchine is in the professional ballet field. Graham's company is by far the most active, both in the United States and abroad. Among audiences that would otherwise not see modern dance, she is accepted and appreciated. Through the many dancers who have been in her company for a period of time and are now choreographers and teachers themselves, her technique and artistic viewpoint are disseminated widely throughout the country. Particularly in dance education in schools and colleges, her influence is pervasive.

What changes have occurred in Graham's approach to choreography and performance through the years? She now creates major works only—dance-dramas that are, in Hering's words, "made to last." There is a sharp contrast between the choreography designed for the rest of the company, which is now "more opulent, more pulsating, more swift," and that which she designs for herself, which is more fragmentary, less flowing, and less demanding.

> Perhaps by way of compensation, the women Miss Graham has chosen to portray have more and more been the super-heroines of Bible and mythology—Jocasta, Medea, Judith, Phaedra, Clytemnestra, Hecuba—all women whose conflicts are big and whose wills are equal to them.[2]

While Graham choreographs no short pieces that might be regarded as "fillers," or pleasant trifles, a number of her works that are concerned with dance are somewhat abstract in mood, or reveal a satirical bite. *Acrobats of God,* a lively and joyful piece about the dance, or *Diversion of Angels,* a bright and virtuosic dance, are of this category. Others, notably *Part Dream, Part Real, Circe,* and *Phaedra,* have a marked erotic quality which is justified by the dramatic content of the work—but which is disturbing to some audiences. Overall, all of her works continue to be impressively staged; they are superbly choreographed and danced by a company of unmatched dancing skill and physical attractiveness.

It should be noted that a considerable portion of Graham's creative work today is supported by subsidy in one form or another. Thus, her 1967 season in New York City, extending for three weeks, was made possible by a grant from the Lila Acheson Wallace

[2] Doris Hering, "What Sorrow Is There That Is Not Mine?" *Dance Magazine,* May 1967, p. 55.

Martha Graham and Company in "The Lady of the House of Sleep." Photograph by Martha Swope.

Foundation. The two new works which were presented at this time, *Dancing-Ground* and *Cortège of Eagles*, were financed by a grant from the National Council on the Arts. Many of the other works in the repertoire—*Appalachian Spring, Circe, Dancing Ground,* and *Acrobats of God* (to name those in a single set of program notes) —were supported fully or in part by grants. Graham's school and entire program are heavily supported by the de Rothschild Foundation.

While she has continued to dance in a limited number of roles—even in the late 1960s—it is apparent that Martha Graham can no longer do so without the risk of damaging her own reputation. Thus, she has gradually been relinquishing roles to members of her company and it seems probable that she will retire from dancing within the next few years. This raises the question of what will happen to the Graham company when its leader, now a "living legend," can no longer be active. For such an important artistic venture to be spearheaded by a single great figure is understandable—perhaps inevitable. It would be tragic, however, if Graham's giant contributions to the American dance theater could not be kept alive for future audiences, when she is no longer there to dance and to choreograph new works.

A second major figure whose reputation was established long before mid-century and who has continued to perform, choreograph, and teach is José Limón. Though lacking the stability afforded by a major school and permanently established company, he has had a number of important affiliations through the years. He has been a director of the Juilliard Dance Theater, where his company has performed both his own works and those by Doris Humphrey. He has continued to be head of the faculty and a leading performer at the Connecticut College of the Dance in New London where, summer after summer, a number of his new works have received their premieres.

Through the years, the Limón Company has carried out a number of highly successful tours of Europe, the Orient, and Latin America, under State Department sponsorship. In 1964, when the New York State Council on the Arts agreed to underwrite two performances of the American Dance Theater at Lincoln Center in New York, José Limón acted as artistic director, bringing together the works of Donald McKayle, Anna Sokolow, and Doris Humphrey on a single program, and performing in a premiere of his own *A Choreographic Offering*.

José Limón and Lucas Hoving in "The Traitor." Photograph by Matthew Wysocki.

However, Limón has by and large been unable to find a consistent audience for his works. In 1966, for example, his dance company was able to arrange only one appearance in New York City, at the Brooklyn Academy of Music, where he performed two of his most recent works, *A Choreographic Offering* and *Missa Brevis*. Clive Barnes commented on this occasion that the inability of the Limón company to have more than a "meager one-night stand" in New York City, despite its distinguished reputation, was "scandalous."[3]

Although he is no longer in his prime as a dancer, Limón is still an impressive and moving figure. His choreography is consistently serene and powerful; unfortunately, there is too little opportunity for it to be seen.

Another dancer-choreographer whose career has bridged the past quarter-century is Merce Cunningham. During the years from 1940 to 1945, he was a soloist with the Martha Graham Company, creating such roles as the Acrobat in *Every Soul Is a Circus*, the Christ Figure in *El Penitente*, March in *Letter to the World*, and the Revivalist in *Appalachian Spring*. While with Graham, he also studied ballet at the School of American Ballet where, during the late 1940s, he taught a class in modern dance.

Since the 1940s, Cunningham has been extremely successful as a choreographer with his own company. He has used the works of a number of contemporary composers, but has collaborated most intensively with the avant-garde pianist-composer, John Cage. His work has varied greatly, and invariably stirs up a strong audience reaction. He is known for his experiments with "choreography by chance," as illustrated in a 1953 work titled *Suite by Chance*. For this long dance in four movements, a large series of charts was made. One gave body movements, phrases, and positions; another chart gave numbered lengths of time; and another gave directions in space. These charts, which defined the physical limits within which the continuity would take place, were not made by chance. But from them, the actual continuity was determined as by a lottery:

> . . . a sequence of movements for a single dancer was determined by means of chance from the numbered movements in the chart; space, direction and lengths of time were found in the other charts. At important structural points in the music, the number of dancers on stage, exits and entrances, unison or individual movements of dancers were all decided by tossing coins . . . .[4]

---

[3] Clive Barnes, "A Master's One-Night Stand," *The New York Times*, February 14, 1966, p. 33.

[4] Remy Charlip, "Composing by Chance," *Dance Magazine*, January 1954, p. 19.

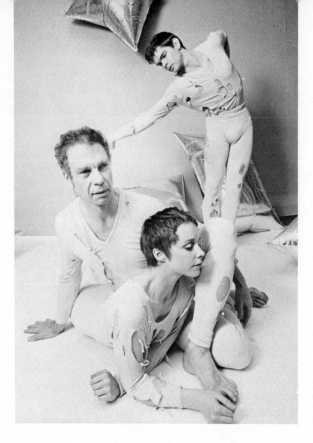

Merce Cunningham, Barbara Lloyd, and Albert Reid in "Riverwind," with décor by Andy Warhol. Photograph by Jack Mitchell.

In another work during the same period, titled *Solo Suite in Time and Space*, with music by John Cage, spots or slight imperfections on sheets of white paper (seen by holding the paper up in front of a bright light) were numbered. From these chance arrangements came the space and lengths of time of each dance. Spots on other sheets of paper, similarly numbered, gave the sequence of the movement. In another work, *Solo*, chance movements were attached to other chance movements; thus, a found-by-chance leg or torso movement would be added to a found-by-chance arm or head movement.

Cunningham has continued to choreograph in an equally experimental vein through the years. He has toured internationally with much acclaim, and has performed at major foreign festivals. In recent years, his works appear to be more carefully prestructured than during the "chance" period, although they still are often jarring to audiences. Light and sound are often used in extreme intensity, blinding and deafening the audience. A recent work, *Place*, is described on the occasion of its New York premiere in 1967:

The sound score by Gordon Mumma relentlessly blares the hideous noises of our modern life . . . . For *Place* sets us down in one spot and shows us with pitiless inexorability the shrinking of the world until there is no space left. There is only this tiny plot of ground into which the dancers huddle. Cunningham is sometimes in sole possession of it, but the others crowd in and he is reduced to cringing in a corner. They inch their way into a vacant place but, with foot in midair, they find that the space is no longer free. Only the air is still without boundary and they flail their arms, creating an illusion of freedom in which to move . . . .[5]

Cunningham has a great range of moods; in another recent work, titled *How to Pass, Kick, Fall and Run*, his dancers caper about in the gayest of spirits. In general, his choreography is an imaginative, no-holds-barred commentary on life, visually exciting, and often highly demanding of the audience. His own dancing and that of his company are of an extremely high caliber. It is always clear to the audience that if what they do does not *look* like dance, as it is popularly conceived, it is by the choreographer's choice, rather than the inability of the performers. And, just as Cunningham was a featured dancer with the Graham Company at the beginning of his career, today several members of his company have become choreographers in their own right.

Among the choreographers who have become widely known since 1950, three names stand out: Alwin Nikolais, Paul Taylor, and Alvin Ailey.

Alwin Nikolais, who today is director of the Henry Street Playhouse Dance Company, in New York City, is an accomplished musician who worked closely with Hanya Holm for a number of years, and who composes his own musical scores, which are usually electronic. He has, since the late 1950s, become noted for a new kind of dance theater which is almost completely abstract in terms of dramatic content, but which represents a unique and imaginative fusing of sound, color, light, bizarre props, shapes, and movement, to create a remarkably theatrical set of illusions on the stage.

The first of his works to be widely seen was *Totem*, choreographed in 1960. This is a full-evening work, consisting of fifteen episodes, in which abstract props seem to extend the performers' bodies. In one episode, *Shadow Totem*, dancers appear to be headless; in another, *Banshee*, dancers create a weird effect as they wave lights about under their huge, shapeless costumes; in still another, titled *Clowns*, figures clad in felt of bright color move heavily, their feet and arms suggesting bells. It is a work that has been described as

[5] "Merce Cunningham Dance Company," *Dance News*, January 19, 1967, p. 9.

"Imago," dance theatre-piece by Alwin Nikolais. Photographs by Robert Sosenko.

deriving from "mysticism, fetishism and fanaticism." Choreographer-designer Nikolais has said of it:

> Ritual and ceremony are like a formula in that certain ingredients, proportioned and mixed, cause a magical result. *Totem* comprises a number of such imagined rituals and ceremonies. I can conceive ritual in the growth of a flower, the kaleidoscopic interplay of geometrical design, the intermingling of people, the flickering of colored lights. Some of *Totem* is fun and foolish ritual, some macabre, and some frightening. To me it shows some of the fanciful moods of nature as it transpires through some of its earthly instruments, including man.[6]

A color film has been made of *Totem;* in addition, it has been seen widely throughout the United States, and was performed in 1962 at the Festival of Two Worlds in Spoleto, Italy.

A second major work of Nikolais's has been *Imago*, a full-evening dance theater piece premiered in 1963. It consists of twelve episodes involving solos, small groups, or the entire Alwin Nikolais Dance Company. Choreography, lighting, and costumes are by Nikolais, and he created the electronic score in collaboration with James Seawright. *Imago* has been variously described by critics as "weird," "fantastic," and "delightful." Since its initial performances, *Imago* has been presented on tour, at the Lincoln Center in New York City, and in a four-week revival financed by the United States National Council on the Arts, in 1967. Like *Totem*, it combines dance movement, color, lighting, and electronic music. Its ten dancers are depersonalized through remarkable costuming, the use of white makeup, and stylized headdresses. It contains both humor and menace, as well as sequences of great visual beauty.

Other important works of Nikolais have included *Sanctum* (1964), *Galaxy* (commissioned by the John Simon Guggenheim Foundation in 1965), and *Vaudeville of the Elements*, first performed in New York in 1966, and described as a "shifting science-fiction world." More than any other modern dance choreographer (except possibly Martha Graham in recent years), Nikolais has succeeded in reaching both an audience of dancers and dance enthusiasts (including those influential in the other modern arts) and the public at large, through several appearances on national television programs. He has appeared at several international festivals, has had his color films shown around the world, and has received a number of commissions for choreography from various universities and foundations. Clearly, his is a major influence in dance today.

[6] Alwin Nikolais, quoted in *Dance Magazine*, February 1962, p. 43.

The single major criticism that is frequently made of Nikolais's work is that it is dehumanized, impersonal—simply a visual and auditory design in which the performers are not dancers as such, but rather movable props, and in which man is not the concern of the dance. To this, he has replied eloquently, pointing out that all the arts have today become freed from the need to portray literal subject matter, and are able to directly translate the "abstract elements that characterize and underline an art object":

> I look upon this polygamy of motion, shape, color, and sound as the basic art of the theatre. To me, the art of drama is one thing; the art of theatre is another. In the latter, a magical panorama of things, sounds, colors, shapes, lights, illusions, and events happen before your eyes and your ears. I find my needs cannot be wholly satisfied by one art. I like to mix my magics. We are now in a new period of modern dance, and it is a period of new freedom.[7]

Nikolais goes on to comment that, while the early modern dance explored the human psyche and was almost a form of psychological drama, today character is no longer dominant. In his view, dance figures speak through motion, shape, time, and space. He points out that man's ability to communicate in non-verbal ways, and to sense meaning beyond literal and materialistic language or visual symbols, is his greatest distinction from the lower animals. Finally, he defends his work against the charge that it is cold, unemotional, and dehumanized by claiming that it is the very reverse; that it has the power to depict man to himself, as no literal image could.

Among Nikolais's leading dancers have been Gladys Bailin, Bill Frank, Phyllis Lamhut, and Murray Louis.

Of these, Murray Louis in particular has emerged in recent years as a remarkable choreographer-dancer in his own right. Performing first at the Henry Street Playhouse with a small company drawn primarily from the parent group, Louis has now appeared in other dance series and in tours of the major cities in the United States. He is widely regarded as a brilliant dancer and a highly creative choreographer whose stage works display a great range of inventive movement, humor, pathos, a suggestion of mimetic meaning, and remarkable sensitivity and choreographic authority. The mood is often mysterious and, while dramatic relationships may be suggested, the overall characteristic of Louis's work is abstraction.

---

[7] Alwin Nikolais, "No Man from Mars," in *The Modern Dance: Seven Statements of Belief*, Selma Jeanne Cohen, ed. (Middletown, Connecticut: Wesleyan University Press, 1966), pp. 63–64.

Among his better known works have been *Interims*, to music by Lucas Foss; *Chimera*, a solo which offers what seems to be a pop-art parody of electronic music; *Concerto*, a much-praised and much-abused interpretation of a Bach Brandenburg Concerto; *Illume*, danced to a score by Toshio Mayuzumi, suggesting strange creatures of the sea; *Facets*, a duet with Gladys Bailin; and *Calligraph for Martyrs*, an impressive piece which reaches great heights of emotion. While his choreography has undoubtedly been influenced by Nikolais, for whom he has been a leading dancer for a number of years, Murray Louis makes much less use of elaborate sets, props, and visual effects, and is much more directly concerned with the recognizable and comparatively unadorned dancer.

Probably the most successful American dancer-choreographer, in terms of having reached a broad international audience in recent years, has been Paul Taylor. Originally a painter, Taylor danced first with Merce Cunningham and then with Martha Graham. Since 1956, when he formed his own small company—

Paul Taylor and Company in "Orbs." Photograph by Jack Mitchell.

now consisting of nine dancers—he has choreographed almost 50 works, has toured widely, and has earned a reputation as one of the world's leading modern dance choreographers. The Paul Taylor Dance Company appeared at the 1960 Spoleto Festival, toured Italy in 1961, danced at the Festival of Nations in Paris in 1962 where Taylor received an international critics' award as best choreographer, and performed in 1963 in performances in Mexico sponsored by the Mexican Government. In 1964, he toured throughout the United States and then through Europe (Italy, France, Belgium, Holland, England, Iceland). In the following years, he has continued to travel widely. In 1967, the company toured the Near and Far East, including Egypt, Korea, and Japan; it was Taylor's fourth tour under the auspices of the United States State Department. Taylor comments himself:

> Most places overseas are hungry for our kind of thing. European ballet seems somewhat outdated, and audiences have begun to look to American dance. They're receptive to new work and they seem to have a marvelous time with us . . . .[8]

Taylor's success, of course, is due to the dancing that his company offers. He is unpretentious about his own work, and has written amusingly on the theme, "Down with choreographers!" Nonetheless, his work is painstakingly developed and permits his excellent dancers to show their strengths in well-mounted pieces. It is both complex and simple, serene and exciting, stylish and witty. Taylor is not afraid to repeat himself to build an effect, and often deliberately limits the amount of invention in his dances, repeating and changing basic movement patterns, and setting them to music with contrasting tempi, in order to develop them fully.

For the most part, his work is abstract although the viewer may perceive dramatic content if he wishes to do so. Taylor seems almost to represent a blending of Martha Graham and Balanchine; his work is authoritative, almost classic, and yet refreshingly new, with emphasis placed on dance first and foremost. Among his dances have been *Party Mix*, a parody on party-going; *Scudorama*, concerned with the grim life of cities; *Aureole*, a bouncing, poetically musical work to a setting by Handel; *From Sea to Shining Sea*, a satirical appraisal of American culture; and *Orbs*, his latest and most ambitious work. First seen in New York in December, 1966, *Orbs* is an examination of man and the universe—the sun, the seasons, God and Man, the planets—all interwoven in a fascinating personalized epic of six major sections. It is set to the last

[8] Paul Taylor, quoted in "Have Troupe, Will Travel," *The New York Times*, July 3, 1966, p. 16-D.

Paul Taylor with Dan Wagoner and Molly Reinhart in "From Sea to Shining Sea." Photograph by Jack Mitchell.

quartets of Beethoven, and has been hailed by critics and the public as a masterpiece of choreography.

It is a curious paradox that Taylor, like other major modern dance artists of today, although he has been well received throughout the United States, finds greater acclaim and opportunity to perform before large receptive audiences abroad. Thus, in the mid-fall of 1966, his company had made only one appearance in New York, at the Brooklyn Academy of Music, and was having considerable difficulty in arranging a brief New York season for a later time in the year. At the same time, he has had no difficulty in obtaining extended bookings abroad, in London and other major cities. Taylor comments:

> We're homebodies and we like to perform our work for American audiences. And for dancers, the constant traveling is disruptive and exhausting. But it's financially impossible to put on a big-city show in the U.S. The expenses always exceed what we take in at the box office. Actually, we're very lucky to be one of the few companies that can exist by performing abroad.[9]

[9] *Ibid.*

Alvin Ailey with Carmen de Lavallade in "Roots of the Blues." Photograph by Jack Mitchell.

Another American dancer-choreographer who has had re-markable success both abroad and in the United States is Alvin Ailey. Originally trained as a dancer by Lester Horton on the West Coast, Ailey has assembled a company of outstanding dancers who perform both his own works and those of a number of other modern choreographers. One of the highlights of the Alvin Ailey Dance Theater is that it was the first Negro company have been sent abroad by the President's International Exchange Program, administered by ANTA under the auspices of the United States State Department. During this 1962 tour, the company presented sixty performances for 146,791 people in twenty-five cities in ten countries—Australia, Burma, Viet Nam, Malaya, Indonesia, the Philippines, Hong Kong, Formosa, Japan, and Korea. Rich praise was heaped upon them; in Hong Kong the dance critic wrote:

> These dancers spin, jackknife, twist, swivel, leap, prance, ripple, flutter, slide, contract, recoil, spring, shiver and quake in a way that makes any other dancing look jaded, wooden and stiff.[10]

[10] Arthur Todd, "Two Way Passage for Dance," *Dance Magazine*, July 1962, p. 39.

One important effect of this tour was that it brought home an understanding of creative dance in America to large groups of artists and intellectuals throughout the East, as well as a more varied and positive view of the role of the American Negro. Edwin Reischauer, American Ambassador to Japan commented:

> In many fields of art and culture we of the United States have much to learn from the culture of Japan, but in other fields—and here I would especially single out the field of modern dance—we believe that we have something of value to contribute . . . . In the entire range of the performing arts, I know of no art form more uniquely American than the music of the American Negro. This music, and the dances which derive from it . . . have about them something of the originality of expression and the vitality that I like to think of as characteristic to the United States.[11]

Actually, the Ailey company does not perform works that are restricted to Negro themes or musical sources. In the Far Eastern tour, for example, the following works we.e performed: John Butler's drama of New England, *Letter to a Lady;* Glen Tetley's *Mountain Way Chant,* an archaic ritual of the Navajo Indian with music by Carlos Chavez; and *Hermit Songs,* a series of solo dances by Ailey, set to ancient poems written by Irish monks, to music by Samuel Barber. Only in the final 40-minute section of the 2-hour program presented by the company were Negro materials used exclusively. This section included one of Ailey's major works, *Revelations,* a deeply felt work based on the Negro experience in America—full of anger, compassion and, ultimately, a moving spirit of celebration. Other pieces choreographed by Ailey included *Roots of the Blues,* a duet with Carmen de Lavallade, with three jazz musicians and folk singer Brother John Sellers on stage; and *Fix Me Jesus,* a starkly effective study.

In recent years, Ailey has toured the United States, and has also performed in a number of European countries. In 1964, his company had a six-week season in London, more than any other American dance group, and in 1966, had an extensive series of performances in Germany and Belgium. In recent appearances in the United States, Ailey has performed works by Talley Beatty, including *Congo Tango Palace* and *The Road of the Phoebe Snow,* in addition to pieces from his own repertoire. It is clear that, far from being a choreographer who deals only with folk materials—in this case dance and music of the American Negro—Alvin Ailey must be recognized simply as a major creative artist of our time. Like Paul Taylor, he has been a superb ambassador for America

[11] Edwin Reischauer, quoted in "Two Way Passage for Dance," *op. cit.,* p. 39.

and, in his own view, has learned much from his tours of other lands concerning the roots of dance and its place in society.

One of the most unusual choreographers of the present day, in terms of her background and the scope of her professional efforts, is Anna Sokolow. This unusual creative artist spans the period from Martha Graham's early days at the Neighborhood Playhouse on the lower East Side, through the present. She has taught movement to actors and choreography to ballet dancers; her works today are performed in foreign lands and by a number of American companies, of both modern dance and ballet.

Sokolow performed in the Graham company during the 1930s; she also appeared in workers' clubs with her Dance Unit, performing works with anti-Fascist themes and other themes of social significance. She worked and performed in Russia in the mid-1930s, and in 1939 was invited to Mexico by the Fine Arts Ministry to appear for a six-week season with a company she had formed there years before. She remained in Mexico, teaching young Mexican dancers, who called themselves "Las Sokolovas" and who later became the nucleus of a large group called "La Paloma Azul." From this group came several leading Mexican choreographers, like Raquel Gutierrez and Ana Mérida. For nine years after this, Anna Sokolow commuted between New York and Mexico City. There, the largest and most impressive theater was hers and she choreographed a number of important works, with the collaboration of Mexico's leading composers and designers. Mexican themes have since pervaded a number of her works, like *Mexican Retablo* and *Lament for the Death of a Bullfighter*.

Drawn back to New York City as a center for her creative work, Sokolow was again involved in another land when, in 1953, she went to Israel, to teach movement to the Inbal group, a company of Yemeni dancers that has since toured the world with great success. Over a period of years, she then divided her activities between Israel and the United States, spending between four and six months in Israel each year, staging theater works. In the early 1960s, she served as director-teacher-choreographer for the Lyric Theater there, a unique form of experimental theater:

> It is in the truest sense of the word a dance theater fusing dance and drama. . . . Essentially, I want to experiment with the spoken word and movement as I have done with Kafka's *Metamorphosis*. Kafkaesque images particularly lend themselves to the style of dance theatre I conceive.[12]

[12] Walter Sorell, "We Work Toward Freedom," *Dance Magazine*, January 1964, p. 53.

Since that time, Anna Sokolow has become extremely active once again in the United States. She teaches the actors of the Lincoln Center Repertory Theater dramatic movement, just as years before she taught choreography to ballet students in New York's School of American Ballet. This crossing of traditional lines is typical of Sokolow's career. In 1967, the National Ballet of Washington performed the Broadway premiere of her work, *Night*, a grim and ominous study to electronic music by Luciano Berio. At the same time, her jazz ballet *Opus 65* was being performed by the City Center Joffrey Ballet, in New York. The Joffrey group also plans to use Sokolow's important work, *Rooms*, in their repertory; the latter dance is also performed by the Alvin Ailey Company and the Netherlands Dance Theater.

In these works, as in others which she performs with her own company, such as *Dreams, Déserts, Lyric Suite,* or *Time +7,* Sokolow shows a deep concern with modern man's existential state. Her view of life is a bleak and painful one, and her dances are bitter, frightening, tragic—and yet somehow compassionate and moving. The choreography of *Night* is described as:

> [a] madhouse delirium of weird night-shapes ... and compulsive night fears ... terrified and lost, full of half formulated gestures and dances either shaking with tension or limp with despair .... [13]

In *Dreams,* there is the shattering imagery of humans imprisoned in an imaginary concentration camp; people running hopelessly in place; falling, despairing; an unbearable message of misery. In *Déserts,* a world of mystery and loneliness is exposed. It begins and ends with the same image: a dozen individuals are seated on the floor, heads bowed, their postures defenseless and exhausted.

> When they move, it is with the frantic quality of people under attack by invisible assailants; they writhe; they spin feverishly; their eyeballs bulge with the pressure of panic. They jump straight into the air, then fall, their arms flailing against bodies which burn with a thousand itches. It is as if each is experiencing a personal inferno, unreachable and unrelievable. [14]

Without question, Anna Sokolow is today firmly established as a major creative figure in the world of dance, and her influence and reputation are continuing to grow steadily.

[13] Clive Barnes, "A Sombre 'Night' Unfolds," *The New York Times,* May 7, 1966, p. 8.
[14] Jacqueline Maskey, "Anna Sokolow Dance Company," *Dance Magazine,* May 1967, p. 36.

Erick Hawkins (right) with Nancy Meehan and James Tyler in "Early Float-ing." Photograph by Jack Mitchell.

Another gifted and original choreographer today is Erick Hawkins. Working to music composed by Lucia Dlugoszewski, he has performed with a company of five dancers in the major modern dance series, and has toured the "college circuit" during the 1960s, with much success. His work is highly experimental and abstract, and stresses the use of unusual music, or "choreo-graphic sound," created during the performance, on sculpturally designed instruments. His best known works include *Early Floating*, *Geography of Noon*, *Naked Leopard*, and *Lord of Persia*, commissioned by the American Dance Festival of Connecticut College and first performed there in 1965. Hawkins also directs his own school in New York, the New School of Dance Technique and Art.

One of the most promising young dancers today, and one who has successfully bridged the gap between modern dance and ballet, is Glen Tetley. He is regarded as a modern dancer, in the sense that he has performed with the Martha Graham Company as a soloist, and often appears with his company on modern dance series. He also, however, has been a soloist with the American Ballet Theater, and has choreographed works for that company and for the Netherlands Dance Theater, resident company of The Hague, over two and a half years.

Tetley's dances include *Ricercare*, created for the American Ballet Theater; *Pierrot Lunaire*, danced by the Netherlands Company; and *The Mythical Hunters*, created originally for the Batsheva Company of Israel. Tetley is regarded as an extremely inventive and subtle choreographer and performer.

Daniel Nagrin, for many years co-director of the Tamiris-Nagrin Dance Company with his wife Helen Tamiris, continues to dance actively in both company and solo recitals in the United States and abroad. An extremely intense and vigorous dancer, Nagrin is known for such works as *A Gratitude; Not Me, But Him; ...Versus...; The Man Who Did Not Care;* and *Indeterminate Figure*—a view of man whose commanding self-image is contradicted by his irrepressible foibles and weaknesses of character.

An outstanding Negro dancer, who has performed with the Martha Graham Company, the New Dance Group, the Anna Sokolow Dance Theater, and the New York City Center Opera Ballet, is Donald McKayle. He has appeared on Broadway in a number of musicals, and has choreographed several successful shows, including *Golden Boy*, as well as many television productions. On the concert stage, his best known works were *District Storyville*, *Rainbow Round My Shoulder*, and *Games*. He has been guest choreographer at the Festival of Two Worlds in Spoleto, has taught and performed in Israel, and has had his work performed as part of the American Dance Theater in the mid-1960s.

Other dancers who are extremely active today include Pauline Koner, Pearl Lang, Katherine Litz, Paul Sanasardo, Sybil Shearer, James Waring, Bertram Ross, Ruth Currier, Stuart Hodes, Lucas Hoving, and Helen McGehee. In almost every case, they have been leading dancers with one or more of the companies or choreographers described earlier, and have since ventured into independent careers as teachers heading their own companies. To do full justice to them, as well as to many other active choreographers around the country, is not possible within the confines of this chapter.

In a number of cases, young choreographers who might otherwise have found it impossible to mount productions have joined together in informal groups or associations to sponsor joint recitals or series of programs. One such group in New York City is the Dance Theater Workshop. Among those who have shown choreographic works as part of this group are Jeff Duncan, Jack Moore, Judith Willis, Gus Solomons, Elizabeth Keen, Judith Dunn, and Bill Dixon.

Frequently, such dance programs are extremely experimental in nature; indeed, a number of these dancers and choreographers represent offshoots from companies that are themselves regarded as avant-garde. Within the dance world, there is something of a split regarding the extreme avant-garde, which many regard as non-dance and as actually harmful to the entire movement. What does *avant-garde* mean, in this context, and what are its implications?

First, it must be recognized that experimentalism has always flourished in modern dance, as in all contemporary art. The essence of modern dance is that it challenges old traditions and must represent a seeking of new rather than a replaying of old tunes.

Essentially, what has happened in the dance of Nikolais, Cunningham, Hawkins, and other highly experimental choreographers is that they have been keeping pace with what is happening in the other arts. The notion of dance being abstract is not in itself at all shocking or controversial. Abstract painting and sculpture have been widely accepted in recent years, and much of the ballet of Balanchine (to pick the most solidly entrenched choreographer in that field) is completely nonliteral. What if dance movement does not fit the audience's expectation? Throughout the history of dance, new techniques and movements have constantly been developed by innovative performers and choreographers. In terms of having dancers disguised as objects, or making use of properties that tend to make the dance something of an engineering phenomenon—these too have counterparts in history (such as the lighting and staging techniques of Loie Fuller) and in the other arts, with the current example of "op art" that makes use of objects that are moved by magnetism and built-in motors. Even the sound that is used to accompany avant-garde dance is paralleled by what is happening widely in the music field itself—the use of "fixed" instruments, electronic sound, or even silence as a form of "sound."

The real stumbling block for many audiences or dance critics comes in the realm of dances that are essentially "happenings." The term "happening" has been defined by one writer as follows:

A Happening is simply anything that happens to more than one person in a sort of half-planned, half-spontaneous way. It is an experience shared, and each individual takes from it what he will. Sometimes there are performers and an audience; sometimes the audience are themselves the participants; sometimes there are participants and no audience. A Happening usually consists of several Events which are totally unrelated—a kaleidoscope of impressions, as it were. Performers do not portray characters in specific environments; they are always themselves in precisely the environment in which the Happening is taking place.[15]

Examples of possible happenings:

A butterfly is let loose in a theater. The audience watches. When the butterfly flies out the window, the performance is over.

Several musicians appear before an audience and sit in perfect silence. The audience listens to the incidental sounds of traffic, coughing, etc.

A mass mural is painted in the park, by having a hundred feet of heavy paper put up and dozens of children and adults splash it with poster paint.

There is something intriguing about all this, but a good part of it has to do just with the novelty of the situation, and with humans involved in an informal process of self-discovery and social contact. How much it relates to art is another question—and the degree to which it represents leg-pulling on the part of the "happening" planner, is a moot point.

In terms of dance, when a "happening" is staged, it usually represents a degree of preplanning and existing structure. Thus, in a work viewed recently, a solo dancer moved around the stage in a dance of five sections. In each section the audience was asked to participate differently. In the first, they rattled paper. In the next, they shouted out numbers at random. In another, they scraped their feet on the floor or cleared their throats. Presumably, the dance was influenced by the sounds they made. After a period of time, the dance was over.

In another dance on the same program, a jazz musician played a series of unconnected, spontaneous phrases on a horn; the sounds were evocative, original, and drew forth a series of vocal sounds from the dancer who sat next to him for the first part of the work. Finally, the dancer began to move about the floor, as the musician explored the possibilities of his instrument with short bursts of sound. The dancer's movement had no strict beginning or end; it seemed to be a cross-section of unrelated gestures and locomotor movement, chosen at random and stopped abruptly.

All of this, as indicated, has a base in the other arts— particularly in recent trends in the graphic and plastic arts.

[15] Jerome Rockwood, "What's Happening," Letter to the Editor, *The New York Times*, January 16, 1966, p. X-7.

There, the surrealist, abstract expressionist, and action schools of painting have given way, through the 1960s, to the "pop" and "op" movements. Characteristic of the latter are that they frequently are based on, or make use of, commonplace objects. Sometimes these may be "found" objects which most would regard as little more than junk. Thus, in a museum one may find on display a crushed automobile, a toilet seat, the replica of the inside of a grimy diner, or the plaster cast of a man driving a car. When it is not the actual object itself, it may be the photograph-like painting of it, as in the painting of giant soup cans, comic strips, or posters. Sometimes it may represent a carefully worked-out abstract design to create visual illusions, or may be based on mechanical contrivances which supply motion to the art object, as in a motor-driven mobile.

Over a period of time, a number of leading choreographers have reflected these approaches. In Merce Cunningham's "chance" dances, the idea of improvisation, based on certain stimuli being chosen at random, results in what might almost be called "found" movement. In Nikolais's choreography, one finds a strong resemblance to "op art." In almost all of the avant-garde works, there is a tendency to avoid literal thematic material, and also to avoid the appearance of dance that is organized, fitted to instrumental musical accompaniment, and consistently danced in the same way.

Thus, dance may be perceived as being within the mainstream of modern art. One might assume that the audience for avant-garde dance would grow as, apparently, the audience for avant-garde art has grown. But there is a real question as to whether this has happened, or whether, in a field which has always been directed to an extremely narrow audience, the most extreme experimenters in avant-garde dance have not in effect painted themselves into a corner by alienating large portions of that audience.

To illustrate the point further, it may be helpful to describe more fully the work of one of the major experimenters in avant-garde dance, Ann Halprin. Her company, the Dancers' Workshop of San Francisco, performed an extensive piece titled *Parades and Changes* in New York, in 1967. Hering describes their work as intended to be fluid and semi-improvisational, yet quite intense in mood. The curtain was up as the audience assembled; the dancers, dressed in trousers and skirts, moved down the aisles and lined up neatly on stage. Then they turned to face the audience and began to disrobe.

. . . one's interest shifted to the cleverly timed device of having some dancers dressing while others were undressing; by having some dancers suddenly contemplate each other or give the impression that they were competing over each other. All of this was understated, almost ritualistic. Endless carpets of brown wrapping paper were stretched across the stage. The dancers, by now all nude, became entangled in the paper. Some punched at it furiously. Some crawled or stood beneath it . . . . By degrees all gathered up huge armfuls of the paper and began jumping into the pit . . . .[16]

At a later point, the company, dressed now in white, crawled down the aisles, ran down, descended from rope ladders which were attached from the balcony, or just stood and swayed epileptically. They trembled, shouted at the audience and flopped to the floor, now and then rearing up like a "mass of beached fish." The dancers embraced wildly but sexlessly. They stamped on little platforms, yelled like jungle beasts, laughed hysterically, threw themselves about with no concern for their physical safety.[17]

In another series of experiments in California, Halprin's dancers joined together with a group of architects exploring the possibility of "kinetic environments." The purpose of this collaboration was to enable members of each group to become aware of the nature and possibilities of the other art. As part of it, they constructed a driftwood village on the beach, each person or small team developing environments that suited their needs. Another involved a "tower and paper event" in which dancers "told stories" either physically or verbally, and the architects designed and immediately put up light-and-paper constructions based on the repeated telling of the story in different locations. Anderson recounts a major event which illustrates the approach to developing the "kinetic environment." It took place in Union Square in San Francisco, and was designed to simultaneously constitute a dance composition, an architectural investigation, an exploration of how environment affects man and man affects environment, and finally, a "theater event." At noon on a July day, forty young people entered the square. They sat about, ate lunch, casually napped, or fed pigeons. At three o'clock chimes from a nearby building struck the hour.

The forty young people immediately stopped whatever they were doing and solemnly rose to their feet, as though for a ceremony in church. Each person scanned the square, attempting to establish

[16] Doris Hering, "Dancer's Workshop of San Francisco in 'Parades and Changes,'" *Dance Magazine,* June 1967, p. 37.
[17] *Ibid.,* p. 72.

eye contact with at least twenty other people from the group. That done, they slowly began walking to the center of the square.

As though they were magnets or modern-day Pied Pipers, their simple act of walking to a common meeting-point drew a crowd of curious followers behind them. Now in the center where all the paths converged, each of the forty inflated a balloon and either let it fly off into the air or gave it to a child. Then the forty mysterious strangers walked away.[18]

The purpose of all this is difficult to assess, as are the outcomes. A comparatively small audience gets to view such works, although occasionally a mass audience may be attracted, as in the case of an unusual production which was given in a New York City armory during the fall of 1966. This program, which combined the arts of music, painting, and dance with a total controlled environment that made use of high-powered sound and lighting equipment, was in effect a nine-day "happening" that drew many thousands as spectators and semiparticipants. Ultimately, it was revealed as a somewhat boring sequence of pretentious but meaningless large-scale episodes to which the audience reacted, in a generally good-natured way, by walking out in large numbers.[19]

One of the most serious problems of modern dance is that, both in colleges and in the community, it is widely assumed that anyone can become a choreographer. As a consequence, many individuals with comparatively little training, skill, or talent have established themselves as choreographers and have presented works through which audiences have judged the field of modern dance. Often audiences have lacked criteria through which to do this, or any sense of perspective, or knowledge of other modern art forms. The result has frequently been that the product is poor and the audience response negative. The temptation of avant-garde dance is that it creates a situation in which there are even fewer standards—in fact, none—which an audience or choreographer can apply. Thus, how intelligently can it be judged by a spectator? How many uncomfortable questions can a choreographer ask himself?

The premises on which avant-garde dance are based sacrifice certain strengths inherent in a more traditional approach to choreography. Self-expression, naive as it may be, at least provides an impulse for the composer and the possibility of meaningful communication with an audience. The selection of thematic

[18] Jack Anderson, "Dancers and Architects Build Kinetic Environment," *Dance Magazine*, November 1966, p. 52.
[19] Doris Hering, "The Engineers Had All The Fun," *Dance Magazine*, December 1966, pp. 36–40.

material which is dramatic, or which is perceptibly concerned with social content or psychological insights, again offers the possibility of holding an audience, or providing the piece with structure. The use of music which has its own form, mood, rhythms, and aesthetic content, lends another kind of strength to dance. The approach to choreography which values the application of traditional principles of artistic construction—balance, contrast, sequence, climax, dynamics—offers a system in which the composer may learn a craft, and through which he may be judged.

Much avant-garde dance tends to lack these elements. It stands or falls strictly on the basis of superficial and transitory audience appeal. And, based on many of the works that have been presented thus far, many of the most experimental pieces have little to offer, once the novelty of freedom in "no-holds-barred" improvisation, or the surprise of seeing dancers in customarily hidden activity or states of dress (or undress) has passed away.

This, of course, represents a personal judgment. Each artist, as well as each spectator, must make his own decisions in matters of artistic taste. However, many teachers and choreographers fear that if the avant-garde approach to choreography assumes dominance in the modern dance field, it will have serious consequences. If an increasing number of choreographers—particularly those who lack real conviction in this area, or whose basic skills are limited—adopt this approach because it is fashionable and they feel it is easy and cannot be judged with rigor, the risk is that modern dance will come increasingly to be judged as a strange and mysterious "put on." Instead of being regarded as a significant art form, it will be threatened, even more than in the recent past, with rejection or disinterest. Therefore, it would appear that an atmosphere somehow must be maintained—both in schools and in colleges where beginning choreography is done—that permits young artists to critically evaluate the trend, to see it in comparison to other styles of choreography, and if they wish, to reject it, rather than accept it blindly.

Finally, it must be strongly affirmed that a movement like this *must* exist if modern dance, like any other art, is to be healthy. It represents the cutting edge of creativity in dance, and it is entirely possible that a decade or two from now, when entirely new possibilities for creative dance have been discovered, what is being done today will appear incredibly traditional and outmoded.

A final area to be explored, in terms of the concert dance field today, is that of the relationship between modern dance and ballet. Obviously, during the early decades of the development of modern dance, there was a considerable amount of hostility between the two. Modern dancers for the most part rejected ballet strenuously, as a foreign, decadent, and mechanical art form. They saw it as meaningless in terms of meeting the contemporary concerns of people. In their view, it was so committed to an obsolete movement vocabulary, and to themes of a distant past, that it no longer was significant to those who wished to view dance as part of the contemporary cultural scene.

Margaret H'Doubler, for example, the leading pioneer of modern dance in higher education, wrote in this vein:

> The ballet is a form of theater dance that continues to be popular in the more urban centers of this country, although as an art form it has never taken root in American soil. Its earliest importations were taught by foreign dance masters, and in essence they were dances of an aristocratic Europe . . . . As a theater art, dance should inspire and thrill, and cause man to think and feel. If ballet were denied its spectacular settings, costumes and orchestra, and were forced to rely upon its movements for conveyance of meaning, it is doubtful if it would carry much significance as drama or dance. Both the technique and the themes seem to have lost touch with life, with common human impulses from which all the arts spring.[20]

On the other hand, Kirstein, writing in the mid-30s, characterized the way in which many of the proponents of ballet thought about modern dance. He described those who create "in spite of and outside tradition" as almost invariably suffering from lack of information, competence, or accomplishment. Ultimately, he saw what they created as becoming a rigid "school of formulated dilettantism."[21]

Even more critically, the English ballet critic Arnold Haskell wrote about an early stage of what was to become modern dance:

> Dancing that gets its inspiration from ancient Greece is also popular today, and doubtless it is of distinct benefit as physical education. So is hockey. (Both have a thickening effect on the ankles.) Its artistic pedigree will not bear close examination . . . . The dancing rebels do provide one fine ingredient—thought. There is a close parallel here with the unlicensed medical practitioner.[22]

Thus there was a mutual hostility between modern dancers and ballet performers; it extended to audiences, teachers, and choreographers. Most modern dancers, although they might have

[20] Margaret H'Doubler, *Dance: A Creative Art Experience* (New York: F. S. Crofts and Company, 1940), p. 38.
[21] Lincoln Kirstein, *Dance: A Short History of Classic Theatrical Dancing* (New York: G. P. Putnam's Sons, 1935), p. 305.
[22] Arnold Haskell, *Ballet* (Harmondsworth, Middlesex, England: Penguin Books, 1951), p. 45.

had a degree of ballet training in their youth, regarded it as a separate and unrelated art, and one in which they had little interest—certainly one which had no part in their own systems of technical training. Most ballet dancers and choreographers saw modern dance as a somewhat obscure cult of enthusiasts who concealed with mystic statements of purpose their lack of ability to really dance. Or, in contrast, they viewed it, as Haskell did, as a fairly vigorous but certainly not artistic form of physical education.

However, even in the early years there were some exceptions. Ted Shawn, who had had ballet training himself, regarded it as a valuable ingredient in the development of a dancer:

> So much has been said and written against the ballet that I feel it is wise to emphasize some of its positive virtues. Nothing has ever taken its place for disciplinary training. There is no technique in any other style of dancing that is so valuable for producing exactitude, precision, sense of form and sense of line. I do not think that it should be used as the sole type of training, just as I would not advocate in an academic curriculum that a student should have nothing but mathematics .... It must be taught wisely and with discrimination ....[23]

On the other hand, an increasing number of ballet choreographers came to be influenced by the approach of the leading modern dance composers. In a number of cases, their works became hardly distinguishable from modern dance itself. Kurt Jooss, in Germany during the 1920s and 1930s, was strongly influenced by the work of Mary Wigman and Rudolf von Laban; many of his important ballet works, including the famous *The Green Table* (lately revived by the City Center Joffrey Ballet), clearly show the influence of the early modern dance. Respect began to grow steadily for the major modern dance choreographers who emerged in America during the 1930s. Thus, in England, which has never had a strong modern dance movement, in spite of Laban's influence there, Lester comments, "The principal pioneers in Modern Dance are a force which has made a formidable impression on the course of theatrical stage dancing...."[24] Gradually, knowledge and respect for the new art grew:

> In Britain, all too little is known, and less is appreciated, about dancing in this genre, despite the presence of the Ballets Jooss

[23] Ted Shawn, *Dance We Must* (London: Dennis Dobson, Ltd., 1946), p. 88.
[24] Susan Lester, *Ballet Here and Now* (London: Dennis Dobson, Ltd., 1961), p. 25.

between 1933 and 1947. The visit of Martha Graham and her company from the U.S.A. in 1954 was a significant introduction to Britain of a unique form, combining highly trained artists, an artistic director and principal choreographer of great ability, and intensely theatrical ballets with finely conceived modern musical scores and décors. The chief barrier between Graham and her public in Britain has been unfamiliarity with her medium and hence, some prejudice and a general hesitation in acceptance.[25]

Others were to follow Graham; by the middle 1960s, the companies of Merce Cunningham, Alvin Ailey, and Paul Taylor all enjoyed extended seasons in Great Britain. In 1964, Francis Mason, Deputy Cultural Attaché, of the United States Embassy in London, described their great success:

> ... audiences were fervent, faithful and articulate .... If there ever was a prejudice here against dance that is not strictly ballet, it is now strictly on the wane.[26]

Both in the United States and abroad, the barrier between modern dance and ballet has been breached in two ways.

First, modern dancers have increasingly come to recognize the value of ballet training. More and more they are incorporating fundamental ballet terms, positions, and movements into their systems of modern dance training. It is becoming increasingly necessary for a skilled modern dancer to take separate classes in ballet as part of his training. This is reflected both in the schools that serve professional modern dance companies, and in the programs that are devoted to dance as a performing art in American colleges and universities. Although most of these are primarily concerned with modern dance as a concert art form, the following institutions are examples of those which offer courses in ballet as well: the University of California at Los Angeles, the University of Colorado, the University of Illinois, Butler University in Indianapolis, the University of Michigan, the University of Wisconsin, Sarah Lawrence College, and Bennington College. A number of years ago, this was not the case.

Ballet, on the other hand, has been chiefly influenced by modern dance in terms of choreographic ideas and approaches. Many of the great contemporary ballet choreographers, including Tudor, de Mille, Robbins, and Ashton, have selected the kinds of themes that modern dance broke new ground exploring—in symbolic works involving psychological insights of human

[25] *Ibid.*, p. 26.
[26] Francis Mason, "London Likes American Dancer," *The New York Times,* December 27, 1964, p. X-19.

behavior. They have also clearly been influenced by the leading modern dancers in terms of their use of dancers and dance groups, in their selection of music and decor, and in their extension of the range of dance movement. In a number of contemporary ballet works, the movement is indistinguishable from what one might find on the modern dance concert stage.

As a consequence of this breakdown of the wall between the two forms, there has in recent years been a widespread use of modern dance choreographers to develop works for major ballet companies. One of the frequently noted problems of the ballet world is its lack of gifted young choreographers. Thus, company directors have felt free to cross the line. American Ballet Theater has premiered new work by Glen Tetley, known as a modern dance choreographer. The Harkness Ballet has put dances by such moderns as Alvin Ailey, Stuart Hodes, and Donald McKayle into its repertory. The Joffrey Ballet presents works by Anna Sokolow and Norman Walker. Martha Graham and Balanchine collaborated on a two-part work, *Episodes*, with music by Anton Webern; it was performed by the New York City Ballet at the City Center as part of the regular 1959 season. Other examples are numerous. In 1966, Merce Cunningham created a new work, *Summerspace*, on commission for the New York City Ballet. John Butler, whose primary background is in modern dance, has composed many works for the Harkness Ballet, the Netherlands Dance Theater, the Pennsylvania Ballet, and the Metropolitan Opera ballet, as well as numerous nationwide television dance programs. James Waring, a highly experimental and creative choreographer, crosses the line so fully in both his teaching and composition, that it is not possible to definitely identify him with either modern dance or ballet.

Yet, will the difference between the two forms break down completely? It seems unlikely. There will be, for the foreseeable future, a group of modern dancers and choreographers who will reject ballet training, or at least be unwilling to accept it as their primary source of technique. They will be determined to pursue such irrevocably experimental directions that they will continue to be recognizable as modern dancers. On the other hand, certain companies will continue to base their repertory very heavily on classic dances of the Romantic period, or on modern works which have a strong classic flavor about them; these companies will be easily identifiable as ballet companies. Somewhere in a middle group, there will probably be an increasing number of modern dance companies that look very much as if they were performing ballet—and vice versa.

This process of cross-fertilization is undoubtedly a good thing for theater dance in America. It does not, for the immediate future, however, serve to solve the pressing problems of professional dance companies—particularly those of modern dance artists. For them, as suggested earlier, there continues to be a minimal degree of support and acceptancy by the public. Although such artists as Graham, Ailey, Taylor, and Nikolais have received high critical acclaim and have traveled abroad with great success, their opportunities to perform in the United States are severely limited.

Many proposals have been made to improve this situation. Some suggest that the solution is the establishment of modern dance repertory companies, which will perform the great works of the outstanding American choreographers and thus ensure their continued availability, as well as provide the field with a sense of tradition, which it has lacked when compared to ballet. Others feel that the primary need is to develop more theaters specifically designed for and available to modern dance companies. Still others believe that the heart of the problem lies in the need for the American public to become more fully attuned to *all* forms of contemporary art. As far as dance is concerned, they feel that this can only be done by bringing high-quality dance programs to "grass roots" regions of the country, and by strengthening the role of colleges and universities in this field.

Without question, the heart of the matter, for both modern dance and ballet, lies in audience readiness for dance, and in the approaches that may be used to bring dance more effectively before the public. The roles of educational institutions, and of government and foundation programs in the arts, are explored in the chapters that follow.

13

DANCE AND THE GOALS
OF CONTEMPORARY
EDUCATION

The preceding chapters have been concerned with the development of dance as a cultural form in American society. Clearly, this has been closely linked to the increasing use of dance as a medium of education in American schools and colleges. On all levels—elementary, secondary, and higher education—some form of dance instruction is today being provided. What is the contemporary rationale for such programs, and what are the actual practices? These questions are considered in this chapter and in the one that follows.

First, it is helpful to review briefly the history of dance in education during the early decades of the 20th century. As described in Chapter Eight, the most popular forms of dance in this period were aesthetic and gymnastic dance, tap and clog, folk and national dance. By the 1920s, the so-called natural dance that was taught by Gertrude Colby, and the creative dance that was taught by Margaret H'Doubler in Wisconsin, became widely influential. These forms were to evolve into what became known as modern dance in education, during the early 1930s.

At this time, women physical educators had considerable interest in dance education. The National Society of Directors of Physical Education for Women devoted an entire meeting to dance at its national convention in Boston in 1930. In the following year members of the American Physical Education Association (later to become the American Association for Health, Physical Education and Recreation, the major professional organization in this field) decided to form a separate Section on Dance. In the decades that followed, the Dance Section, under the leadership of such outstanding women educators as Ruth Murray, Dorothy La Salle, and Mary O'Donnell, became a leading force in promoting effective programs of dance education throughout the United States. At its annual meetings, it sponsored major dance events and workshops. It issued publications on dance in education, provided advisory services to schools and colleges wishing to improve dance instruction, and stimulated research in this field.

A number of women's colleges sponsored symposiums in dance education during the 1930s. The first such symposium was held in 1932 at Barnard College; participating colleges included Smith, Vassar, New York University, and Wellesley. In the same year, the University of Michigan sponsored a Midwestern Symposium, and within two years similar meetings were held elsewhere in the Midwest and in the far West. Increasingly, professional dance artists were drawn into educational programs and workshops. Martha Graham, Doris Humphrey, Charles Weidman, and Hanya Holm began to appear as guest artists or master class teachers at professional meetings, and in some cases taught special courses or institutes at colleges. They toured extensively:

In the . . . 1930s the concert dance artists and their groups were on tour in specific areas and at times on transcontinental trek. At this time it was possible for an interested person in almost any part of the United States to [become] familiar with the repertory of a number of renowned dance artists. Into almost every state came the top American dancers to appear in concert, to give lecture-demonstrations, to spend a day or two on a college campus, or to present a program at a national or district association convention.

One could see Martha Graham in solo performance or with her group; Doris Humphrey and Charles Weidman in duo, or with their company, which then included José Limón; Hanya Holm and company; Ruth St. Denis and Ted Shawn; and a bit later, Ted Shawn and his group of men. From Germany came Mary Wigman in solo concert, to return the following year with her company, and Harald Kreutzberg with his partner, Yvonne Georgi.[1]

Gradually, dance emerged as a distinct and important focus of educational concern on the campuses of a number of colleges around the country. The first to give full recognition to it both as an art form and as the basis for a degree program was the Univer-

[1] Barbara Page Beiswanger, "National Section on Dance, Its First Ten Years," *Journal of Health, Physical Education and Recreation*, May-June 1960, p. 23.

sity of Wisconsin. In the summer of 1934, the Bennington School of the Dance was begun at Bennington College in Vermont under the direction of Martha Hill and Mary Josephine Shelley. Bennington College has had, since that time, a strong program in dance education, as part of its highly experimental curriculum. Its summer school continued as an important meeting place and training ground for modern dance teachers and students until World War II compelled its cessation in 1942. In 1948, a new Summer School of the Dance was begun at Connecticut College in New London, and this has been carried on successfully to the present day.

As dance education became increasingly influenced by professional dancers, and as its content became more and more geared to developing dance as an artistic experience, certain questions were asked by physical educators. They had become intensely aware of the rapidly increasing number of demonstrations and concerts that emphasized dance as a performing art. It was apparent that many colleges had become involved in what was described as a "competitive marathon" of demonstrations, concerts, and other events designed to bring favorable publicity to their departments— just as competitive sports had increased in emphasis as part of men's programs. It was clear too that the original stress on individual creativity and freedom of expression that had been found in natural dance was giving way to much greater emphasis on the teaching of dance technique as a formal discipline.

By the end of the 1930s, the professional point of view toward modern dance had become highly influential in educational dance circles. This posed a problem. Were the goals and needs of college or secondary school students the same as those of aspiring dance artists? Should the teaching techniques used by dance educators be the same as those who taught in professional studios?

> Dance educators, after a ten-year period [1930–1940] of vigorously pioneering and of "selling" modern dance to college administrators, students, and audiences, had succeeded in establishing modern dance as an integral part of the college program. They recognized, however, that they had not succeeded in clearly defining the direction that future development of dance in education should take. Up to this point college teachers in general had thought of dance in terms of professional dance; not until the early forties did they give any serious thought to dance in relation to general educational goals.[2]

In a sense, they were impelled to do so by their co-teachers, physical educators in schools and colleges. In 1937, Eugene C. Howe summarized what he considered to be "the most recent

---

[2] Alma M. Hawkins, *Modern Dance in Higher Education* (New York: Bureau of Publications, Teachers College, Columbia University, 1954), p. 20.

event of major importance in physical education"—the extraordinary rise of the modern dance—and asked some searching questions about the relationship between the two fields:

> It can hardly be denied that the recent adoption by the profession of the leading concert dancers, critics, and counselors as *professors extraordinaire* has been a truly remarkable phenomenon. The dance of the '20s in physical education, though the seed came from the world of art, grew up *in* and *for* physical education; the dance of the '30s in physical education is for and by the concert artist in that he now virtually heads up this activity in a field foreign to his primary interests and about the nature of whose objectives he may, quite naturally and justifiably, be assumed to have no detailed and comprehensive understanding. The situation obviously has possibilities for both good and evil.[3]

After delineating some of the specific issues and problems, such as the need for teachers of dance in physical education to look for a "more systematic and conventional treatment of anatomy and kinesiology," rather than the "piquant and intriguing" but unscientific theories held by various nonacademic specialists in dance training, Howe went on to suggest that serious difficulties might develop in the years ahead.

> The business of modern dance in physical education is evident enough in theory. As a matter of functional integration, it may prove to be a severe test of the dance's practical adaptability to its environment and of physical education's powers of liberal imagination.[4]

World War II enforced a hiatus on all kinds of educational innovation and growth. The grim necessity was to win the war, and education went on an "austerity" basis. Dance, where it continued to be offered in secondary schools or colleges, was frequently given a body-conditioning emphasis, in accord with the national concern about "physical fitness." In community life, dance was widely used as a form of social recreation (folk and square dancing became popular in service centers and community clubs during this period). Dance too was widely employed as a form of mass entertainment for troops at home and abroad, through traveling entertainers and companies. But in schools and colleges, dance education underwent a "holding action."

After World War II, it embarked on a period of rapid expansion, chiefly on the college and university level. At the same time, dance educators attempted seriously to come to grips with the

---

[3] E. C. Howe, "What Business Has Modern Dance in Physical Education?" *Journal of Health and Physical Education*, March 1937, p. 132.
[4] *Ibid.*, p. 188.

important question of identifying their basic objectives. What was the theoretical rationale for dance in education? At a time of considerable ferment in educational thought, it became necessary to clarify this issue.

Certainly, it was not an entirely new question. During the earlier periods of its history, dance had been supported in very specific terms as an activity area within physical education intended to achieve certain outcomes important to that field. Also, it had been praised for its cultural and aesthetic values. Rogers wrote in 1941:

> . . . our major thesis is that dance, earliest of the arts and pedagogies, should become once more a basic educational technique, because it may serve, and probably more rapidly than any other single kind of pupil activity teachers now utilize, to transform children into more healthy, graceful, sensitive, courteous, courageous, cooperative, cultured and charitable citizens. The classic Greeks knew this, and made practice conform to knowledge, as have more ancient and primitive peoples everywhere. But contemporary English and American pedagogy, beclouded by heritages of asceticism, scholasticism and puritanism, has, until very recently, ignored or even proscribed dancing in schools.[5]

Similarly, H'Doubler had suggested that if every child, throughout his entire educational experience, were able to take dance as a creative art, "the enrichment of his adult life might reach beyond any results we now can contemplate." She wrote persuasively about the great social value of dance as a vitalizing experience within human society:

> This element has proven to be an enduring and vitally important power in the cultural life of all ages. It is for us today to rediscover this power and seek its influence.[6]

H'Doubler, of course, had a vision of dance education as a liberating and civilizing force that would contribute to a healthy philosophy of life and an integrated sense of self for all. She commented that while it was not expected that all students would experience dance to its fullest extent as a form of personal artistic expression,

> . . . every child has a right to know how to achieve control of his body in order that he may use it to the limit of his ability for the expression of his own reactions to life. Even if he can never carry his efforts far

[5] Frederick Rand Rogers, *Dance: A Basic Educational Technique* (New York: The Macmillan Company, 1941), p. viii.
[6] Margaret H'Doubler, *Dance: A Creative Art Experience* (New York: F. S. Crofts and Company, 1940), p. xii.

enough to realize dance in its highest forms, he may experience the sheer joy of the rhythmic sense of free, controlled, and expressive movement, and through this know an addition to life to which every human being is entitled.[7]

In the late 1940s it became evident, however, that this sort of statement of purpose, inspiring though it might be to dance educators, would not hold much currency in the marketplace of educational philosophy and curriculum development. There were many other special subjects in the curriculum, all of whose adherents were equally convinced of the merit of what they were teaching. Why were the writings of dance enthusiasts to be considered of any greater value than theirs?

Other factors impelled a rethinking of the purposes of dance education. For one, there was an increasing concern about the extent to which those who taught modern dance in schools and colleges were influenced by the approaches and objectives of professional dancers and choreographers. A leading dance educator, Ruth Whitney Jones, took the view that "studio" and "educational" dance were basically the same:

> The objectives of the studio dance teacher, since she is usually a composer-performer, are dancing as a life career for herself, and the teaching of technique for its own sake to students. The objective of the dance teacher in education is primarily the fullest possible development of the whole personality, as well as the physical ability, of each student. Technique is taught as a necessary tool for the student's creative use of movement to achieve the values inherent in the creative process. In all other respects the materials with which the artist and the teacher work are the same in principle and substance. The well-balanced dance program in education is based on principles underlying all modern dance but adapted to the level of the student's capacities . . . .[8]

Despite such arguments, it was clear to many that there were distinct differences between the goals and techniques of dance education and theater dance.

In the former, dance was perceived as an educational medium or experience which could achieve, through its unique blending of creative, physical, intellectual, and social involvement, important goals of education for all students. These goals, stated in terms of student growth, were seen as primary, rather than the achievement of a high level of performing or choreographic skill on the part of students. In contrast, it is usually the purpose

[7] *Ibid.*, p. 66.
[8] Ruth W. Jones and Margaret DeHaan, *Modern Dance in Education* (New York: Bureau of Publications, Teachers College, Columbia University, 1947), p. 2.

of the professional dance teacher to bring the performing skill level of the student to as high a level as possible. Elements related to the cognitive or social growth of students are not primary concerns.

The teaching process is also usually somewhat different. The educational dance instructor frequently introduces creative or improvisational experiences at an early point, to stimulate the student's creativity and interest in the dance. The professional instructor takes the student's motivation for granted, and rarely uses creative problems in teaching. The educational dance instructor makes a point of getting to know each student as an individual, and of paying particular regard to her individual problems, needs, and abilities. The professional teacher, by contrast, often treats her class as a faceless unit, providing a single, uniform experience for all and correcting, when necessary, in an authoritarian and impersonal fashion.

Gradually, more and more teachers of dance in schools and colleges became dissatisfied with their administrative location in physical education departments. They sought to establish dance as an art form, rather than as an area of activity skill. Jones spoke for this point of view:

> In assessing . . . the hard-earned place of dance in the curriculum, the fact must be stressed that modern dance is an art, not merely a form of physical education. Dancing taught solely for the purpose of increasing bodily control and muscular prowess has no educational value beyond that of any comprehensive physical activity; physical skill is but one part of the development of the body as an instrument of expression . . . . Modern dance, being one of the arts, offers simultaneous development of physical and creative faculties through the medium of the body.[9]

This conflict alone—and it is one which has continued as part of a heated controversy to the present day—would be enough to compel a searching review of the goals and essential focus of dance in education. It was coupled, however, with an extremely critical examination of American education during the 1950s and early 1960s, which made it essential that all educators clarify their objectives.

In essence, this critical review, spearheaded by such individuals as Paul Woodring, Arthur Bestor, H. G. Rickover, and James B. Conant, represented an attack on the pervasive influence of "progressive educationists" during the preceding several decades. In the view of the mid-century critics, American public education had become soft, wasteful, ineffective in terms of bringing about

[9] *Ibid.*, p. 1.

true learning, and dominated by an interlocking directorate of school administrators, state education officials, national educational organizations, and professors of education. Specifically, they were critical of curricula that had proliferated far beyond the "three R's" to include a host of activities that Rickover, for example, described as having "... little resemblance to traditional programs and intellectual disciplines but . . . making the school a sort of gigantic social-service agency aimed not at education but adjustment."[10] In his view, not more than twenty-five percent of what was taught in schools could now be described as "serious learning."

The major fire of the critics was directed against nonacademic courses and school experiences were related to "social adjustment." Thus, Woodring characterized the period of the 1930s and 1940s in these terms:

> The high schools tried in a hundred ways to keep the students interested: easier courses, more "practical" courses, more varied offerings, individual guidance, dances, parties and other social activities supervised by the school, including extensive athletic programs and allowing high school credit for everything from social dancing to camping and fishing.[11]

It was proposed that greater stress be placed upon the fundamental academic disciplines, such as the sciences and social sciences, mathematics, and the language arts. The fine and performing arts—particularly when approached as "doing" fields—were regarded as secondary in importance.

In the face of these attacks, and their influence on the attitudes of the taxpaying public and on school administrators, many educators in essentially nonacademic fields found themselves under extreme pressure.

For one, many of them had accepted the goal of "social adjustment" as a primary objective. Indeed, the entire physical education field had seized upon this as a major aspect of curriculum development, as evidenced by the 1951 yearbook of the American Association for Health, Physical Education and Recreation, *Developing Democratic Human Relations Through Health Education, Physical Education and Recreation*. Typically, in one of the leading texts of the 1940s on modern dance in education, Radir justified dance because it gave students group experiences in democratic living:

---

[10] H. G. Rickover, *Education and Freedom* (New York: E. P. Dutton & Co., Inc., 1960), p. 197.
[11] Paul Woodring, *A Fourth of a Nation* (New York: McGraw-Hill Book Company, 1957), p. 3.

Dance fulfills its function in the curricula of democracy's schools only if group work is so conducted that it is a little laboratory in democratic living. Students, working in groups, should be, in effect, self-directing, with the teacher acting only as a guide in helping them solve the problems of construction . . . [they] talk them over . . . to clarify meaning and find its essence . . . work in groups to objectify their idea in a movement theme, and then build this theme into a dance. In this group composition there is a constant interchange of ideas, opportunity to lead, and to follow, and a kind of informal majority rule . . . the core of the learning experience in a democracy . . . .[12]

By the late 1950s, this emphasis on the life-adjustment goals of education was decidedly out of style.

Similarly, those who had sought to pursue dance primarily as an aesthetic experience also were experiencing difficulty. For, following the first Russian Sputnik and the disclosure of the advanced level of Soviet education in mathematics, science, and engineering, there was a "crash" program of strengthening these areas of education. By default, the arts necessarily received less support and attention. Indeed, as a consequence of the growing numbers of high school graduates in the postwar period and the ensuing pressure for college admission, many high school students tended to concentrate in their elective program on the academic courses which represented the core of college admissions requirements. Elective areas were not valued as highly; similarly, the pressure of more rigorous academic instruction in the high schools meant that many students who might formerly have been deeply involved in school music, theater, and dance activities, found it difficult to fit such activities into their schedules.

What course were dance educators to pursue under such circumstances?

Physical educators found an easy solution. Recognizing that two of the goals which they had widely professed during the previous decades ("social adjustment" and "education for leisure") were no longer hospitably viewed by the educational profession at large, they seized upon recent research findings related to the poor "physical fitness" of American youth. During the 1950s, much of American physical education embarked upon crash programs of conditioning, and on comprehensive testing programs, with support of national and state governments. Surely, in a period of continuing national emergency, the fitness of youth was an important concern; and so it proved to be.

But dance educators could obviously not accept this as a

[12] Ruth Radir, *Modern Dance for the Youth of America* (New York: A. S. Barnes & Co., Inc., 1944), p. 4.

focal point for their efforts. Instead, if anything, those who were leaders in the field pressed even more strongly for the recognition of dance as an area separate from physical education, and one which was essentially an art form. In so doing, they were supported not only by their own conviction of what dance education should be, but also by the growing swell of conviction about the importance of the arts in national life, during the late 1950s and early 1960s.

The apparent growth of public interest and involvement in the arts provided justification for pressing for a fuller place for the performing arts—including dance—at the educational table. In terms of verbal support at least, many school administrators supported this cause. The American Association of School Administrators adopted the following resolution at its annual conference in 1959:

> The American Association of School Administrators commends the president, the Executive Committee, and the staff for selecting the *Creative Arts* as the general theme for the 1959 convention. We believe in a well-balanced school curriculum in which music, drama, painting, poetry, sculpture, architecture, and the like are included side by side with other important subjects such as mathematics, history and science. It is important that pupils, as a part of general education, learn to appreciate, to understand, to create, and to criticize with discrimination those products of the mind, the voice, the hand, and the body which give dignity to the person and exalt the spirit of man.[13]

Nor was support for the arts lacking among many of the leading educational philosophers of the period. In what must be interpreted as a sharp rejoinder to the mid-century critics of modern education, Sidney Hook wrote:

> An unfailing mark of philistinism in education is reference to the study of art and music as "the frills and fads" of schooling. Insofar as those who speak this way are not tone-deaf or color-blind, they are themselves products of a narrow education, unaware of the profound experiences which are uniquely bound up with the trained perception of color and form . . . . A sufficient justification for making some study of art and music required in modern education is that it provides an unfailing source of delight in personal experience, a certain grace in living, and a variety of dimensions of meaning by which to interpret the world around us. This is a sufficient justification: there are others, quite subsidiary, related to the themes, the occasions, the history and backgrounds of the works studied. Perhaps one should add—although this expresses only a reasonable hope—

[13] Resolution adopted by the American Association of School Administrators, Atlantic City, New Jersey, February 1959.

that a community whose citizens have developed tastes would not tolerate the stridency, the ugliness and squalor which assault us in our factories, our cities, and our countryside.[14]

Increasingly too, there has been the recognition of the need for educational experiences which would provide a sense of personal involvement, to counteract the growing tendency toward depersonalization in a mechanized society that is dominated by the mass media of communication. Philip Phenix writes, in dealing with the topic "meaninglessness and modern man" that, in wide areas of modern life, significant personal relatedness has disappeared from view.

> People feel isolated and estranged from nature, from themselves, from one another, and from the ultimate sources of their being. The depersonalization and collectivization of life is far advanced . . . . Another cause of meaninglessness in the contemporary world is the growing mechanization and depersonalization of life. Man has become assimilated to the machine, and in the process has lost his identity as a person. He has merged with the mass in the anonymity of impersonal organization.[15]

Within this climate, and faced by an enormously complex culture, modern man feels increasingly frustrated and impotent, Phenix believes. There is an increasing need for education to provide experiences which will equip the student to become aware of and to develop his own uniqueness, and to help him become capable of making meaningful personal judgments within all areas of life. If it is anything—for either the doer or the audience— art is a profoundly individual kind of experience. Thus, there is increasing support for the arts today as a form of highly personalized creative process.

Exactly what does this acceptance of creativity as a goal for education in the arts imply? Obviously, one may be creative in many aspects of life, including science and technological development, business, or government. However, many educators believe that the arts are in a particularly advantageous position to foster creative development in students.

Although there is no single widely-accepted definition of creativity, one influential view today is that it is heavily based on "divergent" thinking and exploration. As contrasted with "convergent" (which means moving toward a single correct solution or answer), "divergent" involves searching around, changing direc-

[14] Sidney Hook, *Education for Modern Man* (New York: Alfred A. Knopf, Inc., 1963), p. 154.
[15] Philip M. Phenix, *Realms of Meaning, A Philosophy of the Curriculum for General Education* (New York: McGraw-Hill Book Company, 1964), p. 34.

tions, not necessarily flying in the face of convention, but often coming out with unconventional solutions and answers. It is felt that creative people are more likely to excel in divergent thinking and activity, and that the kind of educational experience which is open-ended (that is, which has no single solution or desired response) is likely to lead to creative growth. Creativity is believed to be fostered in education when students are permitted or encouraged to exhibit spontaneity and individuality; when they are not regimented or repressed by imposed restraints or required conformity; when they have the freedom to initiate purposeful behavior, to communicate freely, and to make their own choices of activity or learning experiences.

Most educators in the arts—including dance educators—believe that their position in education today is strengthened because of the current need for creative development of students. But this is only one aspect of a total rationale supporting dance in the curriculum. Viewed broadly, how are educators to define the overall values and educational objectives of dance in the curriculum?

Obviously, this must be done within the structure of a governing philosophical framework regarding the purposes of education within a given society. In the United States, we have seen two prevailing orientations in terms of educational philosophy; these may broadly be described as "traditionalist" and "experimentalist." The "traditionalist" position is generally concerned with the development of the intellect; all other values related to morality, civic or social development, creative involvement or preprofessional training, are viewed as secondary. This philosophical view, stressing as it does the fundamental academic skills, and such subject areas as history, science, mathematics, and languages, is obviously somewhat hostile to the presentation of art experiences as personal creative involvement, within the curriculum.

In contrast, the view of the "experimentalist" is that education must serve to meet the needs of modern man, by helping him adjust to his environment and indeed helping him remodel or reshape it. Within this broad philosophy, human nature is seen as differing widely; since this is so, and since the needs of people change according to geographical and social settings, no one scheme of education can apply universally. John Dewey, who was the most influential of modern "experimentalist" philosophers, held that the study of the past must be made relevant to the needs and demands of the present; that the curriculum must be broad and of great variety, respecting individual needs, interests, and capacities; and that the study of society is at the heart of the school's effort.

Stated succinctly, Dewey's view of education was:

Education is that reconstruction of experience which adds to the meaning of experience, and which increases ability to direct the course of subsequent experience.[16]

Throughout the 1930s and 1940s, the view of education as a dynamic process of change that both improved society and enabled individuals to live effectively within society was established. In several influential policy statements on the goals of American education, the role of well-integrated citizens within democratic society was defined in detail.[17] It encompassed the following areas of needed competence: membership in a family, in an economic system, and in a community. The well-educated person was described as one who was able to fulfill responsibilities of citizenship within his own community and in the nation at large. He should have the necessary skills to function adequately in an economic sense, both as a producer and as a consumer. He should be able to relate effectively to others, and to develop a constructive and happy family life. As part of this, he is expected to have a working command of the basic skills imparted by education—reading, writing, and arithmetic, as well as an understanding of the cultural heritage of the past. Finally, the well-educated citizen is expected to have an intelligent, inquiring mind and to be—so far as his capabilities permit—a creative individual.

These expectations were summed up in the following statement:

> The general end of education in America at the present time is the fullest possible development of the individual within the framework of our present democratic society.[18]

During this period, educators (with the exception of those dance educators mentioned earlier) generally thought of dance as a skills area within physical education. As such, it was expected to contribute to the widely cited goals of *organic development, neuromuscular development, interpretive development,* and *personal-social development.*[19] None of these goals implied any great stress on creative or aesthetic expression. Nor, in the great majority of situations in which dance was taught, was it really approached as an art form.

---

[16] John Dewey, *Democracy and Education* (New York: The Macmillan Company, 1938), pp. 89–90.

[17] See for example *Education for All American Youth* (1944) and *Policies for Education in American Democracy* (1946), reports of the Educational Policies Commission of the National Education Association and the American Association of School Administrators, Washington, D.C.

[18] George Counts, *Education and the Promise of America* (New York: The Macmillan Company, 1946), p. 112.

[19] Charles A. Bucher, Constance R. Koenig, and Milton Barnhard, *Methods and Materials for Secondary School Physical Education* (St. Louis: The C. V. Mosby Co., 1965), pp. 39–43.

The capabilities of most teachers, and the size and degree of motivation of their classes, simply did not permit attempts at work of real quality.

How has the situation changed during the 1950s and 1960s? What new directions characterize education in general? How do physical educators conceive their role today, and what is the prevailing view of dance education in the present setting?

First, it is clear that no new philosophy of education has arisen within the past two decades to dominate the field, as had progressive education during the preceding years. To the extent that there is a powerful, continuing emphasis on the basic academic disciplines, the stress has been a rather utilitarian approach to meeting the practical needs of society. Today, with an increasing number of students completing high school and going on to some form of higher education, it is expected at the same time that they will achieve more advanced levels of skill, competence, and understanding. Michaels points out that there is a "downward thrust" of courses, with more rigorous instructional programs (particularly in mathematics, science, and foreign languages) being introduced in the junior high school and elementary school.[20]

Yet, it is understood that the mere acquisition of presently available knowledge, or skills that are currently required, will not be enough, in terms of preparing American youth for useful and productive lives in the years ahead. Farsighted educators recognize that students must be prepared for a lifelong learning process:

> The student must learn to learn, for he will need to grow intellectually during his entire lifetime in order to avoid obsolescence. Less emphasis should be placed upon high school as a preparation for college and more attention given to the development of an open-ended attitude toward the students' needs and aspirations in a learning society. It has been stated that half of what a graduate engineer studies today will be obsolete in ten years; half of what he will need to know is not yet known by anyone. The total amount of all knowledge will double in the next 15 years.[21]

Thus, what is required is the development of favorable attitudes toward learning, as well as techniques of teaching and learning which bring about comprehension of the structure of subject matter and the essential principles which govern content and learning within each curricular field—rather than place

[20] Lloyd S. Michaels, "The High School's Changing Tasks," in *The Challenge of Curricular Change* (New York: College Entrance Examination Board, 1966), p. 15.
[21] *Ibid.*, p. 15.

emphasis on the mere acquisition of knowledge. Jerome Bruner, in particular, has influenced contemporary educators through his research and writing on the cognitive process.[22] Yet, considerable discontent remains with the rigorous academic programs found today in American schools and colleges. For one, many students— including the most gifted—have begun to question and reject the values that have been imposed upon them. The increasing specialization of learning in particular disciplines and their sub-fields has resulted in an "academic pressure cooker" which, in Kolb's words, no longer provides the opportunity for a search for the self, or for the making of a commitment.

> ... although we do not necessarily pass negative judgment on the successful outcome of this orientation in the person of the highly motivated, highly trained, specialized intellectual who may also have some dimension of breadth in relating himself to his discipline ... and the world, the fact remains that we know empirically that the societal expectations described above can produce docile guilt-ridden individuals; aggressive and uncompassionate people interested primarily in external incentives like grades, money, and prestige, or in internal incentives like abstract knowledge totally unrelated to the human complex in which meaningful knowledge must be rooted . . . .[23]

In more recent years, Kolb points out, we have seen increasing numbers of alienated students who respond either with a paralyzing apathy or with destructive rebellion to parental and societal goals and drives. Sulkin comments that some extremely bright college students revolt against the pressures and confinement of their specialty by fleeing from it, either by failing, or by changing fields. "They say they want to learn more about 'life,' about their own feelings and values and personal relations." The result for many is disillusionment and discontent; more and more, college students seek "authenticity in their education . . . real relevance . . . genuine and dependable commitment."[24]

What does all this have to do with the arts? Clearly, one way for secondary school and college students to achieve a value-shaping personal involvement in life is participation in the creative arts. There is a need for another kind of learning—one which is essentially nonverbal, creative, and open. C. Robert Pace suggests

[22] See, among others, Jerome Bruner, *Toward a Theory of Instruction* (New York: W. W. Norton & Company, Inc., 1966).

[23] William L. Kolb, "Changing the Collegiate Culture," in Lawrence F. Dennis and Joseph F. Kauffman, eds., *The College and the Student* (Washington, D.C.: American Council on Education, 1966), p. 68.

[24] Sidney Sulkin, *The Challenge of Curricular Change* (New York: College Entrance Examination Board, 1966), p. xxvii.

that we must counter the current emphasis on verbal facility and verbal learning by providing a richer acquaintance with universal nonverbal languages of man:

> ... the languages of movement and form, of color, and sequence, and sound, the languages of direct expression and feeling. Throughout history these have been powerful and significant avenues by which man has expressed his knowledge, his aspirations, his beliefs, his insights, and his wisdom. Are these still foreign languages to many of our students? Is the capacity to translate them, to understand their meaning, and to communicate through them teachable? If we must require competence in two languages for graduation from college, why not the languages of painting and sculpture, of drama and dance, or of music?[25]

One major stumbling block preventing a fuller acceptance of the arts within American education has been the sharp distinction made between art and science in the public mind—in an era in which science is viewed as increasingly essential to our survival. Pointing out that basic differences between science and art are widely assumed, Harold Taylor notes that scientists are seen as rational, objective, abstract, concerned with the intellect, and with reducing everything to a formula, while artists, on the other hand, are seen as temperamental, subjective, irrational, and chiefly concerned with the expression of the emotions.[26] He goes on to say:

> One of the most unfortunate results of this misunderstanding of the nature of the intellect is that the practice of the arts and the creative arts themselves are too often excluded from the regular curriculum of school and college or given such a minor role in the educational process that they are unable to make the intellectual contribution of which they are supremely capable.[27]

There appears to be increasing awareness today that the barrier that has been erected between science and art is a false one. Bronowski contends that there exists a single creative activity, which is displayed alike in the arts and in the sciences:

> It is wrong to think of science as a mechanical record of facts, and it is wrong to think of the arts as remote and private fancies. What makes each human, what makes them universal is the stamp of the creative mind. I found the act of creation to lie in the discovery of a hidden likeness. The scientist or the artist takes two

---

[25] C. Robert Pace, in Dennis and Kaufman, *op. cit.*, p. 99.
[26] Harold Taylor, *Art and the Intellect* (New York: Museum of Modern Art, 1960), p. 9.
[27] *Ibid.*, p. 11.

facts or experiences which are separate; he finds in them a likeness which had not been seen before; and he creates a unity by showing the likeness.[28]

More and more, then, the dichotomy between "the two cultures" is being challenged by thoughtful educators and philosophers. Taylor suggests that there is a need to recognize that dance, music, painting, design, and sculpture are all forms of knowledge even though they do not express themselves in words. Further, he protests against adding "more blocks of science and mathematics while we allow the arts and the humanities to languish," by asking:

> Do we not need scientists and engineers who combine with knowledge and skill of a practical kind a sensitivity to human values, a sense of social responsibility, an understanding and appreciation of the arts? The widest sweep of imagination, the deepest level of intuition, the greatest command of insight are as necessary to the true scientist as to the poet or to the philosopher.[29]

The needs to educate feeling, to inculcate sensitivity, to provide a testing-ground for values and personal growth and change, are all related to the search for educational experiences which can counter the stultifying effect of the "high-pressure knowledge industry" of the present. While certainly no definitive statement of this viewpoint has been widely accepted by American educators, it represents an area of conviction which increasingly is influencing the shaping of curriculum—particularly on the college level. It is within this philosophical context that all forms of creative and artistic experience in education, including dance, find their support.

Meanwhile, what of the specific area of the curriculum to which dance has traditionally been attached over the past several decades—physical education? What shifts have occurred in this field, particularly in its philosophical undergirding?

Following the period in the late 1950s and early 1960s during which many physical educators stressed the attainment of "physical fitness" as a primary, if somewhat undefinable, goal of their programs, the emphasis shifted toward identifying physical education as an "academic discipline."

This trend stemmed from several sources. First, it was undoubtedly influenced by the increasing amount of research and publications having to do with learning theory and cognitive process being produced by Bruner, Bloom, and others. In physical

---

[28] J. Bronowski, *Science and Human Values* (New York: Harper and Bros., 1956), p. 35.

[29] Taylor, *op. cit.*, p. 27.

education, there was now a heavy emphasis on psychomotor experimentation—often somewhat remote from the direct concerns of physical education teachers in schools and colleges—but certainly contributing to the profession's knowledge about the nature of motor learning and performance. In both undergraduate and graduate departments of physical education, more and more courses related to motor learning and performance were introduced, as well as supportive sequences in anatomy, kinesiology, and physiology. This development in itself contributed to the view of physical education as an academically oriented field.

Probably too, the trend was a response to the pervasive criticism of physical education as a field which—at a time in which education generally had become more academically rigorous— was concerned with "fun and games." Often singled out for attack, particularly on the college level, where physical education majors suffered because of their association with educationally unjustifiable high-powered competitive athletic programs, leaders in this field sought a new justification and a new basis for respect.

In any case, by the mid-1960s, many leading physical educators now conceptualized their field as one which, particularly in terms of professional preparation of teachers, was heavily based on scientific content. Franklin Henry, one of the most effective spokesmen for this viewpoint, describes an "academic discipline" as an organized body of knowledge collectively embraced in a formal course of learning; it is assumed that the acquisition of such knowledge is educationally justifiable, whether or not it has practical applications. He goes on:

> There is indeed a scholarly field of knowledge basic to physical education. It is constituted of certain portions of such diverse fields as anatomy, physics and physiology, cultural anthropology, history and sociology, as well as psychology. The focus of attention is on the study of man as an individual, engaging in the motor performances required by his daily life and in other motor performances yielding aesthetic values or serving as expressions of his physical and competitive nature . . . .[30]

Henry points out that all of these elements must serve to bring about a comprehensive and integrated knowledge of the motor behavior and capabilities of man. He considers the following areas essential to physical education as an academic discipline: kinesiology and body mechanics; the physiology of exercise, training, and environment; neuromotor coordination, the kinesthetic senses, motor learning, and transfer; emotional and personality factors in physical performance, and the relation of all of these to human

---

[30] Franklin Henry, "Physical Education as an Academic Discipline," *Journal of Health, Physical Education and Recreation*, September 1964, p. 32.

development; the functional status of the individual, and his ability to engage in motor activity, as well as the role of various types of physical activities in past and present cultures.[31]

Clearly, this concept of the nature of physical education as an instructional field is gaining increasing influence. How does it affect dance when carried on as part of the total physical education experience? It is obvious that dance, as activity in which movement for its own sake is of primary importance, must be considered in any comprehensive examination of motor learning and performance. Indeed a number of dance educators have begun to suggest ways of viewing this field as a form of academic discipline itself,[32] and to initiate research in it based on sound scientific procedures. A major difficulty in this connection is that the kinds of research which are now being carried on within graduate departments of physical education are somewhat antithetical to the nature of dance as an expressive art. It is extremely difficult to measure aesthetic value, feeling, or the nature of the artistic process itself.

How may one assess the essential values and objectives of dance in American education today? It would appear that six major areas of purpose may be identified.

1. *Movement Education.* Certainly this area of concern is one in which dance (which shares with gymnastics the element of being an activity in which movement itself is primary, rather than subservient to other goals or purposes) has much to contribute. Phenix, not a physical educator himself, but a perceptive analyst of the curriculum, writes:

> The arts of movement are the foundation for the learnings which take place under the broad heading of "physical education." The program of instruction in this field is ordinarily centered around individual and team sports and gymnastic activities, with the dance being at most one among many options . . . concerned with promoting the vigor of the human organism, neuromuscular skills, good interpersonal behavior, emotional balance and control, and sound judgment. While these objectives extend beyond the aesthetic concern which is proper to the arts, it is still true that the arts of movement, and particularly the dance, provide the main key to methods and meanings in health, recreation, and physical education.[33]

What is the special contribution to be made by dance, in terms of movement education? Elizabeth Hayes suggests that its particular appeal lies in the satisfaction or enjoyment that it

---

[31] *Ibid.*, p. 33.

[32] See Nancy W. Smith, "Movement as an Academic Discipline," *Journal of Health, Physical Education and Recreation*, November-December 1964, p. 64; and *Focus on Dance II, An Interdisciplinary Search for Meaning in Movement*, Conference Report of Dance Section, American Association for Health, Physical Education and Recreation, 1962.

[33] Phenix, *op. cit.*, p. 166.

provides the participant; it is pleasure in the kinesthetic sensation of movement that impels the dancer to move as he does.

> The key to its distinction lies in that the dancer's immediate concern is not with lifting weights, transporting himself through water, balancing on skates or skis, or winning a game, but rather with movement per se—movement that has consciously been given form and rhythmic structure to provide physical, emotional or aesthetic satisfaction. If dance happens also to promote good physical condition or otherwise contribute to the welfare of the dancer, so much the better; but the derivation of such benefits is not the essential reason for the existence of dance.[34]

2. *Development of Personal Creativity.* Dance, like all the arts, offers the opportunity for teaching and learning that is designed to enhance and encourage the personal creativity of students. Through the posing of compositional problems, as well as tasks related to performance and staging, the student is encouraged to produce imaginative and inventive thinking and movement solutions. Uniquely, of course, he does not make use of other tools or symbols in doing so. His body is the instrument with which he works, and movement constitutes the vocabulary; thus the creative expression is a particularly free and open one, unhampered by the need to translate meaning. Such experience, at any age, makes a vital contribution to the growth of the individual. Taylor writes:

> The essence of the modern movement in education is the idea of creativity and its liberating effects on the individual. The modern movement is in fact a fundamental shift in attitude toward life itself. It refuses to accept the conventional forms in which life is presented to us and looks for fresh ways of interpreting facts, for new forms of art, of architecture, of scientific discovery, of literature, of science . . . .[35]

3. *Aesthetic Experience.* At the same time as it develops creativity, dance provides an aesthetic opportunity for students. They are helped to become open to aesthetic experience, both in terms of being able to respond fully and sensitively to artistic stimuli, and also in terms of being willing and increasingly able to express themselves through creative media. The purpose of such experience is not narrowly confined to specially gifted individuals. Robert Henri, the art critic, wrote several decades ago:

---

[34] Elizabeth R. Hayes, *An Introduction to the Teaching of Dance* (New York: The Ronald Press Company, 1964), p. 3.

[35] Harold Taylor, "Individualism and the Liberal Tradition," in Willis D. Weatherford, Jr., ed., *The Goals of Higher Education* (Cambridge, Mass.: Harvard University Press, 1960), p. 12.

Art, when really understood, is the province of every human being . . . . When the artist is alive in any person . . . he becomes an inventive, searching, daring, self-expressive creature. He becomes interesting to other people. The world would stagnate without him— and the world would be beautiful with him. He does not have to be a painter or a sculptor to be an artist. He can work in any medium.[36]

The development of values, and the education of feeling are both important elements of aesthetic experience. In a discussion of the goals of higher education, Brand Blanchard wrote:

> . . . we have been considering the disciplines that aim at knowledge. But what about the study of literature, music, and art? These are now a recognized part of a liberal education, and their primary aim is plainly not only knowledge. Their aim is to satisfy and educate feelings. We sometimes forget that feeling is as educable as intelligence and that, so far as happiness is concerned, its cultivation is even more important.[37]

4. *Intercultural and Integrative Experience.* Dance provides a rich medium for exploring the customs, attitudes, history, and living circumstances of people of other lands. Through the study of folk and ethnic dance, carried on under skilled instructors or sometimes as field assignments, students may venture deep into ethnology and anthropology. On the elementary school level, where the unit-study approach makes use of various forms of educational experience that focus on a single problem or theme, dance is frequently one of the key forms of activity. Similarly, in terms of the integration of various subject areas, dance has strong links with such fields as the fine and graphic arts, music, the language arts, and theater. In many secondary school programs, and in some courses in the humanities on the college level, all of these art fields may be linked in interdepartmental courses which stress the common elements among the arts.

5. *Social Involvement.* Recognizing that "social-adjustment" and "life-adjustment" have become less than respectable terms in today's educational glossary, it is clear that many of the most serious concerns of adults today have to do with the social behavior of school and college youth.

The problems range from a spirit of rebellion against widely accepted societal values to an unwillingness to attempt to communicate with adults on any level. Narcotics experimentation, a radical shift in attitudes toward premarital sexual involvement,

[36] Robert Henri, *The Art Spirit* (Philadephia: J. B. Lippincott Co., 1923), p. 5.

[37] Brand Blanchard, "Values, The Polestar of Education," in Weatherford, *op. cit.*, p. 91.

the rising incidence of mental illness and even suicide on American campuses—all these clearly have both psychogenic and social causes. Commonly, they are related to what is described as alienation (or, more colloquially, "turning off" or "tuning out") on the part of students. While it is not possible to claim for dance—or for any other performing art—any magical quality as a cure for alienation, it should also be recognized that it involves, in a greater degree than more academic forms of learning, intense interpersonal relationships in small working groups. The range of social involvement in theater and dance activities, and the necessity for both providing and accepting critical judgment, is rarely equalled in other courses or student activities. In those forms of dance which are specifically recreational, such as folk, square, and social dancing (all of which are found in many school and college instructional programs), there is the opportunity for constructive and relaxed social involvement for students.

Typically, in an Eastern college which was recently raided by the police and in which a number of students were arrested as narcotics users, the point was made by a college administrator that there were comparatively few opportunities for healthy and enjoyable social involvement in the nearby community. He attributed at least part of the student drug problem to this lack of recreational outlets. While obviously no solution to the total problem, dance can provide one such badly needed outlet.

6. *Carry-over Values.* Clearly, a major purpose of education today must be to prepare for the enjoyable and enriching use of future leisure. Dance—as well as experiences in the other arts—must be viewed as such preparation. Through it, students may gain favorable attitudes and performing skills for active participation after graduation in modern dance or ballet, or recreational dance forms as hobby interests that combine physical, social, and creative values. In other cases, through their school or college dance experience, students may gain an interest and awareness of dance as a performing art that will help them become part of the growing audience for theater dance throughout the country.

In either case, the steady growth of leisure on the American scene compels the recognition and support of varied forms of activity that can help to bring about lifelong participation and pleasure.

These, then, are regarded as the primary values of dance education. They account for the increasing interest in dance and support for it today—particularly on the college level. The following chapter describes specific practices in dance education today, as well as the problems facing those working in this field.

14

CURRENT PRACTICES
IN DANCE EDUCATION

Instruction in dance is provided on all three levels of American education today, although practices obviously vary from school system to school system.

In elementary grades, dance is generally taught by classroom teachers or, in the upper elementary grades, by physical education teachers. In junior and senior high schools, it is the responsibility of physical education teachers. In higher education, it is usually taught as an area of activity within women's physical education departments, although in a limited number of colleges it may be offered through a separate department of dance, or a department of drama, fine arts, or music. On each level, it is characterized by a distinct set of practices and by goals appropriate to the age level of students being served.

How widespread are offerings in dance education on each level?

No scientifically based study of dance education throughout the United States has yet been reported in the literature, although Walter Terry of the *New York Herald-Tribune* carried out a number of examinations of college dance programs, and other directories have been compiled of dance in higher education. However, a graduate student at Teachers College, Columbia University, in cooperation with the author, carried out a nationwide study of such practices during the spring of 1963.[1] Questionnaires were sent to a sampling of 510 institutions (204 junior and senior high schools and 306 junior and senior colleges) which were randomly selected from an educational directory, the only stratification being that each state was represented by at least four colleges or universities, and that an attempt was made to avoid sending questionnaires to obviously religious schools or colleges, or all-male institutions.

Several findings of this survey are reported in this chapter. Table I gives the percentage of institutions on each level that reported offering dance as part of their curricula.

TABLE I

*Does your institution offer instruction in dance
as part of the curriculum?*

Level	Yes	No	Number Responding
Junior High School	23 (63.9%)	13 (36.1%)	36
Senior High School	62 (62%)	38 (38%)	100
Junior College	17 (58.6%)	12 (41.4%)	29
Senior College	108 (82.4%)	23 (17.6%)	131
Totals:	210 (70.6%)	86 (29.4%)	296

This survey indicates that a majority of the institutions that responded, on each level, offered some form of dance instruction. Since they were randomly selected and may be considered to be representative of schools and colleges throughout the nation, they provide an overall picture of practices in dance education. It will be noted that the highest percentage of instruction in dance (82.4%) is found in senior colleges, and the lowest (58.6%) in junior colleges.

Practices in dance education are now examined for each level in turn, beginning with programs in elementary schools.

Dance in Elementary Education

Dance in elementary schools is generally regarded as an important creative experience—along with art and music activities—that contributes to the development of children in their

[1] Joan McGinley and Richard Kraus, *A Comparative Study of Trends in Dance Education*, Teachers College, Columbia University, 1963, unpublished report.

most formative years. It is recognized that children have a hunger for movement that must be satisfied if their proper biological development is to be achieved, and that motor learning provides an important avenue for personal growth that is related to all forms of development and school achievement. Radler and Kephart write:

> The primary process is *motor development*. This is the basis upon which is built the child's ability to control his body . . . . In addition to being the result of an order from the brain, each movement made by the developing child, is in itself, an experience which contributes to the basic store of information held by the brain. In other words, movements are not only output; they are input as well.[2]

It is believed that control and mastery of the body's movement relate to emotional as well as physical and mental development. Murray comments that control of one's own body means the beginning of self-control in general. In bringing his own body under control, the child begins to understand himself better, and to have confidence in his ability to direct his own actions and to control his environment meaningfully.[3]

It is important that, through creative rhythmic experiences, children explore their movement capabilities and gradually improve in terms of physical strength, flexibility, body balance, endurance, and coordination. Dance should be a pleasurable, happy experience, in which children are able to express themselves creatively in free and spontaneous movement, as well as in guided or structured movement experiences.

What should be the content of dance instruction in the elementary grades? Two physical education authorities, Miller and Whitcomb, suggest that there should be three components to the dance offering on this level:

Movement Fundamentals and Variations. This consists of the necessary tools for dance, including such fundamental locomotor and nonlocomotor skills as walking, running, hopping, jumping, leaping, galloping, skipping, bending, pushing, twisting, falling—or combinations of these—all learned and practiced in various rhythms, tempos, and floor patterns or groupings.

Creative Rhythms and Dance. This extends the fundamental movements into creative expression, by having children create dance movement or actual dance, through response to such stimuli as music, percussion accompaniment, stories, songs, pictures, poems, suggestions for pantomime (i.e., sports movements, work

[2] Don C. Radler and Newell C. Kephart, *Success Through Play* (New York: Harper & Row, Publishers, 1960), p. 23.

[3] Ruth Murray, *Dance in Elementary Education* (New York: Harper & Row, Publishers, 1963), pp. 9–14.

movements, familiar characters), moods, colors, textures, etc. On the simplest level, it may involve children moving freely to such stimuli; on more advanced levels, it may involve individual or group compositions that represent more thoughtful and extended solutions to dance problems. In some cases, dance compositions may actually become class projects, for presentation at assemblies or other programs.

Folk Dance. This includes singing games and folk dances of America and other lands, performed in various formations: circles, lines, squares, threesomes, and as mixers and icebreakers. Often the same skills which are learned as part of dance fundamentals are essential to correct performance of folk dances and singing games; similarly, the movements and patterns of such structured dances may be used by children to create their own dance compositions. Thus, all three forms of dance experience are interrelated.[4]

Ruth Murray, whose text, *Dance in Elementary Education,* is the most authoritative and comprehensive in this field, suggests that there are four major categories of experience: *creative movement and movement skills, rhythmic skills* (related primarily to musical understandings and rhythmic competence), the development of *original individual or group dances,* and *learning dances,* such as singing games, play parties, and folk and square dances. She suggests that the emphasis in each of these categories should vary, according to the age level of children being taught:[5]

TABLE II

Suggested Percentage of Involvement

Age Levels	5—7	8—10	11—13
Creative movement and movement skills	50%	30%	25%
Rhythmic skills	20%	20%	15%
Making individual dances	20%	30%	20%
Learning structured dances	10%	20%	40%

Murray's breakdown has the following implications. First, she does not separate creative movement and the learning of movement skills, as Miller and Whitcomb do. Instead, it is obviously

[4] Arthur G. Miller and Virginia Whitcomb, *Physical Education in the Elementary School Curriculum,* 3rd ed. (Englewood Cliffs, New Jersey: Prentice-Hall, Inc., 1969), pp. 228–79.

[5] Murray, *op. cit.,* p. 15.

her view that the fundamental skills of movement may be learned in a creative way. Second, she suggests that greatest emphasis be given to this category of dance experience with younger children. Making individual dances (and later, group compositions) is at its peak during the middle elementary years, and increasing emphasis is given to the learning and performance of structured dances with each succeeding age level.

The final point reflects the fact that older children are more capable (in terms of their physical skills, ability to perform complex tasks, attention span, and social attitudes) of learning folk and square dances. It also suggests that the emphasis on free creative response that is appropriate for young children is no longer as suitable for those in the preadolescent period. It is true that creative movement experiences can be made increasingly difficult and advanced, to add progression to learning and provide challenge to the experience. Creative movement can be related in a more complex way to problems of space, force, musical meter and dynamics, level and direction of movement, mood, and dramatic content. Often other classroom learnings, such as the language arts or the social or physical sciences, may be related to problems of group composition—as part of "core" or unit studies.

In the hands of gifted teachers, children in the middle elementary grades are often able to develop group compositions of surprisingly high quality—as well as to maintain a high level of interest and personal growth. A basic problem at this point is that children, as they move into the upper elementary grades, become increasingly uncomfortable about moving freely or spontaneously. Often, they may feel too big, too awkward, too silly—or they are aware that there is an actual technique involved in dancing skillfully, which they have not mastered. Just as creative writing may become frustrating for them if they do not possess the necessary vocabulary and knowledge of grammar, so, in dance, they may feel limited by the lack of an adequate movement vocabulary.

Many children—particularly girls—may have begun to study ballet or modern dance in classes outside of school. What is being done in school in the form of "creative rhythmic movement" may appear simple and childish to them. With boys, if the teacher is not ingenious in introducing masculine and physically challenging themes and forms of dance, an attitude of resistance may quickly be built up.

For all these reasons, it is important that instruction in elementary school dance activities be highly knowledgable. The teacher of the upper elementary age level should be able to demonstrate and lead children through sequences of warm-ups, stretches, bends, swaying movements, and exercises for different parts of the body, for flexibility, strength, and coordination. In addition, he or she should have a broad awareness of the purpose of dance in education, a knowledge of musical structure, and the ability to work sensitively and creatively with children.

The question must be asked—who teaches dance in the elementary school and how widespread are such programs? When one reads texts in this area and sees impressive photographs of children moving freely and imaginatively, the impression is given that such programs are widely found. The reality is that they are extremely rare, and that actual instruction of dance and creative rhythmic movement in elementary schools tends to be quite stereotyped and limited.

In the lower elementary grades, it is usually the classroom teacher who is responsible for "rhythms," as the activity is often termed. This teacher is expected to be competent in a wide range of learning skills—with the priority usually given to the more academic skills of arithmetic, and reading instruction. She may have had a course or two in physical activities for the elementary school. Usually, this will have placed emphasis on the use of traditional singing games and simple folk dances, as well as other forms of physical activities such as group games, lead-up ball games, self-testing activities, etc. Thus, the dance program in the lower elementary grades tends to consist heavily of structured dances— singing games, play parties, and folk dances. These are somewhat easy to teach, and also easy to control in the sense that they must be performed in a certain way; they do not "overstimulate" children, and they are neatly organized and do not tax the teacher's creative capacities.

As far as fundamental movement skills and creative expression are concerned, most teachers in the elementary grades who provide such activities tend to use phonograph records which have different rhythmic sequences (and sometimes verbal instruction or songs which provide cues for movement) on them. Occasionally, in the lower elementary grades, the classroom teacher may be helped by a music or physical education specialist; such special teachers, however, rarely work directly with children in the lower grades. In general, dance on this level, when taught by classroom teachers, tends to consist primarily of structured dance forms, such as singing games and simple folk dances. Creative movement, when it is taught, (in part because of the lack of musical accompanists) is usually handled in a stereotyped and limited fashion.

What of the middle and upper elementary grades?

It is usually at about the fourth grade level that curriculum specialists in the fields of art, music, physical education, and sometimes science are introduced to elementary school classes. A common practice is for such specialists to work with individual classes once or twice a week, and have the classroom teacher take responsibility for other teaching sessions. The specialist is also expected to provide consultation assistance to classroom teachers and, in many schools, to offer in-service training sessions for teachers.

At this point, in many elementary schools, one finds the separation of boys and girls into separate physical education classes. When this occurs, the boys are usually assigned a male teacher, and the girls a female teacher. The boys' program then focuses on active games and sports, tumbling, gymnastics, conditioning exercises, and similar activities. If they have any involvement at all in dance, it usually consists of special coeducational classes (usually in folk and square dancing), under the direction of the woman physical education instructor. Often, boys have no involvement at all in creative dance forms, after the third or fourth grade, unlike the English system of motor education which was heavily influenced by Laban, and in which both boys and girls participate extensively in creative movement experiences throughout the grades. Thus, it is understandable that many American boys quickly gain a stereotyped view of dance as a feminine activity. Their attitude, as far as participation is concerned, may range from disinterest to a strongly negative view.

For girls, dance activity in the upper elementary grades tends to consist of recreational dance forms and, in some cases, creative or modern dance. It is usually taught by the physical education instructor, and too often tends to be approached as an exercise or drill, devoid of true creative meaning or expressive content. In most cases, physical education instructors on the elementary level are generalists, and have a somewhat limited background in modern dance, which prevents them from offering the solid technical content that children who are approaching the teen years are capable of absorbing.

In a limited number of communities or state educational systems, a greater priority is given to dance education. There is a strong effort to have classroom teachers become more highly skilled, through preservice and in-service training, and to equip physical educators more effectively in dance. Often, at physical education conferences, elementary school dancing programs of very high caliber are seen. In a number of private schools, well-qualified dance and music teachers are employed, and exceptional work has been done in creative dance. However, it must be generalized that in only a very small proportion of public elementary schools do children receive a meaningful program of dance education. Usually those who have a special interest in this field receive training in dance by attending private schools or studies. In many communities, the school system cooperates with other agencies interested in providing special instruction in dance (such as a Parent-Teachers Association, a community arts association, or the municipal recreation department) by co-sponsoring an after-school series of dance classes.

Such programs, while they often are conducted by highly skilled teachers, tend to serve only those children who are well motivated toward dance to begin with, and whose parents are able and willing to pay the necessary fees.

What accounts for this somewhat negative picture of practices in elementary school dance education (a picture which is supported by the reports and observations of many elementary school teachers who have taken graduate courses with the author of this text)? One may blame the obvious shortages that exist in many school systems—the lack of adequate physical education staffs, facilities, and programs, or the limited training of classroom teachers. However, more to the point is the lack of understanding of teachers, school administrators, and parents about the importance of creative experience in general—and dance in particular—during the formative years of childhood. Without such understanding and conviction, it is extremely difficult to develop and support a rich program of dance and creative rhythmic movement in the elementary grades.

Dance Education in Secondary Schools

In public secondary schools throughout the United States, dance is taught almost invariably within departments of physical education. There, as in elementary schools, it differs widely in both the scope of content, and the quality of the experience. In one major school system,[6] the goals of dance for grades seven through twelve are stated as follows:

Objectives

1. To develop a perception of rhythm for greater efficiency and pleasure in the performance of all motor skills.

2. To develop a knowledge of the fundamentals of music and other accompaniments as they relate to dance.

3. To develop an awareness and appreciation of dance as presented in concert and theater.

[6] Board of Education of the City of New York, "Dance Fundamentals, Grades 7–12," Curriculum Bulletin, 1957–1958.

4. To develop a vocabulary of movement and a knowledge of the factors which influence movement.

5. To develop strength, endurance, flexibility, and coordination.

6. To develop a feeling of pride in the body as an instrument of expression, not only in dance, but in life situations as well.

7. To provide greater enjoyment of dance as a recreational activity both in school and later in adult life.

8. To provide an opportunity for creative dance.

9. To provide satisfactory socializing experiences through the use of group activity.

However, one must ask whether these stated objectives give an accurate picture of what is actually offered in the program. It is helpful to turn to the texts of leading physical education authorities in this regard. Bookwalter, who carried out a major study of physical education in the secondary schools, the report of which was published by the Center for Applied Research in Education, describes the recommended content of "rhythmic activities" (meaning dance) in the following passage:

> It is expected that the fundamentals of the dance will have been developed at the elementary school level. This must be kept in mind in teaching the various types of dance in the secondary schools. Indian dancing, and folk and square dancing are particularly valuable in the junior high schools. Social, square and modern dancing are most suitable in the senior high school. There is a dearth of dance or rhythm instruction in boys' programs. Beginning with the ninth grade, some coeducational dance instruction is possible and desirable. Men and women instructors must share that duty.[7]

Although one finds a measure of support for dance in physical education in this statement, the view that creative dance has no place in the junior high school (usually grades seven through eight, or seven through nine), and that, at most, boys may be given some coeducational dance instruction in the later grades, indicates that it is very faint support indeed. The author's reference to Indian dancing as a staple of the junior high school curriculum is a curious one and may reflect the lack of current information on the part of many physical educators in the area of dance. It is doubtful whether 1 per cent of junior high schools today offer instruction in "Indian dancing," or, indeed (even if this were perceived as having important educational value) whether their teachers have received training in this field. In terms of the time that should be allotted to "rhythms," the Bookwalter study recommends:

[7] Karl W. Bookwalter, *Physical Education in the Secondary Schools* (Washington, D.C.: The Center for Applied Research in Education, 1964), p. 52.

Athletic sports should be allotted, collectively, 30 to 32 per cent of the boys' class instruction time, and 21 to 24 per cent of the girls' time in junior and senior high school.

Rhythmic activities (dance) should be allotted from 5 to 8 per cent for boys and from 16 to 18 per cent for girls, in junior and senior high school.

Formal gymnastic activities should be allotted from 27 to 28 per cent for boys, and from 21 to 25 per cent for girls, in junior and senior high schools.[8]

In another recent text on secondary school physical education, Bucher, Koenig, and Barnhard are even less generous. They offer a suggested time allotment for ninth grade girls' physical education classes, assigning the following number of weeks to activities, during a thirty-six week semester:[9]

Basketball	6	Volleyball	3
Field Hockey	5	Tennis	3
Modern Dance	5	Badminton	3
Softball	4	Archery	3
Stunts & Tumbling	4		

Thus, five weeks of the total year (about 13.8 per cent of the instructional period) is allotted to any form of dance activity. No mention is made of other forms of dance, or of coeducational participation on any level, in this schedule. Again, a lack of current interest or understanding of dance is reflected in the recommendation in this text, published in 1965, that secondary school physical education offer the following: "social dancing, folk dancing, rhythms, gymnastic dancing, square dancing, tap dancing, and modern dancing."[10] Gymnastic and tap dancing, as the historical review of dance education in this text points out, had a vogue during the first three decades of this century and have since all but died out in American schools. Only rarely are they found in the programs of colleges that prepare physical educators today.

In an attempt to understand the scope and nature of secondary school dance education, it is helpful to examine the curriculum guides of state departments of education, or school systems. New York State, for example, provides a physical education curriculum

[8] *Ibid.*, pp. 53–55.
[9] Charles A. Bucher, Constance R. Koenig, and Milton Barnhard, *Methods and Materials for Secondary School Physical Education* (St. Louis: The C. V. Mosby Co., 1965), pp. 192–93.
[10] *Ibid.*, p. 205.

with recommended programs for grades seven through twelve. The schedule for two grades (eight and eleven), based on a maximum number of 180 class meetings per year, is as follows:[11]

TABLE III

Periods Per Year

| | Grade 8 | | Grade 11 | |
	Boys	Girls	Boys	Girls
Conditioning and Body Mechanics	3	5	4	5
Aquatics	35	35	35	35
Self-Testing Activities	35	30	25	20
Games (including individual, dual and team sports)	86	79	94	88
Rhythms, Marching, and Dancing	10	20	10	20
Evaluation, Skill and Knowledge Tests (including fitness)	11	11	12	12

It is revealing to note that the category of "rhythms, marching, and dancing" is recommended for only 5.5 per cent of the boys' physical education program, and 11 per cent of the girls' program. It is considerably lower than the time assigned to "aquatics" for example, which suggests the extent to which dance is held in regard; many secondary schools do not possess a swimming pool and are unable to maintain an aquatics program of any kind.

In New York City itself, dance is assigned somewhat higher priority for girls in the junior high school; in a schedule based on 72 class meetings per year, dance is recommended for 18 periods (25 per cent).[12] However, for the same grade levels in New York City, it is recommended that boys spend only 15 of 165 class periods in dance (9 per cent); this is limited to recreational forms of dance, and in the eighth grade, no dance at all is recommended.[13]

While it is true that these guides reflect recommended practices within only one state, they are generally typical of practices elsewhere, as revealed by study of physical education syllabi and the statements of teachers.

In terms of the kinds of dance taught in secondary schools, the institutions responding to the 1963 Teachers College Study reported that they offered the following activities:

[11] *Physical Education in the Secondary Schools*, New York State Education Department Curriculum Guide, 1964, pp. 51, 54.

[12] *Physical Activities for Girls, Grades 7–9*, Curriculum Bulletin of New York City Board of Education, 1961–1962 Series, p. 7.

[13] *Physical Education for Boys, Grades 7–12*, Curriculum Bulletin of New York City Board of Education, 1963–1964 Series, p. 11.

286

CURRENT PRACTICES
IN DANCE
EDUCATION

TABLE IV

Which forms of dance are taught in your curriculum?

Type of Dance	Number of Schools Offering It	Percentage of Responding Schools
Modern Dance	44	70.9%
Square Dance	44	70.9%
Folk Dance	43	69.3%
Ballroom Dance	17	27.4%
Tap Dance	2	3.2%
Hawaiian Dance	2	3.2%
Ballet, Ethnic Dance, and Eurhythmics	1 each	1.6% each

Based on this study, and on the curriculum guides cited earlier, a picture of dance in secondary education begins to emerge.

1. It is viewed as a comparatively minor "skills" area within the majority of physical education programs. Little attention is paid to it as a medium for achieving creative or aesthetic growth. Invariably it is offered within the girls' physical education department.

2. Girls participate in both modern dance and recreational dance forms. Modern dance, when taught, tends to be treated as a technique "drill" or as a form of physical conditioning exercise. Partly because of the size of physical education classes, and partly because of the lack of adequate accompaniment, many classes offer no improvisation or other creative dance activities. While curriculum guides often recommend a certain number of periods during the year for boys in square, folk, and ballroom dancing, in many schools they do not take part in any instructional dance activity.

3. A number of secondary schools have modern dance clubs, in which particularly interested students may obtain more advanced instruction in modern dance, and may be involved in performance. Often this represents a much more demanding and challenging experience in dance as a performing art than is provided in classes. Very rarely (and usually through the special effort of the dance teacher and department chairman or school principal) boys may be involved in the modern dance club—or a special club may be established for them.

4. Sometimes secondary schools may sponsor clubs in recreational dance forms (folk, square, or round dancing). In a few cases, such clubs have developed into performing groups which, as in the case of Lloyd Shaw's *Cheyenne Mountain Dancers,* or the *Silver Spurs* taught by "Red" Henderson of Tacoma, Washington,

have toured the country giving performances. In such schools, dance has become a very popular activity for boys.

5. Just as in elementary schools, there are no special teachers of dance. Instead, in order to teach dance in secondary school, one must meet state certification requirements as a physical educator. As a minimum requirement, this usually means that a teacher has had two or three courses in modern dance and recreational dance forms as part of her undergraduate professional preparation.

6. Often the teacher of physical education in the secondary schools regards dance as a subject of minor responsibility. Only rarely, on this level, is a teacher hired as a full-time dance specialist (with physical education credentials, of course). Usually this happens in large urban high schools, where there are several women teachers in the girls' physical education department, and it is possible to assign teachers to different specialized areas in the curriculum.

All this represents a somewhat negative and disappointing picture; yet it is consistent with practices on the elementary school level as well. To state, as Bookwalter does, that the fundamentals of dance may be assumed to have been taught at the elementary level, is simply not facing up to existing conditions. In part, one of the problems is that many students enter junior and senior high schools lacking all but the most cursory information about dance. Typical responses to the 1963 Teachers College Study with respect to student attitudes, were:

> Among the girls, modern or creative dance has to be taught and developed. Many dislike it because of little or no knowledge of it and lack of experience in performing it. T.V. and movies have helped somewhat but there is still much more to be done before this type of dance can be widely accepted in this locality. (High School, Delaware.)
> I was wondering if you could give me some information as to how to get girls in junior and senior high school motivated in learning modern dance. (High School, West Virginia.)

The point should be made clearly that in some areas of the country, there is a considerable amount of dance interest. In states like Michigan and California, enthusiastic leadership and support by physical educators appear to have resulted in a fairly high level of dance activity in the schools. In such areas, professional organizations hold conferences and meetings, and provide in-service training classes for teachers. Dance festivals are held, and high school students and teachers attend concerts by leading companies at nearby colleges, sometimes taking part in dance clinics and workshops.

In a number of situations, teachers have been successful in involving boys in modern dance activities. At Washington Park High School in Racine, Wisconsin, an all-boys' modern dance club, composed of members of the school's athletic teams, gave impressive performances.[14] In a large coeducational high school in New York City, with many students belonging to racial minorities, boys have participated in a coeducational modern dance program, both in actual dance classes and in an annual school festival.[15] In Novato High School, Novato, California, considerable success has been met in involving boys in recreational dance classes.[16]

Many other examples of successful secondary school dance programs might be cited. However, it must be stressed that they are the exception, rather than the rule. Typically, a suburban county in New Jersey close to New York City includes a number of well-to-do and presumably culturally active communities. However, within this entire county, only one school offers modern dance on the secondary level—and even this is not part of the instructional program, but is offered through a modern dance club. The physical education instructor responsible for dance in this school has been successful in obtaining a federal grant for the upgrading of modern dance instruction in secondary schools throughout the county (see p. 329). Her application was supported by a number of principals and teachers who corroborated the statement that this activity was lacking in their programs.

Thus, there is much to be done to provide more adequate instruction in dance education on the secondary level, and to achieve greater awareness of this as an important part of the program. How can this be done? Essentially, it is a problem that faces all educators in the arts; a number of guides for the development of support of dance education are provided in the following chapters.

Dance in Special Secondary Schools

One unique exception to the somewhat negative picture that has just been drawn lies in the examples of schools which have recently been established which stress the development of profes-

---

[14] Grace C. Piskula, "Boys Like Modern Dance, Too!", *Journal of Health, Physical Education and Recreation*, May 1954, pp. 42, 61.

[15] Mamie Phillips, "The Male Dancer at George Washington High School," unpublished student paper, Teachers College, Columbia University, 1962.

[16] Ralph Cutler, "Dance for High School Boys and Girls," *Journal of Health, Physical Education and Recreation*, April 1964, pp. 36–37, 90.

sional skills in the performing arts. For a number of years, there have been special secondary schools in large American cities that have offered advanced programs in music, art, and other forms of academic experience. In some cases, these have had a vocational orientation.

The first public secondary school to have initiated a curriculum to provide professional preparation in the performing arts was the High School of Performing Arts in New York City. Founded in 1947, this public school was designed to provide talented boys and girls in New York City with the opportunity to specialize intensively in music, drama, or dance, and at the same time to obtain an academic education of high quality. The premise for its existence was that New York City, as a major artistic and cultural center and, in effect, the "entertainment capital" of the nation, offered a considerable amount of employment to professionals in the theater arts, the concert field, television, radio, and night club fields. However, any student who wished to have an intensive professional development in his high school years found it almost impossible to also obtain a rounded academic education at the same time. John Martin commented in *The New York Times*:

Two students in High School of Performing Arts ballet class. Photograph by Victoria Beller.

Modern dance students at High
School of the Performing Arts.
Photograph by Victoria Beller.

Professional dance education . . . has always had to be obtained in
spare time and chiefly after the normal high school years have been
completed. Since dancing is a profession demanding youth, this
means just that many years lost out of the income producing career.
The advantage of getting the professional training along with a
standard high school education can hardly be overestimated.[17]

Competition to enter the High School of Performing Arts
is vigorous. Only one of four applicants can be admitted, and the
most talented of those who apply are selected through auditions
in music, drama, or dance—rather than through academic ability.
Among those who have served on the auditions board for dance
have been Martha Graham, Doris Humphrey, Hanya Holm,
Agnes de Mille, and John Martin. The curriculum itself is a stiff
one, with the first half of the day devoted to academic studies and
the afternoons to work in the performing arts.

The approach to instruction is extremely realistic and practical; the attempt is made to equip students with real skills and
knowledge that will make them as professionally competent as

[17] John Martin, "The Dance: Training," *The New York Times*, November
2, 1947; see also David Boroff, "High School with a Flair," *Dance Magazine*,
February 1962, pp. 29–33.

possible upon graduation. Many graduates have already achieved success in the performing arts. Several of those actually attending the school are members of Actor's Equity; some have performed in summer stock, danced in musical shows on Broadway, played with major symphony orchestras, or performed in concerts. In dance, a number of graduates have joined the New York City Ballet, or leading modern dance companies, or performed on television.

The dance curriculum includes both theory and practice in the broad range of ballet, modern dance, musical comedy, and other theater dance forms, as well as various types of ethnological dance—African, Spanish, and Oriental. During the first year or two, dance majors are encouraged to explore all forms of dance. In later years, they specialize in one of the major areas of dance performance, concentrating on technique, composition, and non-public performance. During the fourth year of study, students take part in public performances, which are of an extremely high caliber.

A number of outstanding dancers have been employed as teachers of dance by the High School of Performing Arts. The New York City Board of Education has made it possible for noncertified teachers to be employed by the school, in order to insure a high caliber of professional instruction. The director of the dance department, Dr. Rachael Yocom, has maintained a flexibility in assignments that permits members of the faculty to take part in concert tours, and then to return to their responsibilities at the school.

A high percentage—approximately 70 per cent—of those who graduate from Performing Arts go on to college. This, coupled with the professional success of a number of graduates, suggests that thus far the school has lived up to its initially stated purposes, and that it is possible to meet both academic and professional needs on the secondary level in public education.

A second example of a professionally oriented secondary school offering high-level instruction in the performing arts is the North Carolina School of the Arts, in Winston-Salem. This school was established by an act of the North Carolina Legislature in 1963, and is open by audition to junior high school, high school, and college students throughout the nation who are considered to have outstanding talent in music, drama, or dance. Professional training in the arts constitutes the major emphasis of the course of study, supplemented by an intensive academic curriculum. The thirty-acre campus includes dormitories, dance studios, rehearsal halls, theater, and classrooms; it serves students from twenty-six

Ballet performance by students of North Carolina School of the Arts. Photograph by Phil Barringer.

states, plus such foreign countries as Bolivia, Brazil, Japan, Mexico, and Hungary. Pauline Koner, who has been a leading performer, choreographer, and teacher, and guest soloist with the José Limón company for many years, is in charge of modern dance instruction. Ballet students work under the direction of Robert Lindgren, formerly a featured artist with Ballet Theater, the Ballet Russe de Monte Carlo, and the New York City Ballet, and his wife, Sonja Tyven.

It is possible that such schools as the High School of Performing Arts in New York City and the North Carolina School of the Arts may be the forerunners of a trend toward providing professional education in the arts in tuition-free public institutions on the secondary level. While this is an encouraging trend, it does not deal with the major problem of providing high quality education in dance for all students, not the gifted alone. The solution to that need is not yet in sight.

Dance in Colleges and Universities

Through the years, a number of surveys have gathered information about dance programs in higher education. They support the view that the major portion of growth in dance education in the United States in recent years has taken place on the college and university level.

In 1940 and 1947, Walter Terry carried out surveys of college dance programs; these were reported in his book, *Invitation to the*

Dance,[18] and in his column in the *New York Herald-Tribune*.[19] He discussed in detail the characteristics of college dance programs with respect to courses offered, sponsoring departments, the background of dance instructors, and the goals of dance education. In 1947, he found that of 123 colleges responding, 105 offered dance in some form. Ninety-two (74.8% of the 123 that replied) offered it for credit. In the 105 institutions that offered some form of dance instruction or experience, the following types were found: modern dance, 102 (98%); folk and square dance, 101 (97%); ballroom dance, 66 (63%); tap dance, 43 (41%); ballet, 15 (14%); rhythms, 38 (36%); ethnic dance, 12 (11%); and acrobatic dance, 4 (4%).

Terry's analysis, although it was not based on a representative sampling of colleges throughout the country, led him to the conclusion that dance in higher education was expanding, that its standards of instruction and performance were higher, and that understanding and acceptance of the goals of dance in education were growing.

Other periodic surveys of dance in higher education have been carried out by *Dance Magazine*, first with the assistance of Katherine Dickson of the National Council of Dance Teachers Organizations, and then Professor Mildred Spiesman of Queens College, in New York City. Through the years, these surveys have revealed an increasing number of such programs. In a directory published in 1954, *Dance Magazine* provided detailed information (including the nature of the dance program, the courses offered, policies regarding academic credit, the nature of departmental sponsorship, and similar information) about 59 colleges and universities. In a directory published in 1961, 69 such institutions were listed. In 1966, the number climbed to 99, showing a steady growth in the number of colleges and universities that were identified as having a significant dance program. In every case, dance was part of a curriculum leading to a degree, although it was not always a dance major.[20]

An even more comprehensive study and report has been made at intervals by the Dance Section (now the Dance Division) of the American Association for Health, Physical Education and Recreation.

[18] Walter Terry, *Invitation to the Dance* (New York: A. S. Barnes & Co., Inc., 1942), pp. 112–15.
[19] Walter Terry, "Survey of Dance Activities in Education," *The New York Herald-Tribune*, March 14, 21, 28, and April 4, 1947.
[20] "College and University Dance Directory," *Dance Magazine*, February, 1966, pp. 43–46.

In 1963, Professor Eugenie Dozier of Springfield College in Massachusetts reported the replies to questionnaires sent to more than three hundred institutions of higher education, which was augmented by information from current college catalogues and from *American Universities and Colleges* (1960 Edition). The responses indicated that there were a number of curricular patterns for dance in colleges and universities:

1. *Educational Dance Program.* A major or minor dance program designed primarily to prepare students to teach dance.

2. *Performing Arts Program.* A major or minor dance program designed primarily to prepare students as professional performing dance artists.

3. *Equivalent Dance Program.* A type of program which in the opinion of the respondents to the questionnaire is similar in content to the educational and performing arts programs, but differs in title.

4. *Dance Concentration.* A selection of dance courses required in professional preparation for a major in a related field such as Physical Education or Fine Arts.

5. *Service Program.* Dance programs which are required for general education and have as their purpose recreation, general understanding, and appreciation of dance.

The institutions reported were then grouped under two major headings: *Dance Programs in Professional Preparation* (in which dance was either the major itself, or an important area of skill related to the major), and *Dance Programs in General Education* (in which dance courses were offered chiefly as part of the service program or as electives not related to professional preparation).

The 1963 report indicated that 145 colleges and universities had dance programs in professional preparation, and 57 had programs in general education, a total of 202.[21]

A similar study published in 1966 reported that 199 colleges and universities had dance programs in professional preparation, and 78 gave programs in general education, a total of 277.[22] This represented a 37.1 per cent increase in the number of colleges and universities identified as having dance offerings.

[21] *Dance Directory: Programs of Professional Preparation and General Education* (Washington, D.C.: American Association for Health, Physical Education and Recreation, 1963).

[22] *Dance Directory: Programs of Professional Preparation and General Education* (Washington, D.C.: American Association for Health, Physical Education and Recreation, 1966).

CURRENT PRACTICES
IN DANCE
EDUCATION

What were the characteristics of the institutions described in this report? The Dance Directory gives a profile of each curriculum, but makes no attempt to tabulate all the kinds of degrees offered, the characteristics of staff, courses given, or similar information, for the total group of institutions. In order to obtain a general picture of practices, the author has analyzed certain aspects of the information given for the first 100 colleges listed under the heading of *Dance Programs in Professional Preparation*.

First, it was found that the departments in which dance courses or degrees were offered, fell into the following categories:

Physical Education Departments	84	(84%)
Theater or Theater-Dance Departments	5	(5%)
Dance Departments	3	(3%)
Others: Department of Music, Division of Arts, Music, and Theater Arts, etc.	3	(3%)
No reply given	5	(5%)

In terms of degree offerings, the institutions reported having the following kinds of programs, on the undergraduate level:

Dance Major (emphasis not specified)	4	(4%)
Educational Dance Major	15	(15%)
Performing Arts Dance Major	11	(11%)
Concentration or Emphasis in Dance	42	(42%)
Minor in Dance	28	(28%)

In four cases, colleges offered both a major in Educational Dance and in Dance as a Performing Art.

A number of colleges offered both a major and a minor program in dance, particularly in Educational Dance. In many of the colleges, degree requirements in other fields (particularly physical education) include required courses in dance. In a number of cases, colleges permit students to take a heavy cluster of courses in dance (amounting to a minor, or concentration), while actually taking their degree in other fields.

What types of courses are offered in these 100 college curricula? A listing of courses given includes the following:

Modern Dance*	91*
Folk Dance	77
Ballroom or Social Dance	66
Square Dance or American Country Dance	60
Rhythms or Rhythmic Analysis**	54
Composition, Choreography, Production, or Performance	55
Courses in Teaching Methods***	47
History and Philosophy of Dance	39
Ballet	22
Tap Dance	13
Labanotation	12
Ethnic Dance	9
Round Dance	5
Jazz Dance	4
Character Dance	3

* It is possible that the number should be higher than this, since several departments listed courses in "body movement," "introduction to dance," "movement fundamentals," or "elementary dance," all of which may have included modern dance techniques; these were not tabulated.

** This category includes several kinds of emphases: rhythmic understanding with focus on musical concepts and skills; developing creative movement skills; and rhythms in elementary schools, for preteachers. It was not possible to distinguish clearly among them, and they are lumped together here.

*** This includes courses designated especially for certain grade levels (elementary, secondary, etc.) and also courses generally described as having to do with "dance pedagogy" or skills courses in special areas of dance instruction.

It should be recognized that the 1966 AAPHER College Dance Directory, while it covered a comprehensive list of institutions, was not based on a *random* sampling of all colleges and universities. Thus, it is not as representative of the total range of college dance programs as the 1963 Teachers College Study. This report showed a somewhat higher proportion of physical education departments which sponsored dance, and a somewhat lower number of independent dance, theater-dance, or fine arts departments in the total group. In general, however, both reports are in agreement as to the nature of dance programs and the types of activities offered. It should be stressed that while a high percentage of institutions offer courses in recreational dance forms, the greatest number of courses and the most varied sequences are offered in modern dance. It is obviously this form of concert dance—rather than ballet—which is at the heart of most college performing arts programs in dance.

To more fully understand the nature of dance programs in higher education, an analysis of several college and university departments is presented on the following pages. Drawn chiefly from the 1966 AAPHER College Dance Directory, it also makes use of information found in the 1966 Dance Magazine Directory.

This sampling of college dance programs includes several of the best known and most highly regarded institutions throughout the country, as well as institutions with more limited reputations.

Certain differences are apparent between the group of private colleges (nos. 1–5) and the public, state-supported colleges and universities (nos. 6–12). Among the private colleges, which tend to be comparatively well-known liberal arts institutions, with fairly small enrollments, there is a greater emphasis on dance as a performing art, as well as a greater degree of flexibility in program structure. In contrast, the public institutions either were, or still are, heavily dedicated to the task of teacher preparation, particularly in physical education. The private colleges tend to house their dance offerings in separate departments of dance, or performing arts, while the public colleges have theirs within departments or divisions of physical education.

The private colleges tend to offer more courses in ballet, and to have comparatively few courses in recreational dance forms, or in the teaching of dance. Public institutions usually do not offer ballet (with some notable exceptions) but usually have a variety of courses in folk, square, and ballroom dancing—reflecting their function in the preparation of physical education teachers. In a number of the larger state universities, such as the University of Illinois, Ohio State University, and the University of Wis-

The Ohio State University Dance Company in a 1966 revival of Doris Humphrey's "Passacaglia and Fugue." Photograph by Harry Blaine.

TABLE V

DANCE EDUCATION IN U. S. COLLEGES	1. Bennington College, Bennington, Vermont	2. Butler University, Indianapolis, Indiana	3. Mills College, Oakland, California	4. Colorado College, Colorado Springs, Colorado	5. Sarah Lawrence College, Bronxville, New York
Enrollment	Under 500	Over 4,000	Under 1,000	Over 1,300	Over 500
Type of Institution	Women (men admitted to Performing Arts)	Coeducational	Women	Coeducational	Women
Department Sponsoring Dance	Dance Dept.	Performing Arts Dept.	Dance Dept.	Dance-Drama Dept.	Dance Dept.
Dance Degrees	Dance Major and Minor	Dance Major Educational Dance Minor (Music Dept.)	Dance Major and Minor	Dance Concentration in Liberal Arts	Concentration in Performing Arts
INTRODUCTORY COURSES					
Introduction to Dance	X	—	—	X	X
Basic Movement	—	—	—	—	X
Rhythms or Rhythmic	—	X	X	X	X
Analysis	—	—	—	—	—
MODERN DANCE					
Elementary	X	X	X	X	X
Intermediate	X	X	X	X	X
Advanced	X	X	X	X	X
BALLET					
Elementary	X	X	—	X	X
Intermediate	X	X	—	X	X
Advanced	—	X	—	X	X
Character or Mime	—	—	—	—	—
CHOREOGRAPHY AND PERFORMANCE					
Choreography or Composition	X	X	X	X	X
Production	X	X	X	—	—
Performing Group or Workshop	X	X	X	—	X
Stagecraft or Stage Movement	X	X	—	—	—
RECREATIONAL FORMS					
Folk	—	X	—	—	—
Square	—	—	—	—	—
Ballroom	—	X	—	X	—
Ethnic	—	X	—	—	—
Tap	—	—	—	—	—
DANCE HISTORY	—	X	X	X	X
Philosophy	—	X	X	—	—
DANCE EDUCATION OR SEMINAR	X	X	X	X	X
Teaching Methods	—	—	—	—	—
Practice Teaching	X	X	—	—	—
MUSIC FOR DANCE (accompaniment	X	—	—	—	—
or percussion)	X	—	—	—	—
LABANOTATION	—	—	X	—	—

298

6. Arizona State College, Tempe, Arizona	7. University of Illinois, Urbana, Illinois	8. Ohio State University, Columbus, Ohio	9. Texas Women's University, Denton, Texas	10. University of California at Los Angeles	11. West Chester State College, West Chester, Pennsylvania	12. University of Wisconsin, Madison, Wisconsin
Under 14,000	Over 33,000	Over 30,500	Over 2,300	Under 20,000	Over 5,000	Over 28,000
Coeducational	Coeducational	Coeducational	Women	Coeducational	Coeducational	Coeducational
Physical Education Dept.	Physical Education Dept.	Dance Area of Physical Education	Physical Education Dept.	Dance Dept.	Physical Education Dept.	Physical Education Dept.
Dance Concentration in Physical Education	Performing Arts Dance Major and Dance Education Major and Minor	Educational Dance Major, or Dance Concentration in Fine Arts	Educational Dance Major and Minor	Dance Major	Dance Concentration in Physical Education	Educational Dance Major and Minor; Applied Dance Major
— — — —	— — X —	— — — —	— — — —	X — X —	— X X —	X — X —
— X X	X X X	X X X	X X X	X X X	X X —	X X X
— — — —	X — — —	— — — —	— — — —	— — — —	— — — —	X — — —
X X — —	X X X X	X X — —	X — — —	X X X X	X — — —	X X X X
X X X — X	X X X — —	X — — — —	X — — X X	X X — X —	X X X — —	X X X — —
X X	X —	X X	X X	X X	— —	X X
— X —	X X X	— — X	— X —	X X —	X X —	X X X
— — —	X — —	— — —	X — —	X — —	— — —	X — —
—	—	X	X	X	—	—

Modern dance performance by Bennington College Dance Group. Photograph by M. Tarnay.

consin, strong emphasis is given to dance as a performing art, and also to the preparation of dance educators. Not shown in this chart, but an important part of the curricula of public institutions, are courses in anatomy, kinesiology, motor learning and performance, and physical education principles and methods, as well as other courses in education which are essential to the preparation of dance educators who expect to find employment within physical education departments.

Butler University is an example of a private college with an extremely professional approach to the preparation of dance performers; it offers a wide variety of skills courses, with a particularly heavy ballet component throughout the four years of the curriculum.

Mills College, Bennington, and Sarah Lawrence all stress dance as a theater art, with emphasis on modern dance—and with a considerable amount of attention placed on aesthetics, and dance theory and criticism, as well as on the development of student choreography and performance. Texas Women's University and the West Chester State College of Pennsylvania are good examples of institutions having well-developed dance programs in physical education departments. They offer considerable emphasis on modern dance and recreational dance forms, but offer no ballet. In many cases, public institutions like these with physical education majors offer much less in the way of dance.

Thus, college programs range very widely from those which offer a broad selection of all dance forms, dance philosophy, history, teaching methods, choreography, and performing experience to those which offer very few courses—chiefly to serve physical education majors, or to provide "service" courses which all students may elect to meet physical education requirements.

Although several of the colleges analyzed in Table V offer the choice of performing arts or dance education majors, they do so as part of related curricula, within single departments. Often, students in the separate majors take many of the same courses together. In a number of colleges, the trend for dance educators to seek independent department status, *outside* the physical education department, has actually resulted in two separate majors which are in *different* departments. Examples of such institutions follow:

The University of Indiana, at Bloomington, offers two completely separate dance majors. The physical education department sponsors an undergraduate Dance Education major, which places stress on modern and recreational dance forms and teaching methods. In the same institution, there is a ballet department in the School of Music, which places primary emphasis on the development of performing skills; students in this program very frequently take part in the school's operatic performances.

The University of Oklahoma, at Norman, Oklahoma, offers an Educational Dance major and minor, in the physical education department, which stresses modern dance, folk dance, and teaching methods. Also at the University of Oklahoma there is a dance department in the School of Drama, which provides courses in ballet and modern dance, production, and stagecraft.

Perhaps the most interesting example of such separate departments was found for a number of years at the University of Utah, in Salt Lake City. There, Prof. Elizabeth Hayes was in charge of a strong modern dance program within the department of physical education, assisted by such specialists as Virginia Tanner, known for outstanding work in children's dance. At the same time, there was a strong ballet program with an attached ballet theater company in the College of Fine Arts, under the direction of William Christensen and Gordon Paxman. Relationships between the two departments were good. Eventually, the modern dance educators sought their independence from physical education;

University of Utah Dance Company in "Sculpture Garden," choreographed by Joan Woodbury. Dancers are Edd Pelsmaeker, Robert Beswick and Rick Rowsell.

in this case, they joined the ballet program in a separate department of ballet and modern dance, in the College of Fine Arts. Although the physical education department wished to retain service classes (classes used to fulfill part of the physical education requirement in general education) in modern dance, all these were assigned as a teaching responsibility to the new department. Folk, square and social dancing continued to be offered by the physical education department.

There was considerable resistance to this move on the part of physical education administrators at the University of Utah. Thus, although the new department continued to offer a teacher education program in dance with the full support of the University's College of Education, the Utah State Office of Education refused to approve state accreditation for dance as an area distinct from physical education. Prof. Hayes comments that "the result has . . . meant that the best prepared teachers of dance are now prohibited from teaching . . . in all-dance positions in existence at many of our major high schools." In other ways, she regards the shift as one which has benefited dance education at Utah greatly; the curriculum has been expanded, salaries have been upgraded, and funds and faculty time have been allowed for choreography and concert direction.

Such moves for separation on the part of dance educators who are presently housed in physical education departments must then face problems with respect to the use of facilities, granting of permission to students to take performing arts dance courses to meet physical education requirements, and, most important, the accreditation of dance as an area of instruction in the public schools. The trend toward separate status for dance is discussed further in the final chapter of this text.

One of the most interesting developments in dance in higher education has been the rapid proliferation of special summer programs and workshops throughout the country—offered for college credit. The University of Connecticut at New London and Colorado College at Colorado Springs have long sponsored outstanding summer workshops of this type. The Perry-Mansfield School of Theater and Dance in Steamboat Springs, Colorado, and the Jacob's Pillow School of Dance at Lee, Massachusetts (associated respectively with Stephens College, Columbia, Missouri, and Springfield College, Massachusetts, for college credit) are two other outstanding programs which many college students attend during the summer.

Each year, however, more and more colleges have established new summer dance workshops. The University of Utah Summer School has an outstanding Modern Dance Workshop each year, featuring such leading professionals as Alwin Nikolais and Murray Louis. Adelphi College, in Garden City, New York, has spon-

The Texas Christian University Ballet Company, with Zac Ward, Barbara Macklen and Julie Rigler, in "Aurora."

sored summer dance workshops with Paul Taylor, Ethel Winter, and Audrey Keane on the staff. The University of Oregon, the University of Pittsburgh, Southern Methodist University, the University of Washington, the University of Southern California, the University of Georgia, the University of Wisconsin, the University of Cincinnati—all these, and many others, have initiated special summer offerings with intensified dance courses and performances. In many cases, students from other colleges attend them to obtain added dance experience; often they are attended by college graduates who are currently teaching and wish to improve their dance skills.

Thus, it is apparent that both the number and the quality of undergraduate dance programs in colleges and universities throughout the United States are on the upswing. Some of the fundamental issues about such programs—including the tendency for them to become increasingly performance-oriented, and to have preprofessional goals, as well as the attached question of departmental affiliation—are discussed in the final chapter.

Dance in Graduate Education

In addition to programs on the undergraduate level, an increasing number of colleges are offering dance curricula for those who already hold the baccalaureate degree. Of the 99 colleges listed in the Dance Magazine 1966 Directory, 32 indicate that they offer graduate programs involving majors or strong concentrations in dance. These include Master of Science and Master of Education degrees (usually for those concerned with dance in physical education) and Master of Arts or Master of Fine Arts degrees (which tend to stress dance as a performing art, and are more often found in departments or divisions of fine arts, music, and theater). Nine universities offer doctorates, either the Doctor of Philosophy or the Doctor of Education degrees, with dance emphasis, although the granting department tends to be either a department of physical education or a department of theater arts.

The lack of uniformity that characterized undergraduate dance programs is even more evident on the graduate level.

Traditionally, graduate study has had such purposes as refining the specialized professional competence of individuals who have had a broad and unspecialized undergraduate program; or of advancing professional competence of students who have already had undergraduate specialization and are already at work in their

The "Tamburitzans," a touring folk dance and music company from Duquesne University, in performance.

discipline. An increasing trend in graduate programs in teachers colleges and schools of education has been to focus on advanced studies and research of a somewhat theoretical nature—rather than to continue to deal with the performing skills and actual teaching competence of the individual. Specifically, this might mean that in a physical education department, graduate students might no longer be permitted to take courses in actual physical education skills (sports and games, aquatics, gymnastics, etc.) but would be restricted to courses in physiology and kinesiology, motor learning and performance, psychological or sociological aspects of physical education, administrative practices, etc. Within the field of dance, it means that in a number of institutions graduate programs are offered in which students no longer take courses in technique to meet requirements. Instead, they become concerned with more theoretical or philosophical aspects of dance in education, or dance as a performing art.

In part this has been done to make a clear distinction between undergraduate and graduate course experiences, and in part because of the principle that graduate study should not involve the learning of fundamental skills, but should deal with more involved or scholarly investigations of subject fields.

To illustrate, a recent bulletin from the University of California at Los Angeles lists course offerings provided for Master of Arts students in dance. Thirteen courses are given; their titles and brief descriptions follow:

Dance 200	*Advanced Dance Notation.* Advanced study of dance notation.
Dance 202	*Research Methods and Bibliography in Dance.*
Dance 204 A-B	*Advanced Choreography.* Theoretical and creative aspects of advanced choreography.
Dance 206	*Music for Dance.* Theory of the aesthetic and functional relationship of music to dance.
Dance 208	*Principles of Dance Theater.* Principles which serve the presentation of dance.
Dance 210	*Aesthetics of Dance.* A critical analysis of aesthetic concepts related to dance.
Dance 220	*Dance in the Twentieth Century.* Concepts, styles, and forms of dance in the 20th century.
Dance 226	*Dance Expressions in Selected Cultures.* Dance as a social and cultural experience in the life of man.
Dance 227	*Advanced Studies in Dance Education.* Concepts relating to the development of creativity and artistic integrity in dance.
Dance 251	*Dance in Rehabilitation.* Dance in the therapeutic setting.
Dance 596	*Directed Individual Study or Research.*
Dance 597	*Preparation for the Comprehensive Examination for the Master's Thesis.*
Dance 598	*Research for and Preparation of the Master's Thesis.*

Clearly, the emphasis in this offering is on courses stressing conceptual rather than practical aspects of dance performance. Similarly, graduate course offerings in dance at the University of Illinois include courses in the history, theory, and philosophy of dance; seminars in music and dance; problems in dance education; choreography and experience in a dance production workshop. Presumably, the latter includes the opportunity to actually perform as part of the graduate experience; however no courses in dance technique are actually listed on the graduate level.

In contrast, a number of other institutions, including New York University, Sarah Lawrence College, Smith College, Texas Women's University, and Teachers College, Columbia University, support the validity of having technique and performance courses on the graduate level. In general, it must be assumed that those who work for graduate degrees in this field are primarily educators, since few individuals whose chief orientation is professional performance are likely to feel the need for graduate study. It must also be assumed that many dance educators have had inadequate preparation in terms of their own performing skills, and that, even if their earlier training were sound, they could profit by continued study and performance. This issue, of course, must be viewed in the context of an institution's overall practices in graduate education. However, it would seem that any graduate program in a performing field which provides courses only in "aesthetics," "principles," "studies," and "research" is reverting to an earlier day when, for example, the fine arts could only be taught as history or "appreciation" and not in the studio.

Clearly, in the years ahead, the essential purpose of graduate education in dance needs to be discussed and more fully clarified.

Other Sources of Dance Education

A final important phase of dance education in the United States is in those private schools, studios, or academies which are devoted exclusively to the performing arts or to dance itself, and which are not part of public school systems, or degree-granting institutions. These may be operated for profit or may be noncommercial; in either case, since it is their major purpose to develop a high level of performing skill in dance, it is here that large numbers of young people receive professional training in the dance arts. In some cases, they may be attended on a part-time basis by students who are attending regular schools or colleges at the same time. In other cases, their students attend on a full-time basis.

Examples have already been given of the major ballet companies which operate their own schools, from which they draw many of their most talented young dancers. In addition, many of the less well-known ballet companies throughout the country maintain or are affiliated with ballet academies in their own communities. There are many other independent schools or studios in which ballet and modern dance are taught; *Dance Magazine* lists over 165 of these in its regularly published directory of schools, colleges, and teachers—not including degree-granting institutions. Often ballet schools are directed by formerly well-known performing artists; similarly, many of the leading modern dancers, like Martha Graham and Hanya Holm, have their own schools of dance in which they teach their own techniques.

In addition to these, there are many arts centers, community centers, performing arts organizations, YWCAs and YWHAs, and similar organizations throughout the country, which offer a high level of dance instruction. New York City offers a number of useful examples:

The Henry Street Playhouse, attached to the Henry Street Settlement, offers an extensive roster of courses in dance for children and adults throughout the year. Directed by Alwin Nikolais, and taught by Murray Louis and others of the Nikolais company, the Playhouse offers courses in modern dance technique, modern dance theory, choreography, pedagogy, percussion, notation, and repertory.

The New Dance Group, which was founded in New York City in the early 1930s, and which places primary emphasis on modern dance, also offers courses on all levels of ballet, jazz, Haitian, Caribbean, and classical Indian dance, and teaching methods. Its faculty includes many leading concert performers, and it has trained such dancers as Pearl Primus and Donald McKayle.

The Clark Center for the Performing Arts, housed in the West Side YWCA in New York, offers a varied group of courses in modern dance, African dance, ballet, mime, jazz, stage movement, and other courses related to stage performance. Alvin Ailey, Car-

Martha Graham teaching technique class at Connecticut College Summer School of the Dance. Photograph by Dora Sanders.

men de Lavallade, and James Truitte have been leading members of the Clark Center's dance faculty, and this school has been a primary center for instruction of the Lester Horton method, which is not found elsewhere in the East.

In other cities throughout the country, similar programs may be found. The Walker Art Center, in Minneapolis, Minnesota, offers a variety of dance courses and has sponsored major summer dance workshops. The Salt Lake City Children's Dance Theater has been directed by Virginia Tanner for a number of years, as part of the Conservatory of Creative Dance which is linked to the McCune School of Music and Art of Brigham Young University. In Cleveland, a famous settlement, Karamu House, has for years offered a variety of courses in all the arts and has been the center of outstanding dance instruction and performance. Similar centers for dance instruction may be found in many other cities throughout the country.

Similarly, there has been an increasing number of special summer workshops in dance which, unlike those listed earlier, do not provide college credit. One of the leading ones has been the annual Interlochen, Michigan, National Music Camp, which offers a high level of instruction in ballet and modern dance. Others include the Mt. Pinnacle Dance Camp in Hendersonville, North Carolina; the Southern Vermont Art Center in Manchester, Vermont; Stonegate Music and Arts Camp in Long Lake, New York; and many other such camps in New England and throughout the country, some of which are devoted to all the performing arts and some exclusively to dance. In the area of recreational dance, annual summer dance camps are held in square, folk, and country dancing in many states. Among the best known programs of this type have been the folk dance camp of the College of the Pacific, in Stockton, California; the Maine Folk Dance Camp conducted by Michael and Mary Ann Herman; the Pinewoods Camp in country dancing and folk music sponsored by the Country Dance Society of America in Plymouth, Massachusetts; and similar sessions throughout the country.

Such schools, studios, academies, and special summer workshops do much to develop highly skilled performers in dance, as well as to provide creative satisfaction to young people and adults alike who are interested in dance on an amateur basis, rather than as hopeful professionals.

15

THEATER DANCE: PROBLEMS AND PROSPECTS

The future of dance education is obviously closely linked to that of dance as an art form in the United States. Therefore, it is necessary to examine realistically the current status of theater dance, and to determine what forms of assistance will be necessary if it is to succeed in reaching a fuller audience in the years ahead.

Since World War II, there has been an unusual and dramatic growth of public involvement in the arts and other cultural pursuits in the United States. Reported at length by Toffler in *The Culture Consumers*,[1] it is marked by the following: greatly increased attendance at art museums; development of a large number of cultural centers around the country; increased purchase of books and phonograph records; the establishment of numerous national, regional, and local organizations to promote the arts; and, most important, a dramatic growth in the performing arts. It has been very widely documented that interest and direct participation—either as audience, student, or performer— have expanded strikingly in all forms of music, drama, and dance.

The term that is usually given to this phenomenon is the "cultural explosion." While there is some controversy as to the

[1] Alvin Toffler, *The Culture Consumers* (New York: St. Martin's Press, Inc., 1964).

real extent and meaning of the explosion, there is no doubt that
it exists.

To illustrate—in the field of music, a 1966 report indicated
that there were now 37 million amateur musicians in the United
States, and that participation in this area had been growing at
over twice the growth rate of the population itself. Since 1939,
the number of symphony orchestras in the United states has more
than doubled; there are now 1,401, more than half the world's
2,000 symphony orchestras.[2] This does not include the 300 youth
symphony orchestras maintained under the training programs of
many adult symphonic groups. According to the annual survey
conducted by the American Symphony Orchestra League, the
total number of concerts and touring programs has also expanded
greatly.

There are now 754 opera-producing groups in the United
States, which gave 4,176 performances of 331 works during the
1964–1965 season, as compared with only 316 such companies in
1950–1951. There is a great amount of youth activity in music;
today, there are more than 12 million school-age instrumentalists,
as compared with only 3 million in 1950, an increase far beyond
the population increase during the same period. The purchase
of musical instruments, classical music records, and performing
rights has grown steadily at a rate much higher than the general
economic growth of the nation. Concert music is programmed more
and more on both AM and FM radio stations, and there are today
more than 63,000 musical organizations in the country—double
the number prior to World War II.[3]

The field of theater has shown a comparable expansion.
While the professional Broadway theater actually dwindled during the 1950s in terms of number of theaters and total audiences,
at the same time the off-Broadway theater expanded from a handful of houses in 1950 to 32 playhouses in 1964. According to Toffler,
the success of this movement has led to the formation of professional resident acting companies of extremely high quality in
cities like Minneapolis, Pittsburgh, Milwaukee, Houston,
Washington, and San Francisco. In addition, large numbers of
semiprofessional and amateur drama groups have sprung up
throughout the country. According to *Variety*, there are now about
5,000 nonprofessional theater groups in the United States, in
addition to nearly the same number of college theaters, and
15,000 theater groups in clubs, churches, and schools. It is

---

[2] "Concert Music U.S.A., 1966," summarized in *Music Journal*, February
1966, p. 94.
[3] *Ibid.*

estimated that 500,000 amateur productions are seen by 100 million spectators each year.[4]

In dance, while no comprehensive statistics are available (since no single organization attempts to assess total activity in this area), there is no question that professional activity has expanded greatly in the large cities. Thus, in New York City, between January 1 and May 31 of 1967, there were at least 425 performances of ballet, modern, or ethnic dance, including programs by the New York City Ballet, the Manhattan Festival Ballet, the Martha Graham Dance Company, the City Center Joffrey Ballet, and American Ballet Theater, with performances also by such out-of-town or foreign companies as Ballets Africains, the Pennsylvania Ballet, the National Ballet, the Royal Ballet, the San Francisco Dancers' Workshop, and Ballet Folklórico de Mexico. In diversity of companies as well as in total number of performances, this far exceeds previous seasons.[5]

The steady growth of regional ballet companies throughout the United States has already been described, demonstrating that the new interest in dance is not restricted to major cities. The remarkable growth of dance in colleges and universities, which was discussed in the preceding chapter, is certainly an aspect of the "cultural explosion" within this area of the performing arts.

Growth of interest in the arts has evidenced itself in many other ways. In the years following World War II, the number of museums, and particularly art museums, in cities throughout the country grew strikingly. Each year, attendance has expanded, and museum directors have commented on what they perceive as a new renaissance of popular appreciation of the arts. In large measure, this has been promoted by the creative vitality of the museums themselves. Instead of simply acting as repositories for art treasures—as in the past—museum directors today offer courses, lectures, special exhibits, tours, highly dramatic displays, school-connected programs, and a variety of other imaginative services that stimulate the popular ground swell of interest in the arts. Many act as well as hosts for concerts, film series, and programs linking the arts.

In a commercial sense, the interest in the arts has been strongly evidenced. In 1950, there were about 150 art galleries in New York City and about the same number spread thinly across the country. By the mid-1960s, the number in New York had doubled, and the number elsewhere has probably multiplied several times. Toffler gives an example: In Phoenix, Arizona, there

[4] Toffler, *op. cit.*, p. 21.
[5] "Presstime News," *Dance Magazine*, June 1967, p. 3.

were 2 galleries in 1950, 4 in 1955, and 15 in 1960. The estimated volume of sales of painting, prints, and sculpture had increased over fifteenfold within the last five-year period. In many other communities, large and small, similar examples are available.

One of the most convincing evidences of artistic expansion has been in the recent development of cultural centers throughout the country. A survey conducted by *Arts Management* in 1962 documents this trend vividly.[6] It describes projects being carried on in over 69 cities throughout the country, involving chiefly museums, theaters, and concert halls, with a planned expenditure of about $375 million. The examples range from the huge and impressive Lincoln Center for the Performing Arts in New York City, with a projected cost of $142 million, to a small art center in Key West, Florida, costing only $10,000. Elsewhere, the State of New Jersey is planning a $6 million Cultural Center in Trenton; a $30 million National Cultural Center for the Performing Arts is being built in Washington, D.C.; there are many examples. All of them are in addition to cultural centers and complexes which have been in operation throughout the country for a number of years. They do not include the many elaborate arts complexes being constructed by colleges and universities, which undoubtedly will contribute significantly to the cultural life of their regions.

Thus, the case for the "cultural explosion" has been widely documented. What brought it about? Lippincott outlines a number of key factors:

> (1) an increase in the amount of... leisure time, (2) an increase in family and personal income, (3) an emphasis on urban living which promotes a climate for the arts, (4) America's continuing [growth] as a consumer ... society, (5) the great stress laid on creativity in education and in daily living, (6) the tax-exempt status of many art objects and gifts presented by individuals and corporations to museums, educational institutions, etc., (7) the financially profitable state of the arts for many dealers and artists, particularly painters, (8) the financially profitable investment possibilities of the arts, and (9) the status symbol syndrome of owning works of art.[7]

Perhaps more important than any of these is a change in American attitudes about art. In the past, art was often viewed as an activity suited only for the highly gifted, or as an outlet only for the wealthy or intellectual person. In either case, involve-

[6] "Cultural Centers Are Springing Up in Cities Big and Small," *The New York Times*, July 29, 1962, Section VIII, p. 1.

[7] Gertrude Lippincott, "The Cultural Explosion and Its Implications for Dance," *Journal of Health, Physical Education and Recreation*, January 1965, pp. 83–84.

ment in the fine and performing arts was perceived as an "elite" activity—not attractive to, or suitable for, the mass of people in society. A second factor was that, until fairly recently, many Americans had the view that any aesthetic product of this country was second-rate, in comparison to the work of Europeans. This was linked to an attitude that art was just not too important, that it was only a peripheral concern of life, and certainly did not justify the serious attention of government, industry, foundations, or educational institutions. In effect, these attitudes were a logical outcome of our history. We have long been a nation that valued material accomplishment highly and aesthetic and spiritual achievement on a much lower scale. In effect, we have always had an inferiority complex about our capacity in the field of art. Our Puritan heritage has had much to do with this negative attitude.

Since World War II, these attitudes have changed very widely. No longer is art viewed as the exclusive province of a comparatively few, wealthy patrons. Toffler suggests that a new middle class of well-educated, professionally or technically trained persons, young and intelligent, and numbering between 30 and 45 million, is now the backbone of artistic support and involvement. They crowd museums, flock to concerts, support drama and ballet, study music, perform in the little theater, join cultural organizations, and spread the base of support of the arts in community life.[8]

John D. Rockefeller, III, president of the Lincoln Center for the Performing Arts, gives his view of what has occurred. He sees the growth of popular interest and participation in the arts as:

> ... another evidence of our national maturity, a natural and predictable deepening of interest in artistic matters. The people want art and are making it for themselves in a characteristically American way. They are taking what is at hand, working hard to improve it, and meanwhile enjoying it immensely . . . .
> A basic cause of this increased interest in the arts is man's need and desire for what I can only call creative fulfillment. It is a need for positive self-expression; a need for modern man to assert, or to reassert, his individuality . . . .
> It is a clear call that we accept the arts as a new community responsibility, that we place them alongside our already accepted responsibilities for the health, welfare and education of our community . . . .[9]

However, there is evidence that the national picture is not as rosy as the preceding pages would suggest. Two major studies

[8] Toffler, *op. cit.*, pp. 26–27.
[9] John D. Rockefeller, III, in Joseph Prendergast, "The National Cultural Center," *Recreation Magazine*, October 1960, pp. 363–64.

were carried out during the mid-1960s, which concluded that much of the enthusiasm about the cultural boom has been over-inflated, and represents wishful thinking rather than solid fact. William J. Baumol and William G. Bowen, both professors of economics at Princeton University, spent several years studying the performing arts in America under a grant of the Twentieth Century Fund. Their report, *Performing Arts: The Economic Dilemma*,[10] does much to dispute the view that there has been a widespread increase of actual attendance at artistic events, or that the "explosion" has truly cut across class and geographical lines, to reach new audiences and grass roots regions of the country. They conclude that the cultural expansion:

> ... is shown to be an extremely spotty affair, with some levels of activity increasing, some declining, and the over-all result amount-ing best to a small and patchy pattern of growth .... In sum, this analysis of the record entitles us to conclude neither that this nation has entered a great cultural renaissance nor that it is lost in an artistic wilderness. Rather, as is so often the case, one is forced to a comparatively colorless in-between position—that over the course of the last decade and a half, the over-all progress of profes-sional activity in the living arts has amounted to little more than a continuation of past trends.[11]

The Twentieth Century Fund report arrived at the following specific findings:

Although "there has been an air of excitement and growth" that may augur well for the future, there has been no sharp increase in the amount of attendance at professional performing arts events. Thus, Americans spent $127 million on admissions in 1929, and $433 million in 1963, which, based on analysis of price levels and income, indicates a 25 per cent decline in expenditure—from 15 cents to 11 cents of each $100 of disposable personal income. Undoubtedly, television, which brings professional entertainment into the home, has had much to do with this. Nor has the growth of interest been as widespread as suggested. New York City alone accounted for nearly 40 per cent of all admissions to classical music performances in the most recent year recorded, and over one half of all theatrical admissions. New Yorkers spent an average of $1.42 on concert tickets and $17.94 on theatrical admissions in 1963, contrasted with an average national expenditure of 29 cents for concert tickets and $1.88 for theater.

The audience for the performing arts, say Baumol and Bowen,

[10] William J. Baumol and William G. Bowen, *Performing Arts: The Economic Dilemma* (New York: The Twentieth Century Fund, 1966).

[11] *Ibid.*, pp. 67–69.

is still drawn from an extremely narrow segment of the population, consisting chiefly of well-educated professional people in their late youth and early middle age. They are remarkably similar in background, regardless of art form or location. Overall, it is probable that no more than 5 million people, about 4 per cent of the population, used the 20 million tickets sold for professional performing arts events in the 1963–1964 season. Thus, in the opinion of Baumol and Bowen, the view that interest in the arts has spread rapidly through all classes is not justified; probably no more than 10 per cent of audiences are blue-collar workers.

The economic dilemma of the performing arts receives the major portion of Baumol and Bowen's concern. They point out that while salaries in music, drama, and dance have risen markedly, this is compensated for by the high level of unemployment or partial employment through the year, in these fields. Thus, of 49 male professional occupations in the 1960 census ranked by income, actors were 34th, musicians and music teachers 40th, and dancers and dancing teachers 48th. They comment that while performers with some top year-round organizations average more than $10,000 per year, the "salary levels of performers in many organizations are still scandalously low." Baumol and Bowen refer to the performer's lot as being "a nightmare world," and suggest that, unless conditions improve, talented youngsters are going to turn to other fields.

Finally, they deal in considerable detail with the actual situation of the major companies, orchestras, and theaters in the country. First, they cut through the very large figures which are generally cited about the numbers of performing groups (which they regard chiefly as amateur), and conclude:

> In no case is the number of professional organizations very large; they range [in 1965] from about 60 metropolitan and major orchestras and 40 to 50 permanent theatrical groups to perhaps 7 opera companies and a slightly larger number of dance groups. In number of performers they vary from a dance company of 6 to an orchestra with over 100 musicians and grand opera with a cast of over 200.[12]

The economic structure of the performing arts makes it clear that they cannot support themselves directly through admissions alone. Taking grand opera as the most obvious example, when one considers that the cast includes leading and supporting singers, members of the chorus, ballet dancers, extras, and musicians (totalling between 200 and 300) who must perform in halls that usually have a capacity of less than 4,000 persons, one realizes

[12] *Ibid.*, p. 32.

that the maximal audience is 20 persons per performer. "It is as though a two person cast in a Broadway play were to try to run night after night before an audience of forty!" The situation for opera is even worse, in the sense that it must have expensive costumes and sets for each of the several works that it carries in its repertoire through the season—plus the need to maintain a number of extremely high-priced stars, who draw the audience. Thus, the 1964–1965 $1.5 million deficit of the Metropolitan Opera is hardly suprising.

In varying measure, each of the performing arts is faced with similar economic hazards. Even Lincoln Center for the Performing Arts, widely regarded as the most professional and prestigious of all cultural organizations in the country (consisting of the Metropolitan Opera, the New York Philharmonic, the City Center of Music and Drama which includes the New York City Ballet and New York City Opera, the Library and Museum of the Performing Arts, the Lincoln Center Repertory Theater and the Music Theater of Lincoln Center) is presently operating at a multi-million dollar annual deficit.[13]

The Twentieth Century Fund report comes to a single major conclusion: that the performing arts in America—theater, opera, music, and dance—cannot live by box office alone. They now need more than $20 million dollars a year in contributions to survive, and by 1975, they will require $60 million a year. Ticket price rises will not solve the problem. Instead, government and foundation support is essential. Thus far, this has been minimal and has served chiefly as a stop-gap measure. Foundations, for example, have typically given grants for a short term (usually three to five years) and have renewed them once and then withdrawn them. While companies have thus been encouraged to expand their efforts, they have been in even more dire need for support as the grants expired.

Baumol and Bowen conclude that professional performance may well survive and even prosper.

> But the cost of its preservation will be high and will rise inexorably. Fortunately the very rise in productivity in other sectors of the economy which lies at the heart of the problem will also provide society with the wherewithal to pay the mounting bill if it is determined to do so.[14]

An earlier report, *The Performing Arts: Problems and Prospects*, published by the Rockefeller Brothers Fund in 1965, is somewhat

[13] Richard F. Shepard, "Lincoln Center: A Business Too," *The New York Times,* January 9, 1967, p. 78.
[14] Baumol and Bowen *op. cit.,* p. 407.

more positive about the "cultural explosion" in general. Its authors comment that a very considerable expansion of the performing arts has taken place in the past two decades, and conclude that the potential for the successful development of the performing arts is tremendous. They write:

> There are millions of Americans who have never seen a live professional performance of any kind. There are untold numbers who might, with opportunity and training, become first-rate performing artists. There are electronic devices, still in a relatively early stage of development, to bring performances to vast audiences at modest expense. And the material resources to do all these things are available if we choose to do them.[15]

Conceding that the figures regarding the growth of performing arts companies are accurate and that they show a remarkable upswing in performance, the Rockefeller Panel Report makes what it considers to be a "sobering" comment—that *almost all this expansion is amateur.* Thus, they comment that the American people may have experienced an extraordinary awakening to the performing arts, but comparatively few are ever exposed to any *live professional* presentations. They point out that the professional, commercial theater has declined in recent years; that, of the large number of symphony orchestras, only 54 are composed predominantly of professional musicians; that only five or six dance companies meet high professional standards and have a real degree of institutional stability; that, of the 754 opera groups, only 35 to 40 are fully professional, and that not more than ten of these provide performances for more than fifteen days in the year.

The Rockefeller Report stresses that the amateur movement in the arts is a vital element in developing an audience for the performing arts, as well as a first opportunity for many young artists to gain valuable experience in performance. If it were not for such amateur or semiprofessional companies, many communities far from the great urban centers would have no opportunity at all to view live performing arts. Through amateur participation in the arts, there has been a vital change in America's entire cultural landscape—a new spirit of interest and involvement. Only a few are likely to see this change from a "cultural elitist" position, lamenting, in the words of Dwight McDonald, "that the segment of the public interested in culture has changed from a "small body of connoisseurs into a large body of ignoramuses." This automatic condemnation of amateur performance and

[15] Rockefeller Panel Report, *The Performing Arts: Problems and Prospects* (New York: McGraw-Hill Book Company, 1965), p. 11.

involvement would seem to rest on the traditional concept that
if standards of excellence are to be maintained, culture must
remain the property of a privileged few.

Nonetheless, the Rockefeller Report makes the following
point very strongly:

> ... it is on the professional performing artists and arts organizations
> that ultimate responsibility for the highest levels of creative output
> and quality rests. Some of these organizations, particularly the
> orchestras, are expanding rapidly, some are actually in declining
> health, others are just barely holding their own, and others are grow-
> ing at a rate much slower than might be. In general, there has been
> no significant improvement in the basic health of the professional
> arts organizations. There is much to be done.[16]

Exactly how does professional dance performance fit into
this picture? What do the Twentieth Century Fund and the
Rockefeller Report say of this art, in terms of its health and prospects for the future?

In general they comment that it suffers from the same difficulties as all the performing arts: difficulty in finding regular employment and maintaining an adequate standard of living for the
performer; with few exceptions, a lack of opportunities for first-
class training throughout the country; the need for more theaters
designed for dance and available to dance companies for seasons
of the appropriate length; a lack of strong and stable sponsoring
organizations, combined with a dependence on "crisis financing";
and, finally, insufficient long-range planning and research.

The Rockefeller Report concludes that from the point of
view of finance, administration, and organization, the professional
dance world is "close to chaos." It points out that there is only
one theater in the country devoted exclusively to dance—Jacob's
Pillow in Massachusetts—and that this is open only three months
of the year. Not more than five or six dance companies, it states,
have both a national reputation and a reasonably stable organizational structure; in addition, there are perhaps "a dozen leading
dancers, who scrape together companies, get up programs on shoe-
string budgets, and hope for a modest performance or two in New
York, followed by a short and usually equally unprofitable road
season."[17]

In analyzing three major dance companies, the Rockefeller
Report praises the New York City Ballet and the San Francisco
Ballet as two relatively successful organizations, from an economic
point of view, which provide full or close to full employment for

[16] *Ibid.*, p. 15.
[17] *Ibid.*, p. 43.

their companies, and maintain schools of high quality for the development of talented new performers. While recognizing the stature of the Martha Graham Company, the report makes clear that it is able to perform only when presented "by a government agency, a foundation, or some other interested agency or individual. At such times Miss Graham and members of her company are paid a fee by the presenting agency, which also pays the production expenses and covers the deficit a presentation inevitably entails. There is no profit or loss to the company, which exists only at these infrequent times of rehearsal and performance."[18]

It is clear that if it were not for wealthy patrons such as Lincoln Kirstein, Lucia Chase, Jean Riddell, Ruth Page, and the B. de Rothschild and Rebekah Harkness foundations, it would have been all but impossible for a number of the major dance organizations—chiefly ballet but also modern dance—to have continued to function, even during recent years of relative prosperity. In the case of a number of other companies, directed by Alvin Ailey, Merce Cunningham, Robert Joffrey, José Limón, and Paul Taylor, it is absolutely necessary that they tour widely in order to find audiences and more or less sustained employment for their dancers.

The Twentieth Century Fund study supports this analysis, pointing out the curious paradox that none of these organizations constitutes the real core of professional dance performance in the United States. Instead, it sees the audience flocking to the glamorous foreign troupes—the Bolshoi, the Royal Ballet, the Royal Danish Ballet, and other visiting companies. Only the New York City Ballet's audience begins to compare with those of the foreign companies.[19]

On the positive side of the ledger, the report indicates that there has been a pronounced though erratic growth in the amount of what it describes as "professional dance activity" in New York City. Analyzing calendars of dance events in *Dance Magazine* and other notices, it points out that the number of performances from 1951–1952 to 1964–1965 has increased at an average rate of 4.2 per cent a year. It points out that the growth in touring activity throughout the United States has been even more impressive. Between 1952 and 1964, the number of dance performances on tour and the total number of communities visited have each quadrupled. Thus, it concludes,

> . . . with the development of the college and university circuit, the dance really seems to have expanded its audience in this country,

[18] *Ibid.*, pp. 46–47.
[19] Baumol and Bowen, *op. cit.*, p. 32.

and the number of areas outside our major cities in which dance performances are available has increased correspondingly. Here is a performing art in which there really seems to be a substantial rate of expansion.[20]

Both studies present a picture of dance as an area of artistic activity with considerable potential for the future, but one which will require the combined effort of government, foundations, and universities if it is to operate on a sounder base. The Rockefeller Report stresses the need to consider and plan for all of the performing arts, as part of a total master plan for support and encouragement. It envisions a situation in the near future in which a number of recognized, major companies and organizations within each of the performing arts would provide their artists—as most do not now—with twelve months of employment, and the public with year-round performances of high quality. Such a program, embracing fifty permanent theater companies, fifty symphony orchestras, six regional opera companies, six regional choral groups, and six regional dance companies, in addition to the two major resident companies (New York City Ballet and San Francisco Ballet) now in existence, would require an annual subsidy of between $40 and $60 million.

It would obviously be dependent on public recognition of the need for such a program. The Rockefeller Report points out that performing arts of high quality are costly, but a decidedly modest financial outlay (in terms of the overall wealth of our country) is all that would be required to provide the needed support. As a long-term goal,

> The panel recommends that the artistic goal of the nation be the day when the performing arts are considered a permanent year-round contribution to communities throughout the country, and our artists are considered as necessary as our educators.[21]

How promising are the prospects of such support for dance? What forms of subsidy have been obtained in recent years from governmental and private sources?

On the basis of practices in other Western nations, one might expect that the federal government would play an important role in support of the arts. In England, for example, the Arts Council of Great Britain has been extremely effective since World War II in providing annual grants to support opera, ballet, and theater. In its Ninth Annual Report, for 1953–1954, the Council stated that if the half-million pounds then being spent annually on the arts as public subsidy were withdrawn, "nearly all the

[20] *Ibid.*, p. 53.
[21] Rockefeller Panel Report, *op. cit.*, p. 49.

national institutions of music and drama in this country would have to close down." It commented further that while all the arts were attracting far greater audiences in Britain than ever before, it was not possible for them to catch up with their rising costs of production and performance. Through the twenty years following the war, Parliament continued to vote increasing sums (now amounting to over six million pounds annually) to the support of the arts, under both Labor and Conservative Governments. The disposition of the funds has been left to the nonpolitical Arts Council, and there has been general agreement that it has acted effectively—without favoritism or bias.[22]

Similar patterns of support are found in the national ministries of culture in a number of other major European countries, with specific grants being given to institutions such as national ballet companies or opera houses, as well as to the training of performers.

In France, there are two national theaters (the Opéra Comique and the Comédie Française) which receive subsidies amounting to several millions of dollars annually, granted by the national Ministry of Beaux Arts. In the provinces, opera is subsidized locally, and there are many national festivals which also receive governmental support. In Germany, each state has a separate ministry of culture; in fairly large cities, theater and opera are in separate houses and performances are given every night of the week for eleven months of the year. Music and theater personnel are, in effect, on government salaries year-round, with pension rights, just as other civil employees are. Government support of the arts is also extended to great annual festivals such as the Bayreuth Festival.

In Italy, the famous La Scala Opera House in Milan is supported by municipal and state funds; such national festivals as the one at Spoleto each year are supported by the Italian government. In Austria, the government aids such undertakings as the Vienna State Opera, the Vienna Philharmonic, and the Salzburg Festival. In the Netherlands, the government sponsors a number of major orchestras, such as the Amsterdam Concertgebouw, theaters, and festivals. In Eastern Europe, the countries in the Soviet bloc all operate networks of performing arts schools, playhouses or concert halls, and companies, as a routine governmental responsibility.

In the United States, the first large-scale effort on the part of the federal government to assist the performing arts came during the depression of the 1930s. It was prompted not so much by a

[22] Howard Taubman, "Through Foreign Eyes," *The New York Times,* July 8, 1966, p. 41.

recognition of the special need of the arts as it was part of a total program to provide employment during a period of national emergency. From 1936 to 1938, the Federal Theater included a dance unit, which helped to promote a nationwide program of dance participation and performance—chiefly modern dance, although some ballet and ethnic dance were involved. The Federal Dance Theater, with Don Oscar Becque as director, and with Doris Humphrey, Felicia Sorel, Tamiris, and Charles Weidman among its supervisors, was founded in January 1936.

Tamiris, Myra Kinch, Ruth Page and Bentley Stone, Katherine Dunham, and Grace and Kurt Graff all produced works which reflected the view of dance as part of "people's theater," and which were concerned both with Americana and with left-wing and minority group themes—as were much of the dance and theater during this period. Thus, Myra Kinch and her company performed *American Exodus*, a dance drama of pioneers crossing the plains. Katherine Dunham's company did *L'Ag'ya*, based on ethnic and folk themes from the Caribbean. Page and Stone produced *Frankie and Johnny*, based on the popular folk ballad. Tamiris created *How Long Brethren?*, based on Lawrence Gellert's *Negro Songs of Protest*.

Like many of the works created for the Federal Theater, or as part of the Federal Arts Project, dancers and dances soon came under political scrutiny and attack. The Dies Committee in 1938 attacked the Federal Theater, charging that it had many employees who were either members of the Communist Party or sympathetic to it.[23] Ultimately, the entire program of support for the arts was discontinued, with the approach of World War II, and no such broad-scale effort to assist the performing arts or provide employment in the arts has been undertaken since by the federal government.

This experience, however, illustrates the fears that many persons share with respect to support of the arts by a national government.

In their view, there are grave risks of government attempting to use the arts as a means of propaganda (and so perverting their essential purposes), or curbing creativity by withholding support or terminating grants. It is feared that even if the attempt to control is not overt, some artists may, in their desire to retain support, unconsciously yield to a form of artistic censorship to avoid giving offense to the establishment. It is also thought inevitable that

[23] Hallie Flanagan, *Arena* (New York: Duell, Sloan and Pearce, 1940), p. 347.

those who are assigned to positions of control in whatever government agency is responsible for distributing funds will favor certain individuals or companies or schools of artistic belief—thus, in effect, permitting their own taste to dominate what should be a free marketplace.

For these and other reasons, there has been hesitation, on the part of many legislators and many professionals in the arts, to support a full-fledged program of government support of the arts. It would seem that, in estimating the likelihood of censorship and control of the arts as an outcome of government subsidy, one would have to examine first the nature of the government that provides the aid, and second the kind of structure that is established to channel and direct it. In the Soviet Union and Communist China, it appears quite clear that the arts are made to serve as handmaidens of the national ideology. So too, however, are newspapers, radio and television, youth organizations, workers' unions, and many other organizations or cultural bodies. On the other hand, in Great Britain and other Western nations, there appears to be widespread agreement that the nonpolitical structure that has been established to administer art subsidy programs has not attempted to influence or curb artistic output. Inevitably, choices for support must be made, and the tendency is to channel the major funds to large, established national companies. Undoubtedly, the problem becomes more difficult when a government attempts to distribute funds more widely, among less well established artists and companies.

Apart from the question of whether government should subsidize the arts (in terms of potential dangers in this relationship) there is the even more basic question of *why* it should do so.

Some have made the point that if the arts cannot justify themselves through attendance and ticket sales, as commercial motion pictures, or stage shows, or ice shows, or the circus, or rodeo, or rock-and-roll shows, then they have no right to ask for support. They imply that government has no obligation to support one level of cultural taste in preference to another, which of course is the basis for such subsidy.

The answer to this, of course, is that government is in a position to support whatever it considers important in national or community life. The provision of parks, health services, sanitation, police, and education are all usually mandated by law—but only because those who make the laws perceive these as essential functions of government, which are not likely to be adequately provided in other ways. Throughout the history of the Western world, the arts have been viewed as essential to society. For centuries, music, drama, painting, dance, and architecture have all been strongly supported in European countries. Indeed, the United States has lagged far behind other nations in this regard. Today, it has become increasingly evident that the arts are essential to the fullest and richest life in both the community and the nation, that they express the highest ideals of a society, that they provide a vital and necessary dimension of human existence.

Within this context, it has become unmistakably clear that the performing arts cannot support themselves independently, through maximum income from ticket sales; costs are simply too great. Thus, government has come increasingly to recognize that if it values the performing arts as part of national life, they must receive a substantial measure of financial subsidy.

In the United States during the 1940s and 1950s, there have been certain specific programs for aid of the arts with which the federal government has identified itself.

1. The government has financed many foreign tours for dance groups. José Limón received State Department support in 1954 under the then new International Exchange Program, which was administered by the American National Theater and Academy. The program, designed to familiarize other countries with our art forms and balance the extensive exporting of performing groups sponsored by other governments, sent Limón with a company of 16 to South America for a month, during which he appeared in Rio de Janeiro during the annual meeting of UNESCO, and in Montevideo during the meeting of the Organization of American Republics. The first major artistic mission of this type under government sponsorship was in 1941, when the American Ballet Caravan, ancestor of the present New York City Ballet, made an extended "goodwill tour" of South America. Later, the Ballet Theater went there and, in 1950, to Europe, with assistance from the State Department. Since then, many modern dance companies, including the Martha Graham and the Alvin Ailey Companies, as well as leading ballet troupes, have toured other countries with government assistance.

Such assistance is by no means an outright subsidy. Emphasis has been placed on assisting only organizations that are able to arouse a high degree of natural interest in the countries they are visiting; thus, the State Department grant serves to supplement the tour's income and to make it possible. In general, dance tours have been well regarded. They are seen as presenting a true cultural image of the United States, and tend to find—as an essentially nonverbal art form—ready acceptance from widely varying audiences.

In recent years, such programs have been administered under the President's International Program for Cultural Presentations, with a Dance Panel screening and recommending the programs to be selected for support. By 1963, twenty-six such companies had been sent abroad.

While such subsidies are important in helping to present a favorable picture of American culture abroad, and also are useful in that they help to provide direct support for dance artists and companies as far as their total program of performance is concerned, they do little to assist the health of the performing arts within the United States itself. Similarly, the Fulbright grants for study abroad (by 1966 there had been 27 of these in dance) and other International Exchange scholarship programs are of personal value to dance students and artists, but are only indirectly helpful to the field itself in the United States.

2. A program with a domestic focus was initiated when, in 1964, the National Arts and Cultural Development Act established a National Council on the Arts within the Executive Office of the President. A year later, the Arts and Humanities Act of 1965 established a National Foundation on the Arts and the Humanities, with separate endowment programs for the arts and humanities, and advisory bodies for each area. The National Council on the Arts serves as the advisory body for the National Endowment for the Arts; it is responsible for providing funds (chiefly on a matching-grant basis) to nonprofit organizations and to state and other public organizations and individuals for the following:

> ... To assist artistic and cultural productions which give "emphasis to American creativity" and encourage professional excellence; to help make available artistic programs of high merit in areas of the country which otherwise would be culturally barren; to encourage and assist individual artists; to promote a general appreciation and understanding of the arts; and to provide assistance for relevant projects related to surveys, research and planning in the arts.[24]

The Arts and Humanities Act of 1965 appropriated funds amounting to $21 million for each of the three fiscal years from 1966 through 1968. Its general goals were to:

Develop a larger, more informed audience;

Help meet the needs of the "new leisure";

Decentralize the arts in the United States;

Encourage the state arts council movement (by November

---

[24] "National Foundation on the Arts and Humanities Act of 1965," *Health, Education and Welfare Indicator* (Washington, D.C.: U. S. Government Printing Office, November 1965), pp. 4–5.

1965 more than half the 50 states had developed state art agencies);

Alleviate the financial crisis in the arts and humanities by providing federal grants;

Stimulate private funding for the arts (through the matching-grant arrangement, and private assistance to state councils on the arts);

Help solve the problem of the scarcity of well-prepared teachers in the arts and humanities.[25]

Through this Act, the Commissioner of Education of the United States Department of Health, Education and Welfare was empowered to make grants and loans to strengthen instruction and to establish teacher training instituted in the arts and humanities.

What specific programs under this federal act have been directed to the support of dance? In some cases, direct assistance has been provided to dancers or dance companies or organizations by federal agencies; in others, the aid has been funneled through state councils on the arts, which have shared in the funding. To illustrate, the National Council on the Arts in 1966 gave a direct grant of $181,000 to the Martha Graham Dance Company to finance the creation of two new works and to permit Miss Graham to take her company on an eight-week tour of the United States. Similarly, in 1966 the American Ballet Theater received a substantial grant of $350,000 on a matching-funds basis from the National Council on the Arts, at a time of great financial crisis.

Through the Office of Education, Nadia Chilkovsky Nahumck of the Philadelphia Dance Academy was awarded a two-year $195,000 grant to conduct research in cooperation with the University of Pennsylvania, leading to the development of a comprehensive graded curriculum in dance for secondary school students. This curriculum, which made extensive use of the historical and cultural backgrounds of dance forms, of Labanotation techniques, and of a variety of specially prepared teaching aids, was field-tested and evaluated at nine special centers in the mid-Atlantic and Southern states. Then, during the summer of 1967, the proposed curriculum and teaching methods were presented to 95 school and college teachers and curriculum specialists at an Institute for Advanced Study in Dance at Wisconsin State University, Stevens Point, Wisconsin. This institute, one of twelve major programs designed to improve the teaching of arts and humanities sponsored by the U.S. Office of Education, was the

[25] *Ibid.*, p. 7.

Workshop in teaching of creative dance to elementary school children, conducted by Nadia Chilkovsky Nahumck, sponsored by U. S. Office of Education. Photograph by Seco.

Secondary School students in dance curriculum project demonstrate approaches to instruction and choreography. Photograph by George Dolan.

first of its kind to be specifically directed to the improvement of dance teaching.

Another federally funded program designed to stimulate the teaching of modern dance in secondary schools was carried on by the North Plainfield school system, in Somerset County, New Jersey. With the aid of $22,000 awarded under Title Three of the Elementary and Secondary Education Act of 1965, Nancy Schuman, a high school modern dance and physical education teacher in North Plainfield, carried out the following "crash program." During the summer and fall of 1967, a series of modern dance workshops for teachers was provided; full-length, professional concerts were given at schools throughout the county by such outstanding dance artists as Lucas Hoving, Pearl Primus, Glen Tetley, Paul Taylor, Murray Louis, and their companies; lecture-demonstrations in dance were given as part of assembly programs in a large number of schools; and a variety of other events and workshops were held throughout the county. The primary purpose of the program was to encourage and enable secondary schools in the county to begin courses in modern dance as part of their regular curricula. While it is too early to tell whether the venture has been fully successful, certainly it provides a useful model for other dance educators who seek to promote local interest in dance instruction.

Recognizing that one of the great needs in dance is to have a permanent service organization which would permit dancers of all types to work together in common causes, the National Endowment on the Arts funded, in June 1966, a planning meeting to help establish such an organization. During a three-day session, 150 delegates from ballet and modern dance companies from coast to coast met in New York City and planned an organization, tentatively to be called the American Dance League. Its purpose, modeled on the American Symphony Orchestra League, would be to help disseminate news and exchange information, advise in business and administrative matters, help member companies in their appeals for financial support, and attempt to increase audience support for the dance. Later in 1966 the organization was formally launched, assisted by a modest $11,000 from the National Endowment on the Arts, with promise of additional funds to be granted on a matching basis. Now officially titled the Association of American Dance Companies, it is intended to serve as an umbrella organization to which will belong such other groups as the North American Association of Ballet Companies, the National Association for Regional Ballet, the Foundation for American Dance (a recently formed modern dance group), and the growing National Dance Guild.

One of the first projects the newly formed Association of American Dance Companies sponsored, along with the New York State Council on the Arts and the Cunningham Dance Foundation, was a one-day seminar on the theme of dance administration and support. Clearly, the problems of management, housing for dance, and financial support are all crucial to the success of any performing arts field, and the efforts of the federal government in this area have begun to bear fruit rapidly.

Through the stimulus of the National Council on the Arts, and with the help of matching funds provided by the National Endowment on the Arts (regarded chiefly ᵤ₃ "seed money"), a number of states have developed thriving state arts councils. Prominent among these are Illinois, Missouri, and North Carolina. New York State has been notably progressive in allocating funds to its Arts Council (federal support amounts to only about 20 per cent of the program's total cost) and its assistance to dance is worth examining as an example of what the state's role in this area may be.

The New York State Council on the Arts made a remarkable contribution to dance in 1964, in supporting the new American Dance Theater, a modern dance repertory company, in a brief series of performances at Lincoln Center. The basis on which this venture was supported was that the state council would underwrite the anticipated deficit of the program which actually turned out to be much less than expected. In its first year, 1962, the New York State body sent professional theater, opera, ballet, and art into more than fifty communities throughout the state. Companies performed on a low admissions scale and, although they played to 90 per cent capacity audiences, they lost money overall, which the Council subsidized. The New York City Ballet Company took part in this program. The Council has also provided assistance to schools, colleges, and universities throughout the state to develop instructional programs in the performing arts. These programs include lecture-demonstrations, symposia, seminars, master classes, workshops, and performances before student audiences.

Specific dance groups included in the school-connected and college-connected programs of the New York State Council on the Arts are: the Alba Reyes Spanish Dance Company, the Korean National Ballet, Paul Taylor Dance Company, José Limón Dance Company, and groups directed by Norman Walker, Sophie Maslow, Erick Hawkins, Olatunji, Jean-Léon Destiné, Merce Cunningham, Jean Erdman, Pearl Lang, Paul Sanasardo, Valerie Bettis, Matteo, and others. In some cases, the focus has been not only on presenting dance as a discrete art form, but also on showing the interrelatedness of the arts. Thus, in 1967, the New York State Council on the Arts sponsored a series of appearances at a number of universities in the state of choreographer-dancer Merce Cunningham, composer John Cage, poet Robert Creeley, kinetic sculptor Len Lye, painter Jack Tworkov, film-maker Stan VanDerBeek, and engineer Billy Kluver. Their purpose was to hold discussions with college students, give demonstrations of their work, and present their own concepts of their art, of the relationship among various art forms, and of the creative process in general.

Similarly, other states have developed tours as a means of spreading understanding and building receptive audiences for dance. In New Jersey, the Garden State Ballet received a $15,000 grant from the new State Arts Council in 1967 to extend its educational program throughout the state; over 35,000 school children saw live ballet as a result of this venture. During the first full year of the Connecticut Arts Commission, ten pilot programs were initiated, including film festivals, technical assistance to theaters and museums, and touring groups and master classes in music and dance. Without question, as state arts councils move increasingly into such ventures, with the help of the National Endowment on the Arts, grass roots audiences will become increasingly knowledgeable and receptive to the performing arts.

A number of other programs sponsored by the federal government have been directed specifically at the arts in education. Under Title III of the Elementary and Secondary Education Act of 1965, a special program entitled PACE—Projects to Advance Creativity in Education—has provided many millions of dollars to promote the arts and humanities. Live Lincoln Center productions of music, drama, and dance have been brought into New York City schools, for example, and many afterschool and Saturday creative arts centers have been established to serve disadvantaged and specially gifted children.

Even more important than government in the direct support of concert dance companies has been the role played by private individuals and foundations. Typically, the American Ballet Theater, which has produced more diversified works than any other American company and has spawned many brilliant choreographers and teachers, has survived largely through the generosity of a single patron, Lucia Chase. Similarly, Martha Graham, through the years, has been assisted heavily by the gifts of a single individual, administered through the B. de Rothschild Foundation.

Through the years, the largest single contributor to the arts has been the Ford Foundation. During the period from 1957 to 1964, it gave $30 million to Lincoln Center and the National Cultural Center, and approximately $30 million more for other purposes, including theater ($8.6 million), opera ($6.2 million), and dance ($8 million) with a later grant of $85 million to American symphony orchestras.

The major Ford contribution to dance consisted of $7,756,750 given in 1963 to eight ballet organizations. The New York City Ballet and its affiliated School of American Ballet, both controlled by George Balanchine and Lincoln Kirstein, were given control of $5,925,000, or more than 75 per cent of the allotment, to strengthen the company and school over a ten-year period and to use in programs that bring ballet to communities and schools in the New York region. The remaining millions went in varying amounts to the San Francisco Ballet, the Pennsylvania Ballet of Philadelphia, the Utah Ballet of Salt Lake City, the Houston Ballet, and the Boston Ballet.

The policy of the Ford Foundation executives was clearly to give heavy support to a few established enterprises, rather than spread itself thinly over a large number of less stable organizations. Thus, it has committed itself to building a solid foundation for ballet, and for the support of training. The Ford Foundation grant has been widely criticized throughout the dance world, however, because it excluded modern dance completely and because it gave such a major portion of the grant to the New York City Ballet and to other ballet organizations that are closely linked to Balanchine and Kirstein—at the same time ignoring American Ballet Theater and many of the smaller but promising companies throught the country. In 1965, the Ford Foundation made additional grants totaling $1.25 million to the Robert Joffrey Ballet, the Pennsylvania Ballet, and the Boston Ballet. In the words of W. McNeil Lowry, director of the Humanities and the Arts Division of the Ford Foundation:

> The new grants are intended to insure the companies' continuing momentum. Though they have passed the first hurdle with artistic and critical success, these companies yet have before them a difficult transitional phase in finding some financial strength from their own communities and their followers.
> They now face the challenge of consolidating their artistic gains while achieving greater security although even the best ballet for the foreseeable future will continue to need local patronage above box office revenues.[26]

[26] W. McNeil Lowry, in *The Dancer's Notebook*, published by Selva and Sons, XII, No. 2 (1966), 1–2, 4–5.

There have been comparatively few other foundation grants to dance; the largest of these was the $1 million given by the William Hale Harkness Foundation in 1964 to help establish and support the new Harkness Ballet for a ten-year period. The same foundation at earlier points had assisted Pearl Primus, Jerome Robbins' Ballets U.S.A., and the Joffrey Ballet. Other major foundations which have given substantially to the performing arts in the past several years have been the Rockefeller Foundation, the Avalon Foundation, the A.W. Mellon Educational and Charitable Trust, the E. and A.E. Mayer Foundation, and the Old Dominion Foundation. However, it is clear that the performing arts have received comparatively little, on an overall basis, both from foundations and from large corporations that are in a position, through tax-exempted gifts, to offer meaningful support:

> The available data . . . indicate that civic and cultural activities together received 5.3 per cent of corporate giving in 1962, and this category clearly includes considerably more than the performing arts alone. Estimates of the portion going to the performing arts range from about 3 to 4 per cent of the total of $580 million given by the corporations in 1964—somewhere between $17 and $23 million, with the lower of these figures the more plausible. Roughly half of the nation's large corporations give something to the arts, but most of them give very little; about half of those contributing allocate less than 1 per cent of their total donations to this purpose.[27]

If concert dance is to flourish in the years ahead, it will be necessary for both government and large foundations and corporations that are capable of providing adequate assistance to do so. This is particularly true of modern dance, which has been almost completely ignored in the large recent gifts just described. In large measure, the foundations and corporations have given assistance to major cultural centers in New York, Washington, and other large cities. It is clear that it is not enough to plan a structure or set of structures (one comment is that corporate donors today have an "edifice complex"). Instead, from the very beginning, thought must be given not only to designing theaters suitable for performance—whether of music, opera, drama or dance —but also to developing and supporting companies that will be able to perform in them. The New York State Theater in Lincoln Center has been a prime example of this. Originally conceived of as a dance theater, and widely referred to in this vein, it actually came into being as a center which would be shared by dance and musical theater. The economics of support for the hall, and the difficulties of scheduling, meant that in terms of dance, it became dominated by the New York City and touring ballet companies.

[27] Baumol and Bowen, *op. cit.*, p. 333.

It was almost impossible for modern dance to be scheduled, even for a brief season in the building, unless it was under a special subsidy.

The danger is that many of the other large cultural centers throughout the country will make little effort to encourage and act as a home for vital resident companies in their own cities, but will, in DeGaetani's words, act as glorified road houses, "pandering to the star-studded wanderings of Broadway and the international Hurok coterie."[28] One solution, necessary from the very beginning, would be to devote a small percentage of the capitalization of cultural centers to the development of companies and programs with which to fill the halls and stages, and through which to spread cultural activity in the community.

This can best be done through the intelligent collaboration of all concerned agencies and people in the community or region. DeGaetani cites an example of such collaboration, the $15 million Convention and Cultural Center being built through a combination of civic and federal funds in Norfolk, Virginia.

> Scheduled for completion in 1970, the Center, consisting of a 14,000 seat arena, a 3,000 seat theatre, and a 300 seat versatile and variable-use space, is employing the services of the world-famous architect Pier Luigi Nervi with Norfolk architect E. Bradford Tazewell, Jr., as collaborator.
>
> Space allowance at the Norfolk Center will allow for the future accommodation of the administrative and rehearsal requirements of a resident symphony and yet-to-be-formed companies in opera, dance and drama. Norfolk's Little Theatre needs are seen as initially being met by the . . . 300 seat . . . space.[29]

To insure that there will be unified direction and full support given to regional arts activity—both professional and amateur—the Norfolk City government has taken steps to establish a Regional Council on the Arts, to cover the entire spectrum of the visual and performing arts in the greater Norfolk region. It is expected that this council will serve to promote widespread cultural activities for both youth and adults in the region and the concerted effort needed to establish strong, indigenous professional performing companies that will find their home in the cultural center, when it is built.

A final important aspect of the growth of dance as a concert art today lies in the role played by national and regional organizations working in this field. In addition to the recently formed

[28] Thomas P. DeGaetani, "Building for the Arts, or A House Is Not a Home," *Dance Magazine*, November 1966, p. 75.
[29] *Ibid.*, p. 37.

Association of American Dance Companies, which was mentioned earlier, there have been several such organizations which have been rapidly expanding their influence. Some of these are broadly concerned with all the arts, with dance being one of the component fields.

Such an organization is the National Council of the Arts in Education, a federation of national associations concerned with the arts at all educational levels. It supports general education in the arts in elementary and secondary schools, in preprofessional and professional education, and teacher education. Members of the constituent organizations are active as both teachers and practitioners in the arts; they include actors, dancers, musicians, painters, and sculptors, as well as composers, museum curators, art critics, historians, and researchers. Member organizations include fourteen national groups concerned with theater, music, art education, ethnomusicology, architecture, and dance. The dance-connected organizations are the National Dance Guild (formerly the National Dance Teachers Guild) and the National Division on Dance of the American Association for Health, Physical Education and Recreation.

Founded in 1958, the National Council of the Arts in Education exists to:

Define educational goals for the arts;

Disseminate views of the artistic community on questions of national importance;

Stimulate research and development in art education;

Keep membership abreast of legislative activity affecting the arts, and develop informed opinion on pending legislation;

Provide contact among artists, art educators, school administrators, government officials;

Promote understanding of the arts and their place in education;

Discover new sources of support for the arts.

The National Council of the Arts in Education has held, since 1962, important annual conferences at universities throughout the country, concerned with major themes related to the status and development of the arts in education and in community life.

A second organization which deals broadly with all the arts is the Arts Councils of America, a national nonprofit group chartered in North Carolina, with headquarters in New York City. This body is a federation of arts councils throughout the United States, which holds annual conferences dealing with the development of the arts. Typically, the twelfth annual meeting, held in New York City in May 1966, dealt with "Planning for Change"; more than 500 representatives of councils, art commissions, and other civic groups met to share information about concerts, exhibitions, festivals, fund-raising efforts, and building plans.

The Arts Councils of America has developed an expanded center of information and referral to assist those in local communities who are designing facilities to house the arts, and generally to provide technical assistance.

The National Dance Guild, whose home is in New York City, is a membership organization designed to meet the needs of creative teachers of dance throughout the country. Its goals are to improve instruction in dance, to develop increased community awareness of dance and a higher level of aesthetic taste ("to combat the impact of commercialism and its corruption of taste through techniques of parent education"), and to further the progress of dance through support from a number of levels: community, state, and federal governments.

Among its program goals, the National Dance Guild seeks specifically to:

Establish basic curriculum standards for varied age groups and forms of creative dance;

Create a Dance Laboratory, a "choreography counseling service";

Improve public relations of the dance through the inclusion of dance on educational television, and through the development of teacher demonstration groups to appear before parent and community organizations;

Establish a basic minimum salary scale and acceptable teaching conditions for Guild members;

Work for certification of Dance Teachers in public school systems; promote maximum employment for members and stimulate new dance teaching situations;

Campaign for Federal support of the arts.

The Guild, whose membership is chiefly in the northeast region of the country, has gradually been spreading its membership and range of influence. It publishes a newspaper, sponsors workshops through local chapters, provides a placement bureau, publishes a magazine, *Dance Scope,* and holds annual conferences of high quality, which attract hundreds of dance teachers who are concerned both with enhancing their own competence and with strengthening the entire field of dance education.

In contrast to the National Dance Guild, which is essentially concerned with the teaching of creative dance on a noncommercial level (usually through small community-sponsored nonprofit organizations), there are a number of large, powerful organizations, which represent commercial dancing teachers throughout the United States. The distinction is that the commercial teachers operate on a profit basis, running large-scale enterprises in private studios which may either be part of national chains or independently owned. Such studios tend to stress not modern or creative dance, but rather ballet and ballroom dancing for children and adults, modern jazz, and tap dance, as well as other forms which are associated with performing dance on a "popular" and non-aesthetic level.

Organizations of this type include the Dance Masters of America, "a professional organization for certified dance teachers only," which holds large-scale regional and national conventions each year. The curriculum of such conventions includes: "ballet, tap, jazz, baby work, children's work, modern, acrobatic, baton, and ballroom dance." Faculty include such leading dancers and choreographers as Robert Joffrey, Leon Danielian, Violette Verdy, Matt Mattox, and other leading dancers—including many who are known as performers or choreographers for movies and television. In terms of levels of taste, the members of the Dance Masters of America are closely attuned to what people generally are inclined to accept as dance. Their studios and business operations tend to be large, flourishing enterprises which emphasize the development of technique and showmanship rather than the personal growth and creativity of the child.

The Dance Educators of America, Inc., is a similar organization, consisting of "qualified dance teachers," who are essentially connected with private and commercial studios and whose orientation is dance instruction or performance on a popular level. It holds major conventions throughout the country, including, in 1967, meetings in Salt Lake City, Utah; Portland, Oregon; and Atlanta, Georgia. There are numerous local and state chapters of the Dance Masters of America and Dance Educators of America, as well as of the American Society of Teachers of Dancing and a variety of similar organizations. Dance Caravan, U.S.A., operates a major tour each summer throughout cities in the United States, offering performing arts courses for both teachers and students, staffed by popular and highly-skilled specialists. Most of these organizations, both national and regional, are affiliated with the National Council of Dance Teacher Organizations, with offices in Elmira, New York.

In contrast to these groups, the organizations that are concerned with promoting dance as a creative, aesthetic activity on a noncommercial basis tend to be much smaller and to operate within a narrower range of influence. Nonetheless, they are attuned to both the interests of government, which seeks to promote dance essentially as an art form (in order to raise the level of popular culture) and to the role played by colleges and universities, which have the same concern.

Within the broad spectrum of dance activity, concert dance as such is now in a position to strengthen itself materially in the years ahead. Without question, although the problems of economics and of the narrow range of public taste continue to exist, there is far more widespread activity in theater dance today than ever was the case in the past. Similarly, there is for the first time a broad acceptance of the place of the arts in community life, and a recognition of the need for support to come from every corner of community life—from businesses and foundations, from government on various levels, from arts organizations, from colleges and universities, and from the artists themselves.

It is a time of ferment and growth. If the promise of the 1960s is realized, theater dance, as well as the other performing arts, stands at the threshold of a new era of much-expanded participation and performance. What is needed above all is the establishment of solidly based organizations connected to centers for performance. Business know-how, financial stability, solid plans for financial support (which must come in larger measure from government and foundations, if the arts are to be healthy), all will be linked to the growth of the individual artist and the establishment of an increasing number of artistically sound ballet and modern dance companies.

Within this framework, the role of educational institutions will be extremely important—in terms both of stimulating general understanding and support of dance and of providing direct experience in dance as an art form to a much broader segment of American youth than before. The following chapter, therefore, is concerned with the task of improving and expanding programs of dance education in schools and colleges.

16

DANCE EDUCATION: THE YEARS AHEAD

It is clear that if dance in education is to flourish in the years ahead, certain basic problems must be faced. These fall under two main headings: (1) the need to clarify the educational purposes of dance as aesthetic, social, and physical activity, and to demonstrate these convincingly to students, parents, and educational administrators; and (2) the question of sponsorship of dance in the schools—whether it is to continue largely within the province of physical education, or under some other arrangement.

To fully understand the way dance is regarded in American education, one must examine its place in American community life. For, unlike other subjects in the curriculum which are somewhat isolated from direct experience in community life, dance is widely encountered in many forms outside the schools. Indeed, much dance education of high quality is provided outside the formal educational structure of the nation. Therefore, students, parents, and educators all have certain attitudes about dance which are based on their contact with it in community life; these in turn influence their attitudes about it as a form of curricular experience. And, because dance has not, within the United States, been typically regarded as a basic educational discipline or subject, it is important that these attitudes be knowledgeable and favorable.

What are the widely-held attitudes about dance in commu-nity life? While they may vary according to region, community, or socioeconomic status, certain generalized views may be iden-tified.

First, for those persons in community life who have an estab-lished interest in culture and the arts, dance is regarded as an important theatrical form. While the audience for ballet and modern dance is obviously only a comparatively small percentage of the total population today, it represents a literate, prosperous, and influential segment of society. The growth of professional and amateur concert dance performance which was detailed in earlier chapters is evidence of this recognition of dance as a significant cultural form. Despite the reservations which were cited, it appears likely to grow even stronger in the years ahead.

Secondly, dance continues to be an important ingredient in popular entertainment. On television, in movies, and on the musi-cal stage, the quality of dancing has grown immeasurably. Years ago, dancing in Broadway shows or in touring companies tended to offer little more than a lineup of attractive but comparatively untrained and untalented "hoofers." Today, few dancers are hired for musical shows, movies, or television programs who have not had extensive training in ballet, modern dance, jazz, ethnic, and tap dance. Thanks to the work of such leading choreographers as Balanchine, Agnes de Mille, Jerome Robbins, Michael Kidd, Bob Fosse, and Gower Champion, public taste with respect to dance in popular entertainment has become increasingly sophisticated. Today, it is not at all uncommon to have the choreographer become responsible for staging the entire work, rather than have him assigned to stage a few numbers, as a minor aspect of the overall production.

Another important aspect of dance in community life is based on its widespread acceptance as a form of recreational and social activity. In the 1930s, sociologists Robert and Helen Lynd found dance to be one of the leading recreational activities in Middle-town; similarly, the Neumeyers wrote, "Social dancing is one of the most common leisure pursuits, especially among young people . . . . "[1]

Today, while the forms of social dancing have changed mark-edly, with "rock-and-roll" or "discotheque" dancing becoming the preoccupation of most adolescents and many young adults, as contrasted to the more traditional forms of ballroom dancing enjoyed by older persons, dancing continues to be a highly popular form of social activity. In hotels, resorts, night clubs, community

[1] Martin and Esther Neumeyer, *Leisure and Recreation* (New York: A. S. Barnes & Co., 1936), pp. 94–95.

recreation programs, secondary schools, and colleges, ballroom dancing flourishes. The teaching of dance in commercial studios has expanded to the level of a major enterprise in cities and towns throughout the United States. Since World War II, other forms of recreational dance, such as square, folk, and round dancing, have also increased in popularity. In many smaller towns and suburban areas, particularly in the far West, Midwest, and Southwest, there are also large numbers of clubs of avid folk dancers, square dancers, and round dancers. In some cases, they represent people of a particular ethnic descent, doing dances of their own nationality, but more commonly they are drawn from a variety of national backgrounds, united in a common interest.

Finally, there is an increasing interest in the use of dance as therapeutic activity. Although this function of dance is historically ancient, today it is finding new and varied applications. Interesting dance experiments are being carried out with the deaf,[2] with inmates of penal institutions,[3] with blind children,[4] with the retarded,[5] and, most commonly, with the mentally ill.[6] Marian Chace of St. Elizabeth's Hospital in Washington, D.C., has been a leading worker in the latter field, but a number of other dance educators and rehabilitation specialists have contributed much to its growing body of knowledge. Since 1956, the AAHPER National Dance Section has had a study committee on Dance Therapy. In addition, a number of mental hospitals have conducted experimental programs in dance therapy.[7] The concept of dance as therapy not only for the psychotic or severely neurotic patient but also for those in a more normal range of mental health, who are suffering from a degree of stress or disability, is being explored. In 1967, a Dance Therapy Center with this broader range of purpose was established in New York City, under the direction of Blanche Evan.

[2] Nathaniel Nitkin, "The Deaf Like to Dance," *Dance Magazine*, June 1955, p. 49; Margaret Murrel, "Dance for the Deaf Child," *Journal of Health, Physical Education and Recreation*, October 1959, pp. 46–47; and Peter Wisher, "Dance and the Deaf," *Journal of Health, Physical Education and Recreation*, November 1959, pp. 68–69.

[3] Mary Ella Montague, "Women Prisoners Respond to Contemporary Dance," *Journal of Health, Physical Education and Recreation*, March 1963, pp. 25–26, 74.

[4] "Light Steps in a Dark World," *Life Magazine*, January 20, 1958.

[5] Since 1964, the Mental Retardation Clinic of the New York Medical College has offered intensive dance therapy training programs under the direction of Liljan Espenak.

[6] See: Elizabeth Rosen, *Dance in Psychotherapy* (New York: Teachers College, Columbia University, Bureau of Publications, 1959).

[7] Marian Chace, "Opening Doors Through Dance," *Journal of Health, Physical Education and Recreation*, March 1952, pp. 32–34; and Joanna Gewertz, "Dance for Psychotic Children," *Journal of Health, Physical Education and Recreation*, January 1964, pp. 63–64.

Another unusual aspect of dance in community life has been the emphasis given it in special antipoverty programs for disadvantaged urban youth—particularly those who belong to a racial minority. Typically, the huge HARYOU-ACT program in New York City's Harlem has had an extensive program in the performing arts, with a highly successful dance group under the direction of Thelma Hill. In similar programs in other cities, it has been found that theater and dance activities have had considerable appeal for Negro teen-agers and young adults. In many cases, talented youth have been motivated toward serious study as a consequence of initial involvement in antipoverty recreation and cultural programs.

These, then, are the most important aspects of dance in community life that lead to its being favorably regarded by the public. On the other hand, there are certain prevalent attitudes of a negative nature, which undermine the possibility of dance becoming more fully accepted as an educational discipline.

The first of these has to do with a continuing degree of suspicion about dance as immoral or sinful. Although it is commonplace today to say that the centuries-old Puritan disapproval of dance has now died out, it would be false to assume that it has disappeared completely. A number of schools and colleges, particularly those in rural areas of the country or those which are affiliated with fundamentalist Protestant sects, still prohibit any form of dancing—as instruction, entertainment, or recreation. To a degree, these attitudes are a throwback to the old Calvinist teachings, or the fire-and-brimstone religious revivalism of the 19th century. But they continue to be fanned anew. A tract that is still published by a religious publishing firm in the South describes ballroom dancing in these terms:

> . . . I flatly charge that modern social dancing is fundamentally sinful and evil. I charge that dancing's charm is based entirely on sex appeal. I charge that dancing is the most advanced and most insidious of the maneuvers preliminary to sex betrayal . . . . The dance has been the downward step for many . . . .[8]

Such condemnatory attitudes stem not only from the traditional religious prohibition of dance, but also from the kinds of settings in which dance has been found in the past and present centuries. Asbury described the so-called dance-houses in the French Quarter of old New Orleans:

> Except that there were no formal programs of entertainment, the dancehouses of Gallatin Street were operated in much the same fash-

---

[8] *The Modern Dance*, Pilgrim Tract Society, Randleman, North Carolina.

ion as the concert-saloons—the main attractions were women, liquor, and dancing. But they were infinitely lower in the scale of depravity . . . .[9]

During the 1920s and 1930s, so-called taxi-dance halls were established in many American cities, to meet the need for feminine companionship of homeless or lonesome men crowded into rooming house districts of larger cities. Often, during the Depression, both the patrons and girls were exploited economically; many taxidance halls became fronts for prostitution, a situation which has existed in some cases up to the present, despite extensive legislation and municipal ordinances controlling these establishments. Even during the 1960s, there was an investigation of commercial dance halls in New York City, in which the Commissioner of Licenses found that ballrooms had provided hostesses for "lewd, obscene, and immoral dancing, and acts and conduct offensive to public decency."[10] In one case, the operators of a dance hall were prosecuted for running a commercialized vice ring.

The very fact that ballroom dancing permits young people to embrace and move about the floor rhythmically together, shocks many who are religiously conservative. The frankly sexual movements of the more recent "rock-and-roll" dances have led some critics, including former President Eisenhower, to criticize them for "vulgarity and sensuality."

Often, too, the dance as popular entertainment has been featured in shows stressing nudity and suggestive themes for commercial, prurient appeal. In the midways of traveling country fairs, in night club performances, and in burlesque shows, dancing has often been the vehicle for frankly bawdy presentations—and its reputation has suffered accordingly. Nor has criticism been limited to this level of performance. In 1963, one of Martha Graham's major works, *Phaedra*, was sharply attacked as salacious and immoral by a New York Congresswoman who had seen it performed in Germany on a government-supported tour; the legislator proceeded to demand that the government impose censorship on ballets and films sent abroad in cultural exchange programs.

While such episodes are of minor importance, and do not reflect on the true worth of dance as an aesthetic or recreational activity, they contribute to a vague aura of sinfulness that clings to dance and which compels some school or college administrators to hesitate to provide dance instruction—because *some* students or parents may find it objectionable.

[9] Herbert Asbury, *The French Quarter* (New York: Alfred A. Knopf, Inc., 1936), p. 244.
[10] "Dance Halls Using Hostesses Under Close Inquiry by City," *The New York Times*, August 9, 1963, p. 15.

Even more harmful, in terms of community attitudes about dance, is the popular concept of it as a feminine activity. Many people assume that if a male is a dancer—particularly a ballet or modern dancer—he is necessarily effeminate. Certainly, this stereotype is a factor which prevents many educators from requiring or strongly supporting dance as an activity for boys and young men in schools and colleges. What accounts for this attitude?

First, one must recognize that in all cultures, certain roles or occupations are assigned on the basis of sex affiliation. Margaret Mead, the anthropologist, also points out that we ascribe a set of stereotyped personality traits to each sex. We assume that a man is strong, aggressive, and emotionally stoical, while a woman is more passive, gentle, emotional, and aesthetic in nature. As part of this view, certain activities within the arts—particularly dance—are seen as essentially more feminine than masculine. How did this prejudice come into being in the Western world? Surely history tells us that throughout the ages man has always led in dance. José Limón writes:

> The male of the human species has always been a dancer. Whether as a savage or civilized man, whether warrior, monarch, hunter, priest, philosopher or tiller of the soil, the atavistic urge to dance was in him and he gave it full expression . . . .[11]

Yet, particularly in the United States today, the man who dances is considered by many to be a sexual deviate. Although some may angrily deny the stereotype, it has become so powerful and widely accepted that it has become self-enforcing. American boys who are entirely normal in their sexual identification and who might wish to take up dance, often hesitate to study it or to embark on it as a career because of the expressed fears and resistance of parents, or the criticism of friends. On the other hand, those youths who are ambivalent in their sexual identification, or who are attracted to sexual deviation as a way of life, find the reputation of dance a positive attraction. Thus, although there is nothing about dance which is *innately* feminine or effeminate, it has, within the American society and through much of the Western world, become largely so in practice.

The roots of this stereotype lie in the past. During the early history of ballet, when boys and young men dressed as women to play feminine roles in the French court, the sexual identification of the male dancer was clearly weakened. Later, during the 19th century, when the ballerina was glorified and the male dancer

---

[11] José Limón, "The Virile Dancer," in Walter Sorell, *The Dance Has Many Faces* (New York: World Publishing Company, 1951), p. 192.

denigrated, dance as a profession lost its appeal for many men. By the time the Golden Age of ballet in Europe had run its course, few men were willing to embark on a career in which they could find little prestige or economic reward. Dance became a field in which the female performer was preeminent—although men, of course, continued to be the leading teachers, choreographers, and impresarios.

In modern times, other factors have contributed to the stereotype. Because dance, as all the stage arts, has been a competitive and economically precarious field, many young men who had the intention of marrying and raising families hesitated to enter it or, in some cases, were forced to leave it because of economic pressures. In contrast, the homosexual dancer, with fewer ties or responsibilities, has been better able to withstand the economic stresses and the demands of touring and performance. Thus, the homosexual remains in disproportionate number in the field, and his appearance and behavior are seen as characteristic, discouraging others from entering.

It is worth comment that the stereotype has not attached itself to men in the more commercial phases of dance; performers like Fred Astaire, Gene Kelly, Ray Bolger, Bill Robinson, and the like have not suffered from it. What is there about ballet in particular that arouses prejudice? Some of the adverse reputation is undoubtedly due to the reaction of the untutored and artistically unsophisticated American to the very appearance of ballet. He tended to be suspicious of this ornate, aristocratic, and graceful art. The exaggerated and flamboyant gestures, the walk which he was bound to perceive as mincing, the tight-fitting and revealing costume of the male dancer—all these aroused his disapproval.

Finally, the view of dance as an essentially feminine activity has been strengthened by the way it has been presented in schools and colleges.

During the late 1800s, when aesthetic dance was developed for women and gymnastic dance for men, the male role was defined as vigorous, strong, and essentially nonartistic. As sports became increasingly important in the program of physical education for boys and men, they tended to displace dance activity. The fact that physical education is today divided into separate departments for boys and girls, with men teachers for boys and women teachers for girls, and with a minimum of coeducational activity, makes it extremely difficult to involve boys meaningfully in dance programs. When boys take classes in private studios, they are usually placed in classes with girls in which they are in the minority. Instruction is usually given by a woman and they learn, in effect, to move as girls. The strongly masculine boy (if he ever came in the first place) usually rebels or quits; the others become acclimated.

All of these are factors which led to the view of dance as a feminine activity. Many dancers and dance educators—particularly Ted Shawn—strove to overcome the prejudice. Shawn, through his all-male touring group, his teaching and writing, had strong influence in supporting male dancing during the 1930s and 1940s. Today, there appears to be an increasing number of boys and men entering dance; certainly, in college and university programs, more and more men teachers of dance are being employed. However, the stereotype is still a pervasive one, and continues to be a serious problem in the field of dance education.

A final negative attitude which is held by many in community life is that dance—particularly modern dance—is a "highbrow" and incomprehensible activity. On this score, ballet tends to be more acceptable to a broad audience, in part because it is somewhat more familiar, and because it is known to have a long and respected tradition. Like opera, it has established a base of support in many communities. Civic leaders serve on the boards of ballet organizations, and ballet is widely accepted as a form of training for young girls of well-to-do families.

But perhaps more important than these factors is that audiences can watch ballet without being disturbed about understanding what they are seeing. On the other hand, modern dance (by definition more exploratory and innovative in movement and theme) often stuns and puzzles its audience. Not knowing what to look for, and accustomed to seeing either frankly abstract movement or else a fairly literal approach to communication in ballet, the unsophisticated audience tends to react badly to much modern dance.

All of these are reasons why dance, and particularly modern dance, has failed to gain a larger measure of support in community life. To these must be added the view that dance is a "frill," a decorative adjunct to education, but not a matter for serious curricular concern. Recognizing the problems which stem from a lack of public understanding and whole-hearted support for dance, what can dance educators, physical educators, and school or community leaders who are interested in this art form do to promote its fuller acceptance in education?

Essentially, the needed steps fall within two categories: (1) programs that will strengthen and enrich dance in community life, both as part of the cultural growth of our time and as a form

of direct recreational use of growing leisure, and (2) actions that
will expand the scope and improve the quality of instruction in
dance education in schools and colleges.

How is the first task to be accomplished?

First, as earlier sections of this book have demonstrated, a
great deal that is positive is already being done. On the federal
level, the government is assisting touring companies, providing
subsidy for performance in a few strategic instances, funding the
initial efforts of a number of dance organizations, and supporting major conferences devoted to the promotion of arts in the
community and in education. Through such programs, as well as
through the increased efforts of state governments, arts councils,
and foundations, much help is being given to the performing arts.
If, in the development of arts centers around the country, greater
attention is given to the need for supporting locally sponsored
performing companies—rather than simply providing an auditorium or theater for visiting troupes—dance in community life
will be greatly strengthened.

Dancers themselves can do a great deal to promote fuller
understanding of the dance, and to improve its public image.

Certainly, it will be helpful for male dancers themselves—
many of whom are virile, masculine, and athletic—to act more
forcefully as spokesmen for their art. America's greatest male
dancer, Jacques d'Amboise of the New York City Ballet, has done
this successfully, both on national television programs and in major
publications, where the special class he conducts for boys (including
his own son) has been favorably publicized. Other dancers are
carrying out similar efforts to promote the acceptance of male
dancing.

Dancers also have an obligation to help audiences understand and appreciate their works.

Erick Hawkins, one of the best-known of today's modern
dancers, has toured widely throughout the United States and
Canada in recent years. In 1966–1967, his company performed in
60 communities from coast to coast; all but a few of these performances were under college or university auspices. However,
Hawkins does not assume that, for this reason, his audiences are
knowledgeable about modern dance. Instead, he and the members
of his company work hard to orient their audiences. On the day
of a university dance concert, a member of the company may give
a master class while Hawkins lectures on dance to students in the
English or philosophy departments. Sometimes his composer-
accompanist, Lucia Dlugoszewski, gives a lecture-demonstration

to music students. Not infrequently, the company may remain in a university community an additional day or two, without charge, in order to promote dance interest and understanding.

The most effective technique used by Hawkins to orient audiences has been to make a short talk to the audience before the performance. Typically, in such an address, Hawkins talks about the arts and American society, about the role of the male dancer, and about how to view all art, particularly dance. Giving the audience some basic principles as well as a sense of security about the works that they are to see, he then goes ahead with the performance. Frequently, when performing before an audience that has seen little modern dance before, he presents a work titled *John Brown,* based on the American historical figure. His purpose in this is to illustrate the function of art as literal communication, and to give audiences a work to which they can relate somewhat more easily than more abstract or symbolic dances.

This sort of effort by dancers and choreographers is extremely helpful in creating a more favorable audience for dance. Local and regional dance organizations also are in a position to promote understanding by sponsoring festivals, workshops, film series, and seminars, directed to both educational and lay audiences. In so doing, strength can be gained by allying dance to the other performing arts. In a number of communities, a variety of concerts, performances, exhibitions, poetry readings, or film showings have combined to draw large audiences and promote total public interest in the arts. In such a setting, modern dance or ballet tends to be one of the most exciting and successful program events.

In a presentation before the Second National Conference on the Arts in Education, Gertrude Lippincott made a number of recommendations for dance educators to promote this field in both the community and in educational institutions. Dance educators in the community were urged to:

1. Establish liaison with dance groups and institutions where dance is taught, such as private studios, YMCAs, cooperatives, regional dance festivals both ballet and modern, conferences, museums, extension divisions, etc., in an effort to promote and further dance as an art form.

2. Encourage art festivals in which dance is included, dance symposiums, programs, etc. Encourage state and local art councils to include a dance performing unit among their activities, both professional and amateur. (Professional units should be sought after first.)

3. Establish a loosely-organized clearing house to aid in

sponsoring professional dance performances in educational institutions.

Throughout, Lippincott stresses that it is necessary for dance educators, like practitioners in all the arts, to be personally active in supporting legislation and other governmental activities that promote cultural activities in American life.[12] Her recommendations, if followed successfully by dance educators, would do much to strengthen the place of dance in community life.

But what of the other problem—the need to improve the scope and quality of dance education itself, in school and colleges?

Dance in Elementary Education

As Chapter Fourteen has indicated, dance education in elementary schools is at best sketchy and inadequate.

There is a pressing need, if this aspect of child development is to be more fully realized, for classroom teachers to become more highly skilled in dance and creative movement instruction. They must be helped to recognize the value of creative rhythmic movement and of structured dance activities, and should be given improved teaching skills in these areas. This can be accomplished both in their preservice training in undergraduate colleges, and also through in-service education and graduate study. Those in allied fields, such as music or art teaching, or physical education on the elementary level, must also become more knowledgeable about dance and creative movement if they are to assist classroom teachers in this field. While special teachers in dance are rarely used in elementary education, they have taught in a few school systems (usually when a classroom teacher or physical educator has displayed a high level of interest and competence). Administrative flexibility in teaching assignments makes possible this highly desirable arrangement.

In terms of the participation of boys and men in dance, it is during the elementary grades that patterns are set and attitudes developed that prevail throughout upper grades and college. Therefore, every effort must be made to involve boys meaningfully in dance experience throughout the elementary school, if the harmful and unjustified stereotype of dance as a feminine activity is to be dispelled.

How can this be accomplished? First, it should be recognized that boys usually have little prejudice against the recreational

---

[12] Gertrude Lippincott, *Proceedings of the Second National Conference on the Arts in Education*, National Council of the Arts in Education, 1963, pp. 12–13.

forms of dance; indeed, they tend to enjoy the lively rhythm and sociability of singing games, play parties, folk dancing, and square dancing when they are effectively taught. This may be a convenient starting point, but every effort should also be made to have boys participate in creative dance activity.

For this to be successful, the activity should be presented in a physically challenging way—almost like gymnastics, or stunts and tumbling. If dance requires strength, coordination, and ability, it will tend to command respect in its own right. For creative improvisation and performance, boys should be given themes of a dramatic and exciting nature. At the outset, movement themes based on sports, primitive dancing, animals, combat, machinery, or similar ideas are likely to have great appeal. Boys should have the opportunity to develop their own accompaniment with percussion instruments or other forms of music and improvised sound. They should also be able to draw their ideas for creative movement from the subjects studied in the classroom—social studies, science, literature and poetry, music, and the graphic arts. Such integration of dance with other subjects not only serves to promote unified learning experiences, but heightens interest and motivation as well.

Efforts should be made to have dance become a prestigeful activity. If performance—as part of assembly programs, parents' day, arts festivals, or other special events—can be a culminating activity at the end of a unit in dance instruction, it will reinforce the interest of children. Obviously, such performances should not be the sole goal of dance instruction and should not be permitted to dominate the actual process of learning to move and of creating in dance for its own sake. However, they provide goals for classes to aim at, as well as a means of demonstrating the outcomes of dance instruction—in terms of physical skills, creative growth, and integrated learning. If they are not approached in a drill-like, boring series of rehearsals, and if they are vital and exciting, rather than stilted and mechanical, they will provide interest and enthusiasm for dance classes.

In terms of the actual teaching of dance techniques in the upper elementary grades, to help children acquire a vocabulary of movement, it is probable that many classroom teachers will be unable to gain the competence needed to do this effectively. Physical educators and other specialists should be able to provide such instruction. In many school systems, it should be possible to bring in specially qualified teachers from the community, as curriculum resources specialists, to give special instruction in dance in physical education classes—even though they may not possess regular teaching credentials. Skilled parents may even be willing to contribute their services, in order to promote better dance education, although this is not a desirable way of providing for such instruction on a permanent basis.

Dance in Secondary Schools

Many persons who are familiar with the problems of dance instruction in secondary schools feel that it would be best promoted by having dance presented in a separate department, taught by highly skilled teachers with special certification in *dance* itself. While this would be an ideal solution to the teaching of dance as an art form, it offers little hope of actual implementation. Though many dance educators have sought acceptance of dance as a separate certification area, this has been achieved in only two states (California and, more recently, Wisconsin) for graduates of special college dance education programs. Nor would many school administrators be willing to establish new departments of dance, or to identify this as a separate curricular field, in the light of the strong academic pressures that exist today, which crowd the curriculum.

Even from a theoretical viewpoint, it is not likely to receive strong support from educators who are interested in the promotion of the arts in education. A leading authority on the curriculum, Harry Broudy, in a speech before the Third National Conference on the Arts in Education, questions the justification for having "studio instruction in any of the arts" beyond a rudimentary level, as part of general education. It is his belief that it is the high school's responsibility for carrying creative artistic experience to a higher level than that in the elementary grades, but that this must necessarily fall short of advanced training. The dilemma, he says:

> ... is evaded by providing opportunities for performance during extracurricular hours. This does not preclude the presence of teachers to whom the student can look for guidance and instruction in the exercise of his particular form of art. A boy wishing to perfect himself in the playing of the piano should be able to take lessons ... without making [this] part of general education required of everyone. Not being included in the curriculum relieves instruction in piano playing from formal requirements, examinations, and much of the other impedimenta so familiar and necessary in the life of the school, but which art educators and artists find especially irksome ....[13]

One might challenge this position by pointing out that advanced classes are offered in other fields of education (languages, science, mathematics, etc.) in the form of "honors" courses. If secondary school educators are serious about wishing to provide aesthetic

---

[13] Harry Broudy, *Proceedings of the Third National Conference on the Arts in Education*, National Council of the Arts in Education, 1964.

education on a more than superficial level, would it not be possible to provide such classes in dance for specially interested or talented students, provided, of course, that they are of sufficient numbers to justify such a sequence? Realistically, most secondary school administrators take Broudy's position. In most high schools, the advanced opportunities for participation in music, drama, art, or dance are found in clubs, choruses, bands, student orchestras, and dance groups—rather than in classes that are part of the actual curriculum.

There is little likelihood that this pattern will change in the near future, except in special schools which are devoted to the arts, such as those described in Chapter Fourteen. Instead, any discussion of dance in secondary schools must realistically assume that it will continue to be taught in departments of physical education, and that it will not constitute a separate curricular offering or academic sequence. If this is so, what can be done to improve its scope and quality?

First, it is necessary to strengthen the teaching of dance. Hayes pointed out a number of years ago that many physical education teachers who are required to teach dance have had a minimum of training in it, and often lack the temperament or creative interest to be successful in this area. Many of them recognize their own lack of ability in dance and are therefore extremely reluctant to teach it.[14] Sometimes they may actually be surpassed in skill by their own students. How can this situation be remedied?

The professional preparation of physical educators who will be responsible for dance should be strengthened on the undergraduate and graduate levels. Not only should a stronger core of basic dance courses be provided in college physical-education major departments, but there should be a wider provision of dance "concentrations," or "minors," for physical education majors with a special interest and skill in dance. Thus, such students could become identified at an early point as dance specialists, and could build their competence in a sustained way throughout their college program. A number of colleges described in the *AAHPER Dance Division 1966 Directory* have established educational dance majors and minors which include enough physical education courses so that graduates meet state certification requirements. Such programs do much to develop skilled teachers of dance who are able to move into secondary education. Beyond this, it would be extremely

[14] Elizabeth R. Hayes, "The Dance Teacher and the Physical Education Administrator," *Journal of Health, Physical Education and Recreation,* December 1954, p. 20.

helpful if state education departments could develop a special physical education certification requirement which gives credit to a large block of courses in dance, and which keeps other skills areas to a minimum.

Though this would not be appropriate for those physical education teachers who must serve as generalists—teaching the entire range of physical activities—it should be recognized as useful for those schools which are large enough so that there are several members on the physical education staff. In such schools, it is common policy to have teachers specialize in different areas of activity—team sports, dual sports, aquatics, gymnastics, etc. The well-developed dance specialist is badly needed in such programs, and a modified certification requirement (still under the heading of physical education) would encourage more students interested specifically in dance to enter this field.

Hayes suggests also that the professional education of dance teachers should be recognized as a distinctive area of professional preparation. The title of college departments in this broad field is usually "Health, Physical Education and Recreation." Could the word "Dance" not be added to those departments offering majors or strong minors in dance? Hayes asks whether it would not be possible to establish it as a separate administrative unit, rather than as a subject area in the women's physical education department, which makes it either awkward or impossible for men to elect it as a field of professional training. Finally, she suggests other procedures to be taken to improve dance instruction, particularly on the secondary level:

> Those individuals who lack the necessary equipment (technical skill, movement sensitivity, and creative spark) to do justice to the teaching of dance should not be expected to do so. The educational curriculum should be made flexible enough to enable majors in other subject areas such as music, speech, or art, to minor in dance; and the administrative organization in secondary schools should be sufficiently adaptable to permit these other trained educators to teach the dance if the physical educators are unwilling or unable to do so. School administrators as well as physical education administrators will need to reorient their thinking along these lines.[15]

A second important step would be to make secondary school dance activity more appropriate and attractive for boys. While it seems unlikely that such a program can be established on a mandatory basis, particularly in terms of modern dance, certainly more schools could establish coeducational recreational dance classes

[15] *Ibid.*

than are doing so at present. Such classes usually include folk, square, and ballroom dancing. While few boys would be enthusiastic, in the present climate, about a *separate* course in modern dance, it might well be feasible to establish a course on an introductory level in secondary schools, titled "Survey of Dance Skills." Such a course might include the recreational forms of dance *and* modern dance as well, although it is possible that the latter should be described by some name that would avoid the stigma that might presently relate to it. The assumption is that once boys became interested and challenged, many of them would gain a more favorable attitude about dance as an appropriate masculine activity.

If at all possible, men teachers should be involved in the teaching of such classes. It might be that the male teacher (if he has the needed skills, as many have) might present the recreational dance forms, with the woman teacher assisting; the roles would then be reversed for modern dance instruction. Under some circumstances, it might be better to have a separate all-boy class in modern dance, in order to provide activities on their level of ability and interest, and to further avoid the "feminine" label of the activity.

If it is not possible, for administrative reasons, to offer such classes on the curricular level for boys, then every effort should be made to develop club programs which include boys on the secondary school level. Many would welcome such a program, if it were effectively presented and did not prove embarrassing to them. Sometimes it might be offered as part of a music program, a conditioning program, or in connection with school dramatic presentations. If the staff itself did not have qualified teachers to guide such club or special programs on an extracurricular basis, capable instructors might be brought in from the community, on a special-teacher basis. There are a number of examples of such special programs for boys and young men today, despite the overall pattern of exclusion from dance (see Chapter Fourteen).[16]

In terms of promoting the overall prominence of dance, many techniques can be used to arouse interest in it in secondary schools.

Recreational dance activities—square and folk dance festivals,

---

[16] In addition to references in Chapter Fourteen, see: Fred Berk, "Creating Interest in Dance for Boys," *Journal of Health, Physical Education and Recreation,* April 1958, pp. 58–59; Carolyn Parks, "Sex: Male, Profession: Dancer?," *Dance Magazine,* April 1953, pp. 42–43; C. Wright Dunkley, "Most Men Want to Dance, But . . .," *Journal of Health, Physical Education and Recreation,"* February 1966, pp. 39–42; Kathleen V. Powell, *Dance Magazine,* March 1967, p. 73; and Bettie Jane Wooten, "Men and the Modern Dance," *Journal of Health, Physical Education and Recreation,* November 1957, pp. 58–59.

jamborees, clubs, and clinics—can all be developed. Students may attend master classes, seminars, and concerts at nearby colleges, or regional dance events. Student choreography may be presented in assemblies and concert programs. Throughout, it is necessary to make every effort to develop the place of the arts in secondary schools. Often, unified programs of the arts, such as special week-long festivals presenting plays, poetry readings, art exhibitions, concerts, and dance events, have this effect. In a number of cases, secondary schools have developed courses in the *related arts* which are required of all students in the ninth or tenth grades. Such courses include general sections on the history of the arts and principles of aesthetic content and design (in which the elements common to all the arts are explored). Sometimes they also involve students in creative experiences in the arts which are related to the more theoretical aspects of the course. It is essential that dance be part of such courses in the arts and humanities.

If all these steps are taken to promote dance in the school program, both as part of the curriculum and in co-curricular activities, it will contribute much to the total aesthetic environment of the school—as well as to interest and skills in dance itself. Particularly, teachers should make every effort to take advantage of the kinds of help which are now available from outside sources. In a number of states, arts councils and special foundation grants have made it possible to bring professional dance companies into the schools. Such opportunities for cultural enrichment as those described in Chapter Fifteen are likely to increase in the future.

Dance in Colleges and Universities

Here, finally, it is necessary to come to grips with the relationship between dance and physical education. Unlike the situation in elementary and secondary schools (where there is really little choice, and dance for the foreseeable future must continue to be offered by physical education departments), there *is* a choice in higher education. In a substantial number of colleges and universities, there are separate departments of dance, or sponsorship of dance majors by departments other than physical education. Therefore, it is necessary to understand the pros and cons of the relationship with physical education.

Historically, it is true that education in dance came into being under the sponsorship of physical educators, and has long been viewed as an important activity area in that field. Many physical educators have strongly supported dance as the "aesthetic side of physical education" or for its social and physical values. Without question, the fact that it has been part of the physical education *requirement* has meant that vast numbers of students have been exposed to dance through the years.

However, those who are dissatisfied with the place of dance in physical education point out accurately that in most physical education departments dance is treated primarily as a form of exercise, rather than as a creative or artistic experience. The stated goals of physical education rarely stress these latter values. When it is sponsored by physical education, dance seldom assumes a role in school or college programs comparable to that of music or fine art. Indeed, dance educators claim that the size of classes and other administrative circumstances surrounding the provision of dance in physical education make it impossible for it to function effectively as aesthetic education.

The point has already been made that dance is often taught by physical education teachers who are poorly equipped in this field (with foreseeably disappointing results), while individuals who have excellent training in dance are usually not permitted to teach it—unless they have physical education credentials. It is claimed that physical educators rarely see dance as a vital concern or promote its interests as strongly as they do sports and other aspects of the physical education program. In college programs, while they support courses in basic dance skills, they rarely are willing to introduce more advanced technique courses, or courses in dance composition, production, history, or notation. Teachers of dance are often compelled to teach courses in other physical education activities, in which they have been inadequately prepared, and may also be required (because of their dance background) to coach drill teams, cheerleaders, marching units, or other forms of dance entertainment for sports events of which they personally disapprove.

Finally, as was mentioned above, the argument is advanced that having dance sponsored by women's physical education departments perpetuates the rigid separation of men and women in this field, whereas having it as a separate department would mean that both sexes would be able to study it with less difficulty.

Essentially, many dance educators feel that these reasons justify taking dance—particularly dance as an art form—out of the administrative sponsorship of physical education. On the other hand, the majority of physical educators continue to affirm the relationship, seeing dance as a valid aspect of physical education and stressing that in this setting it has administrative support that it would not readily gain if independent. In a symposium by lead-

Miller stressed both the appropriateness of dance education within physical education and the problem of administrative support:

> ... there are those who consider dance—in its broadest sense—to be the basic phase of the well-rounded program .... Dance is an area rich in opportunities for meeting the aims of physical education and, except for the lack of the competitive element, it might well be considered the *sine que non* of the field ....
>
> In general, the educational system in the United States is committed to required physical education and to the provision of the necessary floor space, dressing rooms, and other equipment. Dance requires the same facilities, and any separation of this area from a broader unit which already has these costly necessities by fiat is inconceivable at the present time ....[18]

Others stress the point that dance has been increasingly accepted in schools and colleges as a part of the physical education program and therefore as a compulsory experience. If it were not sponsored in this way, many students would never experience dance in an educational setting. Tillotson and Wilson describe dance as being an essential phase of the discipline of physical education, which is the "science and art of movement." The point is made that those who contemplate dance only as an art form, placing it outside the realm of physical education, have only a partial view of the field. Ulrich makes the strongest case for this argument:

> ... movement is our unique means of education. Certainly dance has been recognized for a long time as the purest of all movement expression. It is an activity which fosters the complete utilization of the total body in order to express meaning and interpret feelings. In a sense, dance permits and encourages the sort of body expression that sports activities only allow in rigid and stratified patterns.
>
> To be sure, such expression as dance permits may be thought of as an art form and hence it may be logical that dance ally itself with certain of the expressive art fields. But the more logical attachment is with the department of physical education—a department which is committed to the education of the individual through gross muscular movement patterns ....[19]

[17] "Dance as an Art Form in Physical Education, A Symposium by Selected Educators," *Journal of Health, Physical Education and Recreation*, January 1964, pp. 19–21, 54–55.
[18] [Kenneth D. Miller] *Ibid.*, p. 19.
[19] [Celeste Ulrich] *Ibid.*, p. 55.

Whether or not these arguments are acceptable to dance educators, they represent the viewpoint of influential physical educators today. It seems improbable that on any level of education they are likely to consent, in appreciable numbers, to a severing of the relationship between dance and physical education. On the college level, where both the theoretical justification and the practical aspects of such a shift are somewhat more reasonable than in elementary or secondary schools, one may envision three kinds of administrative possibilities:

1. In those colleges which have strong liberal arts traditions, placing major emphasis on the arts and humanities, there will be an increasing tendency to promote dance as a theater art, independent of physical education. In such institutions, some dance may continue to be offered on a "service" basis for all students by the physical education department, but the advanced sequences in modern dance and ballet, as well as choreography, production, and other specialized courses, will be offered by the separate dance department. Such programs today tend to be found in women's colleges, although Bennington and Sarah Lawrence, among others, have made special provision for bringing male students in as part of performing arts programs. Particularly when dance is attached to drama departments in coeducational institutions, it may become feasible to develop a larger contingent of male students.

2. A second type of arrangement which is likely to grow involves two dance majors: one in dance education (to prepare teachers) in departments of physical education, and the second in dance as a performing art, either independent or in another arts-oriented department. Such patterns are usually found in large state universities which have a tradition of teacher education and physical education, but which also have developed as liberal arts institutions. In general, the dance education major stresses a broad approach to dance (including recreational dance forms and teaching methods), while the performing arts approach emphasizes modern dance and ballet. Administrative arrangements may be worked out between the two departments so that the performing arts department offers the advanced courses needed by dance education majors, thus avoiding duplication. A key problem here is whether courses in the performing arts program should be permitted to meet physical education requirements; in a number of colleges, this remains a bone of contention.

3. The third arrangement is to be found in institutions which lack a particularly strong interest in the arts—either in terms of the background of students or the capabilities of faculty. Here, dance

is likely to continue to be part of the service program in physical education or, at most, a "minor" area of specialization for physical education majors. Even here, however, there should be the opportunity to experience dance as an art form in courses, and to strengthen it as part of the cultural program of the college.

When dance *is* presented primarily as a performing art, and when students major in it as a form of preprofessional activity, certain basic questions are raised.

First, there is the fact that undergraduate liberal education has traditionally been directed to certain general goals of learning, embodying the arts, sciences, and humanities—but not including specific advanced training in any discipline. Particularly in the arts, this has meant that there has been strong resistance to "studio" work. Often, the most acceptable kind of program has stressed courses dealing with the history, aesthetics, and criticism of a given art field—rather than the development of competence as a performer.

A second question which must be raised is whether preprofessional training in dance in colleges is really feasible. Can it be done? And, even if it can, is it really worthwhile?

One may ask whether it is possible to bring a dancer to a level of professional performing competence in a college program. In the past, few institutions have had programs of the required intensity and standard of instruction. Because of all the other requirements of the college curriculum, the dance major may not be able to give enough energy and time to work in dance. A physical educator, Metheny, questions whether the "serious artist" should be in college at all:

> . . . at best, it can only lay the foundation for the later development of the student artist's talents; at worst, it may encourage him to dissipate talents in diversity and quasi-artistic performances at the dilettante level. For the dancer, whose life-span as a performer is limited by the effects of age on the body, this delay in accepting the rigorous requirements of preparation for full use of talent and creativity may well be disastrous . . . .[20]

Indeed, the majority of students who enter college performing arts dance majors today have not had the kind of intensive training that they should have had during adolescence, if they are to have a reasonable expectation of maturing as highly skilled performing artists. Thus, since only a few colleges are able to provide the kind of intensive and highly specialized training that would be found in a professional academy or conservatory of dance, the odds are

[20] [Eleanor Metheny] *Ibid.*, p. 19.

doubly stacked against them. The real professional dancer—particularly in ballet—will already have had several years of intensive training and, at the age of eighteen or nineteen, may well be serving his apprenticeship in an actual ballet company, or on the musical stage.

This relates to the second point—is such a major in dance as a performing art worthwhile, in terms of the goals of the student? Many students, when they select a field as a college major today, expect that it will have actual vocational value for them. Thus, a student who majors in education expects to become a teacher, just as a student who majors in biology, mathematics, or business administration expects (usually with graduate study) to become a biologist, a mathematician or statistician, or a business executive.

Within dance, such an expectation is likely to be illusory—at least in the sense of finding stable employment in the field. In ballet and on the musical stage or television, there are a limited number of positions, with sporadic employment and an intensive level of competition. For such positions, a college degree is not expected or really relevant. In the field of modern dance—which represents the core of most college performing arts dance majors—there is almost *no* full-time employment for dancers as members of companies performing professionally.

Therefore, it is essential that colleges and universities offering majors in dance as a performing art give students realistic knowledge about the place of dance in community life, and information about the limited number of professional opportunities that are available. They should know that the great bulk of performance is amateur and that modern dance performers, in particular, must earn their living in some way other than by performing.

If, recognizing all this, the college still wishes to offer a major in dance as a performing art—and students still wish to take it—the justification becomes miraculously simple. It is to view dance as part of general education, but without specific vocational purpose. One accepts the idea of a college student majoring in philosophy or literature without serious expectation of making a livelihood as a philosopher, novelist, or literary critic. Likewise, the student majoring in dance will regard his field simply as a rich and rewarding form of education—as an art form related to the other arts, to history, ethnology, philosophy—and one that has great potential for personal growth. Thus, there need be no concern about direct vocational outcomes for the performing arts dance major; it is only when the student has unrealistic expectations or is misled by the lack of frank advisement that the institution is at fault.

Finally, the dance major may wish to consider the possibility of teaching dance as a career. Whether this is done through teaching in secondary schools or colleges, or in community centers, private dance schools and studios, or in a host of other settings, the fact is that many thousands of dancers are able to support themselves in this way. The Statistical Abstract of the United States lists over 7,000 establishments for commercial dance instruction alone. Anne Ingram has done a comprehensive study of the role of dancer-teachers in schools and colleges, as part of a doctoral investigation at Columbia University; her analysis reveals a continuing shortage of well-trained persons in this field.[21] Surely, such a career should be of interest to many college-trained dance majors, as a means of combining a major life interest with secure employment.

Indeed, only if the quality and number of dance teachers on all levels of education throughout the United States are increased is there likely to be developed the kind of mass audience for dance that is still lacking today. This, of course, is an essential goal of dance education; the development of a literate, sensitive, and enthusiastic audience, as well as greater participation on all age levels.

When dance becomes more fully a part of education and thus keeps pace with the promising trends in the concert dance field and dance in public recreation, then at last the prophecy of Isadora Duncan will be fulfilled: "I see America dancing."

[21] Anne G. Ingram, "The Dancer-Teacher," *Journal of Health, Physical Education and Recreation*, March 1965, pp. 29, 54–56.

CREDITS
FOR
ILLUSTRATIONS

The following prints and photographs were obtained for reproduction from the Dance Collection of the Library and Museum of the Performing Arts at Lincoln Center in New York City:

Equestrian Ballet, *Guerra d'Amore*, p. 65
Louis XIV, *Ballet Royal de la Nuit*, p. 74
Pas de Quatre, p. 88
Bal Mabile, mid-19th-century Paris, p. 90
Christy's Minstrels, *Skedaddle*, p. 111
Shaker dancing, p. 115
Isadora Duncan in *La Marseillaise*, p. 143
Ruth St. Denis in *Egypta*, p. 146
Ted Shawn and Company in *Kinetic Molpai*, p. 148
Mary Wigman in *Dance of Silence*, p. 159
Mary Wigman and Company in *Der Weg*, p. 161
José Limón in *The Moor's Pavane*, p. 164
Vaslav Nijinsky in *Afternoon of a Faun*, p. 174
Anna Pavlova in *The Dying Swan*, p. 175
Anna Pavlova and Vaslav Nijinsky in *Le Pavillon d'Armide*, p. 176

Credit is given to the following photographers for their work:

Phil Barringer:
North Carolina School of the Arts ballet performance, p. 292

Victoria Beller:
Ballet and modern dance classes at High School of Performing
Arts, pp. 289, 290

Harry Blaine:
Ohio State University Dance Company in Doris Humphrey's
Passacaglia and Fugue, p. 297

George Dolan:
Secondary school students in dance curriculum project, p. 328

Fred Fell:
American Ballet Theater in *Helen of Troy,* p. 199

James Howell:
City Center Joffrey Ballet in *The Clowns,* p. 202

Herbert Migdoll:
City Center Joffrey Ballet in *Astarte,* p. 200

Jack Mitchell:
Merce Cunningham Company in *Riverwind,* p. 228
Paul Taylor Company in *Orbs,* p. 233
Paul Taylor Company in *From Sea to Shining Sea,* p. 235
Alvin Ailey Company in *Roots of the Blues,* p. 236
Erick Hawkins Company in *Early Floating,* p. 240

Barbara Morgan:
Martha Graham in *Letter to the World,* p. 151
Humphrey-Weidman Company in *The Shakers,* p. 155
Hanya Holm Company in *Dance of Work and Play,* p. 163

Dora Sanders:
Paul Sanasardo Company, jacket
Martha Graham at Connecticut College, p. 308

V. Sladon:
Harkness Ballet in *Abyss,* p. 203

Robert Sosenko:
Alwin Nikolais Company in *Imago,* p. 230

Martha Swope:
New York City Ballet in *The Nutcracker,* p. 195
Martha Graham Company in *Clytemnestra,* p. 223
Martha Graham Company in *The Lady of the House of Sleep,*
p. 225

M. Tarnay:
Bennington College Dance Group modern dance performance,
p. 300

Mathew Wysocki:
José Limón and Lucas Hoving in *The Traitor,* p. 226

Other photographs of professional dance companies were obtained from their press representatives:

New York City Ballet, Virginia Donaldson
American Ballet Theater, Samuel Lurie and Associates
City Center Joffrey Ballet, Isadora Bennett
Harkness Ballet, Harkness Company press office
Alwin Nikolais Company, Arthur Zinberg
Paul Taylor Company, Charles Reinhart Management

Photographs of the following college or school dance programs were obtained from professors or directors in charge of each department:

North Carolina School of the Arts, Dean Robert Lindgren
Ohio State University, Prof. Helen Alkire
Bennington College, Josef Wittman
University of Utah, Prof. Elizabeth Hayes
Texas Christian University, Prof. Margaret Moar
Duquesne University, Walter Kolar
University of Pennsylvania, Dance Curriculum Project, Nadia
  Chilkovsky Nahumck

INDEX

Currier, Ruth, 165, 167

Dalcroze, Emile Jacques-, 140-141, 148, 158-159, 162, 167
D'Amboise, Jacques, 183, 186, 347
Dance (see also Ballet; Ethnic dance; Modern dance; Recreational dance):
defined, 4-7, 12-13
in education, 2, 12, 37-38, 100-101, 107, 110, 119-139, 168, 253-309, 349-361 (see also College dance programs; Elementary school dance programs; Graduate education in dance; Secondary school dance programs)
as entertainment, 59, 340, 343 (see also Musical stage dance)
functions of, 7-13, 15-26
in therapy, 12, 24-25, 341
Dance Educators of America, 337
Dance Magazine, 293, 307, 320
Dance Masters of America, 337
Dance of Death, 52-55
Dance Teachers Guild (see National Dance Guild)
Dancing manias, 55-57
Danilova, Alicia, 93, 174, 182, 184, 189
Danish ballet (see Royal Danish Ballet)
De Beaujoyeaux, Balthasar, 70-71
De Camargo, Marie, 78
De Gaetani, Thomas, 334
De Lavallade, Carmen, 308-309
Delsarte, François, 127, 131, 140-141
De Medici, Catherine, 70
De Mille, Agnes, 23, 66-67, 75, 118, 150, 155, 166, 172, 184, 186-187, 189, 193-194
Denishawn Company, 147-150, 154-156 (see also St. Denis, Ruth; Shawn, Ted)
De Rothschild Foundation, 225, 320, 331
De Valois, Ninette, 93, 184, 213, 215
Diaghileff, Serge, 93, 96, 141, 144, 147, 170-182, 188, 191-192, 215
Dodworth, Allen, 110
Dolin, Anton, 93, 174, 184, 187, 216
Dollar, William, 183
Dudley, Jane, 153, 166-167
Duggan, Anne Schley, 135
Dulles, Foster Rhea, 108-109

Duncan, Isadora, 118, 128, 135, 137, 139-147, 161, 165, 171, 361
Dunham, Katherine, 167, 222-223
Durang, John, 102-103, 106

East Indian dance, 17
Educational dance (see Dance, in education)
Eglevsky, André, 185, 187, 189
Egypt, dance in ancient, 28-33
Elementary school dance programs, 276-282, 349-351
Ellis, Havelock, 10, 32
Elssler, Fanny, 85, 89, 104, 106, 178, 209
England, dance of, 26, 66, 79, 91 (see also Royal Ballet of Great Britain; Sadler's Wells Ballet)
modern dance in, 158
Erdman, Jean, 153, 167
Ethnic dance, 4, 14, 20, 22, 24-26, 146

Federal government and the arts, 321-329 (see also U.S. State Department dance tours)
Federal Theater programs, 166, 191, 322-323
Festival of Fools, 50-51, 57
Financial status of dance, 194-195, 219-220, 224-225, 235, 310-338
Fokine, Michel, 82, 96, 118, 144, 165, 170-176, 181, 186-188, 190, 192
Folk dance, 4, 14, 26, 59-61, 128-133, 256, 296-298, 305, 309, 340-341 (see also Recreational dance)
Fonteyn, Margot, 214-215
Ford Foundation, 2, 205-206, 332
Foundations supporting dance, 2, 200-206, 225, 320, 331-333
France, dance in, 58-59, 62-66, 69-91, 171-177, 179-180, 219-220, 322
Franklin, Frederic, 184, 189, 204
Frontier dancing, 108-109
Fuller, Loie, 118, 141-143, 146

Galliard, 68, 70, 101
Garden State Ballet, 331
Gautier, Théophile, 84-85, 87-88, 105
Germany:
early history of dance in, 56-57, 59-61